A3 183 785 7

FATHERS 4 JUSTICE

FATHERS 4 JUSTICE

THE INSIDE STORY

MATT O'CONNOR

Weidenfeld & Nicolson

LONDON

First published in Great Britain in 2007
by Weidenfeld & Nicolson

1 3 5 7 9 10 8 6 4 2

© Matt O'Connor 2007
[www.fathers-4-justice.org]

A CIP catalogue record for this book
is available from the British Library.

ISBN-13 978 0 297 85306 0

Typeset by Input Data Services Ltd, Frome

Printed and bound at Mackays of Chatham plc, Chatham, Kent

The Orion publishing group's policy is to use papers that
are natural, renewable and recyclable products and made
from wood grown in sustainable forests. The logging and
manufacturing processes are expected to conform to the
environmental regulations of the country of origin.

Weidenfeld & Nicolson

The Orion Publishing Group Ltd
Orion House
5 Upper Saint Martin's Lane
London, WC2H 9EA
An Hachette Livre UK Company

www.orionbooks.co.uk

CONTENTS

LIST OF ILLUSTRATIONS

ACKNOWLEDGEMENTS

I am deeply indebted to the following people without whose love, loyalty, help and patience the campaign would never have been realised: Nick Langford, Michael Cox and Gary Burch for contributing to the invaluable number-crunching research and appendices; all the supporters and activists at Fathers 4 Justice across the world but especially in the United Kingdom, the Netherlands, the United States and Canada; my forgiving partner Nadine Taylor for her unflinching love and affection; my brother David O'Connor for his pearly words of wisdom; a heartfelt thanks to my mother Anne O'Connor for her unconditional love and support; Elizabeth Taylor and Tom Taylor for their prayers and spiritual guidance. Posthumous recognition to the following influences that have shaped my life: my father Thomas Patrick O'Connor, my grandfather Glyn Evans and my grandmother Mary Evans, my tolerant landlord at Kimsings the late Tony Pawsey, and to my friend, the late, great Peter Matthews. Thanks also to the following, who are still very much alive and kicking: Jenny Bostock for her unstinting work in the face of insurmountable challenges; Will Minns for the camper van cabriole and the dosh to save me from destitution; Sophie O'Connor for such wonderful boys and being a great mum; Jolly Stanesby for his dedication; Andy Work for his resilience and compassion; Richard 'The Fat Italian' Castle for the films and friendship; Tony Lewis for helping me get the engine started; Darryl Westell for the drama; Guy Harrison for his sheer chutzpah; Glen Poole for his rambunctious words and wit; Michael and Beth Cox and family, including those fearless fellows Elliott, Matthew and Daniel; Gary Burch for his political insight; Wendy and Ian Taylor for their support; Phillippa Louise; The 'Reverend' Ray Barry; Richard 'The Rock' Adams for his persistence; Chris Kelly for his friendship; Tony Heath for counting the beans; Ian Maddaford for the lunchtime of a lifetime; Mark Harris for laying the foundations; Tina Rayburn; Tremendous Paul and the delicious Kate; Eddie Goldtooth; Julie-Ann Harris, Solicitor; and Robin Belbin, Barrister. And a warm thanks to my personal security at Scotland Yard including Adrian 'Watch Yourself Matt' Laurie, Andy 'The Circle Line' Sharp and anybody else in blue for looking after me these last five years; Julie Simms for putting up with me; Alan Critchley; Anthony Douglas; Jo Phillips; my agent, the irrepressible Jonny Pegg; Ian Drury for the opportunity; my long-suffering yet inspirational editor Penny Gardiner and everybody at Orion; Suzanne Mackie and Nick Barton at Harbour Pictures; Danny Brocklehurst, Will Self, Bob Geldof and any other poor bugger I've forgotten or owe money to. Sorry xxx

For Daniel, Alexander and Archie,
and for those children separated from their parents
by the secret family courts.

Nec timeo, nec sperno

A WORD FROM WILL SELF

It's difficult for me to talk about the phenomenon of Fathers 4 Justice, as I observed it develop, given that I've used it as a major component in a lengthy – and I hope, thoughtful – novel. And indeed, since writing the book I've met Matt O'Connor, heard his end of things, and that too has wrought a change on my perception of this unique pressure group.

However, if I had to sum up what I felt about it at the time, it was that there was something historically queasy about, on the one hand, fathers desperate to have contact with their children, shinning up the façades of public buildings; while on the other, Tony Blair, the self-styled 'Daddy' of the nation, was sending young lads, mostly from poor backgrounds, off on a foreign adventure of dubious moral and legal legitimacy.

It's this incongruity that led me to examine the F4J phenomenon. This, and my own experiences as a divorced father of children, who had difficulties with gaining the care and control that I wanted.

I certainly understood the anguish of fathers who were trying to maintain good relationships with their children, and were facing difficulties in so doing, in part because of what they perceived as obstructive and difficult former partners. This being said, I also knew from my own experience that in many ways I had been an inadequate father in my first marriage, and that there was some perhaps poetic justice in the difficulties I was having. The cash-for-kids situation I found myself in in the divorce courts, in many ways replicated my own, warped priorities. My experience had led me to understand that no outside agency – courts, mediation, police – could ever make good the failures of individuals' relationships or their families.

Nevertheless, the combination of pathos and strange, quintessentially male bravado bound up in the F4J happenings grabbed my imagination very strongly, and while I personally doubted that some of the men who were dressing up in the costumes were actually the same men who were most ill-served by the family courts, I still retain sympathy for the cause they espouse.

Will Self, Journalist and Author

In the time it takes you to read this book at least 100 children will have lost contact with their father.

By the end of the week another 800–900 children in Britain's secret Family Courts will have lost contact not only with their fathers, but also with the grandmothers and grandfathers they dearly love.

By the end of the year, the number of children affected will be in the region of 50,000.

Since the Labour government came to power in 1997, at least half a million children have lost all or partial contact with one parent.

INTRODUCTION:

NEVER MIND THE BOLLOCKS

'If there be trouble, let it be in my day, that my child may have peace.'
THOMAS PAINE, *RIGHTS OF MAN*, 1737–1809

It's official.

> You can be a dad.
> You can be a stepdad.
> You can adopt any child.
> You can be a teacher.
> You can see anybody else's kids.
> *Except your own.*

It's impossible for most people to believe that we live in a country where our government denies all parents, not just dads, a right in law to see their children after separation. But then, because nobody can see into a family court, how the hell would you know there was a problem? If it wasn't for some mad dad dressed in Lycra hanging off a bridge by his fingertips, holding up the traffic somewhere, chances are you'd be none the wiser.

But, probably as penance for my years of hedonistic excess, God in his divine wisdom has afforded me the privilege of experiencing first hand the traumatic effects of family law and witnessing what it does to people. Not just once. Not even twice. But a thousand times over.

Family law in this country is a perversion of the course of natural justice. It trashes lives, destroys childhoods, tears families apart, strips them of their savings; it even pitches parent against parent. It criminalises and crushes you before suffocating you with a blanket of secrecy and censorship. It's like being buried alive.

So what, you might wonder, makes a bacchanalian hedonist like me get on to the streets to campaign for a cause I believe in?

Two reasons. One answer. Daniel and Alexander. The children I dearly love, and nearly lost.

Fathers 4 Justice was conceived by me to do one job. To make the injustice visible and prevent it from being concealed by the state from you, from me and from parents everywhere. It hasn't been all darkness, suffering and misery. On the way we've rattled the cages of the rich and powerful and upset a lot, and I mean a *lot*, of people. There have been thrills and spills, men in tights, midnight raids, car chases, handcuffings, handbaggings, powder bombings in Parliament; we've scaled national monuments, nearly been shot, been accused of plotting to kidnap, and had run-ins with politicians, journalists, newspaper editors, archbishops, Special Branch, MI5 and even the FBI. This is my story, my personal journey with the tragic comedy that is Fathers 4 Justice.

This book spills the beans, in every detail, on how the campaign was organised. After they read *Father 4 Justice: The Inside Story* at Scotland Yard it's possible that I could face charges for conspiracy to cause a public nuisance, a serious offence with no minimum tariff. At least I can be sure of the Yard buying a dozen copies, even if nobody else does.

Oh, and apologies to my mother about the language. I know it shows a poverty of imagination and all that, but even I need to work off a little steam every now and then. Or in this case every few sentences.

Matt O'Connor

MAY DIVORCE BE WITH YOU

The end of a relationship or break-up of a marriage can be a difficult time for all parties involved. Naturally, you will be concerned about your current financial and property arrangements and how it will affect any children you may have. We have a skilled and approachable team of family lawyers who will handle your case sensitively and in a constructive and non-confrontational manner.

Solicitors' Introduction to Family Law

The birth of a child should be one of the happiest and most momentous events in a person's life. Our children are the most precious people to us. They love us unconditionally. They make us laugh and cry. They make us happy, angry, sad, frustrated, hopeful. Our children are our future – a precious human resource to whom we entrust our history. But what of our legacy to them?

In twenty-first-century Britain something intangible has changed. In twenty years' time a generation will reflect and understand that at this time the social unit we called the family, that for thousands of years held us together, has broken down, driven apart by conflicting social and cultural dynamics.

The very glue that used to bind us together, father and mother, brother and sister, is dissolving in front of our very eyes, much of it washed away in a tide of greed, selfishness and narcissism. Some of it is a direct consequence of the perverse experiment in social engineering that was orchestrated by my party, the Labour Party, watched by men of the cloth who did nothing but wring their hands as they turned their backs on the dying days of the family.

By any estimate, today, nearly 50 per cent of all marriages will end in divorce or separation. If you are unmarried that figure will be much, much higher. And, as the 'experts' argue over the causes of family breakdown, caught in the crossfire are a nation's children.

No one is in any doubt that we are experiencing a national emergency in family law, both in Britain and in most industrialised nations. The last two decades have seen a succession of government discussion papers, consultations and select committee enquiries on the issue – but no action.

According to Harriet Harman, Minister of State for Constitutional Affairs, over a million people find themselves in the family courts every year.* A frightening percentage of these lose contact with their children. In 2003 the then President of the Family Division, Dame Elizabeth Butler-Sloss, admitted that '40 per cent of fathers have little or no meaningful contact with their children post-separation'. It is a stomach-churning figure.

By my reckoning at least half a million children have been semi-orphaned by the state from one parent, normally their fathers, in the lifetime of this Labour administration. It is a figure that should make anyone pause for thought before inflicting what will almost certainly be a destructive and painful conflict upon their children. Because for all the fine words and noble sentiment at the outset, divorce *is* a dirty business. No matter how civilised you imagine you are, everybody in a divorce court is reduced to the same, debased level, where parent is pitched against parent, where rancid excrement is thrown in ever increasing quantities, emotional weaponry discharged at every opportunity and where children – who just want their fuckwit parents to get on – are emotionally smashed, mashed and then spat out like shards of glass, lacerating the very fabric of our nation as a consequence.

The blood of our children, as I predicted some years ago, is now being spilt in a bloody harvest of bullets and blades on the streets of London.

These kids are the *first* fatherless generation.

The lost generation.

The Generation X.

If that isn't enough to sober you up, don't think for a moment there'll be any winners either. In Britain's Secret Family Courts there are only losers.

How would you like your family served, Sir? Chinese style? Singapore style?

What about North Korean style? Secret oppressive courts, where nobody can hear you scream – because that is the reality of any decision to go to court. This book is a message, a warning, the question is – *Are you hearing me?*

Of course you might think to yourself, hey, what's the worst that can happen if you split up with your partner?

---

* Speech to the National Family and Parenting Institute, 5 October 2006.

In this book, amongst other things, I pull back the curtains on the secret world of Britain's family courts to reveal their decaying edifice and a modus operandi that will make even the hardiest soul flinch and recoil at their butchery of families. Remember, when you play their Family Law Lotto, next time it *could* be you.

It could happen like this: he runs off with his secretary, leaving his home and family with neither warning nor support; she fucks off with the milkman, taking the kids, dog, furniture and, more distressingly perhaps, draining the wine cellar of vintage Chateau Lafitte.

You'll make a cheap joke like that at the beginning to get over the shock, before the reality drags you down beneath the surface. Equally speaking he may arrive home to find the locks changed and his wife shouting through the letterbox telling him that she has asked for a divorce and that he's now been excommunicated from his children, personal possessions and property. Or she comes home to find herself alone with a pile of bills, hungry children and an empty bank balance.

Your first port of call will be a solicitor, who'll advise you on what they think is the best course of action for you. The first session may be free – or it could cost you upwards of £175 – £250, possibly more. That's per hour, by the way.

If you are the parent with care, i.e. the children live with you, the state will view you as the 'resident' parent or what used to be known as the parent with 'custody'. This is generally the mother. You will receive *all* the child benefits, family tax credits, housing benefits, etc., and pretty much unlimited publicly funded legal aid for any contact disputes until the children are at least 16.

If you are the parent without care, you are the 'non-resident' parent and are generally the father. Providing you have signed the birth certificate when your child was born you are (in theory at least) entitled to information about your child's schooling, medical records, etc. This is called 'parental responsibility'. However, if you did *not* sign the birth certificate and are unmarried, you have *no rights in law* to information about your child and will need to apply to a court to try and establish 'parental responsibility'.

That's the good news.

The bad news is that under English law as a parent (mother or father) you have *no* rights in law to see your children. Period.

Your only right is to apply to a court for a 'contact order' to give you 'theoretical' access to your child. This order will define state-appointed times for you to see your children, though some orders are for 'supervised' contact (in a contact centre) or 'indirect contact' which might allow you to send a birthday or Christmas card once a year.

It has occurred to many dads that these orders bear a striking similarity to 'control orders' which are used on terrorist suspects. That would be a foolish comparison to make – terrorists generally have a right to a hearing in open court. You don't.

If you have access problems you will need to apply to a court for a contact order either as a 'litigant in person', i.e. on your own, or through a solicitor. The application fee for this is £175, plus solicitor's costs starting at £175 an hour. The costs for a hearing are roughly about £1,000 – £2,000 for legal preparation, plus barrister costs for the day which might be another £2,000.

That's at least £4,000, just to start the engine.

Oh, and by the way, this will secure an order to see a child you might have been living with up until last week *and* which has a 50 per cent, yes 50 per cent, chance of being broken – a fact that your solicitor, being economical with his explanations, will omit to tell you.

Without an order, even calling your kids can be an exercise fraught with risk. Mum could argue that your making telephone calls to the children constitutes a course of conduct that causes her 'alarm, harassment or distress'. Before you know it, Plod could be on the phone asking you to 'come in for a chat' down at the station – which is policespeak for 'you're going to be nicked, matey'.

If you were married you should have agreed a 'statement of arrangements' in your divorce papers about the children's visiting arrangements. This sounds good, but don't fret too much – it's utterly worthless.

As you don't have the children living with you, chances are you won't qualify for legal aid so you'll end up paying your own legal costs out of your own pocket. Bank accounts will be bled dry, savings accounts emptied, favours from friends and relatives cashed in.

It's unlikely at this juncture that maintenance will figure high on your priorities list, but in the event that you can't pay because of a mounting financial crisis brought on by separation – you are now living in a bedsit a few miles from your old £450,000 home – the Child Support Agency (CSA) will come knocking. Now even if you had the children living with you 50 per cent of the time, you wouldn't get a penny in benefits from the state because you would not be the parent with care. Instead they would still expect you to pay the amount they calculate, despite the fact that 50 per cent of the time you house, clothe and feed your family. In the real world, this is called discrimination.

If you're employed, the CSA will deduct the amount they calculate straight from your earnings regardless of whatever other bills you have to pay and without taking into consideration such fundamentals as rent. I don't want to depress you yet, or get you reaching for the Jack Daniels to wash down handfuls of paracetamol, but I'm just warning you that this is an everyday occurrence for many parents, mostly fathers.

Meanwhile, back in court, if you're lucky, somebody might mention 'conciliation' or 'mediation' or 'dispute resolution'. Don't worry if you don't know what these terms mean – neither does the court.

Mediation is supposed to happen before you go to court, but solicitors are generally not too keen on this as there's a risk that clients might reach an agreement, which is bad for the bottom line. If this does happen – and pray to God it does – you can ask the judge for a 'Consent Order', which binds all parties with regard to future arrangements without an order being enforced upon you by the court.

However, mediation can also happen when you are in the court. Some judges have been 'trained' in mediation and they often like to exercise their skills in court. Trust me when I tell you this isn't always a good thing. Picture Rocky Balboa conducting micro-surgery and you'll understand. By the way, your barrister (if you have one) may also be a judge from time to time and vice versa, and your judge may change more frequently than your underwear. That's what they amusingly describe as 'judicial continuity'. Worse, most judges are not even specialists in family law, switching from family law to criminal law on a daily basis. What jokers those chaps are at the Ministry of Justice.

As judges are not held to account in open court, nor subject to any kind of public scrutiny, they act with unfettered discretion. This can lead to some frankly horrific judgements, such as the time District Judge Hearne decided a boy's future by tossing a coin in court in front of the boy's father, Ray Barry. Inspires confidence, doesn't it?

If mediation isn't offered to you then there is something called 'dispute resolution'. This is run by a meaningful mouthful called CAFCASS: the Children and Family Court Advisory and Support Service. At least, it's normally run by them, but it can also be run by other external mediation agencies who also run 'dispute resolution' services.

Confused?

I know I am – and I've been involved in thousands of cases over the last five years.

Dispute resolution normally happens after you have been to court – it's the same as mediation, but it's got a different name. Don't ask me why. It can also happen before you go to court. Nobody will tell you anything about this, though you may receive some kind of notification to attend a cryptic meeting with CAFCASS before you go into court.

A WORD ABOUT CAFCASS

A CAFCASS or Court Welfare Reporter is the 'eyes and ears of the court'. Sounds good doesn't it? Not necessarily. CAFCASS was launched on April Fool's Day 2001 (you couldn't make this stuff up, I promise you) and was born from the ashes of the Probation Service. This meant that a substantial number of their officers back then were ex-probation officers who were more used to dealing with hardened criminals than with parents going through the pain of separation. Don't worry, they received 'training'.

All seven, reassuring days of it.

Traffic wardens get more.

These days most CAFCASS officers are recruited from Social Services, which many would argue is an even more terrifying human resource base to be tapping into – social workers tend to have a deeply mistrusting view of *all* parents.

A CAFCASS officer might also double up as a 'Guardian Ad Litum', a person appointed to represent the 'best interests of the child' if agreement between the parents can't be reached. Again, this all sounds great, but for the fact that they don't know what the 'best interests' of any child going through the British justice system have been, as they haven't got round to measuring the outcomes for those children.

So much for this profession being so concerned about our children's best interests.

In fact, our Family Justice system has NO records at all to show what happened to the hundreds of thousands of children who have been through the family courts. I'll take a wild stab in the dark then and guess these might be the teenagers who are now slicing and dicing each other on your nearest street corner or playing field.

There are two final matters to cover. The first is allegations. These can be made against you without your knowledge. CAFCASS divides evidence into two categories: soft evidence and hard evidence. The chances are that you won't be told about this or given the opportunity to answer any allegations, but the reality is that in future you will be routinely risk-assessed if you are a father, even if there are *no* allegations or grounds for doing so. The judge will then decide your 'guilt', not using the criminal standard of proof (i.e. beyond all reasonable doubt) but on the 'balance of probabilities', thereby dismantling entirely the presumption of 'innocent until proven guilty'. This means if the judge thinks you are guilty, you are. Somebody once joked that it can only be a matter of time before they introduce ducking stools behind the courts to determine 'truth'. As such, and this being family law, it'll probably happen, provided they can do it in secret.

Finally, most orders break down, which means you will go back to court – again and again and again and again – trying to get them enforced, forever trapped in the u-bend of the family law urinal.

May divorce be with you. Welcome to breakdown Britain.

CONTACT

In family law this is the word that sums up the beautiful, loving relationships we have with our children.

Contact.

It's the word the state uses in its dictionary of gobbledygook to describe your relationship with your children after a relationship has broken down. And if you can't agree 'contact', they'll stick you in a 'contact centre' in some desolate church hall or sports centre for a few hours on a Saturday afternoon once or twice a month – if you're lucky.

A few weeks back, you and the kids were crashed out on the sofa every weekend watching *Doctor Who*, surrounded by the creature comforts that your hard work has earned. If your kids were anything like mine there'd be farting competitions, arm wrestling, and rounds of beating Dad into submission for more chocolate. But in the clinical environs of this state-monitored room, your every move, breath and word is monitored, interpreted and then fed back for analysis.

The question you keep asking is Why? Don't you trust me with my kids? What is going on here? A few weeks back I was their dad. Now I'm a pariah, the leper of the family. The judge in your case might have decided to send you to one of these centres for a 'cooling-off' period, for no other reason than you and your ex-partner simply aren't getting on.

The judge will promise you an order which he won't enforce and demand your silent, obedient consent in exchange.

THE GODFATHER

The growth of divorce has spawned a vast empire of lawyers, welfare officers, social workers, child psychologists and numerous state-funded charities, all of whom have a vested interest in family breakdown and most of whom owe their jobs solely to the impact that divorce has on children. (Cynics argue that the easiest way to ensure continued employment is to secure an endless supply of fatherless children.) It would be a generalisation to say that the most loathed of these is the legal fraternity, though in my experience, this has been the case.

Did you hear the one about the bus-load of lawyers that was hijacked by terrorists? They threatened to release one every hour until their demands were met.

Just what is it about lawyers that everybody finds so repellent? Is it coincidence that sure as maggots become flies lawyers become politicians? Because, let's face it, Parliament is chock-full of the buggers. Is it the way they relieve their clients of obscene amounts of loot in return for richly unrewarding experiences? Or is it perhaps something more fundamental, such as their lack of moral fibre. Either way, I thought I should at least take a stab at finding out, aided by a sadistically inclined barrister friend of mine, Michael Cox, who had invited me to attend a family law conference that was to discuss opening up the family courts to public scrutiny.

His conditions for my attendance were that I wouldn't handcuff a judge, pee in the tea urn or indulge in any inappropriate outbursts. By this time – four years after I had started the most notorious campaign group of recent years – it was fair to say that my reputation as an attack-dog went before me. I was the *enfant terrible* of family law.

Inside the conference an oily slick of the great and the good of family law had washed up in a south coast hotel to press the flesh, rub each other up the right way, massage mutual egos and indulge in an orgy of sycophancy and social intercourse. One solicitor shuffled his bovine features around his table to take a seat at the front of the room. He looked plump and pampered by the system. Clearly, somebody had enjoyed their time at the family law trough.

The air was charged with anticipation as Michael and I bagged pole position, a table right at the front. We were both wearing campaign threads with suitably provocative messages that screamed 'We eat solicitors for breakfast' at nervous onlookers.

The conference started with a speech by Sir Mark Potter, President of the Family Division. This guy was the head honcho, the Don Corleone of family law and lynchpin in the incestuous relationship between the judiciary and the legal profession. When the Don finished eulogising about the family courts, I thought I'd ask a few questions, thinking that, him being a judge and all that, he'd find them easy to answer.

'Sir Mark, what empirical evidence is there to demonstrate that open family courts would damage children? Public confidence in the family justice system has been undermined and open courts would serve the purpose of restoring it. I'm afraid I should point out that I founded the campaign that did the undermining.'

'Er, nothing, but we rely on experts to tell us these things.'

'But surely the courts rely on evidence, not supposition or prejudice? There must be some evidence on which to base your argument, otherwise why are you so resistant to change?'

'Well, that's why we are having a public consultation,' he said, shuffling his papers and nervously looking to the chairwoman to help him out by finding another question.

I turn to Michael. 'What was that Upton Sinclair principle about it being difficult to get a man to understand something when his salary depends on his not understanding it?' I ask him. 'If this guy was chief executive of a private company he'd have been sacked after a performance like that.'

After lunch the debate got under way with speakers for and against open courts.

'Opening up the courts could damage the fragile ecosystem that is family law,' said one leading woman barrister. 'We cannot risk harming children by exposing them to the glare of publicity. Our family justice system is the envy of the world,' she trumpeted unashamedly, as considerate applause filled the cavernous conference room.

This was a barrister in need of an urgent irony bypass.

'But at no time in living memory can I remember such public criticism of the family courts. In no small part I'm afraid this is down to those men in tights, Fathers 4 Justice.'

Then, through gritted teeth, each speaker grudgingly acknowledged the impact of the campaign. But even those who supported opening family court proceedings to public scrutiny were against us. Sarah Harman, Harriet Harman's icy sister, spoke in favour of open courts, but the temperature dropped to sub-zero when it came to Fathers 4 Justice. She cast a sour look in my direction then launched a volcanic flow of scorn on to F4J and our 'ill-deserved column inches'. I turned to Coxy. 'Bet that woman bleeds ice. If they stuck one Harman sister on the North Pole and the other at the South, there'd be no danger of the ice caps melting.'

I thought about a public retort but decided to make her squirm by saluting her efforts in assisting us with our campaign. I'm rewarded by a half-smile. The simple if unpalatable truth is that none of this debate would have been possible without Fathers 4 Justice.

Standing my ground in the face of their obvious hostility, I made the case for open justice: 'Any country that gags parents and children, closes courts to the public, censors judgments and allows judges to act with impunity and without accountability has more in common with North Korea than an open democracy.'

Another speaker, Cassandra Jardine from the *Daily Telegraph*, was sneered at and then laughed off the platform when she argued that family law professionals were failing the very people they were supposed to protect: the children. It made for uncomfortable and troubling viewing and spoke volumes about this so-called profession.

Then, one after another they stood up to make the case against. The room was awash with denial. There was so much denial I felt like starting a twelve-step recovery programme right there and then. But lawyers just don't get it. Unless they get it in their bank accounts.

Even as the shock waves created by our campaign were reverberating throughout the country, the legal world continued to operate in a vacuum, a parallel universe away from the cruel reality of family breakdown and the consequences of their actions.

Every year, a million parents turn to the state for help when they can't agree 'contact' arrangements for their children. Inevitably they are fed, like me, into the family law mincing-machine, where the last remnants of dignity and humanity are mechanically stripped from the bones of that relationship. If you think it's bad when you have just separated, multiply that by a thousand should you fall into the hands of the court system. Without the demilitarised zone of mandatory mediation, parental conflict is, regrettably, inevitable. And solicitors can be relied upon to inflame the unholy conflict so that it escalates like an arms race to the point of Mutually Assured Destruction – M.A.D.

Protracted, painful and secret court hearings can cost tens of thousands of pounds and last several years. As the case drags on, savings are exhausted and equities signed away to the Legal Services Commission. Children's inheritances are hijacked. And the legal industry turns in a hefty profit: the longer the conflict the more bang they get from *your* buck. When it's over, the more cynical solicitors refer to clients having been 'spin dried'. No wonder they were laughing at that hapless journalist.

'We're a family company,' one leading solicitor told me in early 2004 over a couple of glasses of chilled vino at a boozer opposite the British Museum. 'We've turned over at least twenty since the beginning of the year.'

It was February.

'But how do you square prioritising your client's interests with the children's best interests?' I asked. 'Isn't this all some kind of legal spider's web from which neither parent can escape?'

He smiled pityingly at my naïvety and refilled his glass.

Whatever you call it, the only people who win are the lawyers.

Not the children.

The children *never* win.

SOAKED

I was a spindly rake of a seaside-boy. A stuttering, stammering geek who wore his mum's best pudding bowl fringe haircut with acute embarrassment, not knowing why he felt awkward but picking up enough mocking glances to realise all was not well in the style and sartorial departments.

It was only in my later teenage years that I realised my mother had been pioneering, almost single-handedly, the Rodney Trotter look.

'Planet' Thanet was where I lived, except it wasn't a planet but what was loosely described as an island, separated from the mainland by a silted up drainage ditch called the River Wansum.

Thanet was a vast patch of cauliflowers with the cast of Cocoon strung around its pensioner-lined perimeter. The seaside towns of Margate, Broadstairs and Ramsgate were outposts for the elderly and ghettos for the unemployed.

If Kent was the Garden of England, Thanet was its compost heap.

My parents had been two diametrically opposed personalities thrown together in some fateful tryst when they were studying to be teachers at Reading University. Dad was a flamboyant bon viveur from County Kerry, Southern Ireland, and my mother a sober and conscientious academic of Welsh and English parentage. My childhood was peppered with conflict. At times it felt as if I'd be born on a battlefield.

Any aspirations to follow in my parents' footsteps as teachers were misplaced. During my late teens I went to art college in Canterbury and discovered a revolutionary zeal and bags of youthful idealism, campaigning for CND, the Anti-Apartheid movement and Amnesty International.

I was subsequently unceremoniously thrown out of college for a 'deplorable' attendance record. At the time I was going out with a French topless model called Celine whose feminine curves proved too much of an educational distraction. Rather fortunately I stumbled upon gainful employment in the shape of a Prontaprint shop in Ramsgate which gave me a good grounding in all the design basics. Despite developing a taste for adventure and campaigning, my idealism headed underground when, on my first visit to Paris, I met Patrick Bois, Celine's dad, who ran *Le Shaker*, a magazine for the cocktail industry in France.

I fell for the city – glass, bottle and brasserie. After a few historic nights out with an assortment of industry figures, I developed a taste for both Armagnac and for Monte Cristo cigars.

Any lasting prospect of a life of sobriety was swiftly washed away in 1993 when I was introduced to Peter Matthews, a vertically challenged entrepreneur whose carrot-top barnet, schoolboyish wit and extraordinary energy had earned him an encyclopaedia of nicknames. His parties were the stuff of legend, and though he managed to avoid falling foul of the law, he was forever getting embroiled in near-death yet life-affirming experiences that encouraged him to pursue ever more reckless behaviour.

Peter's favourite haunt was a watering hole called the Papermill, a café bar located on Curtain Road in the City of London. Since he spent so much time there, he decided to buy the place and make it his HQ. Our offices were on the third floor, with a small pied-à-terre to accommodate any member of staff who couldn't make it home.

It was work, rest and play, all in the one building.

The work part consisted of launching a series of cocktail bars and restaurants. It was hard work, too, tasting tapas with Jamie Oliver or downing forty-two cocktails in a single lunch hour with 'Uncle' Dick Bradsell, the country's leading cocktail guru and 'oracle of the optics'. Deals would be sealed over Bourbon-laced Kentucky cream teas and deep-fried ice cream balls. Those bacchanalian days would come back to haunt me, but Peter thought it was a hoot.

'We are,' he declared proudly, 'the finest purveyors of food porn in the City.'

Those ten halcyon years with Peter I call my 'wonder' years (as in – I wonder what happened to them). In among the bar crawls and extended tours of duty I found time for all manner of conquests, corpses, indiscretions, embarrassments and unfortunate incidents, right up until the day that fate dealt me a winning hand.

It came after an especially heavy lunch with a mad Irish uncle, that one-man Celtic cabaret, James O'Connor. Holed beneath the waterline and sinking fast, I somehow managed to crawl back to my gaff in Barking to find my brother waiting for me.

'Fuck, Matt, you can barely walk, you fucking soak.'

We set off for the nearest tavern, The Barge Aground, and it wasn't long before I ran aground. Following unsteadily as David threw the saloon doors open Wild West style and sashayed to the bar in his best *Saturday Night Fever* swagger, I lost my struggle to stay vertical and collapsed on to a banquette occupied by a handful of young ladies. After I'd introduced myself with the promise of champagne and fine wines, one of the girls passed me her telephone number. Not for any serious reason, you understand, but for a bet.

She turned out to be my future wife.

A few days later I came across the number in my wallet. Thanks to my advanced state of refreshment, I couldn't remember a thing about the evening in question, so I called my brother to see if he could throw any light on it. The answer was affirmative. Some poor teacher – David thought her name was Sophie – had suffered the pleasure of my company. Fortunately, though I'd circled the cusp of being badly behaved, I hadn't quite crossed the Rubicon on account of my physically being incapable of committing any lewd, offensive or illegal acts.

I decided to call and apologise profusely for being an embarrassing tart, offering an invitation to dinner by way of reparation. She sounded great; two hours of banter, laughter and frivolity later, we arranged to meet at Hornchurch tube station.

To be honest, I was smitten. Hook, line and bloody sinker. In fact, so worried was I by this turn of events, I visited my doctor to check that I was still of sound mind and body.

But then, on the day I was to meet Sophie, I popped into a bar for a quick snifter with a few colleagues and started getting, well, a bit gushy about her. It was at this juncture that my good friend, the Cultural Attaché for Curtain Road, Ian Maddaford, raised a very pertinent question.

'This is all good and well, dear boy, but can you remember what she actually looks like?'

For a second or two I carried on smiling, until the proverbial penny dropped.

'No, I can't.'

'Well, fuck me, how do you propose to find her if you don't recognise her?'

'Shit, oh fucking shit, shit, shit.'

'You're a prize plonker, O'Connor. She won't recognise you either.'

'Why not?'

'Because you're sober. And if we get you lashed up again so she will recognise you, you'll be back at square one.'

In the end I bit both ends and the middle of the bullet and travelled out to deepest, darkest Hornchurch where I stood outside the tube station, praying, yes praying, for divine intervention. This time the Lord answered with a tap on the shoulder and a face that could have been the Madonna herself. I was so relieved.

There followed a whirlwind romance. Sophie was jaw-droppingly gorgeous, a Spanish temptress who mixed several languages with a gregarious, fun-loving nature. In short, she was irresistible and I was insatiable for love.

The sparks flew from the off. Our relationship was a volatile cocktail of Latino and Celtic blood that would inevitably and spontaneously combust at some point in the future.

Oh my imagination! So many ideas, so little time. So what do you do when you want to woo the girl of your dreams? Find yourself a castle. It all seemed such a good idea at the time: a bit of a romantic leg-over at a fourteenth-century pile nestled in the Forest of Dean. Plan A was for a rip-roaring night of love, romance and hanky-panky in a suitably robust four-poster bed. Sophie would be hosed down with a magnum of Laurent Perrier rosé and then devoured mercilessly by her crazed boyfriend. Plan B turned out to be infinitely more interesting.

The castle was holding a medieval night, with locals on horseback clad in armour and authentic medieval threads. It sounded like a hoot and we booked ourselves in. After a riotous evening, I foolishly rose to the challenge of a sword fight with one of the local farmers on the lawn in front of the castle.

Kitted out in knight's armour and fuelled by enough Jack Daniel's to knock out a baby elephant, I took several hits to the head before retiring concussed. Sophie, who, expecting some al-fresco nooky, had rushed upstairs to grab her coat, returned to find me staggering around the lawn in my suit of panel-beaten metal, as if heavily anaesthetised.

'It's not every day you get to meet a knight in shining armour,' she declared with misplaced optimism, not realising how bad I was.

'I fucking love you,' I slurred.

My head began to pound. I sank to my knees, plunging the sword I was holding into the ground, and gazed upwards to the stars. The low throb in my head evolved into a pounding bass beat and my vision became one seamless motion blur. I found Sophie's face in the soup of the night and focused hard.

'I know this might seem an odd question, given what's happened, but will you marry me, darling?'

She paused for a few seconds, staring down at a man who was now using his sword to support his full body weight rather than for any dramatic purpose.

'Yes, I will marry you,' she said in an almost pitying tone, having deduced that I was simultaneously chivalrous and paralytic. 'You give a whole new definition to the phrase "a drunken knight out".'

The whirlwind continued over Easter, when we went to Spain to meet her relatives. After a night out at a local fiesta, I ended up on a bull run in Arcos de la Frontera, Andalucia, with a half-ton of Spanish steak nuzzling my arse.

Back in London, my colleagues were less than convinced.

'Haven't you heard about the three rings of marriage, Matthew?' said Peter, when he heard I'd taken the plunge. 'There's the engagement ring, the wedding ring . . . and the suffering.'

'Funny fucking ha-ha. I know what I'm doing.'

'Yeah, and twenty quid says you won't last six months.'

Some years later, in one of several joint interviews we gave, Sophie said, rather unkindly and with more than a frisson of mischief, 'He sold marriage to me as though it was one of his marketing operations, even taking me to see *Four Weddings and a Funeral* to get me in the mood.' I'll plead guilty to the first charge, your honour, but not guilty to the second. Sophie was as enthusiastic as I was, booking a venue before I'd even set eyes on the place. Sometimes, in love, these things happen. Just as I'd been dragged kicking and screaming down the aisle to see *Four Weddings*.

I have rarely been so nervous as I was on our wedding day. I had arranged to meet Peter, Ian and the lads at a pub in Hornchurch close to the Registry Office. Peter was on fine form, plying stiffeners on everybody. Even though we were barely half a mile away, we managed to turn up late, the car ripping up the drive as Peter pulled a semi-handbrake turn, nearly wiping out half the guests in the process. It was like a scene from *The Sweeney* as people ran for cover and the boys spilled out in front of the building.

'Don't worry, dear boy,' said Maddaford. 'We'll leave the engine running if you need to make a quick getaway.'

'Christ, Ian, don't let Sophie hear you say that.' Which of course, she had.

It was, so they said, one of the greatest ever wedding bashes. A small room packed with friends and family enjoyed lunch at an Essex manor house, followed by a big evening bash with a full-blown twelve-piece Blues Brothers' style band that had guests dancing on tables and ended with most people being unceremoniously dumped in the hotel pool. Departing guests universally declared the bash 'historic'.

Sophie hated it. The pianist played 'The Wild Rover' instead of 'It Had to Be You' as our wedding song – a switch I suspect had been instigated by one of my colleagues as a laugh. She thought I hadn't been paying enough attention to her during the evening. Even our wedding video ended up being copied over with an episode of *EastEnders*, the memories lost to Dot

Cotton and another bloody pub, the Queen Vic. The omens did not look favourable.

Honeymooning near Olu Deniz in Turkey, my new wife threw up into my lap on a boat trip, while I managed to inadvertently lose my wedding ring while swimming down a river gorge. But we laughed, we joked and Turkey seduced us with her Ottoman charms. Back then we simply sat back and absorbed as much hospitality as she could offer, without any of the baggage that life was inevitably going to dump on us.

On our return, we indulged in a series of culinary capers, travelled, socialised and embraced the intoxicating spirit of bonhomie. So it came as a hefty reality check when Sophie fell pregnant. I took it in my stride without really contemplating the consequences, for this was the woman of my dreams. Despite a few minor misgivings, which were probably mutual, it seemed that life had never been more beautiful.

We did take the precautionary step of acquiring a dog – a bit of enforced discipline and training in preparation for parenthood. 'Basil' was a nervous, timid dog with a bit of a twitch and a tendency to involuntarily defecate on the spot at the first sign of trouble. Perhaps if he'd been called 'Oregano' or 'Tarragon' which sound like *hard* herbs he might have had more self-confidence, but in a manor where the dogs were nutty mutts with names like 'Tyson', 'Jake' and 'Razor', he was so worried about his canine neighbours, he just kept shitting.

I had always been desperately insecure in relationships, never really having the confidence to make them work. When you don't have confidence, somehow you always end up being shat on. Perhaps that's why I used to over-compensate, relying on bravado and humour as a bit of protective armour. But Sophie stripped all that from me and exposed me for who I was. For that reason, the chemistry was extraordinary. And for that reason she became my friend, my lover and my wife. That's why I'll always regret what happened to us. Looking back gives those memories added poignancy, perhaps because during the divorce I had ring-fenced them, unable to confront those feelings.

In March 1996 we moved from East London to a modest but charming nineteenth-century weatherboard cottage in Downe, Kent. I had sunk my savings into buying the property and Peter helped out with a loan to ensure we could afford it. I couldn't thank him enough for his help.

In preparation for the birth, I spent my time painting the house, making a workmanlike job of it. Our first child Daniel was born a few weeks later, on 13 April 1996, at Farnborough Hospital. Sophie battled through the most excruciating, knuckle-biting of labours and I stayed by her side right to the bell – or at least until the surgeon started juggling unconvincingly with a scalpel blade, at which point my legs crossed involuntarily.

'Christ, is that really necessary?' I asked. No wonder women think men are wimps.

'Absolutely, your son has got caught with his umbilical cord around his neck. Every time there is a contraction, the cord is suffocating him. We need to create some room so we can untangle him. He's like a little yo-yo.'

More like a bloody bungee jumper, I thought, the way his head kept popping in and out.

Within ten minutes the drama was over; Daniel was born, leaving Sophie absolutely exhausted. The labour had taken an eye-watering twenty-three hours.

Those first few months with Daniel were precious and every moment was treasured. Sophie radiated maternal warmth and love. On our first Christmas morning in the house, we lay in bed playing with Daniel. I looked out of the window and it was snowing; polar-white flakes of Disneyfied ice tumbling from the sky. We stumbled into the garden, which had been transformed into Narnia. At moments like that, life pulls you by your heartstrings and doesn't let go. Sophie and I threw snowballs and laughed like children.

But the pressures of having a young child levered open cracks in the relationship. Sophie grew resentful that I was away in the City, working and socialising long hours, while she felt trapped in the confines of our new house. Feeling unsupported, she rapidly fell out of love with me. With hindsight, I can't blame her. My behaviour was inexcusable.

Despite this, Sophie fell pregnant again and on 27 November 1997 Alexander was born.

With two children, the marriage came under even greater pressure. The chills and thaws in the relationship turned to permafrost. I wondered whether she might be suffering from an undiagnosed post-natal depression, adding stress points to the relationship, but she dismissed this out of hand. By this time I was having to travel to Prague and the Netherlands, handling projects for clients. Coming home was like being banished to an emotional Siberia. It was so sub-zero, you could carve out conversations with an ice axe.

Feeling rejected by Sophie, I embarked on several affairs. One of these was a liaison that proved as dysfunctional as it was emotionally empty. It was to come back to haunt me. Not surprisingly, I felt sick to the core about the whole damn business.

The marriage seemed to have been a disastrous mistake, but with two children to consider we made a last-ditch effort to save it by finding an old farmhouse in Kent where we hoped to make a fresh start. But no sooner had our offer been accepted than the deal fell through. The survey revealed that the property was riddled with damp. It was the final death knell to the relationship.

LAST RITES

In January 2000 Sophie asked for a divorce.

Maybe it was her plea for me to become a better husband but I couldn't read the message. Perhaps it was coded in some reverse psychology. We've all been there, but the path to relationship breakdown never gets any easier to walk. You stroll past the signposts pointing in the opposite direction thinking it's all going to be alright, then you run into the oncoming traffic.

That day it was my turn to get hit. I was reluctant to agree to a divorce, but the heart-to-heart that followed was as sobering as it was draining. In the end, I couldn't face yet another confrontation with Sophie. I didn't have the stomach for another fight in front of the children. All I wanted was to make her happy, but standing in front of me was a woman who was so demonstrably, unspeakably unhappy.

In the front living room of our house in Cross Ashes, Downe, I scanned the grim domestic scene. All that was missing was a suitably sombre sound-track like Samuel Barber's *Adagio for Strings*. Sophie sat staring out of the window across towards the fields where I used to walk with the children. She explained that she felt let down, that she didn't love me any more and couldn't carry on. All she wanted, she said, was a nine-to-five husband who would be there for her, but, according to her, I didn't do normal.

I couldn't stand 'normal'.

When she got up to walk towards the kitchen I remonstrated with her for playing the victim when, in reality, our marriage wasn't quite the disaster movie she portrayed it as. Nor was I entirely to blame, given her own subsequent admission that she had stopped loving me three years earlier.

But what had started as a civil conversation erupted into bitterness and rancour at this. 'Like father, like son,' she said to me, stabbing her finger towards the floor, telling me that I'd be dead soon enough. Just like my father, who died of a heart-attack when he was 49 years of age. 'I wanted a husband, not an act of contrition,' she spat as she marched out of the room towards the kitchen.

In a last, desperate act of *mea culpa*, I pleaded with her, asking that we avoid divorce for the sake of the boys and make a go of things again. I genuinely believed that the relationship could be salvaged but Sophie wouldn't hear it, brutally beating my words into silence with a harsh, bitter language that was both vengeful and hateful. In a corner of the kitchen, the boys had emptied out a box of Lego onto the floor, trying to carry on playing at being normal.

It was time for me to go.

Upstairs I filled a bag with some toiletries and clothes in almost indecent haste, trying to vacate the property, to escape the storm. I ran back down the stairs and passed her again in the kitchen.

'I still love you, Sophie. I'll always love you.' She turned her back on me. I scooped the boys up in my arms and kissed them goodbye.

'Sorry boys, Daddy's got to go. I'll be back soon. Always remember, Daddy loves you. Daddy will always love you.' I drove down North End Lane, found a small car park to pull in to and sat in the car, shaking and crying uncontrollably, my hands gripping the steering wheel.

I was dead inside, and I didn't even know it.

My first instinct was to escape. Bury my head somewhere where I couldn't feel it. I embarked on a series of fun but perfunctory relationships, travelling the globe. Yet the more girlfriends I had, the emptier I became. And no matter where I went, I couldn't shed the burden of emotional baggage. No matter how hard I tried, I couldn't shake the nightmare off.

Calls to the boys were fraught with difficulty, getting past Sophie being the first obstacle. But every conversation with them pulled me down, no matter how much humour I injected into the calls. When the boys were laughing, I was silently sobbing on the other end of the line as I struggled to come to terms with the malign impact the divorce was having on me.

Not seeing them hurt the most. I used to see them every day.

Every fucking day.

I was there every weekend. Sure, I was working a lot but I *was* there. I washed them, bathed them, shopped for them, played with them – for all my faults, I couldn't mentally embrace the concept that I could become severed from my own flesh and blood overnight. I began to feel sick at different times of the day. My legs would buckle for no reason. There wasn't a day I didn't cry. Worst still was being in the same room as other people's children, hearing their laughter, seeing them, but not being able to see my boys.

What the fuck was going on? I was becoming emotionally disabled by my separation from the boys, but far, far worse lay in store for me.

Sophie was befriended by my ex girlfriend. They say hell hath no fury like a woman scorned.

Try two. It tipped the divorce from two parents struggling with the detritus of separation into something altogether more unpleasant. As the divorce began to escalate, so the first of several 'incidents' occurred.

One weekend in June 2000, a French girlfriend of mine, Christel, and I took the boys to Thorpe Park. It was a glorious day out and we returned the boys on time at 5 p.m. that Saturday afternoon. During the day the boys had told me that mum had a new 'friend' from the village who, they told me with much relish, bore more than a passing resemblance to what they described in my language as a 'knuckle-dragging Neanderthal'. In a moment of excitability at believing my wife had discovered the missing link in the village which had been home to the author of the theory of evolution, Charles Darwin, I mischievously nicknamed the boyfriend 'Bubbles' after Michael Jackson's chimpanzee. On the way back I purchased the boys a bunch of bananas to hang off the central wrought-iron chandelier in the house. Within seconds of me dropping them off, an apoplectic Sophie was on the phone.

'But the kids love bananas, darling ...' I argued, but Sophie's Latino temperament had hit a Chernobyl-style melting point. I pulled into the local pub for a drink with Christel who started bemoaning the over-abundance of drama in my life. However, as we got up to leave and drive off, Sophie arrived in her car and boxed us in, preventing us from exiting our parking space. For several minutes she shouted abuse at Christel in a vitriolic French patois from her driver's side window, before I flipped. In a fit of pique I got out of my car, literally going ape. Shaking a discarded banana at her that I had found on the floor of the car I gave her car door a hefty kick to try and send her on her way, and she promptly left. The reward for this monkey business turned out to be a caution for criminal damage. For a car I owned. It was the first of several run-ins I was to have with Her Majesty's Constabulary.

Then Sophie went on to have me charged with harassment for calling the children and sending four letters to four neighbours, informing them that, contrary to village gossip, I had not abandoned my family. I won the subsequent trial, lost the girlfriend – but then came the bombshell. I called Sophie to make arrangements to see the children and she said, 'I've been to see a solicitor. Things are going to change, Matthew, regarding you seeing the boys.' I sat down on the bed, trying to absorb everything she was saying, but I couldn't make head nor tail of it. Why? Why now? Why, when we have agreed everything already?

I realised at once that I was in serious trouble. My life as I knew it had come to a sudden, dramatic and profoundly unpleasant end.

THUMPER

At my father's school there used to be a lad with the nickname 'Thumper'. Not because he kicked like a belligerent bunny, but because he'd throw a punch right between your family jewels before you'd even seen the little fucker coming. Going to a solicitor for the first time is a bit like that. It hurts.

'Three fucking grand!'

On a Monday morning in October 2000 I found myself sitting in the nondescript offices of a legal firm in South London, scaring the bejesus out of the secretaries and rattling the bone china in the cupboard beside me.

'Would you like some more tea, Mr O'Connor?' the solicitor offered.

When Sophie told me she wanted a divorce, things had got off to an amicable start. We both hoped for a good-natured transitional period with no dispute over access to the children. In fact, in our divorce papers the 'Statement of Arrangements' said that I would see the children three or four days a week. I was stupid enough to think that nothing could possibly go wrong.

After things soured between us, I decided to take action, firstly to establish, then defend, my rights. Being an ignorant so-and-so, I trotted off to the most useful-sounding solicitors I could find in the Yellow Pages. You'll find the majority of lawyers wear double-barrelled names like 'Right Hassle & Co' that imply they'll stand in as a comedy double act or funeral directors if required, both of which are careers just one step outside their professional briefs. The sums they were reeling off had my jaw dropping.

The costs run like this:

Three grand legal prep.

Two grand for one day in court with your barrister.

If you are forced to go back to court to enforce an order, five grand becomes ten grand becomes twenty.

'But all I want is to see my kids,' I pleaded. 'I must have some right to see them. I signed a Statement of Arrangements when we agreed to divorce, surely that must count for something?'

Solicitors, you'll soon discover, don't always tell the whole story. They never mention that court orders for contact are not enforced.

If your children don't live with you, you can forget legal aid. Moreover, even if your other half manages to qualify for legal aid, a charge will be put on the family home to ensure that the lawyers get their pound of flesh when the house is sold.

Even if you hate each other, you will both get skinned alive by the legal profession.

Hate them more.

It's the kids' inheritance, after all.

SAD DAD CAFÉ

In desperation I rang an organisation called Families Need Fathers and spoke to a chap called Tim Rait. It turned out they were just at the other end of Curtain Road so I shot up to see him. He seemed a good egg, very helpful and supportive, and I joined up immediately.

My first Families Need Fathers meeting was a shocker. A huddle of men in a decrepit room above an East End boozer, crying in their beer under a stale fog of cigarette smoke. It was like a departure lounge for dispossessed dads. A variety of 'self-help' books and leaflets were displayed on a table in the corner. Self-help? They were so depressing they should have come with a free packet of razor blades and a rough guide to Britain's suicide hotspots.

I tried to breathe some life-saving air into the room by arguing that dads needed to shake off their stupor and start rattling a few cages. We had to expose this scandalous state of affairs, perhaps by a little civil disobedience. But my attempts at agitation fell flatter than the warm beer that was served as liquid anaesthetic and I ended up being ejected after just half an hour.

I joined another group called the Equal Parenting Council run by Tony Coe, a.k.a. 'El Presidente', although president of what I don't know as it's only him and one other chap. On the plus side I was introduced to two helpful individuals: Gary Burch and Michael Cox. Burchy was the spitting image of Hugh Bonneville the actor and a silver-tongued diplomatic emissary for equal parenting. The debonair, savvy Mr Cox turned out to be a bit of a legal eagle and closet radical, and one of the few decent barristers either you or I may ever meet.

They told me about a big case involving some chap called Mark Harris, who'd been banged up in Pentonville for six months for saying hello to his three daughters in a DIY store car park. This apparently put him in breach of a court order defining the only times he could speak to his girls. At the time, I didn't believe a word of it, but it turned out to be true. I visited him in Pentonville Prison and left shell-shocked at what he told me. It was then that I began to have a very ominous feeling about my own fate in the family courts. It's fair to say that the first foundation stone of what would become the most notorious of campaign groups was laid on that day.

In November I learned that the Children and Family Court Advisory and Support Service, CAFCASS, had been appointed to my case. At my first meeting with case officer Maggie Derreck in Croydon the atmosphere was tense and strained as she broke the news that it could take months for the matter of contact to be resolved. I was incandescent with rage and she responded by bollocking me for my impatience.

'Impatient?' I spat. 'What? After six months of barely seeing the boys, I wouldn't trust you lot to look after my pet goldfish, let alone the best interests of my children.'

The final indignity of 2000 came on Christmas Eve. A few weeks earlier, Sophie had been involved in a car crash that had left her car a write-off, so in the spirit of goodwill I had lent her mine. That Christmas Eve we set out together with the boys to Sainsbury's so I could buy them some food for the holidays before travelling up to Birmingham to stay with a girlfriend, but when I went to put my bag in the back of the car, I found half my belongings had been rammed in there.

'What's going on, Sophie?' I demanded. 'I lend you this car to help you out and is this how you repay me? Dumping my gear in here when you know damn well I have nowhere to put it over Christmas?'

'I thought you'd want it back.'

'Don't fucking screw me over like this. I can't believe it! I just can't believe you'd pull a trick like this – on Christmas Eve, of all days!'

With that Sophie and the boys started to walk into Sainsbury's, but my festive spirit had evaporated and I called her back.

'Let me just spend some time with the boys on my own. I don't think it's a good idea for you to be here for that.'

She started getting agitated. 'You won't bring them back, will you? You're going to punish me for what I've done, I know you will, Matthew. You won't bring them back.'

By this time she was crying hysterically and nervy shoppers were firing concerned glances in our direction. Within seconds two security guards came over.

'Look, my wife is upset, she thinks I'm trying to snatch the kids,' I told them. 'I've got an agreement here saying that this is my time with them.' And I yanked out a letter that showed Sophie had agreed to contact. But by now events had overtaken any kind of common sense. With the kids bawling and clinging to their mum, I realised that there was nothing I could do but walk away from them, out of the store. I drove back to my old house and left my bags on the step. It would be my first Christmas without the boys.

THE WORST CASE SCENARIO HANDBOOK

The New Year got off to an equally grim start. My new work assistant, Jenny Bostock, had the hapless task of trying to keep my marbles together long enough so that I could run what we amusingly described as a 'professional' operation.

Luckily 'artistic' licence is factored in by clients when dealing with 'creative types' like me, and despite the fact that my mind was a mess, I still managed to get out of nearly every scrape I found myself in, producing some half-decent design work for the likes of Cadbury and Marks & Spencer. I lived a charmed existence in this respect at least, and was blessed with some of the most forgiving clientele a deranged designer could wish for.

Jen was a godsend and bacon-saver. She hailed from a small town called Pingelly in Western Australia. Not only did she turn out to be one of the most genuine and nicest people I have ever had the privilege of meeting, but she also became one of the foundation stones for the campaign group I was later to set up.

For my birthday she bought me *The Worst Case Scenario Handbook*, but by the end of the year my entire life was like Ground Zero. Learning how to give a shark a bloody nose in the seas off Western Australia is no help when you are facing the sewer swimming piscatorial delights operating in Britain's legal backwaters. Nor did it prepare me for my increasing dalliances with the Fuzz.

I'd been in Canterbury, working on a new restaurant project with head chef Jim 'the Close' Shave. Lunch got out of hand. To cut a long story short ... well, I was charged on four different counts, including 'drunk while in charge of a mechanically propelled vehicle' and 'stealing a motor vehicle belonging to Kent County Constabulary while under the influence of alcohol'. Eventually I agreed a plea bargain reducing the charge to 'drunk and disorderly' on the understanding that I wouldn't go to the press with the story.

A few months later vandals barbecued my company car. To add insult to injury, as I made my way by train to Croydon for my state-appointed twice-monthly session with the boys, I got mugged for my mobile. By this time I wasn't allowed to call the kids without permission of the court and was spending my nights dissolving into wine-induced self-pity alone in my flat.

LIVING BEREAVEMENT

When somebody has died, you know they are gone, never to be seen again. But when you know that your children are alive, going to school somewhere, it fucking kills you, again and again, day after day, to know that you can't see them. It's like a living bereavement. It hurts. Every day cuts deeper than the one before. Even the laughs start running dry when the tears start flowing.

With an army of solicitors at our backs, Sophie and I were now at war.

The greatest challenge posed by divorce must be to try and stay human. At least that was the mantra I kept repeating to myself.

I started going to a few demos with different campaign groups and began to work up a few ideas for a groundbreaking national campaign. It was clear that something radical needed to be done but my ideas were at an embryonic stage. I couldn't figure out how we could fund this, or produce something with the necessary scale to make any kind of impact. On paper, the ideas looked great. Turning them into a reality looked like mission fucking impossible.

One Saturday in April, along with about fifty other protestors, I arrived outside the Kennington home of a curmudgeonly judge by the name of Munby feeling very inhibited and, frankly, a bit fucking stupid. I'd kitted myself out in a not-so-subtle suit I'd had silk-screened with various slogans. I must have looked like a human billboard.

On that demo, I met Mark Harris's mum, Sheila. Mark was the father I had met in Pentonville, who had been locked up for breaching an order by waving hello at his daughters. Sheila Harris looked frail, her face etched with anguish at not having seen her granddaughters for five years. 'It's double the heartbreak,' she told me. 'I go through it for my son, and I go through it for my grandchildren.'*

---

* Two years later, having been denied access to their dad against their wishes for six years, Mark's daughters finally left their mother to go and live with him. Tragically, Sheila Harris died shortly afterwards.

Others had similarly horrific experiences to relate. Several guys had court orders to see their children, but these had never been enforced.

'I spent twenty grand for this –', one guy ranted, shoving a thick wad of paper into my face. 'Ain't worth the fucking paper it's written on. What do you do? You can't publicise it, you can't get it enforced, 'cause the judge doesn't want to come down hard on Mum. Why don't he just transfer the residence then? Wouldn't cost 'em that way. I'm nothing but a fucking McDad to my kids now.'

Afraid he was about to lose it, I drifted away to mingle as best I could.

There was a barrister, of all things, who'd been told by a judge that in seeking more than two hours' contact per fortnight he was being 'too possessive'. A teacher who'd been prevented from seeing his children solely on the basis that contact between him and the kids made the mother 'anxious and depressed'. As a result it was judged not to be in the children's 'best interests' for them to see him. Imagine, I thought, the insanity of a teacher spending his entire week with other people's children but not being able to see his own.

Another guy looked so resigned to his fate that it seemed he could barely muster the will to talk, let alone live. It turned out he was a former £100,000-a-year IT consultant, now living on the breadline in a squalid Canning Town bedsit. Lady Justice Hale had issued a judgment informing him that 'Father should be satisfied with one day of contact per year . . . father should appreciate that any happy contact, no matter how brief, no matter how infrequent, is of benefit to the children'.

Father after father, case after case, the litany of injustice grew. As unbelievable as these stories sounded, they were all true and verifiable: the unacceptable face of British justice, hidden from public view by a veil of secrecy that purported to be in the child's 'best interests'.

Then there were the tragedies – the horror stories. One man threw himself from a bridge in Taunton at 3 o'clock in the morning after being denied access to his stepdaughter, Skye, 5, and his 1-year-old son, Leo. A friend who'd gone to try and talk him out of it could only watch helplessly, along with several police officers, as the 25-year-old father plunged 60 feet to his death.

His mate later told reporters: 'I begged him – I was literally on my knees, pleading with him for ten minutes, but there was nothing I could say . . . He was saying how much he loved everybody and couldn't cope without his children. I was in pure shock when he jumped. I didn't know what to do. I was with the Army in Kosovo, but not even that could prepare me for what happened.'

Shortly before he jumped, the distraught dad left a voice message on his mother's mobile. Sobbing uncontrollably, he told his parents, Graham and

Debra: 'I really can't take any more. Whatever I'm going to do, I'm sorry. I love you so much and don't want to die, but I've got no choice. I can't take the pain any more. I love you. Bye.'

His wasn't the only suicide. Other fathers in Europe set themselves on fire in tragic acts of self-immolation (http://www.familyrights4europe.com). Vasilica Iulian Grosu was a 35-year-old Romanian who died after setting himself alight in front of a Romanian government building to protest against a ruling of the Spanish courts that took Andrei, his 6-year-old son, while the two of them were travelling in Spain. Despite the fact that Romanian courts had already ruled that the father was the child's legal guardian, the boy was handed to his mother, who lived there. Vasilica's protest was the final result of desperation when weeks of effort to regain his son had failed.

Another abomination that had been concealed from the public involved Harry Forder, an 11-year-old boy who, in defiance of a Family Division judge, had refused to go and live with his mother. The judge held the father in contempt of court and sent tipstaff (security) to remove the child from the house. Two grown men spent the best part of two hours smashing down the door to the bedroom where the boy was hiding under his bed. Cowering, and with tears pouring down his reddened cheeks, the child was bundled into the back of a waiting car. Severely traumatised, he was then forced to go and live with his mother. After two days he ran away and spent that Christmas in foster care. He has since been reunited with his dad.

And they say the family courts are acting in the child's best interests.

I kept asking myself: if it's this bad, why has nobody done anything about it? I couldn't fathom it. I couldn't pretend these guys were all saints, but then neither was I, and neither, probably, were the mothers. These broken men just wanted to be good parents, but the state and its entire arsenal of legal weaponry were ranged against them. The question I kept coming back to was: How far would you go for the people you love the most?

Would you break the law? Would you get arrested? Would you go to jail? Wouldn't you handcuff yourself to the Queen's carriage if it meant you could see your kids?

A million people took to the streets in early 2003 to protest against our going to war; half the country came to a standstill in protests about the price of fuel; how many would take to the streets for their children? Surely we as parents would be just as radical in fighting for them? Would we?

The answer had to lie in exposing the family courts to public scrutiny and smashing the culture of secrecy.

*

It was March 2001, and it had been a fortnight since I had last spoken to the boys. Despite having a court order enabling me to speak to them, the reality meant getting past Sophie, an obstacle which in itself was distressing enough to overcome. She had also told me she had been taping calls as 'evidence' as she put it, should she need it. Whatever that meant. Now I couldn't even speak to my kids in privacy. Every call I did make meant trying to stay calm for the boys, peppering each conversation with jokes in some vain attempt to make things seems as normal as possible for them. But as soon as I spoke to them, I was engulfed in a surging tide of emotion. That night in March I was in my office in Curtain Road when I called the boys at around 7 p.m., but within seconds of speaking to them I collapsed.

'Don't cry, Dad,' pleaded Daniel. 'I don't want you to cry . . . I want you to come home.'

'I can't, mate. It's not my home any more . . .' The phone sounded as if it was suddenly snatched before the line went dead. Nothing about my relationship with them was sacred.

On another occasion Daniel left a message on my mobile. 'Hi Dad, it's me Daniel. Can I speak to you one more time . . . and then you'll never have to see or speak to me again.'

I was heartbroken. There I was, battling through a barbaric system, and now my eldest son who I dearly loved had left this message. The thoughts ran through my mind – what had he been told? Had he been instructed what to say in this message? In the midst of this maelstrom of confusion and pain, I decided to write a letter to the boys to let them know I was thinking of them and still loved them.

All I could do was hope that they would receive it.

Hi boys

Hope school is going well and that you've stopped picking your nose in class assemblies, Alexander. Daniel, never forget to ask the teacher an impossibly difficult question you know she can't answer like, Where is Vanuatu? It will unfoot them for the rest of the day. I know, because your grandparents on my side were both teachers and nothing annoyed them more than a smart alec kid.

Pick up a decent paper as well when you can and start reading something meaty about current affairs. That doesn't mean the News of the World or some tits-and-arse comic, boys.

I'm sorry I can't see you more often but me and Mum are having a few problems which means we have to go see a judge who wears a woollen syrup festooned with crop circles. I'm not sure if he realises, or perhaps he is a shape-

shifting alien from outer space who has morphed into human form. He certainly behaves like it.

As ever I'm in trouble with Mum, the court, the police – in fact it's easier to ask who I'm not in trouble with, but this isn't a licence for you guys to follow in my footsteps.

I miss you both so much, especially our culinary forays and time spent crashing out on the sofa watching Star Wars, though I still want to run a light sabre through that bloody Jar Jar Binks.

And remember, for better or worse, you only ever have one Dad. I'll always do my best for you and will always look out for you.

All my love, your Dad xxx

P.S. I'm trying to swear less, but over the last few months have probably ended up swearing more. Stick a few quid in the swear box for your dad to cover this. I'll pay you back when I see you xxx

TEA AND JAMMY DODGERS

During 2001 I continued to network with members of Families Need Fathers, who for the last thirty-something years had done a magnificent job providing pastoral care for dads with contact problems; but the diplomacy of tea and jammy dodgers of groups like FNF and EPC left me cold, angry and frustrated. It was clear to me from the outset that these groups were being mugged, bamboozled and strung along by the government.

That summer I had attended a meeting with what was then called the Lord Chancellor's Department, now the Ministry of Justice. I locked horns with senior civil servant, Sally Field (dubbed by many in the fathers' movement as 'the mistress of misery' because of her refusal to accept that there was any problem whatsoever with the family justice system that caused them such pain), and with another civil servant called Warren Davies, over the Public Services Committee set up to look at ways of increasing 'safe' contact. I wanted to know why the committee were starting from this presumption that 'contact' wouldn't be safe, and why we were still using this obscene language.

I discovered that nine of the ten people sitting on the committee were women. Over the last hundred years the pendulum in family law has swung from a patriarchal extreme to matriarchal one. Tellingly, in 1990 the Institute for Public Policy Research produced a document, 'The Family Way', which argued: 'It cannot be assumed that men are bound to be an asset to family life, or that the presence of fathers in families is necessarily a means to social harmony and cohesion.' It was written by Harriet Harman and Patricia Hewitt, two early practitioners of the new, insidious gender apartheid.

I entered the room with a threat. I told them that the current system was untenable, and that I'd blow the lid off the fucking thing, starting with my own case. I promised the biggest campaign this country had seen in years and a shed-load of publicity, starting with an article which would be accompanied by a picture of the boys and me. Actually, I didn't believe a word of what I was saying, but what the hell I thought. I had nothing else.

'Mr O'Connor,' Miss Field declared authoritatively, 'discussing your case would be in breach of Section 97 of the Children Act. It would,' she purred, 'be treated as contempt of court. You could be convicted and sent to prison.'

'If telling the truth has become a criminal offence, book me a room at Her Majesty's now. All Section 97 does is gag parents from speaking out.'

'Further,' she added with a withering look, 'parents have no right in law to see their children after separation; only a right to *apply* to a court to see them.'

'Can you repeat that?' I asked, incredulous.

'The government does not believe that a legal presumption to contact would be helpful, Mr O'Connor.'

We have a lot of law in this country, but very little justice. Incredibly, this was the first time anyone had got the Lord Chancellor's Department to admit this: *all* parents – mothers and fathers – had no right in law to see their children.

Davies interjected with his trademark disparaging tone: 'Despite your rhetoric, Mr O'Connor, I should point out that every case is different. You have to *prove* it is in your child's best interest to see you.'

'What?' I snapped. 'Every case is different? That's bollocks. Every murder case is different, but the law is the same. Relationships, Mr Davies, are never black and white, but the law should be. It must be. I'm getting divorced from my wife, not my kids. What's changed? How come my wife is free to bring home the next Roy Whiting, Ian Brady or Peter Sutcliffe, yet I have to leap through burning hoops to see children I was living with until recently?'

'But the child's bests interests *are* paramount,' said Davies.

'How do you know? How is it that I can live with a girlfriend's stepson, invite any of his playmates round to stay, have any amount of contact with anyone else's children – but not my own? I just can't see how you can say that this madness is in the child's best interests.'

'Because the judges work to a welfare checklist.'

'So I presume that the judiciary and CAFCASS know what happens to

these kids afterwards? I presume there *are* records of the outcome for children?'
There was a long pause.

'You do have records, don't you? Because if you haven't, what you are
saying is mere conjecture, a meaningless mantra. A wicked deceit.'

With a nod of her head, Miss Field indicated that the meeting had
concluded. 'Mr O'Connor, it might be an idea to consider what we have said.
Go away and think about it and then give us some feedback.'

'You think I'll roll over, don't you? That if you tickle my belly, I'll just roll
over like every other fucker you've skewered on your family barbecue. But I
won't. When I come back, there will be a hundred more behind me. I ain't
playing by your rules any more. I've got some new ones of my own.

'What would you do, Miss Field, if somebody took your kids from you in
the street? Eh? Would you just stand there? No, you'd fight and do everything
you could to protect them. Where is your humanity? Where is your compassion? You really don't give a shit, do you?'

With that I was launched towards the door, ranting demonically. 'And you
can shove your jammy dodgers!'

Quiet diplomacy and constructive engagement were never my forte and
would play no part in any campaign I was involved in. I decided there and
then that, if I played by the book, we'd get nowhere.

DEBUNKING THE THREE MYTHS OF FAMILY LAW

'The state must declare the child to be the most precious treasure of the people. As long as the government is perceived as working for the benefit of the children, the people will happily endure almost any curtailment of liberty and almost any deprivation.'
ADOLF HITLER, *MEIN KAMPF*; TRANS. RALPH MANNHEIM (HOUGHTON-
MIFFLIN, 1943)

H ere are three of the major porkies expounded in court propaganda, none of which stand up to any scrutiny.

1. THE FAMILY COURTS ARE WORKING IN THE CHILD'S BEST INTERESTS

Sticking to the old adage that if you repeat a lie enough times people will believe it, this line is trotted out more than any other. The truth is that neither the courts nor the government have kept any records on the outcome for the hundreds of thousands of children whose futures have been determined by court judgments. They do not even monitor whether ordered contact is taking place. There is no evidence to prove that positive outcomes have resulted, so it is impossible to prove that the courts have in fact acted in the child's 'best interests'. The evidence actually suggests the opposite: there appears to be a direct correlation between the explosion in young offending and the epidemic of fatherlessness.

2. OPEN COURTS WILL DAMAGE CHILDREN

As somebody once said, justice must not only be done, it must be seen to be done. Never in the history of British justice has there been a field of jurisdiction where this was more relevant. There is not a shred of evidence to support the claim that open courts will damage children. According to one family court judge, Mr Justice Munby, it is 'in significant measure speculative'. Are we to believe that children are being 'damaged' in other jurisdictions where open justice operates, such as Florida, New York or even Scotland? Closed courts were actually introduced in the Administration of Justice Act 1960 to protect adults' privacy, not children's interests. Of course, if they really wanted to prove Fathers 4 Justice wrong they could test the open justice theory in a handful of courts so that they could evaluate and measure the outcome. It begs the question: just what have they got to hide and who are they protecting? The children or their secret system of justice?

Former President of the Family Division, Dame Elizabeth Butler-Sloss, once argued that secret courts protected children from being teased in the playground over the release of information about their parents' divorce. Well, if that's the case, what about the daughter of Paul McCartney and Heather Mills, or any other celebrity for that matter? Or the children of any criminal or individual whose trial is reported in either the local or national press? It's a load of baloney.

3. THE COURTS BASE THEIR DECISIONS ON EVIDENCE

Call me old fashioned, but weren't we brought up to believe that courts relied on something called 'evidence' to make their decisions? Instead, family courts operate on the basis of something called the 'balance of probability', i.e. you are innocent until proven to be the father.

LOOKS LIKE I'VE LANDED: GROUND ZERO

My year drew to an end with a life-threatening blitzkrieg. On Sunday 7 October, shortly after joking that I had become a 'vortex of bad luck', Ian Maddaford rang to tell me that my friend and business partner Peter had been killed in a 15-foot fall from a hotel balcony at a boat show in Annapolis in the United States. I was shell-shocked. My world was literally collapsing around me. Pete had only just turned 40 and seemed invincible. He'd once told me that nothing could be worse that a mediocre death – like that of T. E. Lawrence in a motorbike crash. I couldn't fathom it, my mind flooded with random thoughts. Did he really fall? Was he pushed? Worse; did he fake his own death?

At the time the group of companies he ran was in all sorts of financial difficulty but Pete's death was a cataclysmic event that would spur me on to overcome the seemingly insurmountable obstacles that lay in front of me. At the time though, the litany of disasters was such that I could feel the shadows of an ominously dark depression descending upon me for the first time in my life.

Two weeks later, the group of companies he had founded went belly-up. I found myself with no job, no money, no home, no means of getting what property I had left out of my own house and, thanks to my ongoing purgatory in the family courts, two children I could barely see.

As the late radio interviewer and DJ John Peel was to say to me in an interview on Radio 4's *Home Truths* in mid 2003, 'You were effectively on the streets with just £15 in your pocket – it doesn't get much worse than that does it?'

My next court hearing was at the Principal Registry of the Family Division of the High Court. I went in with unrealistically high expectations. I believed that I had an inalienable right to the society of my children. After all, I was divorcing my wife, not my kids. Fuck the law, I thought, be positive.

It was at this juncture that I realised my popularity had plummeted to a new low. From the outset I was subjected to character assassination, which, given the material they had to work with, didn't require much effort on the part of Sophie's team of sabre-toothed tormentors. If divorce was like a burning house, then using solicitors was like emptying a plane-load of napalm on the separation. WHOOSH!

And boy, was I getting burnt. They had accused me of never being at home and being unreliable. Apparently I didn't even bother calling the kids any more, a fact, which as I pointed out to them, was made quite tricky when your ex was trying to get you banged up for harassment when calling 'home' to speak to them. Much of the mud that was thrown at me contained nuggets of truth, but these had been exaggerated to the point where I had become a caricature of myself. It was a deliberately false representation, created by her solicitors in order to undermine my 'suitability' and credibility as a parent. If her barrister was to be believed, I made Darth Vader look like 'Dad of the Year'. I knew I was allergic to marriage and made a shite husband, but did that make me a bad dad?

As the case unfolded, I sat in court stunned by the barrage of hostility. It suddenly dawned on me that to prove who the best parent is, you have to prove who is the worst. I was getting fucking hammered.

If that was bad, the next court hearing was even worse. Despite providing a written undertaking that I would be permitted a visit to the property in the company of my legal representatives and conduct an inventory of all my personal effects, Sophie had denied access. Her barrister, Mr Seamus Kearny, argued that, rather than have me traipse through the house, it would be better if I wrote a list from memory; a legal version of the *Generation Game*, if you will.

I pointed out that the house was mine, as were many of the belongings inside it, including several valuable family heirlooms. My volcanic temperament erupted when I left the court and out of the corner of my eye caught Kearney laughing with colleagues in a side room. I marched over, intending to wish him well in forging a close relationship with a London bus, but instead tripped on a loose piece of carpet, fell forward and, reaching out for support, fell – entirely accidentally you'll understand – on Mr Kearney. As it turned out, the surface of the table he had been sitting on had been highly polished and Kearney slid across, and then over the end of the table.

Recognising that not everyone might see this as an accident, I thought it was best to make my excuses and exit stage left. 'Call security!' he shouted. In a panic I could think of nothing better to do than to go to the toilet, pouring myself into a cubicle. I sat on the seat for a few minutes shaking like a blancmange in rehab. I could hear the commotion outside but once it had passed I quickly gathered my gibbering self together, stepped out into the corridor and out of the court.

After several more emotionally charged handovers I decided not to see the kids until the next court hearing. It simply wasn't fair on them and it was ripping the guts out of me. Naïvely, I thought that I would be commended for sacrificing my time with them, for doing the right thing. But that's not how things work in the warped universe of family law.

The hearing had been transferred to the Royal Courts of Justice. The judge declared that a 'cooling-off' period was needed. For the next three months I would be permitted to see the children for just six hours a month in a contact centre in Croydon. I was shattered.

On my return to the office, propelled by a kinetic anger to do something creative, I scanned a picture of Daniel on to the Apple Mac. Using some of the effects filters in Photoshop, I played around with the contrast and converted the file into a solid black image with thousands of micro-dots that, from a distance, comprised the full picture. I then cropped it down so you could just see one of his eyes and half a smile set at a slight angle. I reproduced it four times against vividly different colours to create a Warholesque screen-print effect. The design was finished in less than five minutes. I printed it on to a 15 by 10-foot canvas and installed the result at a restaurant I was working on so that every day when I'd walk in I could see him smiling at me.

'Even if I don't see you boys ever again,' I said to myself, 'at least one of you will be here every time I walk past.'

HOUSTON, WE HAVE CONTACT

That first Saturday I travelled down to Croydon consumed by anger and bitterness. The contact centre was a church hall. As I made my way from the station I could see huddles of disenfranchised dads standing in the rain waiting for the centre to open. When the doors were unlocked, the men entered and dispersed into various corners.

In the centre of the room was a pile of toys, most of them broken. Three volunteers sat at a table on one side making notes. There was a small tarmac courtyard at the back. It was a fucking prison in all but name. A zoo without bars, where the kids would enter and get to play with the animals, only in this case the animals were their fathers.

The children drifted into the hall in ones and twos, making a beeline for the toys, seemingly oblivious to the desperate figures loitering on the periphery.

Then, one by one, fathers emerged from the shadows and tentatively approached their children.

Had I been reduced to this? A bit-part player in the lives of my children, criminalised, marginalised, dehumanised? What sort of environment was this, if the intention was to promote a normal relationship between children and their fathers? There were no sofas, none of the warm furnishings of home, just an inhospitable landscape of Formica dinner tables and the cold, hard plastic of twisted school chairs.

When I saw Daniel and Alexander I choked back hard, trying to swallow my tears. I hadn't seen them for a month. They looked confused and uncertain. Poor Alex looked empty, a lost soul running on sadness. Daniel, who was older and more confident, looked the same as he always had.

'It'll be all right, Dad,' he reassured me. 'Mum's angry. She says you hit her barrister.'

'Sorry, Dan, but it's been a bit hellish,' I said, embarrassed by his frankness.

He spoke with an uncharacteristic maturity, as if he had suddenly grown up in my enforced absence. Fuck, I thought. He's talking more sense than the adults in his life.

'Any chance of smuggling out my CD collection?' I asked jokingly. 'No. Maybe not – don't want to dump you in the gulag with your old dad, eh?'

We laughed. We hugged. The group hug of the O'Connor clan.

For the first time in months, I could feel love.

As we engaged in conversation and banter about school, we threw a few high fives and play punches. From the corner of my eye I saw the volunteers scribbling furiously, eyes focused in our direction.

Nobody fucking trusted me.

From father to pariah in a matter of months.

My crime? Being a shit husband.

My sentence? If I didn't get out of this, I'd lose my family, period.

Worst of all, I could see that I was already losing Alexander. Not just in the physical sense, but in the emotional. I could see in his eyes that he was drifting away from me. This man he knew as his dad was being replaced by some other, transient stepfather. Soon I would be consigned to memory, stored away for rediscovery in the future, but not now, not during his childhood.

That afternoon I went back to the company flat and cried. Behind the jovial façade I had constructed, my insides were crumbling, dissolving away in anguish as everything around me was being lost. Curled up on the sofa, I buried my head in a cushion. My humiliation was complete. I'd lost my family, my home, my children. I'd lost everything. Enveloped in a dark, dank pit of despair, I wished I was dead.

BLACK DOG

Caught in a vertical tailspin, I did what I always seemed to do when the chips were down. I ran away.

The next day, with a Churchillian black dog barking in my ear, I made straight to the offy and grabbed a bottle of Sir Jack of Daniels. Fear and self-pity were setting in. This living bereavement was like a serrated blade being dragged back and forth across my heart. I missed the boys. I missed the boys so much. As the alcohol seized me in its grip, I drifted to the dark side, to that place where you can't feel the hurt.

Somehow I ended up on Waterloo Bridge, curled in a crumpled heap against the railings with a torn bit of paper, a pen and a picture of the boys. I wondered how they were. Whether I needed them more than they needed me. Whether they missed me. I made two lists. The first: reasons for carrying on. The second: reasons to make my exit. I didn't ever want to go back to that god-forsaken fucking court again.

As I staggered to my feet, I knew that I had single-handedly wrecked my life and the lives of my family. But the family legal system had delivered the final coup de grâce. I mounted the railings. Passers by just kept walking as I groaned, semi-conscious and swaying, 50 feet above the Thames. I kept running through the lists over and over, trying to make sense of it all. I looked again at the picture of the two smiling boys. 'They need me. Don't they?' I asked myself.

I stared deep into Old Father Thames and saw death staring back at me. Strange shapes and figures contorted in the waters of the twilight rip tide, beckoning me in. I thought about those poor wretched dads who had leapt to their deaths. Disposable, unwanted and all so fucking unnecessary. Do this, O'Connor, I told myself, and you'll be running away for good. Somehow I knew that if I could get through this pain barrier then perhaps, just perhaps, I might be able to make something out of this misery.

Instead of jumping from bridges, maybe we dads could aspire to something higher.

To start climbing them.

It was that night, in the grip of that crushing despair on Waterloo Bridge, that I experienced my own personal epiphany and the idea for Fathers 4 Justice was born.

I dropped Jack into the well of darkness and caught a cab back to the flat.

On reflection, I was as impoverished as the next man who might have taken my place on those railings that night. But the most crippling poverty, I reminded myself, was a poverty of ideas. I was lucky. That night the power of the idea that struck me was so overwhelming. Ultimately it was that idea that saved my life.

A ROLL OF THE DICE

November was a tumultuous month. Pete's death continued to hang heavily over me. I needed to work out an escape route that would save not only me, but my friend and confidante, Jenny, too. On top of that there was another hearing at Royal Courts of Justice. I decided it was time to play what's now known as the retreat strategy.

A last resort, all-or-nothing gambit, threatening to retreat – i.e. walk away from the court and your children – is a high-risk tactic which requires considered analysis. If a 'resident' parent (the parent with custody) wants to deny the 'non-resident' parent, there are generally two simple reasons for this: to punish an unfaithful partner, or a partner who has let them down or failed to meet their expectations; or to replace them completely with a new partner.

If it's the latter, do not under any circumstances adopt the retreat strategy.

After telling CAFCASS officers Eileen Ford and Maggie Derrick that I was at the end of my tether and was going to walk away from the kids, I was left pacing up and down the waiting area outside the courtroom.

Sophie's little-miss-hoity-toity barrister approached and began berating me: 'Contact is not just about times and numbers —'

'Excuse me? You're damn right it isn't about times and numbers, it's about my own flesh and blood who I've barely seen in a year and a half. You can take your judicial buggery and fuck off back to your client and tell her that I'm out of here today. This party's over and you ... you can administer your black alchemy on some other poor hapless bastard.'

The barrister recoiled in shock. By this time I was shaking with raw anger while at the same time steeling myself against the prospect that I may never see my kids again.

In court I tell the judge that I'll put her out of a job, whatever it takes. My shredded emotions had short-circuited any kind of self-control. 'One day,' I tell her, 'you'll rue the day you ever met me. It's the beginning of the end for you and your kind.'

I was lucky my diatribe didn't land me in the cells, but I was past caring by then. I'd grown sick of this grotesque pantomime that passes as family law: CAFCASS officers sitting there, writing reports as the family goes up in smoke; parasitic solicitors feeding off the detritus of divorce; barristers and judges masquerading as arbiters of justice – so many of them cold-hearted and devoid of any moral compass.

I'd have laughed. If I wasn't already crying.

I'd had enough. It had got to the point where I had to risk walking away from the kids for ever.

But in an unexpectedly seismic reversal of fortune, oiled, I suspect, by the fear that Sophie's one financial lifeline was about to be permanently severed, my case worker Maggie Derrick managed to secure an agreement from her that there would be no restrictions on overnight-stay contact, providing my car had the right type of seatbelts and that the property the boys would stay in was 'suitable'.

'Whatever it takes,' I say, 'whatever.' Provided we could reach some kind of closure on this, I was past caring about the semantics.

A PHEASANT PLUCKER

At around this time I was saved from financial destitution by a benevolent friend named Will Minns, who stumped up £10,000 cash, plus the use of his beaten-up camper van. I had the cash and the wheels, now all I needed were the clients and somewhere to live.

After Peter's tragic death I had only a few days to find somewhere to live before the bank foreclosed and turfed me out on to the streets. After many fruitless days travelling through Kent and Essex, Jenny and I came upon Kimsings, a picture-book, rambling, fourteenth-century farmhouse for rent in the idyllic village of Cavendish. Perched on the north bank of the River Stour in Suffolk, it was the perfect retreat. With luck it would pass inspection when the CAFCASS officer came to visit the house on behalf of the court to check its 'suitability' for the children.

God knows these fuckers never trust that you'll live somewhere halfway decent, so out they trot on a day's jolly to ensure you aren't living it large in Sodom and Gomorrah with a crack-guzzling Pete Doherty and his chums.

Kimsings reputedly once belonged to Sir John de Cavendish, Chief Justice of the Kings Bench in 1381 and, if the house was good enough for a Chief Justice, then CAFCASS ought to agree that it was good enough for my boys. What could possible go wrong?

I was about to find out.

Minutes before the CAFCASS officer was due, disaster struck.

The air crackled and fizzed with the whistle of live ammunition and snap of gunshots. First one or two. Then a full volley. I ran to the front of the house but could see nothing. I ran to the back and looked out of my office window. In the fields beyond, a pheasant shoot was in full swing.

'Fuck, fuckety fuckety fuck. I'm fucked, fucked!' I shouted. 'I don't believe this! Why today, of all the fucking days?'

If the camper van's seatbelts weren't enough to nail me, live ammunition would have Sophie in palpitations on the phone to her solicitors.

The doorbell went.

'What an amazing property you have here,' said the CAFCASS officer as I greeted her.

She followed me through the kitchen into my studio, which enjoyed an outstanding vista of Suffolk's gently undulating landscape – and a dozen armed men in tweed. A shot cracked overhead, rattling the windows, making both of us flinch and duck for cover. As we looked up, the body of a large pheasant dropped like a winged breezeblock into my garden, followed by a blanket of feathers. My heart stopped. This was my last roll of the dice and thanks to lousy timing my attempt at get overnight-stay contact was as dead as the pheasant on my lawn.

'Fantastic!' she declared enthusiastically. 'The boys are going to love it up here.'

RENAISSANCE MAN

All you can do is try and work as much as you can to make your child feel that it's a normal weekend and that you love them very much. And when you put them to bed, all the thoughts about who they are, how they are growing up, what their school is like, what they do during the day, and what they think … I'll have to admit that, when he comes to our house for a weekend, I don't sleep for about forty-eight hours, because those moments are the most special moments in my life.

Howard Bashford, Businessman

With access to the boys agreed, 2002 became my renaissance year. I cleaned up my act and started behaving. Business was good. My long-suffering clients stuck by me despite the soap-operatic dramas that had plagued the previous two years. These included Britain's largest independent ice cream company, Frederick's Dairies, run by irrepressible ice cream magnate Frank Frederick and his team. I was in fine fettle and the boys could come up as much as they liked. We cooked, played chess, went fishing, and my fantastically sympathetic and tolerant landlord, the splendiferous Tony Pawsey, even took the boys for rides on the farm's quad bikes and tractors. In the evenings we crashed in front of the TV watching DVDs and rekindling our relationship. During the cold winter months we built mountainous log fires in the inglenook fireplace and toasted marshmallows from the two church pews parked either side.

In late June I held a celebratory 'Divorce – hey, who needs furniture?' survival bash with full-blown Berber feast prepared by my chef from the Papermill bar in Curtain Road, the indefatigable North African prophet of gastronomy, Bounti Khountichef. Guests wore djellabas and deposited their good selves in a Berber tent, ready to imbibe a Kasbah-rocking refreshment of bacchanalian excess. Yours truly prepared a harem-quenching oasis of intoxicating elixirs, while Bounti knocked up seven-hour slow-cooked mechoui lamb.

So far as I was concerned at the time, the evening drew a line under everything I'd ever have to do with the family courts for the rest of my life. As I sat back on the cushions at the back of the tent, surrounded by friends and colleagues, I thought I'd at last found peace in my life.

My plan was to launch a restaurant and parachute in Bounti and his girlfriend Jo, manageress of the Papermill, to run it. I'd found a quaint little place called Vickers for sale in Coggeshall, Essex, which seemed perfect for my purposes.

Life had settled back on to an even keel. After the turmoil of the last couple of years I needed to feel normal again with the boys. I needed to touch them, feel their warmth, to believe they were with me again.

Perhaps most significantly, Sophie and I were beginning to learn to forgive each other for what we had done.

In a belated act of contrition, I accepted responsibility for fucking up the marriage. We kissed and made up, vowing to stay out of the gladiatorial arena of the family court for ever more.

'No way to spunk the kids' inheritance,' said Sophie, 'least not to solicitors and the like. Despite what they say, how can that be in their best interests?'

I told her that, of all the lessons I'd learnt, forgiveness was the most precious. But while I could forgive her, I couldn't forgive the system. The best way of punishing somebody who has been unfaithful or let you down is to stop them seeing the people they love the most, and the system encourages that. It has to change, otherwise our children could suffer the same agony when they become parents.

'If anything positive is to come from this experience,' I told Sophie, 'perhaps I can make a difference by taking the law into my own hands.' She cast me a quizzical look, ignorant of the plans fomenting in the back of my mind.

THE FATHERS' REVOLUTION

B y the middle of 2002 I had abandoned plans to buy the restaurant. The place in Coggeshall didn't have enough covers to make a sensible return and, besides, I wanted to spend time with the boys. Over the next few months I concentrated on my design and marketing work, signing over the family home to Sophie so that the boys would have financial security. I figured that if I'd managed to weather the last few years, I'll be financially solvent somehow without the equity from the house. But all the while, the bitter aftertaste of injustice was gnawing away at me. Every so often I'd get a call from one of the dads I'd befriended, reminding me that I was perfectly placed to start something new: a radical campaigning force for equal parenting, financed with a currency of ideas and hard-won resources.

So I began to research what was involved, even testing out ideas for a campaign concept called 'In the Name of Love' – subsequently ditched for sounding too pretentious and nondescript. But deciding what the thing was to be called was the least of the hurdles I'd need to overcome. The misleadingly entitled 'fathers' rights' movement had been paralysed by infighting for the last thirty years. Worse still, it had left a legacy of impotent campaign groups, splintering into ever-decreasing and ineffective organisations. The result was a proliferation of one-man bands.

Create something that has a committee and we won't get past first base, I thought. As an old boss of mine used say, 'You can't design by committee'. Something ground-breaking was needed to raise awareness and help fire debate about the secret family courts. But how could we get people to join our campaign if they hadn't heard about the injustices being inflicted on fathers?

When I was a child I had been hauled round the country to various historical sites by my well-intentioned mother. One of these was the village of Tolpuddle, cradle of the modern trade union movement and home of the Tolpuddle Martyrs. That trip had had a profound effect on me. Sitting on the grass under what was thought to be the ancient sycamore tree where the agricultural workers had gathered, the knowledge that people had been sent to the other side of the world for defending their beliefs caused me to question authority even more. I had been indoctrinated in political agitation, born and raised in the Labour Party, a movement forged in the very fires of civil disobedience. My late, wickedly argumentative Welsh grandfather, Glyn Evans, had once given me a book entitled *The Long Walk Home*, detailing the rise of the Chartists and the part played in that movement by one Fergus O'Connor. The significance of history repeating itself hadn't been lost on me: that O'Connor, my namesake, wound up losing his marbles by the end of the campaign.

I concluded that, if my campaign was to succeed, I needed to research extensively the methodology of civil disobedience, which was the only hope we had of making the injustice visible. After all, if it was good enough for the Chartists, the early Labour movement and the Suffragettes, it was good enough for us.

Around this time I had the good fortune to be introduced to Tony Lewis, a lion-hearted man with a loveable, hound-dog face like an abandoned St Bernard. Unusually for a dad in his position, Tony had residency of his two fantastic boys, but blessed with an appetite for justice as big as his hunger for fast food, he was ready to commit himself to getting a new equal-parenting campaign group off the ground. I had been formulating a number of ideas, mostly scribbled in one of the many notebooks I carried with me and Tony suggested that we gather together a group of dads for a brainstorming session.

About twenty people turned up to the first meeting, which was held in Gorleston, Norfolk, near Tony's home in October 2002. Afterwards we retired to a local hostelry to discuss our activities further. I had learned from experience that a modicum of Jack Daniels could be most efficacious in transforming a room full of depressed dads into a bunch of convivial men bristling with a sense of injustice and purpose. By the end of the second round, the campaign had been mapped out in my mind.

With my history in campaigning, understanding of marketing and PR, a small pot of money and an unhealthy dose of insanity, I was convinced that I could make a significant contribution. And so, much to my bank manager's abject horror and my accountant's chagrin, just months after losing every-thing, I decided to try and change the law, to make equal parenting a reality, with the launch of a 'Greenpeace for dads'. For a while I wrestled with the notion of going all PC and calling the new group something anodyne like 'Parents 4 Parity', but in the end settled on the name 'Fathers 4 Justice'.

Concerned friends did their utmost to discourage me, arguing that I needed time to let the scars of battle heal. After all, I was only just back on my feet with a healthy bank balance after a lengthy struggle. Why now, when

I had access to the boys after last year's momentous final court hearing, would I want to plunge into something that might cost me my livelihood, even my liberty?

'You're not seriously going ahead with this?' asked 'Uncle' Tony, my accountant and longstanding advisor.

'Wouldn't dream of it, Tone,' I replied facetiously.

'Changing the law – it's impossible.'

'No, it isn't. I can do it.'

'But, Matt, it could cost you everything. Is it really worth that much to you?'

One after another, people lined up to dissuade me from my madcap plan.

My mum reckoned I should be sectioned. 'Matthew, you don't really need to be doing this. It doesn't seem like a good idea to me, in the circumstances, when you've just come through your divorce.'

My brother David took an equally dim view. 'Fuck sake, Matt! Go round the world a few times and work off the steam,' he snapped. 'You're burning up with injustice.'

But I couldn't. I was being driven by something beyond my control. Perhaps it was loaded in my DNA, passed on to me by my Irish father. Celts like a fight; Kerry men even more so. But there was also some other key driver. I'd been bullied at school. I suffered from a bad stammer for many years as a result. I'd decided somewhere in my psyche that I wasn't going to be bullied into submission ever again.

'David, I'm putting my faith in God,' I tell him, 'And clean underpants every morning.'

Uncertain whether I was mentally cut out for such a potentially savage journey, I turned to Jenny, my friend, colleague and confidante. A few years back she'd started working with me on bar and restaurant design projects; now she'd found herself in business with a man hell-bent on taking on the legal establishment. Was I being selfish in pursuing this agenda?

'I know you want to turn this negative into a positive, to give something back. Perhaps it's your penance for being a shit husband. Maybe you could make a difference ... Equally, it could destroy you,' she said. 'And what do we say to clients if you get nicked? For that matter, what do I say to anyone? They'll think we're all barking.'

'Maybe it's all about guilt, Jen, but it's something I think I need to do.'

It was her tacit support that made me to decide to press ahead, regardless of the consequences.

What did I have to lose? I'd lost everything before. If it happens again, I thought, I'll just have to keep my fingers crossed for another Lazarus-like return.

Later, I would be accused of setting up the campaign as a money-making enterprise. Of all the accusations that had been levelled at me, that was the one that saddened me most. I'd worked fourteen-hour days doing two jobs, the campaign and my design company. In fact, for the first six months to a year, we didn't even charge membership yet we were running at full pelt. What did people think the campaign ran on? Thin air?

CAMPAIGN VIAGRA

'What this campaign needs, Matt,' said one father in an email that seemed calculated to appeal to my vanity and ego, 'is campaign Viagra – and you're the man to administer it. You guys could be the suffragents.'

The Rubicon was finally crossed when Bob Geldof appeared on Granada TV's *Tonight* show in a Fathers' Day special, verbally cremating the family justice system, it was as if the trigger had been pulled. I decided to take the £50,000 I'd put together to buy a restaurant and plough it into the campaign. Every last fucking penny. Geldof would soon be tied up with his Africa campaign, and it was clear nobody else was going to do anything.

Several deep breaths and generous swigs of Red Bull later, I was on the mobile making plans, stomping up and down the garden trying to rouse supporters from the slumber of their armchairs.

The research, though a bloody tedious slog, proved a necessary evil. The deeper I dug, the more damning the evidence I uncovered.

At least one hundred children a day lose contact with their fathers in the family courts. At that rate, we calculated, around half a million children had lost contact with their dads in the lifetime of the Labour administration. A million parents go into the family courts every year; 40 per cent of fathers lose contact with their kids within two years of separation; 50 per cent of all contact orders are broken, most children being held hostage to fortune by vindictive mothers, but, as I was to discover, this was not an issue about gender, but about the thin line between love and hate.

Why was this happening? The underlying social dynamics suggested that an explosion in relationship breakdown was to blame. Some mothers would stop all contact for no 'good' reason. According to a Department of Social Security report published in 1998, 40 per cent of mothers had admitted to stopping contact to punish a former partner. Others simply wanted to air-brush the father out of the child's life and replace him with a surrogate dad.

The next few weeks were spent working through campaign planning, theory, methodology and strategy. Several key principles underpinned my work. The first was an old marketing mnemonic: AIDA. Awareness, Interest, Desire, Action. The second was 'Satyagraha', Mohandas Gandhi's philosophy of non-violent resistance famously deployed by him against the British. This incorporated three basic tenets: truth, non-violence and penance or self-sacrifice. Above all, though, it was, as Gandhi said, about making the injustice visible.

However, my new campaign would also use ridicule, satire and subversion to expose the system. Civil disobedience would be our weapon of choice. Our targets would be the main institutions of the United Kingdom. There we would deploy our 'shake, rattle and roll' tactics.

Shake – We would awaken Britain's slumbering democratic structure and create a parliamentary stir with our unique brand of 'shake and wake' guaranteed to get elected representatives off their backsides pretty damn quickly.

Rattle – It's time to rattle more than the collection plates of the Church of England.

Roll – No family has been more affected by family breakdown than the Royal Family. Could we roll them over into engaging in a public debate?

I decided that rather than follow the conventional lobbying route, which could take fifteen to twenty years to get any results, we would use dramatic events to accelerate change. I worked up a concept that could run on the hill of beans we had at our disposal. On a budget that came straight out of my back pocket we couldn't stretch to a touchy-feely advertising campaign. Instead this would be a campaign that was both iconic and ironic. Something that would resonate from Romford to Rio. A vision that people would identify with immediately.

A few years back the filmmaker M. Night Shyamalan made a movie called *Unbreakable*. The plot involved a father, the sole survivor of a train crash, whose son began to believe that his dad was a superhero. From there I developed the tagline 'Every Father is a Superhero to His Children'. Shyamalan's melancholic vision of real-life superheroes who weren't that super played on many levels. If we played it too straight, we would come across as taking ourselves too seriously, so I came up with 'The Men in Tights' – a title shamelessly plundered from the Mel Brooks film of the same name.

I ran the idea past Jenny first, who liked it, before presenting it to Tony Lewis. 'Get this, Tony,' I said. 'F4J is a tragi-comedy. It will employ humour unlike any other campaign group. Think of it as an homage to Monty Python, Citizen Smith, Austin Powers, and later Bob Parr, a.k.a. Mr Incredible – past his prime, a bit flabby, clinging on to tall buildings for dear life. What's not to like? Who can help but crack a smile at fat guys in polyester?'

'There's nothing incredible about us,' Tony responded despairingly. 'Perhaps we should call it "The Impossibles", because we are.'

My hope is that the campaign will unfold like the famous line by Gandhi: first they ignore you, then they laugh at you, then they fight you, then you win.

'They'll certainly laugh if they see me in polyester tights,' said Tony with a nervous laugh.

'It takes a man to wear tights, Tony, though it might raise our voices by a couple of octaves, especially when you and me put them on. We'll make great stocking fillers.'

'Let's hope it makes a great headline filler too.'

It was time to swing into action, slip into our Lycra and get nicked.

'THE NAME'S CHRISTMAS. MR CHRISTMAS.'

We started working on our 'wardrobe' and 'special effects' department at the back of Kimsings, but Sophie was unimpressed when the kids reported what their mad dad was up to.

'Just because you act like a 7-year-old, doesn't mean you have to dress up like one.'

'But I'm in touch with my inner child. Besides, lighten up, you knew what I was like when you married me. Don't forget we got engaged when I was wearing a suit of armour. There should have been a clue in there somewhere.'

'I knew you were crazy, but dressing up in Lycra? Most people mature with age, but you, you just ...'

'I know, I just get younger every day, don't I? Besides, by the time I finish, satire will be the new protest.'

'You're just an insufferably smug bastard, O'Connor.'

'Look, Sophie, you're right, but I'm willing to take the humiliation and have the shit ripped out of me for a principle. I don't see anyone else out there who can make that difference, so I guess it's down to muggins here to start something.'

After plundering every fancy-dress shop in the area, we managed to assemble:

Father Christmas outfits and beards
Elvis jumpsuits circa 1972
Easter Bunny outfits
Batman, Robin, Spiderman outfits
priest's cassock and dog collar
monk's robe
cardinal costume
Pope costume
Tony Blair masks
decontamination jumpsuits
monkey outfits

Purple Phantom costume
purple stilt-walker outfits
painter's overalls
Simpsons' fancy dress

In addition we found suppliers for the following:

Purple paint
set of reliable wheels, van with space for ladder and room to
    change into superhero garb
numerous ladders, including a 54-foot window cleaning ladder
a double-decker bus – good for just two trips
one Sherman tank from Tanks-a-lot
gigantic polystyrene turkey
Ann Summers leopardskin handcuffs (as seen on Margaret Hodge
    MP)
giant heart-shaped balloon (from Air Artists, who did the inflat-
    ables for the last Rolling Stones tour)
1940s air-raid siren
high-visibility jackets
large quantity of bananas
100-plus banners
assortment of fireworks and flares
air horns
whistles

I HAVE A CUNNING PLAN

Right now, listen up. I love it when a plan comes together, but if you want
to grab the headlines you'll need several cunning stunts up your sleeve. There
are certain fundamentals any self-respecting campaigner should know. Most
campaigns are po-faced, miserable affairs. Why? Campaigning can be serious
fun. It can also be theatrical and showbizzy.

The rules of engagement are as follows:

DO

Keep it simple, stupid – The best campaign ideas are those that involve
    less than six people and a cunning plan that will hit the public's
    funnybone. Don't bother trying to get a million people out on the

streets unless they're prepared to go the extra mile and do something to get arrested, like sitting down and blocking a road.

Make it eye-poppingly theatrical – Real life can be duller than watching a party political broadcast. Why else would the nation want to live vicariously through reality TV shows? Everyone likes a little dramatic licence and it's true that a picture speaks a thousand words. Create something that you know newspapers will want to print. The brighter your plumage, the better your coverage.

Use ridicule, satire and subversion – You want to start a campaign? Take my advice and don't do conventional. Explore the outer extremities of the law, but keep it funny. Find something that will make the authorities react with a pea-sized intellect, which, inevitably and joyfully, they generally do.

Research, research and research – Scope venues, vet activists, Google the background of any interviewers. Know your enemy!

Objectives – NEVER lose sight of what it is you are trying to achieve. If it's awareness you're after, go big picture. If it's something more political, keep on the right side of the law and read the press carefully to see if you can piggyback any hot topics.

Plan Z – Inevitably, not everything will go according to plan. You'll need at least two back-up plans to cover every eventuality, from people and equipment not turning up to problems with the police, especially on demos.

DON'T

Do things by committee – Unless you like tea and biscuits, navel-gazing and setting dates for more meetings, just get on with it. With a committee, the only thing you'll end up changing are the seating arrangements.

Use an elephant on a demo – We never did use a fully-grown African Elephant on a demo, but at one point it was being seriously considered. A meeting between Scotland Yard, the RSPCA and F4J was called, but it all sounded too much like hard work. The prospect of shovelling elephant excrement from the streets of Westminster was just tooooo much. We used a tank instead.

Organise a nocturnal gallop to Sandringham on Christmas Day – No-ho-ho. Any Father Christmases that managed to evade MI5 would be picked off by the flesh-hungry Alsatian dogs.

Use Mates condoms – Turns out they're indestructible – no good for our purposes!

Bring bantam hens into Parliament. We weren't chicken but decided against 'death by poultry' in Parliament on the grounds it would constitute cruel and degrading treatment of fowl, setting them to free-range in a pit full of vermin. (Some of us are still hanging out for an outbreak of Avian flu in Westminster, though.)

Try to join Her Maj and the Duke of E in their carriage at the Trooping of the Colour. You could try and cadge a lift with Lizzy and Phil, but in the interests of your own personal safety, we recommend you stick to a black cab.

Offer membership for all – All human life will join. The animal, the vegetable, the criminal.

Aim for global domination – Simple idea. Mammoth migraine.

Down too many Dirty Martinis – Always keep a clear head so you can see your enemies coming. Mine often got a couple of body blows in first because I was still numb from the intoxicating pleasures of a Dirty Martini. (Freeze 15oz martini glass for one hour; pour three measures of gin, gently top with one of vodka and add a splash of Vermouth. Quaff. Never shake. Never stir.)

THE NAME'S CHRISTMAS – MR CHRISTMAS

On 17 December 2002, approximately one year after that fateful night on Waterloo Bridge when the original idea was conceived, Fathers 4 Justice was catapulted into existence. Our inaugural demo would settle a few old scores and rattle the cages of my adversaries.

My plan was to invade the lobby of the then Lord Chancellor's Department in London with two hundred Father Christmases. Jen thought it was a cracking idea and helped me order as many Santa suits as Smiffy's, the fancy-dress people, could supply.

'I think it's great, Matt,' Jen said, pondering the spectacle I would be making of myself. 'And, let's face it, you won't need any supplementary padding.'

'How I suffer for my art,' I replied mockingly. 'Are you telling me that, with my beef-and-bourbon physique, I'm in danger of being typecast?'

'Why don't you go the whole hog and change your name to Mr Christmas? Now that's what I'd call method acting.'

With that inspirational suggestion, I change my name by deed poll and, lest anyone should doubt my identity, I knocked up a business card with a picture of me in a Santa suit on one side and my CV on the other:

Available for Xmas Parties, Hen Nights, Restaurant Openings, Next-Day Deliveries, Extreme Snowboarding, Synchronised Bell Ringing, Roof & Chimney Surveys, Formation Sledging, Reindeer Wrestling, Elf Throwing, Mothers Snogged, Fathers' Demonstrations, Penguin Smuggling, Facial Hair Care Products, 'Stunt' Santa, Turkey Stuffing, Cracker Pulling, Igloo Conversions, Personal Shopping Consultant and Authorised Used Sleigh Reseller.

With our first mission organised, it was time for the gloves to come off and the Santa suits to go on. The week before the event I began to recruit unsuspecting bodies for our mission from the many fathers' forums on the net. One of the dads I contacted was Jolly Stanesby. But the man who would later turn out to be our campaign's answer to Crocodile Dundee wasn't convinced by my plan.

'I don't know,' he told me. 'I think I'll stick to the courts for a while as I seem to be getting somewhere. It might damage my case if I do something like this.'

Give him time I thought, and he'd be sure to come round to my way of thinking.

Preparations continued apace. I hired two open-top London buses for the princely sum of £1,000, and collected the 150 Santa suits and beards that my merry band of Bad Santas would wear to storm the lobby. The idea was to get everyone arrested and fill the following day's papers with pictures of Father Christmases being bundled into the back of police vans a week before Christmas.

We rendezvoused at Potters Bar service station on a ball-shrinkingly cold December morning. The turnout for our first demo was impressive, far surpassing my expectations. By the time we hit London, both buses were rammed to the baubles with two hundred plus psyched-up Santas. We spent twenty minutes in Oxford Street waving at shop workers before hooking a sharp right at Oxford Circus, down Regent Street, through Trafalgar Square, around Parliament Square and up Victoria Street towards the Lord Chancellor's Department. En route I gave an old acquaintance a call.

'Sally? Sally Field?'

'Yes.'

'It's Matt O'Connor. You may remember me, we met a while back. I think

I mentioned that I'd bring a few friends with me next time I dropped by. Well, we should be there any minute now. Ciao!'

'You all right, Matt?' asked Tony Lewis, pressed up beside me at the front of a crammed top deck.

'Not really, mate. I'm shitting myself. This is it, position impossible. Now, where's my megaphone?'

As the buses pulled up outside, I shot off and through the revolving doors of the building, praying like mad that everybody else would be stupid enough to follow me. At the reception desk a nice man in a white suit asked if he could help.

'I'm here to see the Lord Chancellor.'

'What's your name?'

'What the bloody hell do you think it is?'

The man lifted his weary head and looked me up and down.

'The name's Christmas – Mr Christmas. I'm the visage of seasonal goodwill, which I'm hoping will be reciprocated by my friends in the building.'

In the background a few raised voices could be heard, then all hell broke loose with shouting Santas and the sonic assault of a battery of air horns piercing the air. I turned to see a security guard running to block the revolving doors; he managed to hold them for a matter of seconds before the kinetic energy of two hundred Santas forced the door, ejecting a volley of Father Christmases across the floor.

'We want justice! We want justice! We want justice!' The cacophonous chant was turned up to maximum volume, amplified in the foyer as more Santas piled in to block the entrance to the lifts. I gestured with a jabbing elbow for an activist across the room to hit the fire alarms, and the place descended into mayhem. Calmly I strolled back to the reception desk.

'Can I ask that you put out a call out for the Lord Chancellor. Tell him Christmas has come early, courtesy of Fathers 4 Justice.'

'Never heard of you, mate.'

'Don't worry, you will.'

'Now listen, chum,' he growled. 'The police will be here in a minute and you're all going to get nicked.'

'That's the spirit, mate. Now you're getting it.'

But our plan failed to materialise. Only a few nonchalant cops rolled up from the Yard and it transpired that the Lord Chancellor had absconded through a rear entrance. Instead we were offered the Director of Public and Private Rights, Amanda Findlay, who came down to try and placate us.

'You have no right, Mr O'Connor, to see your children.'

'That's why we're here, Amanda. That's exactly why we're here.'

JOIN DAD'S ARMY

Within days of the Christmas demo I got into a contretemps with Tony Coe from the Equal Parenting Council, on discovering that I'd been removed from their forum and turfed out of the group for posting incendiary comments on their web-page. I was at a bit of a loss to understand why the moderator simply didn't just email me to ask me to curb any over-excited literary thoughts, especially given that a few months earlier I had created a new corporate identity for them, gratis. When Coe's sidekick, the diminutive, fidgety Paul Duffield had offered to do the website for Fathers 4 Justice, I'd paid him up front, knowing he was an undischarged bankrupt at the time. These acts of goodwill were repaid in such a way as to shake my faith in the people who were supposed to share our goals, to be working with us rather than against us.

The catalyst for my ejection, according to Coe, was their uneasiness with my so-called 'militancy'. Tellingly, the only person on the Santa demo not to wear a Father Christmas outfit was Coe, who turned up in a raincoat.

When I called him to find out what was going on, despite the lashings of what I took to be fake sincerity in his voice, nothing could conceal his loathing for Fathers 4 Justice.

'Matt, it's like this. . .' he said, delivering the words with his trademark glacial speed. 'We are not entirely comfortable with this confrontational approach you are adopting. It could undo all the years of hard work and effort to get to where we are today.'

'But where are you, Tony, exactly? A couple of meetings with a government Minister, a few crumbs from his master's table, and you think you've cracked the jackpot. Tell me what you think I should do.'

'Reason,' said Tony. 'You have to reason with these people so that they understand that what they are doing is wrong. Once they understand, then things will change.'

'Ah, yes, reason,' I replied mockingly. 'The great voice of reason. Constructive engagement, changing things from the inside. If it ain't happening after five years of you bashing on the door, Tony, it isn't going to start happening now. Change has to come from the outside, through public pressure. And the only way we can mobilise that is through a high-profile campaign.'

'But, Matt, you're new to this. What you need to understand is that your actions will simply cause them to cease talking to moderate groups like us.'

'I think you'll find the opposite will happen, Tony. People will flock to us because we will be doing something. The government will respond by engaging more with groups like yours and Families Need Fathers. There might even be a few quid in it for you. But whatever else, maintaining the status quo is not an option. History favours the brave, Tony, not the jammy dodger.'

Within hours of our conversation the Fathers 4 Justice web site mysteriously went down, and disinformation started to be pumped out on the net. Somebody was trying to sabotage the launch of Fathers 4 Justice, but it backfired when members of other groups jumped ship and came across to the new group. Clearly somebody acted as they did because they perceived Fathers 4 Justice as a threat. It's a shame, because I had endeavoured to keep good relations with most groups including EPC and Families Need Fathers.

THE COLOUR PURPLE

Despite the qualified success of our first piece of non-violent direct action, we still had the problem of overcoming the 'fear factor'. We live in a society where the establishment trades in the currency of fear. Fear of arrest, fear of court, fear of jail, even fear of being shot. Walls intended to defend us have become prison walls; watchtowers erected so that the authorities could look out to protect us, now look inward, to control us. Overcome fear, I argued, and everything is possible.

One morning I woke up and decided that the time was right to go and get arrested. I hooked up with two supporters who had worked tirelessly to get the campaign off the ground, Shaun O'Connell and Sarah Ashford. Both were prepared to join me in a deliberately defiant act of provocation.

The first arrests in the history of Fathers 4 Justice took place at the Ipswich offices of CAFCASS on 5 February 2003. The three of us had painted the door purple, the international colour for equality. It took several phone calls to the police and a wait that lasted twenty buttock-clenching minutes in freezing temperatures before the Old Bill finally arrived to play their part. While we waited, to ensure that we were caught 'purple-handed', we pressed our palms into the wet paint.

In the custody suite I was checked in under my new name, Mr Christmas, much to the bemusement of the custody sergeant.

'You've either arrived early or late,' he scoffed.

'You mean my name?'

'Yes, it's a bit odd, to say the least.'

'Every day is Christmas where I come from,' I told him. 'Think of it as my dramatis personae. A little novelty drama acted out for the boys in blue.'

Nine hours later, they hauled me out of my cell for an interview that consisted of an endless tirade of facetious comment.

'So, Mr Christmas, what's this all about?'

'Well, I guess it's a metaphor.'

'A metaphor?'

'I see some of your cells look like they might be needing some attention, but unlike CAFCASS we don't do whitewash. You can't put a gloss on something that is failing so badly. Think of it as a political protest,' I said, apologising that the standard of workmanship on the door at CAFCASS wasn't what it might have been. The older copper bit back.

'OK, right,' he snapped. 'Did you have permission to paint the door?'

'Well,' I said, 'I don't believe we were invited, so we won't charge. Look on it as a gesture of goodwill. We are trying to raise awareness about an issue that affects you guys professionally and personally. I'm a 35-year-old businessman, I see my two children now, but if you want to know why I am doing this, it's because of the kids.'

'And whose idea was it to paint the door purple?'

'It was a collective effort. See, purple is the international colour for equality. It was used by the Suffragettes. It's also my favourite colour. Do you like it?'

We were subsequently charged with criminal damage and, after a three-day trial, given a conditional discharge and a £600 fine each. I almost managed to save us all from conviction on a point of law – since CAFCASS did not own the building, it should have been the landlord pressing charges. I argued that in the absence of a complaint from the landlord there was no case to answer, but Sarah Ashford's defence barrister took it upon himself to find a piece of case law that would sink my argument.

'Are you out of your tiny cranium! What are you fucking doing?' I snarled at the arrogant little upstart. 'I thought you were supposed to be on the defence side, not the prosecution?'

'My first duty is to the court,' he replied nonchalantly.

'What, leafing through legal books trying to find an argument to convict your own client and us along with her? Even the prosecuting barrister has admitted defeat!'

I called our barrister Michael Cox from outside the court. He informed me that all lawyers are officers of the court and that whilst the defence barrister was going beyond any reasonable duty to the court in bringing relevant cases of law to its attention, he was still scrupulously right in discharging his duty in this way. From that moment onwards, I developed a deep-seated aversion to lawyers.

Either way, it had been a useful first exercise in getting arrested and facing trial. And most importantly, we had proved that you could get nicked and live to fight another day.

LOVE ME TENDER

Our second demonstration was planned for Valentine's Day. I was desperately trying to secure some kind of national coverage to raise awareness about Fathers 4 Justice and our campaign, but initially it was proving a tough nut to crack.

On Valentine's Days past I'd been inclined to spread the love around, but this year I was saving it all for one special girl. I wished I'd saved myself the bother when I woke that morning to find *The Times* running F4J's story under the heading 'Split parents seek end of "heartbreak hotel" court'. If I'd known, I wouldn't have gone to the bother of organising the delivery of a single Violet Carson rose to Dame Elizabeth Butler-Sloss, President of the Family Division at the Royal Courts of Justice, accompanied by an envelope. Inside was a Valentine's Card informing her of the imminent arrival of the Fathers 4 Justice, Barking & Dagenham Chapter, Flying Elvis – circa his 'Aloha from Hawaii' comeback Tour of 1973.

'Dear President,' the billet-doux began. 'Love me tender, don't be cruel, I ain't nothing but a hound dog at the heartbreak hotel.' And thus it continued in humorous vein. Later that morning a 30-foot inflatable heart was delivered to the Royal Courts of Justice by thirty of us in Elvis jumpsuits. It was not a flattering look. The giant inflatable had been produced at a knock-down rate by a company called Air Artists, who created the inflatables for Pink Floyd, the Rolling Stones, etc.

Later that month, Sally Field, at the Lord Chancellor's Department, again threatened me with contempt of court after the long-promised article about me and the boys was published in the *Evening Standard* under the heading 'I spent £10,000 fighting to see my kids', alongside a picture of me, Daniel and Alexander taken at Kimsings. My letter in response to Ms Field was concise and to the point: 'Rearrange this popular Anglo-Saxon phrase: *off* and *fuck*.'

BBC *News 24* called, inviting me to do my first live interview with Family Minister, Rosie Winterton. I was shaking with nerves as Sian Williams put me through my paces.

Tony Lewis came with me to press the flesh in Westminster. Our first meeting was with Tory grandee Bill Cash, who told me that it would take fifteen years to get anything changed.

'Fifteen fucking years?' I replied, aggrieved. 'My kids could be dads by then.'

Taking a long breath, he delivered a rather snotty and disdainful reply. 'Dear boy, I'm afraid you'll have to use the usual channels. You know, wining, dining, schmoozing, that sort of thing. My daughter's going through a messy divorce, though obviously she's batting on the other side to you chaps. That's just how this place works, I'm afraid. But you have my sympathy.'

'How very perspicacious of you, Mr Cash. But we don't have fifteen years and I don't want sympathy – I can't change the bloody law with sympathy.'

Afterwards we hooked up with Ann Widdecombe in her office overlooking Parliament Square. Not only did she turn out to be a sympathetic blanket of huggability, she's also switched on about the family courts and fatherlessness. In fact, it was to be the subject of her next book. At the launch of her book *Father Figure*, a year later, she admitted that F4J had done more for equal parenting in one year than the Tories had done in the last ten, though other Tory MPs like Tim Loughton would slam us for doing more harm than good. Well, at least people know about it now, I thought.

RETURN OF THE RAMPANT RABBITS

On 18 April we held an 'Egg on your Face Easter Bunny' demo at a West Country hotel owned by the late Mrs Justice Bracewell, one of the most senior judges in the Family Division.

As half a dozen man-sized Easter Bunnies sprang into action in front of the hotel, I pressed my furry mask and ears up against the glass of the conservatory. Minus my glasses, I'm as blind as a myxomatosis-hit rabbit can be, but I can still make out twenty jaws dropping simultaneously on to the breakfast tables of the hotel. An old friend from my pre-F4J days had also joined us. 'Big' Ron Davis was already so hairy we deemed it unnecessary for him to dress up. With an orange-juice fuelled bombastic braggadocio, Big Ron went on the prowl, letting rip over a loud-hailer with a hysterical public information broadcast as I walked round to the front door. An agitated old chap answered my knock.

'Get off my land, you, you, bloody vermin!'

'Fathers 4 Justice, actually. It's just a little performance activism we are putting on to both entertain and inform your clientele about the nature of the owner's other line of work. This is Justice Bracewell's hotel?'

'Get off my property now or I'll get my gun.'

'Is that a cue for that old ditty –?' The door slammed before I could name the tune.

'Easter egg, anyone?' I shouted through the letter box, dropping in a handful of Cadbury Creme Eggs.

As I turned to gather the troops I was accosted by a very agreeable lady who asked what we were doing. I apologised and informed her that we had made our point and were leaving to allow everybody to enjoy their Easter Day.

'He sent you,' she said, gesturing towards the sky.

'Who?'

'God. He sent you.'

'He did? If you say so, I'm happy to take your word for it, thank you. Can I ask who you are?'

'I'm the judge's sister-in-law.'

Crikey, I thought. Could be an interesting Sunday roast at their place.

About twelve months later Bracewell took the seismic step of opening her court to the public as she delivered judgment, transferring care of the children from their mother to the father. It was a case where the mother had obstructed all contact. Bracewell decided that her ruling might at least afford the children the opportunity of maintaining a proper relationship with both parents. It was applauded by us not least because, up until then, we had been among her most vociferous critics. I believe that she genuinely recognised that family law was failing, and failing badly.

The media coverage continued to grow. I was asked to do John Peel's *Home Truths* on Radio 4. With the voice of a man who understood what it felt like to be relegated from premier league to division four overnight, John dryly asked me during the interview if it was like being on the substitutes bench after the birth of Daniel. I answered that yes, it was tough, but not as tough as what had happened in the last few years. It was a very agreeable interview, with Peel gently coaxing fragments of my story out from under my radar and it seemed to play well with everybody who listened to it, despite the fact that when it came to doing press, I was still a bundle of nervous energy. At least, I figured, I seemed to have lost my stammer.

Our campaign of non-violent direct action continued through May, when activists Jolly Stanesby and Andy Murray scaled the roof of Plymouth County Court. Huge regional media attention. Jolly – a streak of fermented West Country cider piss – remained cheerfully optimistic even when being cuffed, congratulating his captors, telling them he was grateful for the offer of free grub and accommodation care of Her Majesty.

BACK IN ACTION, BACK IN BLACK

About a fortnight before Fathers' Day 2003 I came up with a plan to shut down the UK's largest family court, the Principal Registry of the Family Division of the High Court. The majority of the population had no idea that the place existed, let alone what it did, so we felt duty bound to devise a demonstration that would convey its purpose.

First I met up with Dr Michael Pelling, who founded the campaign for open justice in the family courts back in 1995. A 50-something sandal-wearing former maths lecturer of shy demeanour, it's fair to say that Michael's modus operandi was the diametric opposite of my own. Where I wanted to mobilise public opinion through creating awareness, Michael persisted with his belief that you could change the law by using the existing legal framework. That said, he was a man of considerable fortitude and intellect. Whatever our disagreements about tactics, our endgame was the same. I wanted to pick his brains about the ramifications of what might happen if we shut down an entire court, so I ran the plan by him.

'In a nutshell, Michael, I have a cunning plan that involves storming Court 1 and informing the judge that the court is now open to he public.'

'It's very, very dangerous.' Michael gave me one of his studious stares as he evaluated the consequences. 'Contempt of court – you could go straight to prison.'

'But what if there are fifty of us? Would they lock up fifty of us, even grandparents?'

Even though I was now pretty certain we could all get banged up, I decided to take the gamble.

And so, on Friday, 13 June 2003, we launched our Fathers' Day 'Men in Black' demo. That morning I told a whopping porky on GMTV, announcing that we were heading for CAFCASS headquarters. As a result, a small army of police set out to wait for us there.

We rendezvoused at my old watering-hole, the Papermill café bar in Curtain Road, just up from the City, dividing ourselves into two groups: those prepared to be arrested, who would travel by bus; and everyone else, who would make their way by tube.

Yet again I was shitting myself. It was a glorious sunny day and we'd got a good turnout, but I was very aware that this protest carried a very real risk of arrest, making it our most hazardous to date.

As the bus hurtled along Gray's Inn Road, I spoke to the driver.

'Change of plan, mate. We ain't going to CAFCASS now, we're going on a bit of a detour. Hook round to Holborn.'

'What's going on, Mr O'Connor? We seem to have attracted some attention.'

In the rear-view mirror I could see two cop cars tailing us. I rummaged in my pockets and rustled up £100 extra cash for the driver to encourage his complicity.

'Listen, mate, we're on a bit of a mission. I need you to pull up outside a court building in Holborn, but you must follow my instructions. Will this help?'

He took the dosh and stuffed it in his trousers.

'Fucking hell, mate, what if they put their lights on?'

'Just keep driving, my friend, just keep driving.'

As we rolled slowly around the one-way system at Holborn, I got on the phone to a team who were already in the building, standing by to hold open the exit doors, where we would be making our entry, and guide protestors up to the first floor and Court 1, which was in session. One of the 'insiders' was a new guy, a father of four called Eddie. Ed was my contact for the protest and as we approached, police cars in tow, I gave him a quick call to ensure everything was all set.

'Ed, it's Matt. You ready?'

'Fucking right. Security all up the other end at the entrance. They look like a bunch of fucking nancy boys. Probably kick like girls.'

I told the bus driver to slow down to walking pace and pull into the bus lane. Everybody on the bus was now kitted out in trademark black with shades, and armed with purple flags.

'Hold it, hold it!' We cruised another 20 feet until we were right outside the exit of the court. 'Kill the engine!' I yelled. 'Kill the engine!' Protestors were jostling beside me, shoulder to shoulder as the doors slid open. 'Go! Go! Go! Fuckkiiinng shift iiiitttttt!'

A cluster of bodies launched themselves from the vehicle and piled in through the exit doors, but within sixty seconds it was carnage in the building as security guards began rugby-tackling the marauding men in black.

'Fathers 4 Justice! Fathers 4 Justice!' protestors screamed.

I got off the bus a few seconds later and my ears were assaulted by the wall of sound as I entered the mêlée: screams, air horns, shouting – the works. Fuck me, I thought. The floor was a mass of seething flesh and East End Eddie had managed to attract an interesting appendage in the shape of a security guard clamped to his back; the two of them were spinning round like a Catherine wheel.

I shimmied through the kerfuffle and on to the staircase. In the adrenaline-charged atmosphere some of the protestors had failed to follow instructions and were racing all the way to the top of the staircase. I craned my neck and hollered, hoping they'd hear me on the fifth floor. 'Down here! First floor, you fuckers!'

As we poured into the court the judge made his exit through a door at the back. Entering stage left, a 6-foot 4-inch reconstructed caveman called Andy

Murray sprang into the judge's seat. One of the women protestors sat on his lap and Andy lifted a carafe of water from the judge's desk, raised it to the packed courtroom and took a swig. Another protestor placed a sticker in the middle of the Queen's crest on the back wall. Meanwhile a hapless court official, face swollen with rage and sweating profusely, tried to remonstrate with protestors, only to be hounded out of the room. I grabbed the megaphone and declared, 'This is now an open court. It is open to the public so that justice is done, and justice is seen to be done. Fathers 4 Justice!'

It was a court I'd had the misfortune to experience on numerous occasions, so this was payback.

But the police were in a foul mood. A chief inspector from Scotland Yard, who has never forgiven me for slipping him a dummy when I'd said on GMTV that morning that we would be protesting at the CAFCASS headquarters, turned up with a small army behind him. Outside, several hundred protestors had lined up waving purple flags. Incredibly, the Old Bill let us out two by two and there were no arrests. The day had been an unprecedented success. The action sent shock waves through the legal system. At the time it was impossible to judge what effect, if any, these protests were having, but with the passage of time, rumour and then story filtered through that the legal profession had been shocked by both the scale and audacity of our campaign. We were having an effect.

In twenty-first-century Britain conventional protests don't work. If you play it by the book, you will be policed into oblivion. You can't even hand out leaflets. The police intelligence team will take video and photographic recordings of you to help construct their so-called intelligence profiles. If you break loose, you'll end up with four on your tail for the rest of the day.

Forget it. The best time to protest is when the police least expect it. How I felt for the anti-war protestors when they marched on London. Same old same old. If a hundred thousand people had simply sat down at midday on London's tarmac for an hour and threatened to stay there, the results could have been very different.

Away from the madness, Daniel and Alexander came up and stayed with me the following weekend. I'd fired up a barbecue at the ranch for us to enjoy, regaling them with tales about Horatio Thudstumper and the Yonk, a mythical creature who lived in the stream at the end of the garden. I had invented the story when the boys first came to stay in Suffolk and I was still able to enthral them with my hammy amateur dramatics. To anyone watching I probably looked like a deranged scarecrow, my windswept hair spiked in different directions. To them though, it added to the aura of mystery that hung over Kimsings, its ramshackle silhouette framed by the setting sun and the air filled with dancing bats.

THE PRISONER

In July of 2003 I received a call from the mother of a man who was alleged to have abducted his 7-year-old daughter and taken her to Portugal. Simon Clayton's daughter had since been returned to her Polish mother in Wales, but he remained languishing in a legal blackhole and seemed set to remain there, baking in a sweltering cell while the Portuguese legal system shut down for its summer break.

'Matthew, we need help,' pleaded his mother, trying to maintain her composure in the face of despair. 'Simon's legal team are doing their level best, but we don't seem to be making any progress.'

'I'm not sure it's our bag,' I told her, wanting to let her down gently. 'We don't get involved in individual cases, especially ones that are hot potatoes like this. What if he is guilty and we are seen to be helping him? It wouldn't play well for us.'

But she was insistent and, after talking it over with Tony Lewis, we decided that we would assist, on humanitarian grounds. (If the roles of the genders had been reversed and Mum had buggered off, Dad would no doubt have been told by the police that it was a civil matter and that he should get advice from a solicitor.) So we pressed the red button and came up with a plan to get him out of jail. Sensing that media interest in the case would make the Portuguese authorities more eager to cooperate, we invited journalist Jan Onoszko and a cameraman from ITV's Central Television to join us on the trip.

The one thing we hadn't counted on was Simon Clayton's non-cooperation. On the first day there I was allowed in to see him on my own. From the outside, the prison looked like a bunkered-up concrete holiday resort that had been displaced from downtown Beirut. Inside it was clean and cool in the downstairs rooms, but the cells were like brick ovens, especially when the sun hit them between midday and 3 o'clock in the afternoon.

The guards ushered me into a small room with a wooden desk. A few minutes later Clayton entered, looking tired and gaunt.

'How are you doing, Simon? My name's Matt O'Connor, I'm from a campaign group called Fathers 4 Justice and I'm here to help.'

Clayton lit up a fag. 'So what are you planning? A jailbreak?' he said sarcastically. It wasn't a helpful start.

I asked him to tell me his version of what happened. After separating from her mum, he'd decided to take his daughter Esti on a four-week holiday. Although he'd been the primary carer, he knew from what he'd read in the press that, in a dispute over residency, chances were her mum would win and he'd have very limited time with Esti in future. When they got to the south of Portugal, their camper van had broken down. Unbeknown to Clayton, back home the Welsh media were in a frenzy over Esti's 'abduction'. When the Portuguese police found him, they went in hard. Seven-year-old Esti was paddling in the shallows of the sea and Clayton was fiddling with the engine of the van when around fifteen armed police tackled him and put him down on the floor with a gun to his head, shouting at him in Portuguese. Within minutes they had found Esti and the two were separated, never to see each other since.

'Simon, for this to work I'll need your cooperation.' I was asking for his help, but his arrogant tone and belligerent demeanour told me that he simply wasn't interested in playing ball.

'They need footage of you, Simon. Perhaps when you are walking around the courtyard we can get a shot there, and also from your cell, but we'll need a signal – a piece of blanket or something hanging out of the window. If we can mobilise some publicity, we should be able to get you out of here a lot quicker.'

'No, I don't think so.' He rolled his head back and threw it forward while adroitly balancing a lit roll-up in his mouth. 'I don't want to play this sort of game. You don't know how it is, how the system works here.'

'Excuse me?'

'I think we should leave it to the lawyers. They're making good progress. They know how it works.'

'But, Simon, I know how it works, too. I know you are here sitting in front of me in a sewer pit of a Portuguese hell-hole sharing a six-by-ten cell with three other guys, and you're only allowed out one hour a day. Your cell hits 44 degrees centigrade every afternoon, and if you don't cooperate you're going to be incarcerated in this frying pan all summer until the judiciary get back from their siesta, which should be some time in September. By then you'll be charcoal.'

'In the meantime,' I blast, 'I'm not here for the fun of it. I'm here to do a job. The sooner you start playing the game, the sooner you'll be out.' But still Clayton wouldn't play ball. 'What is it with you? It's like trying to push water up a hill. I mean, how hard can you make this, Simon?'

The answer is, very. Outside, the guys from Central TV were dumbstruck when they heard that Clayton had spurned our help. The whole purpose of their trip had been to secure some footage of Simon in the prison. We decided to try and secure an appointment with the local judge in charge of Clayton's case. Thankfully, he bought into the whole enterprise. With his perfectly coiffured grey hair and tweaked moustache, the judge seemed pretty chic – well, for a judge at any rate. He even flashed a smile. After half an hour of agreeable negotiation he agreed to an interview. We were indebted in no small part to Jan, who was fluent in Portuguese.

It turned out that the judge was remarkably positive about Clayton's early release or extradition back to Wales. Once he'd done a piece to camera, I filmed an interview in the town square before heading back to the prison to try and pressure Clayton into giving the crew from Central something to go back with.

'We had a meeting with the judge on your case, Simon, and it went well.'

'You should leave it to my legal team, Matt.'

'Oh yeah, that would work a treat. I had to fight my way past them to get in here. Let's face it, Simon, you're in deep shit. Everybody is about to fuck off for their holidays and the only thing you are likely to get between now and September is an intensive course in how to learn Portuguese.'

When we discussed his daughter it was clear that he cared deeply for her and feared the consequences of his actions. I made no judgement as to his guilt or innocence because, frankly, I didn't want to know. As far as I was concerned, the sooner we got him out, the sooner he could get back to Wales and face the music. Tony Lewis, though, had other things on his mind.

'Matt, Jan reckons we are being followed,' he told me that evening as we got stuck into sangria and tapas at a café in Giraldo Square. 'See that couple over there? They're British and they're staying at our hotel. They were at the airport and have been at every café we have been to. We even saw them at the prison earlier.'

'Whereabouts?'

'Just walking past. But they seem to be with us the whole time. Think about it, how many other Brits have you seen?'

'None.'

'Right, and it just so happens that we are smack bang in the middle of Portugal, seriously off the tourist trail, and yet we have these two with us.'

'Fucking hell, Tony,' I said disbelievingly.

'Think about it, Matt. It's all very odd – and that isn't just my opinion. The journalists were the people who picked up on it first.'

With time, however, Simon turned what had seemed to be a hopeless scenario into one that inspires. In Clayton v Clayton [2006] EWCA Civ 878 on 28 February 2006, Simon Clayton, who by now was converted to the Fathers 4

Justice campaign, applied to the Court of Appeal to be able to discuss in public the agreement for shared parenting which he and his former wife had come to at the conclusion of proceedings concerning Esti.

Simon, to his immense credit, also wanted to be able to debate issues about the family justice system in public with reference to his own case, and to campaign for better and more open family justice, including the sharing of Tax Credits and Child Benefit where there were shared parenting arrangements.

In this landmark ruling he was allowed to openly publicise his case. It was an astonishing turn of events, that here was this man who but not a few years earlier had been so obstinate in rejecting out efforts and campaign, and yet now was one of our greatest advocates. Better still, he had turned a monumental disaster into a personal triumph for him, his ex-wife and his daughter Esti. I was delighted.

Being back at home did nothing to allay Tony Lewis's paranoia. He reported having seen a man in a car outside his house for the last two days. 'He's either police or the tax man,' he told me. Tony had never been prone to histrionics or exaggeration, so it was disturbing to see him so unsettled by a growing trail of coincidences.

PORN TO RUN

In September 2003 I was invited to a family law book launch. Sir Bob Geldof, who had contributed a chapter, was guest speaker. In the 1990s, Geldof and his ex-wife, Paula Yates, fought a bitter battle over access to their three daughters. Tonight, with his trademark passion and verve, Bob attacked the representatives of the family law industry gathered in front of him.

'Our system is adversarial, designed to spiral into acrimony, rage, bitterness and hatred. It is creating a nation of feral children and feckless adolescents, and vast pools of unhappiness and discontent. I had no idea there were so many of us out there, destroyed by this system.'

I chatted briefly to a caustic Cherie Blair. She probably used to be very nice.

Later, I discussed tactics with Bob. 'Just keep the fucking nutters out and keep it fucking funny,' he advised. Bob had the attention span of a goldfish but was sharp, analytical, and passionate with it.

A few weeks later, at Bob's suggestion, we shelled out £5,000 for a stand at the Tory Party conference in Blackpool. We pressed the flesh with Theresa May, William Hague and Michael Howard, who immediately grabbed F4J political coordinator, Gary Burch.

'I want a word with you,' said Howard. 'You know it's not down to the politicians, this problem is in the courts. It's down to how the courts apply the law.'

But Burchy put him right. 'Mr Howard, the will of Parliament has not been enforced. The judiciary are applying their own version of law.'

At a bash at the hotel bar where the faithful were camped out, the then Tory leader Iain Duncan Smith gave an interview for *Newsnight* then turned bang into my arms amid a firestorm of light flashes.

'You're one of those Fathers 4 Justice boys, aren't you?'

''Fraid so.'

'No, good, good. Glad to see you.' We shook hands and he departed, surrounded by his posse. Oddly enough we also bumped into a young David Cameron, but then we were probably better known than him at the time.

While we found general sympathy for our cause, we encountered a 'Problem, what problem? What can we do?' malaise among the delegates. After much wringing of limp hands, they were later to experience a Damascene conversion.

In early October the Grosvenor Hotel on Park Lane in London was to host a Family Law Conference for industry luminaries. Hoping to disrupt the event from the inside, we sent a team in to case the joint. At around 9 a.m., as the rest of us gathered across the road in Hyde Park, we saw the cop cars begin to arrive and it became clear that we'd been rumbled.

I immediately got on my mobile and called East End Eddie to warn him. It turned out that he was hiding from hotel security in a walk-in freezer down in the Grosvenor's kitchens. Ed's a brawny lump of beef, with a marbled red complexion that makes him look as if he's been boiled alive in Hackney marsh water and embalmed in malt vinegar. In true gangster-chav style, he's also afflicted with a gob filled with flash golden lead and a grade-two cranium crop. One thing he wouldn't be mistaken for is a Michelin-starred chef.

'It's fuckin' freezing in 'ere, mate,' he announced with his Cockney lilt. 'Place's crawling with Bill.'

Ed liked to brag that he lived in 'Nam' – Dagen-nam, to be precise.

The Bill were always dropping by his gaff, generally using the 'universal key' a.k.a. the battering ram. Many was the time I'd get a 7 a.m. call from Ed: 'Oll right, Matt? It's Ed. Gotta fuckin' loada filth round 'ere. They're gonna smash me fuckin' door down. I'm gonna call 999 and ask 'em what to do, then I'll be out on me toes, dahn the drainpipe, into the neighbour's garden and offski.'

In a previous life, it was believed that Ed had been a failed armed bank robber and getaway driver with all the directional sense of a London cabbie south of the river. I couldn't help but imagine him driving away from the scene of some dastardly crime with a bag of swag over his shoulder and a ball of string in his hand. He also had a disconcerting habit of recognising apparently complete strangers in the street: 'I know that bloke! Dartmoor 1979.' That said, Ed now had unlimited access to his kids, which spoke volumes about his rehabilitation back into society.

We decided to abandon the Grosvenor mission and return to base, but it quickly became apparent that a four-man intelligence team from the Yard were on my tail.

'Taxi! Taxi!' I howled at the traffic in Park Lane. A cab rumbled up and I piled in, along with a freelance documentary maker who was filming F4J's activities. 'Marble Arch, please,' I told the driver, but as the cab yanked out into the oncoming stream of traffic, a vanload of cops fell in behind us. At Marble Arch we hopped off and made straight for the underground station, the police in hot pursuit. While we lost valuable seconds buying tickets, the Bill simply flashed their cards at the barrier. We jumped aboard the next tube, but they were stuck to us like two-day-old Hyde Park doggy-doo.

As our guy filmed their guy filming us, bemused passengers looked on, agog at the bizarre stand-off.

'I feel like Bill Clinton, now I've got my own security,' I joked nervously, trying to inject a little humour into proceedings, but it fell on stony ground.

At Oxford Circus we were off like a shot, sprinting up the escalators. 'Police! Police! Stop that man!' I screamed, the crowds parting in front of me as I pursued my non-existent quarry, closely followed by the real police. Outside the station we climbed into another cab, only to be boxed off by two cop cars that had been following above ground. We sprang out the other side of the cab and burned down towards Regent Street, dodging oncoming buses and cabs. For a moment I thought we'd shaken them off, with their cars caught up in traffic at Oxford Circus as we continued running into Soho. Seconds later another cop car spotted us and two cops hopped out. We took a sharp left, straight into a sex shop.

Down the stairs we breezed, into a basement area rammed full of pornographic material and marital aids, yet still the boys in blue remained in dogged pursuit. Now that's what I call professionalism. I thought about making a purchase for a laugh, but instead picked up a copy of *Asian Babes* magazine and opened it, lifting it high to semi-mask my face. My guy was still filming as I set about creating a distraction to throw the Bill off the scent. Sauntering over to a freestanding rack of vibrators, I casually leaned against it, sending a Bertie Bassett assortment of vividly coloured tickle-pleasers raining down around me. With that, all hell broke loose.

'What you doing? Get outta my fucking shop!' In the confined space of the basement, customers jostled around the mêlée. As I picked myself up, the boys in blue found themselves on the wrong side of the throng and we took the opportunity to make our escape via a rear entrance. Before our compadres could catch up we clambered aboard a passing Routemaster bus and bid the Bill adieu with a few choice hand signals as the bus sped down Shaftesbury Avenue.

Back at the Papermill we rendezvoused with the rest of the team. A new guy called Darren bought everybody a round, which was very generous of him, given that most people in F4J don't have much dosh. We later found out he was undercover Bill.

'At least he gotta round in, Matt!' said Ed.

'Yeah, after being chased like a piece of Spanish bull-steak round the streets of London for an hour, that makes me feel a lot better.'

The next day I took a call from our Bristol coordinator, the indomitable Jeff Skinner. One of their guys, Alan Ford, had seen his son for a sum total of seven hours in seven years. Now he had cancer. While the family court system hadn't crushed his spirit, the disease was threatening to finish him off. I asked Jeff to give Alan as much support as they could until, God-willing, we could all catch up at the next demo.

By this stage in the campaign we were being overwhelmed by demands for help, to the point where it was impossible to cope with the sheer number of calls. Still we soldiered on in the vain hope that we could somehow help every lost soul who turned to us for support. It was a Herculean task.

It sounded like more of the same old same old when Jenny took a call one day and said, 'Matt, I've got another sad dad who says he wants to talk to you. He sounds Irish.'

'Find out who he is, Jen.'

Seconds later, she was waving furiously at me.

'It's Sir Bob Geldof! Sorry, I didn't know.'

I had a discussion with Geldof about tactics. It was clear that he understood the academic side, but I wasn't sure he grasped the simple fact that we didn't have a pot to piss in and I was running the show on beans. Now more than ever we needed to start ramping up our campaign of non-violent direct action. The next protest was to signal a year-long run of unprecedented political protest across the country and the first world. When I told Bob I'd booked a tank for our next demo, the 'Rising', he didn't sound too keen on the idea.

'Can't you paint it white or something? It's too militaristic. We should keep it funny.'

'But we are, Bob; we are. You need to see what happens next.'

K'POW!
INTRODUCING THE MEN IN TIGHTS

T he next day Jolly Stanesby rang me up. He was livid, having received a letter from the court that curtailed his contact with his daughter Rosie. Jolly's case was as interesting as it was illustrative. A registered childminder, Jolly had been embroiled in a long-running feud with the presiding judge in his case, Judge Tyzak, who was based in Plymouth Court. Jolly wanted equality of treatment and an equal division of parenting time. Why, he argued, when he was a registered childminder, could he look after other people's kids all day, but only have defined contact times with his own daughter? But Tyzak wasn't having any of it. Jolly's involvement with Fathers 4 Justice was impacting negatively on his case – in fact it was positively damaging his position with the court. Jolly's response was that he wanted to go one step further and I had just the location for him.

Every Fathers 4 Justice protest was meticulously planned. They still went tits up, but they *were* meticulously planned. Whilst many newspapers had F4J down as a slickly run military machine, in reality it was a shambollocks. Everything seemed to happen in spite of our precision planning, not because of it, and our first serious piece of high-wire work was no exception.

On Saturday, 18 October 2003, Andy Neil and John Levis dropped round to my country pile to model garments for our 'Superheroes' campaign. Andy was a committed activist and London coordinator for F4J. A thin and wiry 30-something with an unswerving sense of equality, he was intent on helping us create the publicity we needed to bring our message to the public's attention. John was a different kettle of fish altogether. A softly spoken man, his life had become saturated with sadness and despair because of his inability to gain access to his children. Even with us rolling up outside court to offer our support, and multiple court orders authorising him to see his children, the children's mother had effectively severed their relationship with John by repeatedly flouting the court's orders – at least until the children reached an age where they could decide for themselves. Even then there was no cast-iron guarantee. While weathering this emotional storm, John remained resolutely committed to the campaign, quietly beavering away building support throughout East Anglia. Both John and Andy were game for a laugh when it came to trying on ridiculous supersuits for a publicity shot. Boys being boys, they played up for the cameras and the resulting shots convinced us that 'Men in Tights' might just hang together as a campaign theme.

The plan was to have Batman and Robin, complete with capes, shin up the front of the Royal Courts of Justice on the Strand and stay there for the week. The aim was to raise more publicity about the campaign in advance of our 'Rising' protest a few days later that October. Every demo we planned at this stage involved incremental increases in the 'dare' factor. With limited food and bedding, the protestors might have been able to last a week on the roof.

At 3 p.m. the following Monday a lorry was to deliver Britain's longest ladder – a beast of a thing, 50-feet long – to the Papermill. At 8 p.m. Andy Neil would assemble the support squad of twelve men.

We thought we'd allowed for the worst-case scenario by working on the premise that only six of the support squad would turn up. In fact, Andy had started with a list of two hundred names, of which thirty we considered 'committed'. The Fathers 4 Justice commitment scale divided volunteers into the following categories:

Model citizen: willing to participate in demonstrations but not direct action. Very sensible and eminently intelligent. Probably joined Fathers 4 Justice by mistake.
Armchair general: keen on the idea of protest, but not the reality. Will sometimes talk the talk but would never walk the walk.
Reluctantly enthusiastic: committed when it came to organising protests but not when it came to an encounter with the boys in blue.
Borderline activist: ready to get stuck in if push comes to shove. At the very least could be counted upon to be actively involved in any support team.
Fully certifiable activist with all the paperwork to prove it: totally fearless to the point of insanity and beyond. One hundred per cent committed.

On paper, the plan seemed idiot proof. Too bad we hadn't tested it out on any idiots.

At 5 o'clock on Monday afternoon, Andy called to say that one of our guys had picked up the wrong ladder – a 35-foot effort that wouldn't reach the roof of the Royal Courts. I went apo-fucking-plectic.

'Hell's fucking bells, it's a fucking ladder, it needs to be 50 feet otherwise it won't reach. How difficult can this be for somebody to understand?'

Andy had no answer. He'd done all the leg-work, and I could sense that he was as pissed off as I was. I got off the phone and Jenny began calling round hire shops trying to source a 50-foot ladder before they closed for the day. Thankfully she struck gold with minutes to spare, but by this time our lorry driver had chickened out and the Papermill, where the gear was to be stored, was under police surveillance. In the end we had the ladder delivered to Andy's London flat. Meanwhile another guy went to pick up the lorry and bring it back to Andy's.

At 8 p.m. a support team of five showed up and started practising putting up the ladder – a considerable feat, when you're dealing with a ladder of that size. Once erect at full stretch it only took a small tip for the thing to go completely, wiping out anyone in the vicinity.

Around midnight, Jolly and Eddie rolled up. There were always disputes in Fathers 4 Justice, but none were more hotly contested than the tug of war over who got to wear which costume. Our 'Men In Tights' campaign kicked off with a tussle between Jolly and Eddie over who would get to wear the Batman cape. It ended with Jolly playing Robin to Eddie's Batman.

I called them up for a quick pep talk. 'All right, Jol?'

'Nice one, Matt. Should be good. I mean, what can go wrong?'

'Everything that can go wrong has gone wrong already, so I hope our luck will change from here on in.'

At 3 a.m. Fathers 4 Justice pumped the high-risk quotient up to max and set off from Andy's pad with the ladder attached to the roof of the lorry. The bloody thing was so long it started bouncing up and down in front of the windscreen and nearly scraping the road. But it was too late to do anything about it. All the lads could do was close their eyes and roll down through the City towards the Royal Courts.

The first indication court security had that something was afoot was when our lorry rolled up outside and the boys spilled out on to the pavement. I'd given specific instructions for them to try the front gate to see if it was open, but instead the boys took the path of most resistance by scaling the 5-foot-high railings. Unsurprisingly, Eddie got himself stuck, legs akimbo, his face gurning away in frustration with gibbering flashes of gold tooth.

Within thirty seconds security were sprinting towards the main entrance followed by a handful of police officers. With a heave and a ho, the lads got Ed over and the ladder erected. Jolly shot up it like the proverbial rat up a drain pipe. Ed's hulk was a little slower to rise to the vertical challenge; before he could reach the top the police, having entered the courtyard via the open front gate, had made it to the foot of the ladder. A copper began climbing, but Ed made it to the roof and began shaking the ladder while the hapless copper hung on for dear life.

'You wanna be careful, mate, this ladder is 'ighly unstable, a bit like me,' shouted Eddie, and the copper beat a hasty retreat down to terra firma.

At 3.15 a.m. I got the call I'd been waiting for.

'The eagle 'as landed,' crowed Eddie from his eyrie, his cape flapping in the early-morning breeze in what would subsequently become an iconic campaign image of ramped-up cartoon bombast. The lads were to enjoy a three-day run entertaining the crowds from a rooftop one hundred feet above the Strand. The event received wide coverage, with Radio One taking a particular interest [http://www.fathers.ca/batman–and–robin.htm].

We discovered that it's all very well coming up with themed campaigns – men in tights, Lycra lads and caped crusaders – but the harsh reality is that being a fully unpaid superhero requires one secret ingredient: balls.

Big brass balls in the summer. Pingpong balls in the autumn. And marbles in the winter. At the risk of sounding sexist, embarking on a superhero safari is man's work and once you've read this, you'll be thankful for that. As you throw your cape over your shoulder and unleash your inner hero, you'll be struggling against the enemies of equality while facing extreme discomfort and fear in a pseudo-Jackass act of exhibitionism, whether it be scaling a tall building, clinging to a crane, or simply bringing the traffic to a standstill. But worse, far worse than that is the humiliation that comes with the costume you have to wear.

Few men will understand the pitfalls of wearing tight, stretchy polyester garments and superhero garb. Firstly, glasses are a no-no. Not only are they nigh on impossible to wear, but with sweaty Lycra comes the sort of steam normally seen condensing around a pouting Nigella Lawson's boiling broccoli. Secondly, your pants will disappear up your crack in a spandex wedgie and your spare tyre will overhang your utility belt, making you look more like the Michelin Man than Superman.

There are five fundamental rules to donning your supersuit and engaging in freelance voluntary superhero work:

1. *Use talc.* You'll be itching all over if you don't use good-quality talcum powder inside your supersuit. Get some. Use it.
2. *Put a sock on it.* It's generally fucking cold up there. By the time the wind chill hits freezing, your bits will have shrunk to the size of raisins and your knob will have curled up for some self-loving and warmth. It's long been suspected that superheroes 'pad out' their lunchboxes to

compensate, and I can confirm that cosmetic sock-enhancements were not unknown on F4J demos.

3. *Wee freely.* Worst of all is the inevitable call of nature, just when the police are climbing up the gantry or motorists' are shouting up at you to let you know they're on their way to shag your ex wife. But when a man's gotta go, he's gotta go. And, to be honest, if it is a bit nippy there's nothing more satisfying than the warm run of pee down the inside of your leg to raise your body temperature by a few degrees.

4. *Get ready to run!* As Sky Masterson said in *Guys and Dolls*, the only time you need to be in a hurry is when the police are coming up the stairs. This is sound advice for wannabe superheroes in tight spots, if you can do a Jolly Stanesby and slide down a rope into a moving vehicle under the very noses of the boys in blue. One final point: it's not the way you fall boys, but the way you land.

5. *Evidence? What evidence?* It's also a good idea, before setting out on a mission, to remove ALL your computer equipment and any materials of an incriminating nature from your home. The boys in blue love nothing more than a bit of forced entry in an effort to retrieve 'evidence'. And there are several no-no's when it comes to conversing with your fellow superheroes, too. Email is out because it's easily monitored. Nothing should be stored on your computer. Everything I ever organised was always done on paper and subsequently burnt in my fireplace. Mobile phones are very leaky too, but thankfully 'telephone intercept', as they call it, isn't admissible as evidence in UK courts.

Sticking to these five golden rules will ensure that any mission stands a better chance of success.

RISING CAMP

The peachy thing about the Batman and Robin protest was that our Rising demonstration, scheduled to take place a few days later, by strange coincidence would finish outside the Royal Courts.

At the time we'd been engaged in a series of increasingly futile meetings with Lord Geoffrey Filkin, the then Minister for the Family Courts, trying to establish some common ground between the government and us. At the time Bob Geldof had also been attending conflabs with the Minister. The afternoon before our Rising demonstration, Bob called me to unleash his views on Filkin.

'Now tell me how you really feel, Bob,' I said, after a ten-minute pneumatic tirade of profanity had been drilled into my left ear about Geoffrey Filkin.

'I kept telling Laurence,' said Bob, 'The family justice system simply can't fucking continue like this. I mean it's just fucking cuntish – it's a fucking outrage!'

'Who's Laurence?' I asked bemusedly.

'Laurence, you know Laurence, the fucking minister, what's his fucking name, er, fucking Filkin.'

'His name is Geoffrey, Bob,' I said, correcting him.

'Fuck me,' said Bob, 'I thought he was giving me an odd look.' And Bob started laughing. 'Just shows what a spineless cunt he is. He didn't even have the balls to correct me about his own fucking name. Cunt.'

Our largest gathering to date, the Rising was powered by raw passion and hard wonga. It cost me about £3,000 to hire all the gear, produce the flags, placards, rent a bus and DJ, but at least it made it look as if we meant business. I'd even hired a fully operational 17-ton tank to complete the Dads' Army theme. Fast and manoeuvrable, it was like a big boy's dodgem, and came complete with a 105mm Howitzer gun with a range of over 9 miles. According to Nick Mead, the owner, Abbot tanks are still in use by several armies around the world. I couldn't help thinking of the possibilities if it were to be 'tank-jacked', but quickly dismissed the notion.

Even though Scotland Yard had agreed to let us bring the vehicle on the demo, they looked a bit nervous when I took it for a spin down Whitehall and back. As I rolled past Adrian Laurie from the Met doing my best Citizen Smith pose astride the top, I couldn't resist shouting, 'Downing Street here we come!'

Meanwhile our army was gathering back at Trafalgar Square. Several thousand protestors, including many children, grandparents and mums, were standing by for the off. The tank would lead the way, followed by a decontamination unit (guys in white cleaning overalls with brushes), a battle bus complete with DJ, purplehearts (women and relatives of those experiencing contact disputes), and regional groups.

I caught up with Adrian, our man from the Met.

'How are you doing, Matt?' he asked.

'Rather magnificently, actually. Fine and dandy, Adrian, fine and dandy. I can smell revolution in the air, can't you?'

'Now don't get ideas, Matt, it's only a demo.'

'I'm only joking, Adrian. After all, how much damage could you do with a tank?'

He laughed nervously as I shot him a cheery smile before heading back to the battle bus.

Once we got under way I kept topping and tailing the front of the demo to ensure that we proceeded at a leisurely pace, thwarting police efforts to keep things moving as quickly as possible in order to minimise traffic delays. As I hopped on and off the bus, I was constantly tailed by police intelligence officers.

Our first stop was in the Strand, adjacent to the Department for Work and Pensions, home to the universally loathed Child Support Agency. Around twenty guys removed their shirts and threw them to the ground in a symbolic protest before we moved off again. I caught sight of a group from Bristol, led by Jeff Skinner, who was pushing Alan Ford up the Strand in a wheelchair. I headed over to join them and discovered that Alan was now in the advanced stages of cancer. Against doctor's orders, he'd discharged himself that morning in order to attend the demo. The boys had picked him up from the hospital at 6 a.m. for the trip to London. It was clear that Alan was gravely ill, and I remonstrated with Jeff for bringing him.

'But he insisted, Matt,' said Jeff.

'You're a belligerent bugger, Alan. You should be in bed, mate.'

'No, Matt, I wanted to be here. I want you to use my name in whatever way you can to advance the cause.' I looked at Alan and then Jeff, not knowing what to say, feeling a lump in my throat. I took Alan's hand and we continued towards the Courts in a reflective silence. The next day, the *Bristol Evening Post* would publish a picture on its front page of the three of us walking stoically along the Strand, hand in hand. That was all we were left with to remember Alan. He passed away three weeks later, having seen his son for just seven hours in his entire life. The boy wasn't even allowed to attend his funeral. Alan's tragic death was to be the catalyst for invigorating the Bristol group in a way that would subsequently catapult them into the national headlines.

Outside the Royal Courts the circus rolled up beneath Jolly and Eddie, who were still acting up on the roof. We dished out several hundred pairs of underpants, planning to burn them in protest. But plainclothes police in the crowd got wind of what was happening and I was warned that such an action would be highly dangerous. I remonstrated with Adrian.

'But women were allowed to burn their bras. What's wrong with this?'

'It's dangerous. Somebody could get hurt.'

'Don't tell me, let me guess: health and safety?'

In the end I gave an undertaking that we wouldn't burn our pants, but it was too late. Our new PR maestro, Glen Poole, had seized the microphone and launched into one of his rabble-rousing speeches. A white man's answer to Lenny Henry, Glen was one of the most impressive campaigners I'd ever met, firing on six cylinders of off-the-cuff humour.

'Burn your pants!' he shouted into the mike. 'Burn your pants! Say pants to injustice in family law. Burn your pants! If it's good enough for the ladies, then it's good enough for us!'

I was furiously shouting 'No, no, no', but there was no way Glen could hear me above the cacophony of cheering. From the back of the bus I could see twenty to thirty pairs of white extra-large pants that had been kindly donated by a benefactor in the undergarments industry going up in flames atop wooden flag poles. Fucking hell, I thought, I'm going to be seriously in the doghouse with Plod now.

As the crowd got whipped up into a frenzy things began to turn ugly. Around twenty demonstrators sat down on the zebra crossing in front of the Royal Courts and the police moved in to pen everyone in on an island in the middle of the Strand. One copper came up to move me away and mashed my glasses into my face. I was about to send him back to where he came from when our barrister, Michael Cox, pulled me back.

'That got a bit fruity,' he joked, trying to calm me down. 'Could have ended badly, Matt, if you'd have gone for him.'

'Bastard! What he did was totally unnecessary.'

'They're nervous. We're on the roof of the Royal Courts and could easily storm the entrance. Somebody's head would be on the chopping block if it went wrong.'

After the protest, the *Guardian* took a dislike to us for some reason, slamming the melodrama of our protests. 'But we're not afraid of melodrama, or a bit of pomp and over-thought circumstance for that matter,' I told them. I suppose an F4J protest with lashings of humour doesn't exactly fit the editorial brief of a serious broadsheet.

Later that month, PR man Glen Poole, political coordinator Gary Burch and I agreed to meet with Geoffrey Filkin again, the Minister for the Family Courts, for what would turn out to be the final occasion. Filkin was a personable chap but utterly gutless, with the spine of a jellyfish and a mouth that seemed to work as if he were a glove puppet for the Whitehall mandarins that sat beside him in meetings. On the way to the meeting, we passed a 200-foot crane sited by Tower Bridge, and East End Eddie mentioned that a chap called Dave Chick wanted to scale it. To me it looked like a vertigo-inducing metal toothpick skewered in the north bank of the Thames. Personally, I get dizzy going up a house-ladder; even safely on terra firma, my legs turned to jelly as I craned my neck up at this edifice. Fuck me, I thought. That's a long way up.

We arrived at the meeting to encounter the usual skin-crawling assortment of brown-nosing civil servants.

'Do we have your attention?' I demanded.

'Yes, you have and we are always willing to engage in dialogue,' said Filkin.

'But are you listening? Are you willing to grasp the nettle and take action over the flouting of court orders?'

'Well, any court that doesn't enforce its own orders is a sham.'

It seemed a promising start, but the meeting rapidly descended into farce – not because of the civil servants, but because we failed to stick to what we had agreed beforehand would be our line.

Each of us broke the cardinal rule by bringing up our own individual cases. With no consensus between us, they were able to wriggle off the hook, dismissing our examples as one-offs. The meeting ended prematurely without them having answered a single one of our questions. Glen later accused me of 'out-swearing Geldof'.

'We'll get back to you,' they told us.

Save yourselves the bother, I thought. I have another idea.

SPIDERMAN

Over the next few days I could feel the temperature of the campaign rising, along with my blood pressure. The only time I felt I could truly switch off was when Daniel and Alexander were up at Kimsings. The office, though, was becoming besieged with email enquiries, and increasingly desperate phone calls. I thought I'd take a day off just to escape and go and watch the machinations of the family justice system myself for another time, just to remind myself, as if I needed reminding, of the task in front of us. I attended Bournemouth court with one father as his 'McKenzie friend'. A McKenzie is a friend or colleague you can bring into court if you have no legal representation. During the lunch break I sat in the public area outside of the courts scrolling through text messages when I overheard a female solicitor and a male barrister barracking a father over his alleged 'violent' behaviour.

This was in the public area and the pair seemed to be attempting to shame him by berating their hapless victim in a very public and vocal fashion.

'You abused your wife,' the solicitor shouted. 'You need to go on an anger management course, and you'll have no contact with your daughter until you do.'

The barrister waded in with all the subtlety of a nightclub bouncer. 'There is no point arguing. You have to accept what we are saying – or you'll never see your daughter again.'

I was gobsmacked. In the full glare of everybody in the public area, two legal professionals had overstepped any ethical boundaries. It turned out that they represented the man's ex-wife. I didn't know who he was but felt compelled to walk over and tell the father not to be intimidated and suggest that he needed to get advice from one of the fathers' support groups.

'This has got nothing to do with you,' spluttered the barrister.

'Yes it has. You have publicly humiliated this man in the public area so it is my damn business.'

'Who the hell do you think you are?' said the woman.

'You know my name,' I said calmly.

There was a collective pause as they focused on my face before the penny dropped.

'Matt O'Connor, Fathers 4 Justice. Might have bloody well known,' said the barrister, lifting his head back, nostrils inflated, chins hanging over his collar.

I turned to the dad. 'I don't know what you have done, but I do know that this behaviour constitutes professional misconduct. You should report them to the Bar Council.'

As I spoke the solicitor's face became tightly scrunched like a fistful of rubber bands and the barrister's blood vessels flowed ruby red across his flabby face.

It transpired that the father concerned had lost his temper once with his wife during their separation and lashed out. He admitted this in the family court though the police were not called and no charges were pressed. It was the sort of mistake that in the heat of separation many parents, mothers and fathers, have made, but this man was being torn apart by these hyenas. He had run out of money to pay for legal representation and was now representing himself.

For this one misdemeanour, he had not seen his daughter in two and a half years. His punishment was that he might never see his daughter ever again – and the legal representatives concerned made sure that everybody in the building knew it.

This incident cemented my every instinct and confirmed in my head what I already knew in my heart: we had to increase the pressure through bigger, more high-profile protests.

By now I was on a hi-octane mission to achieve our three-year plan. We'd already stirred enormous passion, drive and belief in the movement. I had led from the front and created an environment where ordinary people were prepared to go to extraordinary lengths because they bought the dream and wore the T-shirt. So it seemed appropriate to sanction a protest that would be our biggest yet, one that would go off like a Chinese firework – but one that we would also handle at arm's length for fear of the ramifications.

Originally the plan had been for Jolly, dressed in a Spiderman costume, to scale a crane being used to construct a new court building in Exeter. It should have coincided with a protest we'd organised back in September, but we couldn't get the superhero threads in time.

Thus it would fall to Dave Chick to be first to use the concept. Chicky had scaled several cranes previously but with little or no publicity. We gave him a costume, an 'In the Name of the Father' banner, and a set of specific PR instructions. Ironically, our team strolled in through a gap in the fence next to a 'Danger, Don't Climb' poster. In the small hours, they ferried all the gear up to the top of the crane and Chicky was set.

The November 2003 demo went stratospheric, giving us our first taste of a press scrum. For the next five days London was gridlocked, caught in Spiderman's web as the police deliberately closed all surrounding roads in an attempt to turn public opinion against us – at a cost of £9 million. Sadly, Chicky had a head for heights, that was about all. Despite specific instructions to keep his identity secret, he began gassing to the press. Soon various unsavoury skeletons came dancing out of his closet.

It turned out Chicky had a predilection for wacky-baccy and once indulged in a spot of cottaging in his local gent's toilets that would have made George Michael proud. The *Sun* ran the headline 'Spiderman is a Pervert'. Glen Poole, my fellow PR man, thought a better headline might have been 'Superqueero'. Chicky's ex-wife was quoted, wanting to know, 'Has he fallen off yet?'

Even the Mayor of London, Ken Livingstone, waded into the controversy, commenting on Dave Chick's demo he said that Chick's actions were 'amply demonstrating why some men should not have access to their own children ... and why women don't always feel they want their partners to have access to their children.' It reminded me of the arguments used against the Suffragettes when women were campaigning for the right to vote – how can they be trusted to vote when they chain themselves to the gates of Buckingham Palace or throw themselves under the King's horse?

Still, we got some positive media coverage on the back of the protest. When Dave sold his story to the *Daily Mail,* Glen found himself coaching Spiderman in the art of talking to the press. He had to be taught how to speak about his ex without coming across as bitter and vitriolic. When Glen suggested that he use her Christian name rather than calling her the bitch or the cow, Dave said he couldn't remember what she called herself – was it Jules or Julie? In the end they agreed that he would pick one name and stick to it.

Finally, in a desperate attempt to bring the best out of the man, Glen came up with the idea that he should approach the interview as if it were a first date and he was trying to make a really good impression because he wanted to have sex with the woman. Just to be on the safe side, he then made it clear that there would be NO sex with the journalist, and off we went.

A few weeks later, Jim Parton of Families Need Fathers invited a few of us, Spiderman included, along to a book launch at the Bulgarian Embassy. By this time Chick had made the celebrity Z-list. Other 'stars' included the Marquess of Bath plus wifelet, and the disgraced MP Neil Hamilton, who was wearing Rupert Bear trousers and a bow tie. I couldn't decide who looked more absurd, Hamilton or Spiderman. Eddie turned up intent on 'stickering' the gaff with F4J logos, then got stuck into the spit roast with the table manners of Vlad the Impaler at an all-you-can-eat barbecue. Chick, now dressed in his civvies, hailed a taxi home and immediately got into a row with the driver.

'Do you know who I am, mate?' he ranted. 'I'm Sshhhpppiiiderrrmannnn!'

In that moment you could see that his moment of infamy had really gone to his head. With common sense and a management he would listen to, Dave 'Spiderman' Chick could have made a small fortune in the twelve months that followed his protest. Instead his behaviour cost us support. When we approached the comedian Stewart Lee at the Edinburgh Festival in 2004 and asked him to back the cause, he told us that meeting Spiderman at a gig in London had turned him off the group.

And there in a nutshell was the dilemma between mass protest and lone protest. Mass protests made the case for the general problem but received less coverage, whereas lone protests attracted more coverage but exposed the individual to media scrutiny. Never mind that Dave Chick had court orders to see his daughter that were never enforced, it was always much easier to dish the dirt and smear the name of any activist.

The lingering fallout included a plethora of hostile and unpleasant emails from frustrated drivers and cabbies who had been caught up in the chaos that resulted from the road closures. 'I fucking spit on your organisation,' said one. Thanks!

GET PLUCKED!

Our next gig was a demo timed to coincide with our second Fathers Christmas protest. This time our target would be Tower Bridge. Andy Neil helped organise a team of activists who rendezvoused at a café near London Bridge Station. I had produced a huge fuck-off banner, 50-feet long and 20-feet wide, with a picture of Children's Minister Margaret Hodges' head transposed on to the body of a naked turkey with the words 'Get Plucked, Minister!'

The banner was cunningly smuggled past security and into Tower Bridge inside a baby's pram beneath a life-size baby doll. Once upstairs, access to the external walkway was easily gained through a window that had been conveniently left open. For the next few days a team of four activists – Jolly Stanesby, East End Eddie, Steve Battershill and Mick Sadeh – braved the fierce winter elements 150 feet above the Thames.

This time, police had kept the road open. It didn't prevent Jolly from dancing across the roof of the walkway in a hair-raising, death-defying, watch-it-through-closed-eyes jig one morning for the supporters gathered on the

South Bank, watching proceedings through binoculars. That afternoon, he phoned me with a request.

'All right, Matt?'

'Great, Jol. How are you doing?'

'Fucking freezing. Any chance of placing an order?'

'What do you fucking think this is? Domino's Pizza?'

'We'd love some warm grub, Matt.'

'But you're nigh on 200 feet up, mate. How the fuck do I get it to you – EasyJet?'

'There must be something you can do.'

'Give me five, Jol, and I'll buzz you back.'

I discussed the possibilities with Andy Neil and a guy called John Judge who had done some sterling work for us in the early days of the campaign. In the end we plumped for the old-fashioned route. The boys on the bridge would lower a rope and we'd tie the order to it from a moving car on the bridge. I handed over fifty quid for Chinese and fish'n'chips, but just as they were about to set off my mobile rang. From outside City Hall I gazed up at the walkway through my binoculars and saw Ed pulling a monkey grimace.

'Matt, can I change the order?'

'Fuck sake, Ed, what do you want?'

'Well, you know it's fuckin' freezing up 'ere and all that . . . can you git us some booze, like?'

'Like what?'

'Well, a nice bottle of Courvoisier would assist medicinally with my bad chest, and a bottle of Bell's would help us through the cold nights . . .'

On our first run, the rope got caught in the wind and was blowing around some 50 feet above the car. Second time round we hit paydirt. The boys had weighed the rope down with bottles of urine (nobody wanted to be accused of urinating or defecating on the officers standing below, so they'd gone armed with bottles and buckets for the purpose). As our car pulled over towards the middle of the bridge, the cops realised that something was going down: the F4J Tower Bridge Takeaway.

Suddenly the rope was caught in a violent gust of wind that swung it into the path of an open-top sightseeing bus. One of the bottles broke on impact, showering the passengers in fermented protestors' piss. As it swung back across the road, the boys in the car leapt out and grabbed it. With cops running up either side of the road towards them, they had seconds in which to remove the bottles and attach an order of five fish and chips, four mushy peas, four chicken chow mein, one crispy aromatic duck, one bottle of brandy, one bottle of whisky and as many beers as the bags would take. The entire haul weighed a ton and it took the guys on the walkway ten minutes to haul their bounty up. Right above the helmets of some seriously pissed off police.

A month later the irascible Jolly was back again. This time it was the Tamar Bridge, where he spent four days enduring snow and ice storms. We were testing a highway robber concept but it died a death. Everybody took him for Zorro or the bloody Lone Ranger, so I quickly reverted to Plan A and rolled out the superhero campaign nationally with my tagline: 'Every father is a superhero to his children.' Jolly evaded waiting police by sliding down a cable into a moving car in rush-hour traffic. The police didn't even realise he'd escaped until a female journalist Jolly fancied rang up to see how he was doing and Jol asked her out for a drink. She tipped off the Bill, who ordered a nationwide manhunt for him.

STAY UP AND PLAY UP

On Sunday, 1 February 2004, a group of us got together at Steve Battershill's gaff to plan the next stunt. My 'fire in the belly' pep talk didn't do much for one guy, who began shaking and shitting himself before bottling it completely in Steve's toilet. He was hyperventilating so much he could barely speak, so we had to drop him from the op. From then on I resolved to leave it right until the last minute to tell activists what they'd be doing. That way they'd have no time to think about it or to phone their mum, girlfriend or mates to ask whether it's a good idea to climb a 150-foot bridge dressed as a spandex superhero.

My latest plan, 'Operation Highwayman', was for a series of superhero road protests across London and Bristol. I had calculated a way of severing the main road and rail links into the capital by using activists at key stations and gantries over arterial roads including the M4, A40, M1, A13, Blackwall Tunnel, A23 and M3. The plan was astonishingly simple, but in the end it got filed in the 'Plan Zero' folder for ideas that were only to be used in the worst-case scenario, i.e. if activists started being sent to prison. In the meantime we decided to embark on a dry-run, testing response times of the authorities and gauging their reactions. Unsurprisingly, they weren't amused.

I ran the operation from my Mini alongside Michael Cox, who was busily multi-tasking, giving interviews and navigating as we hurtled from site to site like a ricocheting pinball. Plucky new boy Jason Hatch led the charge, shutting down the Clifton Suspension Bridge with a posse of superheroes giving it the full Vaudeville theatrics. Another team simultaneously shut down four main arterial roads coming into London during the rush hour, causing traffic chaos. The strategy for the day: Stay up and play up.

The Met responded by sending out a snatch squad that looked as if they'd stepped straight out of central casting for *The Bill*. They discovered Jolly delivering a vintage performance from a gantry over the Blackwall Tunnel, despite a broken rib from his Tamar Bridge escapade the previous Friday. In painful scenes caught by an ITV camera crew, the police wrestled him down. God knows what the man's made of; he brings new meaning to the old cliché 'you can't keep a good man down.'

Our resident thespian and plucky plank of a drama student, Darryl Westell, hanging on for dear life from a gantry on the A40 opposite the BBC's main studios in White City, was on the verge of tears when he called me.

'Matt, Matt, there are a load of 'em here, about twenty vehicles including an ambulance. They've shut down the A40 and they don't seem to want to negotiate, I'm just hanging here like an oversize gibbon with one hand on the gantry and the other holding the mobile.'

'Who is the negotiator, Darryl? This team have been trying to get people down and, apart from the Blackwall Tunnel, they haven't been too successful. Put me on the phone to the negotiator and I'll get them to back off.' Darryl slid the phone across to the copper 20 feet away from him.

'Back off, please,' I pleaded. 'We don't want anything happening, but you are forcing Darryl into a corner and an accident could happen. He could be killed. Please, just back off . . .'

'My instructions are to remove him by force.'

'I'm asking you, please back off. He'll come down under his own steam.'

'Those aren't my instructions.'

As he gruffly repeated the words, I lost it.

'Listen, you cunt, here's my negotiating position: if anything happens to Darryl, I swear to God I won't be responsible for what happens next. Do you want me to shut this fucking city down? Back off, now!'

The phone was passed back to Darryl.

'I'm afraid the negotiations broke down, mate. I lost it. I'm really sorry. Listen, we'll get there as quick as we can.'

'But, Matt, they're leaving. They're climbing down. I don't know what you said, but it worked.'

Half an hour later we made it to the A40, checked he was OK, then shot off to the A13 where new recruit Graham Manson was holed up in a gantry dressed as Batman.

Canning Town was in darkness by the time we arrived and the pavement adjacent to the A13 was lined with gangs of feral youths, some of whom couldn't have been much older than four. We ran an unedifying gauntlet of eggs, cigarette butts, spit and abuse as we walked up to the gantry to check that Graham was all right. I tried to befriend one hoody-clad lad who looked as if he'd been studying hard for an ASBO. Never have so few words spoken so much.

'How old are you, mate?'

'Seven.'

'Shouldn't you be at home? It's gone nine.'

'Shouldn't you just fuck off?' he spat.

'I don't think so. I'm with Batman.'

'What's he doing up there?'

'Campaigning to give kids like you a right to see their dads.'

'Don't know my dad. He left my mum.'

'Your mum and dad, they fuck you up, don't they? What do you think he'd do if he knew you were here?'

'He'd fucking kill me.'

'You know what, mate? Families like yours don't need parenting classes; what you need are some bloody fathers.'

I looked him hard in the eyes, digesting this wasted youth, who seemed to have been casually abandoned by his parents on the streets of East London. What these boys needed wasn't some troubleshooting supernanny imposed by the state, but the love and care of their fathers. Ironically, the very kids we wanted to save were heaping abuse on us, trapped in a vicious social cycle of fatherlessness. In my eyes these lost children were the guinea pigs in a fucked-up social experiment that was now reaping a bitter harvest.

Later I would undertake an investigation into young offenders that would bear out the notion that most came from fatherless families. For many of these kids, losing one parent was an emotional amputation no less catastrophic than losing a leg. Without both parents to hold on to, they're in danger of falling, especially boys.

It's acknowledged by children's charities like Chance UK that many boys have their self-esteem knocked out of them by their mothers when the father is absent. Some are told repeatedly throughout their childhoods that they are 'a bit of a bastard' and no good, simply because they remind Mum of her ex-partner. They are brought up by women, taught by women, with the result that, in the absence of any male role model, they have no idea how to be a father and no aspirations beyond becoming a gangsta rapper, footballer, or Big Brother contestant. Worse still, many cling to the male-dominated gang culture in this female-dominated environment. For their part, girls grow up not expecting men to stick around, and their first contact with a man is a sexual one.

No wonder we live in such a dysfunctional society. And here it was, staring me bleakly in the face. The cold, hard reality of breakdown Britain: children who were impoverished in every sense, disintegrating and fragmenting before my eyes, right beneath one of our protests. And yet, according to research carried out in the state of Michigan, every dollar spent helping young children by means of early interventions saved the state nineteen dollars in dealing with the consequences of fatherlessness at a later date. No welfare scheme could fight poverty better than a two-parent family.

'THE F FACTOR'

The nature of the relationship between a father and his child is a special one for which there is no substitute. Their role is absolutely critical to the welfare of children. The love of a father for his children might be different to that of their mother, but is the absolute equal.

Dads give their kids tenderness. They give them another viewpoint; let them see that strength and gentleness can go hand in hand; instil social and moral values that help children develop their own codes. They help kids test their strength and boundaries, and, through games and rough and tumble, enable them to develop both confidence and self-esteem – kids can have fun with their dads. Accepted social norms with regard to fatherhood are rapidly changing: according to the Equal Opportunities Commission, a third of all childcare is now provided by fathers. So much for the deadbeat dad stereotype.

But increasing numbers of children are now growing up without a father: 1 in 4 kids is now raised without a dad in the UK. When it comes to black children, that figure is a staggering 1 in 2 children. There is, whichever way you carve up the figures, a depressing statistical association between fatherless, criminality and other social ills. Children who live apart from their biological fathers are, on average, at least two to three times more likely to be poor, to use drugs, to experience educational, health, emotional and behavioral problems, to be victims of child abuse, and to engage in criminal behavior than those who live with their married, biological (or adoptive) parents.

Where forty years ago fathers were held up as respected pillars of the community, today politicians, social commentators and the media in general persist in raining a hail of abuse down on fatherhood. These terms of abuse include the phrases 'deadbeat', 'dodgy', 'runaway', 'failed' and 'feckless' – according to our politicians we are now a nation of *junk males*'. Though such men exist, the issue has been grossly distorted and exaggerated in order to justify the greatest denial of basic civil rights since apartheid: the capricious and unwarranted wholesale severance of fathers from their children. So entrenched has the stereotype of the 'deadbeat' dad become that it is used in effect as a synonym for 'divorced father'.

But some women's groups go even further. They talk about 'dangerous dads', in the way you would talk about 'dangerous dogs'. True, there are heart-rending examples of dads *and* mums taking the lives of their own children, but according to the Home Office, these figures are roughly equal. This isn't enough for the myth merchants, the fanatical feminists who campaign for the elimination of all patriarchy and eradication of 'fatherhood'. Any opportunity to inject another dose of 'father fear' into the body politic is exploited and then sold through the various charities and groups – that are funded by government – to lobby government.

This fanaticism is a key driver in the breakdown of society. By denigrating and then removing the father, the state creates an endless succession of problems: a carousel of transient stepfathers, child poverty, child abuse, increased crime, and thus secures a continuing role for itself whilst at the same time generating a massive and uninhibited expansion of power: a monstrous Supernanny state no less.

And beneath this stigmatisation festers the consequences of this gender apartheid. Increasing knife crime, gun crime, gang culture, drugs, alcohol abuse, gambling, pornography and the distasteful and troubling commercialisation of childhood.

In May 2006, Tony Thomas, the father of Adrian Thomas, the ringleader of the gang sentenced to twenty-five years for raping and murdering Mary-Ann Leneghan, said he wanted to set up a black fathers' group. He said that Adrian's mother had been determined to obstruct him from having any involvement with his son and that, had he been allowed to be a father to his son, there is no way he would have let him get involved in Class A drugs and the gang scene. He said:

We're losing our kids at a rate of knots and they're ending up in crime: then everyone's blaming us and saying we weren't there when we were there all the time. Black dads are the most alienated from their children. The legal system is not on any dad's side, but for us black guys our women are against us too. Half these young boys haven't got a clue what being a man is. Their idea is to get a knife or a gun or a baseball bat and thrash it out over stupidity. I'm really passionate about black British kids. My advice is don't give up on your children. It's an emotional rollercoaster, but keep going.

The following morning after the protests I felt drained but elated: Fathers 4 Justice had been dubbed the hair-raising high-wire act of protest groups in the media. *The Times* went as far as to describe us as 'the fastest growing pressure group in the country, if not the world'. John Walsh at the *Independent* wrote a piece called 'Revenge of the Angry Fathers', in which he asked 'Who are these guys? What does it all mean – the Marvel Comics costumes, the orchestrated gantry stunts, the banners, the Santa outfits, the desperate measures?' But we were to discover that operating without a safety net had its price.

In an interview filmed on a windswept Clifton Suspension Bridge, I was asked by GMTV's Fiona Phillips how I could defend the protests. They ran an amusing Mission Impossible cartoon intro with a montage of the F4J protests to date, though we came out looking more like extras from Dr Teeth's Electric Mayhem Band on the Muppet Show than serious superheroes.

I couldn't help but revel in the absurdity of what we were doing. The entire enterprise was like riding a tornado. Jim Parton at Families Need Fathers seemed thrilled at the coverage, likening F4J to the country's first ever white-knuckle rock n' roll protest group. I could only hope that the public would pick up on the humour and irony. My namesake, John O'Connor, former head of the Flying Squad, was also interviewed. Nice chap, but he took the view that I was bringing the family name into disrepute.

Alongside moments of euphoria there was a downside to my role with F4J. Within a month of 'Operation Highwayman' I had to eject one coordinator from our coordinators conference for repeatedly breaking his coordinators' agreement – a document all coordinators had to sign. The trouble with F4J members, as opposed to those in other campaign groups, was that they were directly affected on a daily basis by whatever was happening in their case. Instead of hitting out at our collective enemy, the result was that they inevitably started hitting the people standing beside them in F4J. We were working with damaged goods, people who were suffering a living bereavement; a perpetual sense of personal pain, loss, anger and betrayal. The white middle-class male was being dispossessed of his family in a way that would have been unthinkable thirty years ago and he was floundering like a drowning man in quicksand.

In all honesty though, if I had still been going through the trauma of court hearings, it was unlikely I would have had the cool rationale to run an effective campaign. Somehow we had to harness that negative energy and channel it into a positive force for change.

SUPERVILLAINS VS SUPERHEROES

SUPERVILLAINS

Common sense has no place in these courts where experts' opinions – based largely on fashionable theories by academics (whose own child-rearing often doesn't bear too much scrutiny) trying to make a career for themselves – tend to decide the case. For God's sake end the secrecy and let the world see how these dreadful people operate.

Philip Walling, barrister

These are my arch nemeses, the family law 'flat-earthers', fiercely resistant to change and the reforms Fathers 4 Justice have advocated in our 'Blueprint for Family Law in the 21st Century'.

The Judiciary
How many judges does it take to change a light bulb?
None. They all want to stay in the dark.

Dressed like the victims of a head-on collision with the wardrobe department of a BBC costume drama, Family Division judges have developed what Martin Mears, former president of the Law Society, has called a 'virtual new legislation'. They act without reference to Parliament, without reference to legislation and apparently without reference to the rule of law.

The judgments they make are often made based on points of law, rather than any desire to quickly resolve protracted family conflicts which are profoundly damaging to children.

In fact this unelected and unregulated judiciary, work family law in such a way that they actively, deliberately and systematically promote litigation, rather than settlement. In doing so they have created a harrowing legal black hole that is like entering a First World War battlefield, complete with trench warfare.

To many, they are the true villains of the piece. Britain's judiciary have engaged in a 'conspiracy of silence', shamelessly using the discredited 'child's best interests' principle to excuse a multitude of inexcusable judgments and to keep the doors on the family courts shut from public scrutiny. With no independent audit of their work, no assessment of the judgments made, no records kept on the outcomes for children and no evaluation of the system, the unaccountable emperors of the gladiatorial bear-pit that is family law are simply not fit for purpose.

Many fathers joke that their contact orders are often filed in the bin marked 'hazardous waste' such was the toxicity of their content. One father famously wrote to a judge about one of his orders with the words, 'I am in the smallest room in the house. I have read what is before me and I have now put it behind me.' Another father emailed us to say, 'These judges could seriously damage the welfare of your family – avoid like Polonium 210.'

Britain's Judiciary: In their own words.
Just a handful of judgments have been made public since 2000. These include the following:

> *Mr Justice Munby sentenced Mark Harris to four months in prison for giving his children Christmas presents (a bike, a camera and a Walkman) during a scheduled contact meeting. Upheld on appeal by Thorpe LJ and Butler-Sloss LJ.*

> *District Judge Kenworthy-Browne said in a judgment that a boy of three will have developed no Christmas associations with his father, and even if he has spent Christmases at the father's home, he will not remember them. As such, he will not expect increased contact with his father over the holidays.*

> *In the case of G (A Child) [2003] EWCA Civ 489 in Northampton County Court. HHJ Mitchell recognised that prior to any contact mother 'went to pieces,' and so ordered a five-year bar on further contact proceedings concerning a 2-year-old child on the basis that 'everyone needed some peace and a breathing space'.*

> *Judge Milligan to a parent who had been unsuccessfully trying to see his child for two years: 'This is a father who needs, in my judgement, to think long and hard about his whole approach to this question of contact and to ask himself sincerely whether in fact he seeks to promote it for his own interests dressed up as the child's interests.'*

> *Judge Goldstein ordered that all contact between a father and his children be stopped for three years after the father filed a complaint against the judge.*

The NSPCC
The sacred cow of charity groups has in fact consistently worked against a presumption of contact, equality and shared parenting, not least by putting pressure on Lib Dem peers in the House of Lords when the Child Contact

Bill was being read in the chamber in November 2005, thereby scuppering an effort on the part of the Conservatives to include a 'presumption to contact' as part of the Bill. The NSPCC argued that such a presumption would put children at risk – an argument that contradicted all its own research. (See appendices for further information.)

Conservative MP Tim Loughton who, though no fan of Fathers 4 Justice, condemned the 'disgraceful remarks' made by the NSPCC in their briefing paper. He said, 'Their briefing is alarmist, sensationalist, misleading, empirically flawed, completely irresponsible and highly reprehensible ... it is not worthy of an organisation such as the NSPCC which claims to stand up for our children'.

Blair and Co.

Family Butchers and masterminds of the 'McDad' generation. As mentioned above, we calculate that a minimum of half a million children have lost contact with their fathers between 1997 and 2007. The real figure may be much, much higher but, of course, in the absence of any official records it's impossible to know. Tony Blair rode into town on the back of his soundbite 'tough on crime, tough on the causes of crime'. What a delicious irony, then, if an indictment of New Labour's tenure proved to be the Crime Minister's role as a catalyst in the explosion in young offending. Tony liked to talk about 'respect' and 'joined up government' when discussing these social issues. In reality they couldn't join the dots in my 1-year-old's CBeebies annual. Thankfully Fathers 4 Justice will still be here, even when he is long gone.

Harriet Harman

A leading instigator in New Labour's failed Frankensteinesque social engineering experiment, which has seen an unprecedented explosion in family breakdown and fatherlessness. She later refused, point blank, an offer of talks suggested by Fathers 4 Justice in 2006 in an effort to break the impasse.

Margaret Hodge

Has a personal history of failing children when, as leader of Islington Council, she was engulfed in a child abuse scandal. So what did Tony Blair then make her? You guessed it: Minister of Children. Hodge was subsequently handcuffed by Fathers 4 Justice activist Jolly Stanesby who got up close and personal with her when he performed a Citizen's Arrest in a case of 'cuff justice'. He is still recovering from his ordeal.

Bruce Clark

About as popular as a divorce lawyer at a wedding, civil servant Bruce Clark works for the Department for Education and Skills. Clark effectively scuppered the only credible 'Early Interventions' (EI) scheme designed by campaigner Oliver Cyriax to funnel warring parents away from the family courts. The two core elements were to encourage written Parenting Plans and mandatory mediation. However Clark rejected the proposals without discussion and introduced his own scheme 'Family Resolutions' where the priority was not continuing contact, but protection from harm. Any application for contact under his scheme would trigger an automatic risk assessment. Where the quality of contact was deemed to be satisfactory there would be no need to increase it; where the quality of contact was indeterminate there would be a cessation of contact while the case was deferred, and where it was considered bad, contact would be terminated.

The final Family Resolution Pilot Project which encouraged 'optional' mediation cost over £1 million. Sixty-two couples were referred to the scheme and fifteen agreements were reached, at a cost to the taxpayer of over £66,000 per couple.

Whether those agreements are still in place is open to speculation as (you probably guessed by now) nobody has kept any records on the outcomes for those families and their children. Cynics argue that the entire enterprise, which was roundly condemned as an 'unmitigated disaster', was deliberately engineered in an attempt to discredit any form of mandatory mediation, especially that proposed in the eminently sensible Early Interventions scheme which it had replaced.

The Archbishop of York

We are still waiting for the Archbishop (and the Church of England) to make a statement with regard to fatherlessness and family breakdown some three years after our first protest at York Minster, despite his being very outspoken on issues as diverse as the Israel/Lebanon conflict and Guantanamo Bay. He slammed Fathers 4 Justice for their 'pranks, theatricality and dressing up', which seemed odd, coming as it did from a man with a penchant for theatricality and dressing up, be it wearing the most colourful threads in Christendom, camping out in York Minster or having African drummers and dancers at his inauguration. Bizarrely, he likened me to the late African despot Idi Amin after a protest at York Minster when I was dressed as a priest.

Fathers Direct

Otherwise known as 'Uncle Tom Direct', Fathers Direct is sponsored by the government to the tune of half a million pounds a year, a substantial part of which is to counter the impact of the Fathers 4 Justice campaign. Fathers Direct blithely tows the government line that there is no problem with family law, whilst demonstrating a breathtaking disregard for the welfare of its own clientele: fathers and their children caught in the family justice system.

In 2006 they were lambasted in the national press for producing a cartoon-laden information pack for fathers-to-be which included advice on cleaning, washing up, taking children to the playground and how to cope with the lack of sex after their baby's birth. The pack contained rip-roaring chestnuts such as 'Bite your lip, not your partner, when she is ratty', and 'Don't have an affair'.

Norman Wells, director of the Family Education Trust attacked the packs as 'patronising'. He said 'The Government is throwing money at a problem its own policies have helped to create. In previous generations, fathers were well able to fulfil their responsibilities without state-funded advice.' He added: 'The advice against fathers engaging in an affair during the pregnancy of their wife or partner – as if it might be acceptable at any other time – is quite extraordinary.' Fathers Direct produced a staggering 10,000 copies of *The Dad Pack*, which cost £50,000 of taxpayers' money, half of which was paid for by the Department for Education and Skills. Bonkers.

SUPERHEROES
The brevity of the list of candidates qualifying for this distinction gives an indication of the insurmountable odds we faced. However the following deserve our utmost respect for their efforts in challenging both the government and the courts.

Sir Bob Geldof
Sir Bob is the foul-mouthed foe of the supervillains. Passionate, articulate and ferociously critical of the family courts, Bob has threatened to spontaneously combust on several occasions when discussing 'contact' between fathers and their children. Famously summed up the experience of 'contact' as a 'holocaust of the heart.' Rock on Bob! Make family courts history.

Ann Widdecombe
The unlikely darling of the equal-parenting movement who once said that Fathers 4 Justice had done more for equal parenting in three years than the Tory party had in thirty. Warm and cuddly with bags of vision, Widdecombe cuts the mustard as a formidable woman of substance in the quest for equality.

She has also written a book on the subject called *Father Figure* which I will plug by suggesting you purchase at least one copy for every member of your family.

Glenn Sacks

Good morning injustice! Glenn Sacks is a US columnist, commentator and talk-radio host who has consistently supported Fathers 4 Justice. Ever the voice of reason, he articulates the argument for equality eloquently and with bags of common sense in the face of often withering criticism from both sides of the divide.

N.B. Over the last five years, I can count the number of decent and compassionate family law professionals on one hand, though they deserve recognition. These include Celia Conrad, a few solicitors and barristers who are named further on in the book and some decent, well-intentioned people at CAFCASS such as Alan Critchley and Anthony Douglas. We don't always see eye to eye, but we are at least able to find a way forward and for that, I am very grateful.

THE FUNPOWDER PLOT

God I knew this day was coming but nothing, but nothing can prepare you for the prospect of a national newspaper preparing to smear your reputation with the effluent of your life.

When I took the call from Sam Coates, a *Times* journalist who had been rummaging through my dirty laundry for a while, I sensed that it wasn't a nice touchy-feely interview he had in mind. Until then, the media backlash had mostly been confined to the pathologically hostile *Observer/Guardian* camp (which seemed ironic, given that we were a bunch of lefties for the most part), but it was inevitable that it would spread.

Coates' call came on the day we had been invited to attend Channel 4's Political Awards – amazingly, Chicky was among the nominees, thanks to our stage-managed Spiderman protest – so I suggested a pub opposite the Channel 4 studios as a venue. I took our PR man, Glen, along. Would it be OK if he sat in on the inquisition? I asked.

'You might not want that. The nature of the allegations are ... well, er ... very personal.' A half smile crept across Coates' flabby chops.

'I'll live with it. Shoot.'

The hack had been door-stepping people from my past. What he had to show for it seemed fairly petty: apparently I'd once brought the kids back half an hour late causing Sophie to think I'd kidnapped them. I'd also had an affair. Coates produced an article in the London *Evening Standard* where I claimed I'd come home and bathed the boys every night; apparently rumour had it that I was often to be found elsewhere, in a bath of champagne with another woman.

'His wife says the *Standard* article isn't true,' Coates crowed triumphantly to Glen.

'Then get on the phone to your editor and hold the front page,' said Glen. 'Fathers 4 Justice founder didn't bathe kids every night shocker!'

'So,' Coates prodded, 'what do you have to say to these allegations?'

'Is that it?' I said. 'After two weeks exhuming the grave of a dead relationship at the whim of your editor, that's the best you can come up with?'

'Why, is there more?' he asked, sitting forward, fidgeting excitedly with his pen.

'Yeah, there is, actually. Haven't you got a proper job to go back to, you shitbag?'

We might have won the first round, but I knew it would be only a matter of time before *The Times* launched their assault. Glen remained characteristically untroubled. He had a plan to get me out of the news and into the fluffy features pages. One of his freelance press contacts, a guy called Steve Boggan, would do an interview with me and Sophie involving open-heart surgery on yours truly with lashings of humble pie. By offering this exclusive 'warts-and-all' piece to *The Times* feature editor, Glen reckoned we could outmanoeuvre Coates and his boss, the home editor.

That night at the political awards, while Burchy worked the room, warning *Private Eye* editor Ian Hislop that he'd be sitting beside 'Spiderman' ('What's he going to do?' asked Hislop. 'Scale me?'), I proceeded to get very drunk, melancholic, maudlin and morose. When Glen caught up with me later and asked what my strategy for F4J was, I had the sense that, fifteen months in, he was losing faith. It wasn't clear to him how we were going to change the law with my twin-track strategy of headlines and hangovers. Fishing a pen from my jacket pocket, I drew a parabolic curve on a napkin.

'Ahhh,' said Glen, nodding sagely. 'The parabolic curve. Now I understand.'

And rather incredibly, it looked as if he did.

'I like it,' said I. 'Simple. Easy to understand.'

But in all honesty I was making half of it up as I went along, looking to others as much as myself to generate new ideas and develop strategy.

Sadly no new ideas were forthcoming. Most people like Glen – who was one of the few dads in F4J who had a shared residency arrangement for his daughter Josie – were beginning to lose faith, whether in F4J or me. Some were simply burnt out and had lost the stomach for the fight. By early 2004, deep down I knew that the three-year plan was doomed to failure. We simply didn't have the money or the talent to make the plan a reality. Instead of the sprint to victory I had envisaged, this was going to be a bloody, laborious, long-distance slog. A test of emotional and physical endurance.

Underscoring this was the fact that the defensive walls of the establishment appeared impenetrable. No matter how much I scanned and probed the system for weaknesses, none were visible. All we could do was aim high with big noisy statements, hoping that the public would grasp the seriousness of the problem and the risk it posed to their own families' welfare.

That week the smear story was halted, much to the chagrin of *The Times* home editor. We got a positive double-page spread and the front cover of *The Times'* T2 section. Glen got an enormous kick out of that victory, knowing that one journalist had had his nasty story spiked. But it was to be a pyrrhic victory.

Within weeks it became clear that, while I was planning on ways of moving us up the political agenda, Glen had decided to move on. An immensely talented and charismatic PR man, I felt that his talents were being squandered. He had the ability to take F4J so much further, but perhaps in the end it was my chaotic style of leadership that dissuaded him.

'The blind drunk leading the blindingly optimistic,' he once remarked after an F4J meeting. 'You've led us to the door of the establishment, Matt, opened it for us . . . and then shat on the carpet and run away.'

But I wasn't interested in playing the political game. I wasn't interested in persuading the establishment to reform the law. I wanted to beat the fuckers into submission. I wanted every family law professional strung up by their bollocks and hung from a lamppost until they apologised or rotted.

I'd paid for my mistakes. Now it was somebody else's turn.

THE FUNPOWDER PLOT

Remember, remember, the fifth of November,
Gunpowder treason and plot.
I know of no reason
Why the gunpowder treason
Should ever be forgot.

Anon

In March 2004, Big Ron Davis was given the opportunity to speak to Tony Blair in a phone-in on LBC Radio. Blair promised action in Ron's case, but nothing came of the promise. Ron decided that, should the opportunity arise, he would get involved in direct action.

As a result of his divorce, Big Ron had been reduced to living in a place that looked as if it had been designed using nanotechnology. Sure, his bungalow in Shoreham appeared nice from the outside, but it turned out to be a bedsit of model village proportions. Ron occupied two microscopic rooms. One was a rabbit hutch, the other a shoe-box. You couldn't swing a hamster in either of them for the flotsam of divorce that occupied nearly every available space. Worse still, Ron was embroiled in a Herculean struggle to see his two children, their mother having denied all access. This conspiracy of events was crippling him, but Big Ron wasn't short-changed when it came to optimism. Against my advice, he kept chugging away at the court system, hearing after hearing, order after order. But it was a farce.

I attended one hearing with Ron as his 'McKenzie Friend' – a lay person who is allowed to assist somebody who isn't legally represented. As evidenced by his accommodation, Ron was exhausted economically and needed all the help he could get, but the hearing was a sham. He had been granted a series of orders to see his children, but their mother had refused to comply. This time around the judge gently berated her legal team.

'You must respect the order of the court. If you do not respect the order of the court then what respect will anyone have for the rule of law? Children need to retain the love and care of both their parents.' It sounded like something I might have written, but then, unbelievably, he proceeded to discharge that order and replace it with another order for a further hearing. So much for upholding the rule of law.

Outside court, Ron struggled to remain upbeat, but I was spitting feathers.

'Ron, you must get involved in some direct action. These hearings are a waste of fucking time. It's bankrupted you financially and now it's going to bankrupt you emotionally. At least if you do something you'll get some dignity back.'

On 2 May Ron called to let me know that a friend of his, millionaire businessman Guy Harrison, had placed an auction bid for lunch with Baroness Goulding, a Labour peer. The winner would be given a tour of both the Commons and the Lords, a chance to watch the PM's question time, followed by lunch in the Pugin Tea Room.

Guy was a charming, wealthy, daredevil dad based in West Sussex. Separated and now divorced from his wife, he had found love with his partner Emily, sister of the pop star James Blunt. But in the five years since his marriage had ended he had not seen his daughter Issy once. Not even the big bucks of a millionaire could fix this tragic situation.

It just went to show that family law did not discriminate. Rich or poor, barrister or bouncer, sane or insane, celebrity or nonentity – they didn't give a shit. If you were a father, you were disposable.

The bones of the Funpowder Plot were assembled in time-honoured tradition by a small ensemble of key players. The major player was Gary Burch, who normally didn't dirty his hands with this sort of thing, being a diplomatic emissary. But the chance to cause uproar in the House of Commons proved irresistible.

We'd both previously been to Prime Minister's Questions as guests of Eleanor Laing MP, so we knew the landscape. And while I'd heard on Radio 4 that the glass panelling which had been erected in front of the public gallery since my visit did not extend to the VIP area, it was still a bloody long way from the gallery to Tony Blair. The only obvious way to create a stunt would be to lob something – a crass method of protest that would lack the charm and humour that had become the trademark of F4J.

Despite obvious obstacles, the stunt became like a cream cake sitting on a plate right beside you. You knew it was bad for you, but you wanted it all the more for it.

I mentioned it to my brother David, who suggests injecting eggs with purple dye and then smuggling them in. A momentary lapse of reason had me contemplating smuggling in bantam hens – a thought I blamed on the egg idea. Christ knows. One afternoon, as I was fishing with my boys, Ron called in a flap, wanting to know what sort of protest it would be.

'I don't bloody know. Could you jump on the Prime Minister?'

'No, Matt, I'd wipe out the Cabinet. Besides this is your department. We need your creative talents to dream up an idea.'

'Knowing your luck, Ron,' I laughed, 'you'd land on Prescott and you'd both be paralysed.'

The Funpowder Plot very nearly came off the rails courtesy of the VAT man. Ron was the key to the stunt; getting him to put himself in the line of fire was crucial. But having agreed to do it, Ron suddenly pulled out on the grounds that he was behind with his VAT.

Communication in the run-up to the stunt was tricky at the best of times, but now Burchy was in charge of coordinating a major political outcry using two fathers with no experience of this sort of thing. We couldn't use landlines or mobiles, so public phone boxes or face-to-face meetings were our only real options. This involved placing one call to a known line, followed by a call back from a 'safe' line. Having negotiated this protocol, call waiting kicked in. When Ron pulled out it resulted in a series of calls that put communication at a maximum, rather than a minimum. So much for our slick Mission Impossible enterprise. I promptly went ballistic.

'Fuck sake, what is this? Do I have to call in the Women's Institute to help sort this shit out? Will everybody just stop calling each other?'

Having decided to follow through on the stunt, the next question was: And what do we want to throw? Somewhere in my subconscious the memory endured of the late American comedian Bob Hope being flour-bombed by feminists at a Miss World contest at the Royal Albert Hall in 1970. Throwing stuff at politicians used to be a national pastime, but post 9/11 it presented a real challenge. The missile had to be compact, soft and benign. Mates condoms seemed to offer a perfect solution.

The other problem nagging at me the whole time was what would happen if it was thrown wrong and instead of hitting its intended target, struck somebody else, a woman MP, for example. Or if it hit Blair on the side of his mush. We could end up looking very bad indeed.

As ingredients went, flour seemed the obvious candidate. But even this posed a problem. In the Commons, white powder was unlikely to be assumed to be flour. Let's be honest, they'd run from it or try and snort it before they'd think of baking with it. In the end, I think it was one of girls in the office who came up with the genius solution of dyeing the flour purple, et voilà, our recipe was complete.

CONDOM BOMB À LA TONY BLAIR

400g self-raising flour (any brand will do)
100g purple icing colourant (available from all good food stores)
100g purple glitter (available from Clinton Cards and all good party shops)
1 packet of unlubricated Mates condoms (available from Boots chemists)

Sift the flour to remove any lumps. Crumble the icing colourant into a fine powder then, using a whisk or wooden spoon, gently beat the flour, icing colourant and purple glitter for around half a minute. Pour mix into an unlubricated condom (don't use lubricated otherwise it will become a sticky, nasty mess). Tie knot in the end and attach to inside of trousers using your belt buckle so that the condom hangs neatly alongside your wedding tackle.

When ready to launch, pull from trousers and gently score the rubber by pressing your finger nail down the sides of the condom to ensure correct impact delivery. Please note: You will look like you have cojones the size of a Spanish Bull who hasn't got his rocks off since the last Fiesta, but nobody in national security is ever going to squeeze your balls to check.

The colour purple, international symbol of equality, had become synonymous with our campaign. Glitter would add a dash of theatricality to the whole protest, and self-raising flour would hopefully get our elected representatives off their arses quicker than you could shout 'breach of security'.

The next day's testing started badly. The condoms wouldn't split on impact. We tried Boots' own brand, Durex, Trojan, an entire arsenal of contraceptive rubber, but none would split. Then we tried cutting further into the sides of the condoms using our fingernails. The results were impressive: on impact, the condom disappeared in a powder puff of purple haze. Hendrix would have been proud.

It was time to call the team. Rather than use my phone, which was probably being monitored by the police, I nipped next door to my unsuspecting landlord's house and asked to use his. After much persuasion, Ron succumbed to the allure of self-raising flour. My three co-conspirators and I agreed the final plan. The countdown was on.

Ask anyone who ever tried to organise anything in F4J what the biggest challenge was and the answer will come back: getting people to do as they were told. It was the same with Ron and Guy. Tell them not to use telephone landlines because they might be tapped and you get Ron ringing you at home. Tell 'em to stick to a simple line of communication – Gary to Ron, Ron to Guy – you get Guy ringing up to check that what Ron had told him was correct. Stand in a public telephone box waiting for a call, your mobile goes off. It was the same on the day of the stunt.

It was essential to the plan that the condoms must be concealed in Ron and Guy's underwear. In my many visits to the Houses of Parliament, security had always been very thorough. The only place where the condoms could be concealed to avoid detection was close to their nether regions. Naturally, it was important that they wear knickers with elasticated legs.

So Guy turned up sporting a fine pair of Gap boxer shorts.

Another F4J masterstroke!

That morning I was a nervous bundle of anticipation and dread. No news filtered back to Suffolk, and such was my scepticism that I had pretty much written the whole thing off, giving it a 5 per cent chance of success. As my silver Mini sped through the narrow back lanes heading homeward from Ipswich, Prime Minister's Questions were being broadcast on Radio 5 Live. I told the unsuspecting colleague sitting beside me that two Fathers 4 Justice activists were about to attempt one of the most audacious stunts ever witnessed in the House of Commons.

As the Prime Minister fended off questions from the leader of the opposition, the seconds turned to minutes. Time was ebbing away: 12.15 p.m. came and went. Then, at 12.18 p.m., Simon Mayo's voice suddenly crackled excitedly down the airwaves.

'Something's been thrown! It looks like purple powder!' he yelled excitedly. 'The house has been suspended.'

Within seconds my mobile burst into life.

'Matt, Sky News here . . . Purple powder has been thrown at Tony Blair in the House of Commons. Is this a Fathers 4 Justice demo?'

Everything stood still, the countryside became a blurry haze, my foot stayed hard on the accelerator and the road began to arc to the right. The car kicked up a storm of gravel and dust as it banked up the side of a cornfield.

'Yes,' I said. 'It is, it fucking well is. And you can quote me on that.'

One condom filled with purple flour had hit the Prime Minister's jacket smack between the shoulder blades live on national television, changing the course of my life for ever. Ron had been supposed to be the one to do the throwing because of his link to Blair, but it turned out that he'd never learnt to throw, whereas public schoolboy Guy was a whizz at sports. So the boys swapped roles, a fact that could not be allowed to get in the way of a good story. While Guy used his skill to launch three condoms at the PM, Ron's job was to hold up a paper banner extolling the virtues of parental rights, a key element in ensuring the protest was not misinterpreted as something more sinister.

But Big Ron, bless him, managed a spectacular fuck-up by holding the 'Flour Power for Dads' sign upside down so no one could read it. His only task on the day and he got it wrong!

Back at base, nobody had cottoned on yet that something momentous had just happened. The first they knew of it was when my Mini came crashing towards the house on a handbrake turn, spraying gravel across the garden and I leapt out, yelling my head off.

'It's fucking showtime, everybody. Off the fucking phones,' I screamed as a volunteer chatted sympathetically to a caller. I switched on the box and, half watching it from behind the sofa in case it's a PR disaster, I couldn't believe that Guy had been so accurate with his throw.

'With an aim like that he should be in the England Cricket Team.'

Jenny came running in to see what the all commotion was about.

'Matt, what have you done now?' she asked, her voice weary with resignation.

'Look, look, it's a perfect strike, a perfect strike, right between the Prime Minister's shoulder blades!' For a few minutes I was like an agitated schoolboy, jigging up and down on the spot like I was queuing for the toilet.

'That self-raising flour worked a treat. I've never seen MPs get off their backsides so quickly!'

In fact, our parliamentary representatives had dropped a clanger. Commons' security etiquette dictated that in such an event they were to remain seated, not leg it out on to the streets and possibly infect the capital with some deadly chemical weapon such as Anthrax. Only the 'quiet man' of politics, Iain Duncan Smith, remained resolutely glued to the spot, cautioning the departing Conservative benches that they really should follow protocol and remain seated. Sadly it was apparent that the quiet man couldn't find his volume button even when admonishing his colleagues.

Within the hour, satellite trucks had parked up and begun feeding live broadcasts from Kimsings. The following day it was clear that the 'Funpowder Plot' had been our biggest demo yet. We hit every front page. A Downing Street press spokesman allegedly described F4J as 'the worst campaign group I have ever heard of'. But at least you've heard of us, I thought.

I had reassured Big Ron prior to the demo that he'd be out by teatime. Yesterday.

According to solicitors, at that time Guy and Ron were in Paddington Green maximum-security nick being stripped of their clothes.

Big Ron was subsequently tried for a Public Order offence. Baroness Goulding took to the witness stand and gave evidence that, in the Pugin Tea Rooms before the protest, Mr Davis had left the table to go to the toilet, followed five minutes later by Mr Harrison. Apparently, she became concerned that something was amiss when fifteen minutes later the men still hadn't returned. Just as the Baroness was about to go and fetch security, they reappeared. Mr Davis was sweating profusely, a fact that gave rise to concern that a homosexual act might have occurred in said toilets with Mr Davis doing the giving, and Mr Harrison the eager recipient of a Commons knee-trembler. Not an uncommon event in said establishment, one might imagine. Of course, we knew the truth. The boys had been adjusting their 'tackle'.

Ron hit the headlines of every national paper. Guy, who had bought the tickets and thrown the condoms, barely got a mention. Guy didn't have a personal link to Blair, but Ron did. His story made sense, it was human and it was saleable. The small puff of purple powder on Tony Blair's left shoulder led the *Daily Mail* to dub Ron: 'The man who could have killed Blair'. Some might say that missing such an opportunity was the worst cock-up of all.

Two days after their arrest the boys were released from Paddington Green nick. After a de-briefing they agreed to hold a press conference. Unable to secure a hotel room for the event, we plumped for the Papermill café bar instead. The place was rammed to the rafters with press and a bit of a mêlée ensued when a lawyer for Ron's ex tried to serve a gagging order preventing him from talking about his case. The bar was immediately invaded by vanloads of police who had moved in at the request of the manageress. Not unnaturally, she was concerned that things were getting out of hand.

The main protagonists all retired to the Great Eastern Hotel at Liverpool Street station to reflect on the events of the last few days. As ever, my brother David remained the most lucid among us.

'Matt, things have changed now, you're becoming a public figure. That means you've got to be whiter than white – no more sex, no more booze and no swearing,' he warned.

'Fuck me, I'll drink to that,' said I as the fatigue began to set in.

'We don't want you turning into the Boris Yeltsin of Bury St Edmunds,' said Dave, laughing.

'Fuck it, bro – they're all wankers anyway.'

'Who?'

'The bloody politicians, that's who. They've had it coming to them – a bloody powder bomb. We send all these fathers off to die as cannon fodder, fighting a phoney war in a foreign land on behalf of a country that doesn't even afford them the right to see their own children. How fucked up is that?'

David ordered himself another large Jack Daniels with a whisker of water. 'Fact is,' he said, 'politicians are scum, and solicitors and barristers are the fungus beneath the scum.'

With that, sensing that we were on the verge of an all-night rant against the forces of injustice, I climbed down off the bar stool, my head blitzed with booze and anger, and headed off to bed for a good night's kip.

The following day *Private Eye* produced a 'Flour Power' special for their cover but not everybody was so enthusiastic. There were pockets of extremely critical coverage. A radio interview with Henry Kelly turned into a bout of verbal fisticuffs:

'Why do you feel it's necessary to engage in such high-profile and provocative protests?'

'It's an antidote to thirty years of suffocating secrecy that's allowed the family justice system to fester and miscarriages of justice to go unreported.'

'Don't you think your stunt in Parliament will lose you support for your cause?' asked Kelly.

'I can't see how we can lose support for a cause that most people hadn't heard about until yesterday,' I responded.

'But you did break the law, didn't you? Do you feel comfortable breaking the law, Mr O'Connor?'

'I don't know if we did break any laws because nobody has been charged yet, but in answer to your question, "am I comfortable?" the answer is, extremely.'

'Isn't it irresponsible, what you are doing?'

'Irresponsible? As Churchill said, I'd rather be irresponsible and right, than be responsible and wrong. It's no different to what Peter Hain, Secretary of State for Northern Ireland and Wales, did when he poured oil on to the pitch at Lords back in his anti-apartheid days. By my reckoning, if it's good enough for a Government minister, it's good enough for me.'

But still Kelly kept harping on about law breaking as if civil disobedience was a hanging offence. 'But you are breaking the law.'

'I think we have established that. Are you being stupid, or am I? We are talking about parents who have court orders to see their kids and those orders are not enforced. If the law isn't upheld in one area, how can anyone have any respect for its authority in another?'

'So you think everybody should break the law then, if something doesn't go their way in court?'

'I don't think you're listening to what I'm saying. I've just said that most of these dads have legally-binding courts orders to see their children and they're not being enforced. Secondly, we also have a long and honourable tradition of law-breaking in this country. You seem to have forgotten that this government was forged in the very fires of civil disobedience you so disparage, and if it wasn't for fucking idiots like me who stood up to defend basic rights then women wouldn't have the vote and we'd still have slavery. You'd be happy then, wouldn't you? Just because one man-made law took a higher precedent over a moral code?'

By the end I realised the line was dead but I was still very much alive and spitting brickbats. I'd given over thirty interviews that day and Kelly's patronising tone had ignited my keg of unexploded munitions.

Some in the media thought they could ride roughshod over F4J. We had been in discussions with the BBC about a documentary for their *One Life* strand, but the whole thing ran aground because of the insensitivity of the production company, Films of Record. Without securing permission from us or the people they were going to film, they went steaming in and wrote to ex-partners involved in ongoing proceedings. When these letters were waved in front of some very unimpressed judges, the fathers concerned came off rather badly. When Films of Record's Roger Graef called to discuss the situation, our conversation ended with a 'go forth and multiply' response from F4J as a whole. A few months later I ran into him at an awards bash. He'd just won a BAFTA and I offered him a few suggestions as to where he could put it and get it chocolate-coated at the same time.

In mid June I travelled into London to film an interview with Geldof for a Channel 4 documentary he was making about the family courts. He ripped into me straight away.

'Fuck, Matt, what's happened to your hair?' he snarled, referring to my guano-tinged veranda. 'It looks like it's been used as a runway for fucking seagulls.'

'It's de rigueur in hairwear on the Côte D'Kent, Bob. At least I've seen a hairdresser in the last twenty years.'

We spent the next few hours sitting round a table being filmed navel-gazing with Jim Parton from Families Need Fathers and Tony Coe from EPC. I just wanted to get on and campaign. We all knew how bad things were, what we needed was a plan that would get us out of this mess.

THE DAY OF THE DAD

The Friday before Fathers' Day, BBC's *Newsnight* team showed up at the ranch to film a piece on us. I was up to my neck, trying to write, design and produce our 52-page manifesto, 'Blueprint for Family Law in the 21st Century'. The document was vital if we were to demonstrate that there was substance behind the style. It would set out our key proposals: mandatory mediation, a presumption of shared parenting, and open family courts.

A few days later we held our Day of the Dad demo, marching from Lincoln's Inn Fields to Parliament – protestors speaking from the heart, marching to the heart of government. Attended by several thousand people, all kitted out in purple, it was our biggest demo yet.

The evening of the demo, the boys called. Alexander confided that he was being bullied at school after helping a girl who was being picked on.

'One boy punched me, Dad.'

'Did you punch him back?' I asked. I had shown him how to handle himself, though his mother might not have been too pleased at my tactical advice.

'No . . . I thought . . . that, that might be the wrong thing to do?'

'Well what should you do in a fight then, Alex?'

'Join in?' he suggested hopefully.

'Jesus, Alexander! Defend yourself. Fight back!'

'But Mum says that's wrong.'

'Well, Mum is right and I'm right. If you're defending yourself, it's fine. Never let anyone push you around. If you don't defend yourself, he'll carry on because he thinks he can get away with it. See, in life, Alex, you get two types of person. Those that hold their ground and defend themselves and try and help other people when they are in trouble, and those that simply roll over. I rolled over for a long time when I was your age, until one day I decided it wasn't going to happen to me again.' As a teenager I'd been bullied at Grammar School until one day I decided to take my tormentor out. I was never bothered afterwards and I didn't want our children experiencing any problems.

Oddly the boys had overcome their initial 'Oh my God, Dad's on the telly again' quibbles and rather taken to the cachet my notoriety had brought them at school. Especially Alexander, who seemed even more of an exhibitionist than his old dad, God help him.

When Sophie and I went along to GMTV to do a joint interview, the boys had taken it in their stride, larking around with the soundmen offstage and tucking into free breakfast with other guests in the green room.

During another joint interview, for the *Daily Mail*, I was taken aback by Sophie's contrary comments, on the one hand demonising me, which was understandable, but on the other lavishing me with kind words. We were both sitting at the old family home in Downe when she came out with an unexpected outpouring of praise.

'Today, we have a great relationship – we get on well, and communicate frequently about the children's needs. He's a great father. I'm incredibly proud of Matt for setting up Fathers 4 Justice. I do feel for fathers who find themselves in a position where they're unable to see their children.'

'Blimey, Sophie, steady on, you'll have me choking on my HobNob,' I said, but she rambled on and for once I was happy to be sidelined.

'The ironic thing now is that, despite the worthwhile cause, the group has affected Matt's parenting time. It leaves him so exhausted that I often long for him to walk away from it. He is so busy shouldering other fathers' problems that sometimes I worry that, once again, his own children will be the ones who suffer.'

'That's a fair comment.'

'But how will you reconcile it, Matthew?' asked Sophie.

'How can you? I could walk away and nothing would change, and then one of our boys might end up going through what I went through . . . Imagine it, you'd be a grandmother with access problems. I have to balance that against sacrificing some time with them now. I guess, now I've started, I'll have to finish.'

Rummaging through the remnants of our marriage with a complete stranger felt weird, but afterwards I felt that I had a better insight into what went wrong and Sophie's thought processes.

Later, the interview done and dusted, the boys rolled up from school.

'Dad, we've been thinking,' said Alexander. 'What if you get arrested and put in jail?'

'Well, I'll admit it's probably a bit overdue, but I could do with the rest.

You know, free board and lodging, care of Her Majesty . . . I might even have time to write a book or something.'

'But isn't it dangerous?'

'It's called a calculated risk, boys. I could have stayed at home and done nothing, but you might not thank me for it when you are older. There are some things you can't learn at school, boys; this is an education learnt at the university of adversity.'

And with that Daniel launched himself at me, arms clamped round my neck.

'Bundle, let's bundle, Dad!'

God, I thought as I was floored by the dynamic duo, either I'm getting old or these guys are getting bigger.

The next day, 'Big' Paul Watson, our North Eastern coordinator, had fixed up a meeting with his local MP – Tony Blair. A passionate firebrand, the archetypal 'Braveheart' Scotsman who wears his heart on his sleeve and tartan jocks outside his trousers, Paul was on the phone to me the moment the meeting ended with a blow-by-blow account.

'What would you do in ma shoes?' Paul had asked Blair as he passed him a copy of F4J's 'Blueprint in Family Law for the 21st Century'. 'Would you give in? Imagine you thought your child was next door, in another house. Would you break the door down and risk getting arrested? Would you do that, as a decent dad? Of course you would.'

Apparently Blair nodded and Paul continued, probably because, knowing Paul, he was now in full flow.

'Because you would do anything for your kids, even if it meant you overstepping the mark, right?'

Blair replied, 'Yes, I would, Paul, I would.'

Paul paused for a second to collect his thoughts.

'Matt, I said to him, "Tony, it's like this, you are nay different to me and I'm nay different to you. We both would do anything for our kids."'

SEVEN WAYS TO SAVE YOUR FAMILY

If you can't save your relationship, at least save your children. Remember, maximum mediation = minimum conflict. But if you fight on to the bitter end, that's exactly how you and your family will turn out. Bitter and twisted.

Don't listen to your solicitor. Best rule of thumb is to do the opposite of what they advise. If you don't avail yourself of this advice, I can assure you that within twelve months your pockets will be several thousand pounds lighter. Your savings, the children's inheritance, pensions, the lot, will be spunked and the Legal Services Commission will slam a charge on the family home so that, whatever you've spent, you'll end up paying back when you next move house.

Don't go to court. Two parents fighting is a mug's game. Don't kid yourself there are any winners. My advice is to avoid all conflict and eat lots of humble pie. Remember, profound damage can be done to young children through parental conflict.

Go for shared parenting. Kids are not there to be carved up like material possessions – they are your flesh and blood and deserve the best of BOTH parents. Draw up a parenting plan and stick to it.

Don't leave the family home. Whatever anyone says and no matter how much you think you are doing this in the children's interests, leaving the family home is a big no-no. You'll find moving back in nigh on impossible. Set out demarcation lines with your partner and, whatever else you do, try, try, try to find a way of resolving your problems without using solicitors. If you think things are bad now, multiply that by a thousand, because that's how it will be once these vermin get their noses stuck in the family trough.

Do mediate. It's not big and it's not clever to think that mediation sucks. Unless you and your partner are hell-bent on inflicting a lifetime of conflict on your family, sooner or later you will have to sit down and talk. Try and deal with the difficult personal issues in your relationship first so that these can be set aside, allowing you to concentrate on making arrangements for the children. One day your children will thank you. They won't thank you if you fuck up their childhoods just because you can't learn the 'F' word: Forgiveness.

Do provide support for your kids. No matter how much you hate your ex, you should always provide both emotional and financial support for your children. However, if you are being denied access for no good reason and being fleeced for the privilege, I'd recommend paying this money into a savings account or trust fund for your children to draw on when they are older. But whatever you do, keep paying it!

Don't denigrate the other parent. Denigration can lead to the alienation of a child from the other parent. Remember half your child is your partner; hate them and you hate half your child.

Finally, NEVER hate your partner more than you love your kids.

BASH THE BISHOP

Now, as I understand it the word 'father' was introduced with the advent of Christianity so it's odd that an institution that ends prayers with 'In the name of the Father . . .' seems to be oblivious to the absence of Dad when it comes to christenings. Like, aren't we missing somebody here? Fathers going through a break-up get virtually no help from the Church of England. I know, I've been there. Tim Hatwell, the vicar who christened my two boys, offered plenty of tea, plenty of sympathy, but when it came to real help he was about as much good as a poke in the eye with a blunt crucifix. I turned to the church in the belief that it was the original social service for families, providing communities and families with moral and economic help and guidance. At the heart of its teachings was the value of fathers and fatherhood.

After the introduction of the welfare state, the church retreated towards focusing on offering services on Sunday mornings and at special events – be it weddings, christenings, funerals or at Easter and Christmas. But I had held out hopes that they be able to provide some sort of pastoral care for the family and help to navigate the uncharted moral geography of divorce. I was sadly mistaken. With this in mind, I was determined to bring F4J's own form of enlightenment to our Christian brothers, if only to confront them with the 'name of the Father' anomaly.

In mid July 2004 an old churchgoing girlfriend let slip that the Church of England's governing body, the General Synod, were meeting that weekend in York Minster. 'Operation Father Ted', an idea that had been on the back burner for the past year, suddenly sprang into action.

It was shamelessly based on a Peter Tatchell demo at Canterbury Cathedral a few years earlier – only with a dash of humour. I had discovered during the course of research that the Bill were forever citing the Ecclesiastical Courts Act of 1886, as if to demonstrate their unlimited knowledge of all aspects of the law. They were particularly fond of quoting some of the punishments, like the lopping off of one ear for the offence of disrupting a church service.

Never mind, I thought. Always got another one.

The Church was in dire need of a new prescription to deal with family breakdown, but they didn't seem at ease with dealing with the bread-and-butter issues that affect their flock. They had debated everything from gay and lesbian priests to the Middle East, but the breakdown of families, which was happening on a Biblical scale, hadn't been debated by the Church of England's ruling body, the General Synod, since as far back as 1992.

The day before the stunt, Jason Hatch and I picked up our theologically themed wardrobe from a fancy-dress shop and went to case the Minster. Inside, the ker-ching of the cash tills reverberated down the cloisters. We found our religious coordinator, the 'irreverent' Ray Barry, having a good gawp at an itinerary somebody had posted on a wall for tomorrow.

'Nice of them to put that up, isn't it, boys?' I said, brimming with confidence, thinking that a bit of bishop-bashing might just rattle more than their collection plates.

'Better still,' said Ray, 'the Archbishop of Canterbury will also be here.'

'Is that to pick up the takings?' asked Jason in his West country twang.

'Fuck me, look at this place,' I muttered. 'In the name of the Father, my arse. In the name of the checkout, more like it. It's a fucking theme park for counterfeit Christianity. They should stick a cashpoint in the pulpit and a bank sign above the main doors.'

'What about having parishioners swipe their bank cards on the way in and having their pin numbers ready for the collection?' said Jason.

'Yeah, they'll probably whack a 12$\frac{1}{2}$ per cent service charge on top for the privilege.'

'Matt, pipe down for Christ's sake,' hissed Ray, trying to reign me in from an on-the-spot soapbox sermon. To no avail. Faced with the sight of capitalist enterprises separating tourists from their wonga at every turn, I was off on one of my rants.

'Next thing they'll be on the telly advertising "I can't believe it's called Christianity" or "Our Father? Not any more he fucking isn't." Talk about the milk of human kindness – all they want to do here is milk you dry.'

That night we bedded down in a Travelodge just off the M1 between York and Leeds. At 7 o'clock the following morning, as we started dishing out the religious threads, it was apparent that a big crew had turned out. I gave the Press Association a quick call to tip them off that something might be kicking off at York Minster in a couple of hours. Then it was off to get changed in the car. Jolly had got there ahead of me.

'It's goodbye dignity then, Jol. What you wearing?'

'Monk, I think,' he said, pulling a scarlet satin cardinal's robe from the bag.

'Monk? More like Shirley bloody Bassey!' I laughed.

As we took off our tops, Jol couldn't resist a dig. 'You're looking a bit chunky.'

'Don't bloody start. It's from that humble pie diet I've been on the last few years.'

A few minutes later we were all assembled and I gave them their mission for the day. Then it was down to the nitty gritty.

'Right, who's got religion?' I shouted. 'Who's ready to be arrested?'

A unanimous show of hands was the response.

'Right, boys, you only live once, so let's make it count. Now, who's ready for our Sunday Service?'

Shouts rang out, hands were thrown in the air, cassocks were tugged as, laughing and joking, we all set off. The original plan had been to enter the Minster by the front door, foxing anyone guarding the door with the authenticity of our clothing. But as we emerged in full ecumenical glory, a journalist was already on our case.

'You look like the Reservoir Reverends,' he said excitedly. 'Wait till I tell my picture desk.'

I realised that the tip-off I'd given the press could backfire if the Minster got wind of our imminent arrival. As we crossed the green behind the building, Jason and one of the other boys were already scaling the scaffolding that covered the rear. Even if no pictures were taken inside, we wanted to be certain of a happy snap of Jason dressed as a Cardinal with the 'In the Name of the Father' banner on the roof.

As we made final preparations for our grand entrance, a security guard from the God Squad approached us.

'Nice and steady boys, everybody pretend to be normal,' said Jolly calmly, wrapping his Monk's belt around his waist while casting a watchful eye over our freaky-looking ecumenical mob.

'What are you boys doing here then?' inquired the security man.

'What do you think we're doing here?' asked the monk.

'Well, you look a bit odd, what you're wearing, like.'

By now the man seemed completely flummoxed and increasingly twitchy.

'Is it any different to what they're wearing in there then?' asked Jol. 'I mean, we can go one better – we've got the Pope with us today,' he said, nodding in the direction of our pontiff.

'I better go back and tell 'em, then.' With that, the guard turned and began to shuffle back towards the Minster, but it was too late.

'Showtime, boys! Let's go now, before the buggers shut the door,' said Jolly.

Like a shot, we were off, sprinting at full pelt towards the door with TV crews and photographers racing to catch up.

When we reached the door an altercation rapidly turned into a brawl, with our priests pulling their priests. What with all the flaying cassocks, arms, legs, and exchanges of very un-Christian language, it was impossible to tell who was batting for whom. Caught in the epicentre of this unseemly and unplanned ruckus, I somehow managed to crawl through multiple pairs of jigging legs and sprint up the aisle, shouting, 'In the Name of the Father!' About halfway down, two large priests rose from their pews and hunkered down in a defensive rugby-tackle position. Fuck it, I thought. That's all I bloody need now.

Being an ex prop-forward in my tempestuous but short-lived career for the school rugby team, I was confident that I could take them out. But it was not to be. Next thing I knew, I was being felled on hallowed ground. My ankles were hoisted unceremoniously up into the air, while my body mass and sheer momentum catapulted me over my two adversaries and sent me sliding a good 6 feet up the aisle on my belly like an old prostate walrus.

'In the Name of the Father! In the Name of the Father!' I bellowed, using everything left in my lungs.

As I came to a stop and rolled over, I looked up to see a shocked biddy with a lavender rinse staring at me in disbelief.

'Nice hair colour . . .' I whispered. 'Purple is the colour of equal—'

Before I could finish, the Christian brothers yanked me unceremoniously back down the aisle by my ankles – I was about to be defrocked.

'OK, boys, calm down, I'll come quietly,' I said, standing up and dusting myself down as best I could with their hands locked round my arms. Then, without warning, I used my full body weight to throw myself to the ground, pulling them down on top of me. A hail of fists and boots started raining in on me. As my carcass was half-dragged, half-carried towards the doors, all I could do was try and curl up in a defensive position.

'This is a once-in-a-lifetime opportunity for me, boys,' I grunted, 'getting beaten up by priests. That's it, a little harder! Right a bit – oh yes, yes, that's very Christian of you!' I took a blow to the side of my head and suddenly I was being catapulted out of the door and down the Minster steps to the media throng awaiting my arrival.

'Did that go to plan then?' asked David O'Neil, who had captured my undignified exit on film.

'Does it fucking look like it?' I rasped, tugging at the arm hanging off my cassock and trying to straighten my dislodged dog collar. 'Fucking hell, I took a beating in there. They haven't seen that much action since Jesus turned the tables of the moneylenders over. Where are the others?'

'No idea. We think they're in there somewhere. Jason's up, though.'

'Thank fuck for that.'

We ran round to the other end of the Minster in time to see Hatchy erect the banner upside down at the wrong end of the building. I called him on his mobile.

'I'm fucking sweating, I'm fucking sweating,' he gasped. 'That's a long fucking climb up here, that is. How'd it go at your end?'

'Disaster. And this is a disaster,' I said, pointing at the banner. 'It's upside fucking down and you are at the wrong end of the building. Can't we get anything right? It's this side, now – shift it!'

I turned to David, my head bowed, wheezing like some old geriatric struck down with emphysema. 'I'm too old for this kind of malarkey. It's just too much. There have to be easier ways of changing the bloody law.'

Before he could answer, Welsh activist Jim Gibson ran up shouting, 'Matt, you've been invited back in by the Archbishop of York to address the congregation.'

'Christ, does that mean we have to run all the way down to the other end? Shit, I'll need a stretcher to get me back up that aisle. Guess it's lucky I'm the peak of physical fitness then!' I laughed as we jogged back round.

At the door, the then Archbishop of York, David Hope, was waiting for me.

As I walked up the aisle, heads in the thousand-strong congregation craned to see this blasphemous figure's re-entry. Drawing closer, I began to make out the fuzzy forms in front of me. Without my glasses, it's difficult to be sure, but with every step it gets clearer.

I could see a monk. A cardinal. Two priests and a pope. Several activists had got through and formed themselves into an ecumenical human shield in front of the altar. They had refused to leave unless I was allowed to give my sermon from the pulpit. As I walked past the Archbishop of Canterbury, I bade him good morning, but his gnarled face wore an expression like a crumbling gargoyle.

Panting, I climbed into the pulpit and surveyed my fellow brethren. I paused for a few seconds, not for any theatrical effect or additional gravitas, you understand, but simply because I was so short of breath I couldn't speak.

The cold, stony faces of the General Synod seemed to bear down on me with 'burn in hell, Beelzebub' stares.

I began my sermon in the same inflammatory vein as my entrance.

'The Archbishop of Canterbury is the Arthur Daley of the Christian world ...'

There was a collective sharp intake of musty Minster air.

'He flogs you this thing called marriage,' I said, referring to the Church's new marketing drive to encourage more people to marry in church. 'A few years later, when it breaks down, there is no roadside recovery and no after-sales service.'

My first sermon, in my finest estuary English, had begun.

I concluded by asking forgiveness for disrupting the service and thanking them for the opportunity to speak. But why, I asked, should it be necessary for us to go to such extremes to raise the issues of family breakdown and fatherlessness?

As I left, the congregation broke into a round of applause. I was stunned, shocked, shaken and stirred.

Once outside, we assumed the excitement was all over. We gave a few interviews, and Jason was about to make his way down so we could all go home when suddenly the Old Bill arrived mobhanded and started nicking people.

Inside the man-bag slung over my shoulder were detailed plans of how to bring the M25 to a complete standstill. There was only one thing to do. As they moved in to grab me, for the second time in the space of thirty minutes I threw myself to the cobbled ground, hurtling the contents of my bag across the nearby grass.

As I sprawled flat out, the press surged around me and the two coppers called for back-up.

'God you're heavy!' puffed a WPC who, for some insane reason – probably equal opportunities – had been given the task of helping to cart me off.

'You don't think I carry round this extra weight for the fun of it, do you? It's defensive ballast for occasions such as this.'

I was shoved into the back of a paddywagon, but they didn't shut the door properly so I kicked it open to wave my fist defiantly and shout 'In the Name of the Father!' at the media scrum one final time.

After a hearty nine-hour sojourn care of Her Majesty's Constabulary, we were released without charge, but not without incident. Some rooky PC demanded my clothes, saying they wanted to test for DNA. When I refused, they served up a meal that looked like something that had been dragged up from the bottom of the River Ouse. And not so much as a sniff of sacramental wine. But at least our 'no comment' Get Out of Jail card seemed to be working.

In a subsequent interview with the *Daily Telegraph* later in 2004 the then Archbishop of York Dr David Hope said, 'I recalled a conversation on the train from York to London about four weeks before the protest with a single father who had been denied access to his child. I felt very strongly for that man,' he said. 'His treatment seemed to me to be wholly unjust. I think that their [Fathers 4 Justice] point about mediation, involving the whole family and including the father in question regarding the future of the child is actually very important.'

By pure coincidence, the following week the Government produced a Green Paper about changes to the family justice system – despite protestations just months earlier that there was nothing wrong with it. Clearly, we'd rattled them. Civil servants contacted Families Need Fathers to ask what they should do to combat our publicity machine, later slipping them £250,000 in grants for their capitulation. For the first time, FNF have been taken seriously – and it's down to us.

A HANDBAGGING

In the wake of the Green Paper I embarked on a marathon media jaunt around the studios doing about fifty interviews in a day. It kicked off with a 3.30 a.m. start to get down to GMTV for an interview alongside Margaret Hodge. Fathers Direct, a government-funded bunch of poodles, had been wheeled out to counter the F4J onslaught. The group's head honcho, a Julian Clary lookalike called Jack O'Sullivan, had been camping it up in interviews with all the gravitas of an androgynous metrosexual pygmy. Small wonder he cut a twitchy figure in the Millbank restaurant when I eyeballed him that morning.

In an explosive encounter later that afternoon, Conservative MP and Shadow spokeswoman on the family, Theresa May, tried to handbag me at Millbank studios in front of David O'Neil, who was shooting scenes for a fly-on-the-wall documentary about us commissioned by Channel 4. I had incurred her wrath by saying in an interview on Sky that she had experienced a Damascene conversion.

The previous year, May had visited our stand at the Tory Conference in Blackpool and expressed the view that family law was 'a very complex and difficult area that you couldn't legislate for'. I remember her words exactly because I'd shelled out £5,000 for the privilege and couldn't believe my ears.

Yet when I reminded her of this she went abso-fucking-lutely bonkers and came springing towards me in her leopardskin stilettos, her handbag clasped tightly in her right hand. Forced to engage reverse gear at speed, I staggered backwards while O'Neil gleefully carried on filming. After taking a serious swing in my direction, May was restrained by one of her aides. Having bundled her out of Millbank, the lackey returned not to apologise but to bark, 'None of this footage is to be used, you understand me?'

'No, I don't. Who the fuck do you think you are? Your boss has just gone all Scary Poppins and tried to handbag me, and now you think you can start throwing your weight around? Beat it, Tory boy.'

After words with O'Neil, he left the ITN office none too happy.

'She was really upset, Matt,' said David. 'Do you always have this effect on people?'

'Not always. But what I said was true. What is it with these people? Can't they just say they changed policy rather than go fricking bananas?'

Gary Burch, our political coordinator, wasn't impressed. Not only had I rubbished Tory leader Michael Howard in a recent interview, now I'd upset another Tory bigwig in Theresa May.

'It's politics, Matt, it's a fucking game. You know how to play it, but you are so stubbornly belligerent you simply refuse to go along with it.'

When David Cohen from the *Standard* dashed up to my ranch in Suffolk for an interview to discuss the week's events, Burchy put through an urgent call.

'For God's sake,' he said, 'don't call Howard a hypocrite again.'

But it was too late. I'd already done the interview.

'Sorry, Gary. It's worse than that.'

'How can it be worse than that?'

'I called him a fucking hypocrite.'

'Fucking hell, Matt, what are you trying to do? Piss off the only people who might give a damn?'

18 SECONDS FROM BEING SHOT

I once acquired an African carved wooden totem in the shape of a British Bobby. Standing about 4-feet tall in his boots, he cut a fine dash, albeit he was probably made from illegally harvested jungle hardwood. But what the hell? He was a bit more animated than those involved in the national security of Westminster, and probably a lot younger. I got him as part of a job lot which included a black colonial judge and an archbishop. Very nice they looked too. Both were the spitting image of the Archbishop of York, John Sentamu. I toyed with calling the totem 'Plod' but decided that 'Bill' sounded a little more personable. He stood guard at the top of my stairs so that, come the day his colleagues kicked down the door and streamed in, the first thing they'd see would be an effigy of their good selves. Make 'em feel at home, I thought. On the other hand, they might just think I was taking the piss.

Relations with Bill's colleagues varied from good to ... well, perhaps not unsurprisingly, more strained than the face of a constipated turtle.

The first thing you discover at Scotland Yard is that being in possession of a sense of humour is liable to be considered a criminal offence. Try asking if they've seen one of your colleagues come by wearing a Batman outfit and you'll get short shrift. Wear one of our 'Don't Shoot, I'm a Dad' T-shirts, as I did about a month after the Stockwell shooting in 2005, and you may come close to spending a night in the cells.

These days they record meetings. Or at least they have the courtesy to tell you they are recording meetings, to which my standard response is 'bollocks'. I have never warmed to authority and authority has never warmed to me. Instead, I prefer to raise two fingers in the general direction of the estab-lishment whenever possible. Immature? Yes. Satisfying? Immensely.

And the more trouble you cause, the higher up the food chain you climb. Despite some nervousness on their part, I assured my contacts at the Met that, in spite of our activities, I was for the most part house-trained and able to behave at meetings with senior officers.

I generally dealt with the Operational Planning Department. I had assumed that they were responsible for handling the 3,000 protests held in the capital every year, but it turned out that these dark horses were also involved in hardcore police ops like the one in East London where the guy got shot in the shoulder running down the stairs after he thought his property was being attacked. The police search of his house came up empty; just as nothing could be found against Jean Charles de Menezes, the Brazilian shot at Stockwell tube station.

Sometimes police intelligence seems a rare commodity. I just hoped they were keeping some saved up for us.

My principle contact was Adrian Laurie, an amiable chap who did his best to rub his charm offensive off on to me. Likewise his colleague, Andy Sharp.

Most of our demos were good-natured theatrical spectacles with an obligatory double-decker bus, street drummers, DJ and a 10,000-watt sound system that blasted out the theme music to *The Professionals* and *The Sweeny* as we crossed the capital.

But for all the good-natured banter that went on with Adrian and Andy, phalanxes of police intelligence officers would swarm through the crowds, haranguing activists and trying to provoke a confrontation in an effort to get somebody arrested. Like the time a Father Christmas was asked to remove his beard so he could be ID'ed – only it turned out his beard was genuine. There was also the time they tried nicking Big Ron Davies by ushering our battle bus from the Camden side of the square at Lincoln's Inn Fields to the side which falls within the London Borough of Westminster, thereby breaking his bail conditions. An unsavoury stand-off followed as we went head-to-head with them to prevent his arrest on the grounds it had been deliberately and maliciously contrived.

It's at moments like this when the façade crumbles away to reveal the manipulative nature of authority and the establishment. In their demands for ever more stringent restrictions on our right to protest, Scotland Yard had crossed the line from being law enforcers to lawmakers.

'We get on well, don't we, Matt?' said Adrian one day.

'Listen, Adrian, you're a top chap, but people higher up the food chain are calling the shots, literally. Business is still business. You have your job to do and I have mine.'

We were frequently warned about the risks we took as an organisation. Every time we did a demo the bogus argument that we were somehow assisting terrorism would be trotted out. Yet even back in 2003 it was my belief that trains and football stadiums were the easiest targets for would-be Islamic terrorists. Besides, I'd lived with the threat of bomb attacks in London for fifteen years. In February 1996 when the IRA blast went off in Canary

Wharf, I was caught in the vicinity with Sophie, who was heavily pregnant with Daniel at the time.

But underlying the tug-of-war battles with the Yard was the unpalatable truth that – as we proved time and time again with a few dads, a van and a ladder – 'national security' was but a smokescreen. Even when they did act, they often got it wrong. Mostly it seemed they hadn't the faintest clue what was going on.

IT'S A DRAG BEING A DAD

That August I took a trip to a bus graveyard out in the marshes of East London, hoping to acquire a double-decker. While I was there, a call came through on my mobile. It was TV presenter Vanessa Feltz, worried that her husband might be making an appearance in a documentary that was being made about F4J. She offered me a variety of inducements, which I declined, reassuring her that the programme had absolutely nothing to do with her family.

Having found a bus that was good for two trips and no more, we set about painting it purple. Our plan was to stage a cocks-in-a-frock demo in the middle of the M25. Giant 'It's a Drag Being a Dad' banners would festoon the exterior of the bus and 100ft purple lamé streamers would trail behind us as thirty-odd 'Doubtfire Dads' stood on the open upper deck in an homage to the film *Priscilla Queen of the Desert*. As roadblocks went, it would have been a stunning spectacle, if not a tad unpopular.

I had run the idea past Glen. 'In the words of the film, it's cocks in a frock on the block.'

'Will everybody dress up?'

'Well, anyone who doesn't is going to look even more stupid than the rest of us. I've even spoken to a transvestite drag queen from Madame Jo-Jo's nightclub who'd love to help us achieve fully authentic sartorial elegance.'

'Matt, if you're going to bring traffic to a standstill you might as well do it in style. Sky News are close so they can get aerial shots quite easily. What about parking it in Downing Street?'

'That was Plan B, but I think it's just too risky. We might get shot. Or even clamped.'

But, as ever, the course of events did not run smoothly. When Ed picked the bus up for the drive to Guy Harrison's farm on the south coast, it turned out the engine was shot to pieces.

Eddie, who used to be an engineer, volunteered to take a gander, see if he could start the old girl up. After twenty minutes fiddling with her bits, he climbed into the cab. A couple of turns of the ignition and still she stubbornly refused to start. It seemed that, where this bus was concerned, two trips had been wildly optimistic.

18 SECONDS FROM BEING SHOT

As always, I had another idea up my sleeve. I had drawn up a logo and basic costume design for our own superhero, the Purple Phantom, and after speaking to several theatrical designers about the concept I'd found a lady on the south coast who agreed to make it.

The idea was for the Phantom to jet into London on a powermotor, a parachute that has a seat with a giant motorised propeller fixed behind it. Taking off from the hill at Greenwich Observatory, he would glide up the Thames, loop the loop at Big Ben, cruise past Lord Nelson, up the Mall and over the top of the Palace before landing at one of Her Maj's garden parties at Buck Palace.

It was an idea everyone loved. But, oddly, nobody wanted to volunteer for the part.

'You'd have to be certifiable to do that,' said Guy. 'Absolutely fucking nuts. It's a kamikaze mission.'

'What, and this from a man who powder-bombed Tony Blair?' I teased, poking him in the side.

'What if we get shot down?' asked Jolly, not unreasonably.

'Well, providing we tell the Gold Room at Scotland Yard as soon as we have lift-off, hopefully we won't have any problems.'

'What do we say when we land?'

'I don't know. I'm making this up on the hoof. "Fathers 4 Justice at your service, Your Majesty"?'

All these plans were examined and then abandoned either because: they are even more insane than our other insane ideas, or they'll piss too many people off.

So I dusted down Plan Z, a protest which would result in much less public inconvenience.

The target: Buckingham Palace. After all, if there is one family in the country affected by family breakdown, it's the Royal Family.

Ray Barry had staked out Her Maj's pad a few weeks earlier on a Palace tour. We'd assessed the options and then left the final detail down to a team I'd assembled the previous weekend. They had in turn run a last-minute assessment of their own.

The night before I called documentary maker David O'Neil, who was making the film about Fathers 4 Justice for Channel 4.

'David, it's Matt. You need to get yourself to Docklands.'

'Why, what's up?'

'You know that idea I've been toying with? Well, it's happening – tomorrow. If you want in, you better shift it.'

'Which idea?'

'The one they could stick me in the Tower of London for. Put your coat on, we've got a date in the City.'

'Fucking hell. Are you serious? I'm just chilling with a glass of wine.'

'Deadly. But you know how these things go. It's dangerous and anything could happen. If you're making a documentary about us, you should be there. Either that or watch it on the telly tomorrow with the rest of the nation.'

'I'm on my way.'

There was one contingency I had to build into the plan. The 'Fuck, what if. . .?' factor.

'Fuck, what if. . .' being – what if somebody gets shot?

Everybody knows the risks, but an activist would be gambling with his life here and I would have to sit in the hot seat if things went pear-shaped and somebody ended up taking a bullet.

That night I gave Robbie Williams wannabe Jason Hatch, who'd volunteered to do the protest, a bloody great bear hug and wished him well as he prepared to embark on our most dangerous mission to date.

'Remember, Jase, if you get in shit, there ain't no cavalry coming to rescue you – or us, if they start shooting and kicking down doors looking for who planned this. If you go down, we all go down together. Good luck.'

Whatever the mud they'd sling at Jason afterwards, this was a feat that required lashings of insane courage. I couldn't help but admire his sheer chutzpah.

Back at base, all computers with client work on them had to be moved out of the office in preparation for the state to come down on us like Bernard Manning swan-diving into a tub of custard.

On Monday 13 September Fathers 4 Justice would turn into a supernova, the world and its landmarks our stage. Big Ron was due in court that day, charged with a breach of the peace for the Funpowder Plot. With everybody, *Time Magazine* included, gathered at Bow Street magistrates' court, it was the perfect cover for our Buck Palace stunt.

The boys agreed to meet up at a member's flat in East London. One of the coordinators there had been a source of concern to me for some time. Despite his useful contributions and his sporadically amenable disposition, you couldn't escape that intangible feeling that something malevolent about him was lurking just beneath his skeletal exterior.

The fact that he didn't use his real name. That he had no children. He hadn't even stepped foot into a family court. He also lived in a reasonable part of the capital with no apparent income and didn't work. None of it added up, so the lingering finger of suspicion remained and when trouble started, all roads inevitably led to one person. All these misgivings weren't helped when a journalist from the *Guardian* called up on the morning of the Palace job trying to root out information about him.

'How much do you know about him?' he asked

'Not huge amounts other than where he comes from, but I don't know his back story'.

'Do you know he doesn't use his real name?'

'Well I was aware of that, but it isn't a crime to change your name.'

'Do you know if he has links with anyone in the security services in Northern Ireland? You know that Special Branch regularly hire informers from there?' At this I begin to get quite defensive about our team, if only because I trusted the press even less than I trusted some of our members.

'Look I'm afraid that if you have something concrete then present it to us and we'll deal with it.'

'But that's the point Mr O'Connor; the man seems to have no history.'

No matter, I thought, we had too much going on to get involved in a wild goose chase. With F4J you were working with damaged goods and infiltrators from the press and Special Branch and that made for some odd pairings and uneasy bedfellows. But when it came to getting the job done we simply knuckled down, closed our eyes and hoped, even prayed, for the best.

Ron's case broke for lunch at 1 p.m. I was immediately on the blower to Jason.

'Where are you?'

'At Graham's.'

'Why are you still there, for Christ's sake? You ought to be on your way up the side of the Palace by now. You know the plan, 1 p.m. till 7 p.m. Hit the early evening news, then come down.'

'But, Matt, it's not as simple as that. Everybody is shitting themselves. We could get shot.'

'We all know what might happen, but if you stick to revealing your costume immediately and shouting "F4J", you should be OK.'

'I know that, but the others are worried ...'

'But the others aren't doing it, you are. We either shift it now, or we pull it.'

When I got off the phone, I began to panic. Should I pull it? In the end, I decided that, if it was going to happen, it would happen.

I caught up with Ron in a bar round the corner.

'Pint, Matt?'

'Nahh, Diet Coke, please.'

'Something wrong? Did my ears trick me, or did you just say "Diet Coke"?'

'I'm supposed to have something happening. There's a woman from *Time Magazine* who has turned up for your hearing, but I'm using your trial as a decoy for another operation. No offence taken, I hope?'

'Not at all. Can you tell me what it is?'

'Well, if it all goes to plan, you might find the public gallery will empty of F4J supporters in about an hour's time. I'll give you two words – not a dicky bird to anyone, understand? – Buckingham. Palace.'

'Fuck me!' said Ron, giving me a conspiratorial wink as he swigged the dregs from the glass. 'If you ain't having one, think I'll have one for you. Might need it for medicinal purposes. But if you don't mind me saying, Matt, isn't it a bit dangerous even by our mad standards?'

'I'll admit there is the small risk of death . . .' I started laughing. A panicky staccato titter.

'Jason's only titchy; if they shoot, they'll probably miss him anyway, whereas with you and me, it would be like shooting an elephant in your living room.' Ron's words had a strangely soothing effect on me, but it was clear he had other things on his mind.

'Matt, can I ask though, what if something happens to me if something goes wrong?'

'You should be OK, just a fine to pay. We'll help out as best as we can. If anything serious happens, don't worry, we'll get you out.'

Back on the street I was tailed by two coppers from police intelligence, easily identifiable thanks to the reflective blue flashes emblazoned across their shoulders. I couldn't resist baiting them with an impromptu and suitably cryptic street interview.

'I'm afraid, boys, you are in the wrong place at the wrong time. But if you provide the popcorn, I'll provide the entertainment.' With that I dashed off into the court toilets and, cupping my mouth with my hand so nobody could hear, I called Jason again.

'Where are you, Jase?'

'We're on our way.'

'Have the others checked the security out front?'

'Yes, it's thick. In every sense, apparently.'

'Great. What's the traffic like?'

'Clear as anything, we should be there in a few minutes. Matt, I'm not afraid to die, but I don't want to,' said Jason, nerves picking away at his confidence.

'Hopefully it won't come to that. Whatever else happens, Jason, you'll always have my respect for this.'

'All systems go then, I guess,' he said.

'OK, book 'em, Danno. See you on the telly. Good luck.'

The moment I hung up the phone went again. At the height of our activities, people used to joke that I'd had the mobile surgically attached to my left ear, such was the volume of calls. This time round it was a client.

'Matt, I'd like to discuss next year's campaign.' It was David Taylor from my clients, Frederick's Dairies, the ice-cream manufacturer that holds the licence for Cadbury ice cream in the UK. I'd been working for them since 1998 and they were great clients, but the timing of the call was inopportune to say the least.

'Er, David, I'm in a meeting at the moment.'

'How long are you likely to be?'

'A few days.'

'Is something wrong?'

'Not exactly, but I'm wearing my other hat. My campaign hat.'

'Are you up to something, Matt?'

'Possibly. Probably. It's all a bit hush-hush. Can I get back to you later?'

'Can't you say what it is?'

'Best not, David. Ignorance is bliss and all that.'

'Well, I need you to start working up a few ideas as soon as possible. Any chance of something by the end of the week?'

Even though David had let me off the hook, I immediately began working up concepts for an ice-cream campaign while drafting a press release for the Buck Palace job that would be flexible enough to cover every eventuality. My brain was fucking fried as I tried to juggle Batman, Buck Palace, Cadbury's Ice Cream and press releases in a cerebral vortex.

At 2 p.m. Jason's 'Bright Ideas' painting and decorating van rolled up the Mall, the ladder on the roof drifting at a dangerous angle as if it was about to come off. When they reached Birdcage Walk and the north-eastern end of the palace where an annexe juts out from the main building and butts up to the exterior wall, Ed slammed the brakes and the boys hopped out. But before they could remove the ladder, Ed, in a state of panic, put the pedal to the metal and sped off towards Hyde Park Corner in a blaze of burnt rubber. Luckily the ladder came away in Jason's hand and he clambered over a small fence and ran across a patch of grass leading up to the exterior wall of the annexe.

The ladder slid up against the wall and Jason scampered up.

'Give me the banner, the banner,' he called down from halfway, then rattled up the rungs to the top. Removing his jacket to reveal his Batman costumer, he shouted, 'Fathers 4 Justice, Fathers 4 Justice!' before running across the roof of the annexe and on to the ledge that would carry him round the side of Buckingham Palace to the Royal Balcony.

Dave Pyke was right up Jason's arse on the ladder, but an armed response officer positioned out of sight behind the wall began screaming his head off.

'Get down that ladder! Get down that ladder now! I will shoot, I will shoot!'

On the subsequent Channel 4 documentary, *Fathers 4 Justice: The Men Who Stormed the Palace* the sound of the gun being cocked was chillingly captured on tape.

In the courtroom, my mobile burst into life and Jason spoke the words I'd been waiting to hear.

'I'm up, I'm bloody up. Get your arse down here, it's kicking off.'

I jumped up and shouted 'Fathers 4 Justice have taken Buckingham Palace! Everybody with me! Go go go! Move it!'

Ron turned to give me the thumbs up and we were off down the stairs.

Along the way, I grabbed Helen Gibson from *Time Magazine*. As I bundled her into a cab, she said, 'What's happening, Matt? I don't understand.'

'Sorry about this, but one of our guys is on the Palace dressed as Batman.'

'Buckingham Palace?'

'Yes, that one.'

'Seriously? That's exciting.'

I got on the blower to Jenny and Julie in the office. Jen had just returned from a holiday in Oz and neither of the girls knew about the stunt.

'Hi, Jen, it's Matt.'

'How are you today, Matthew?'

'Effervescent, my dear, effervescent.'

'Oh God. What's up now? You're sounding unbelievably smug.'

'I can afford to be.'

'Matt, just tell me what's going on.'

'Can you fire out a press release with the following headline: "Breaking News: Batman's on Buckingham Palace".'

'You are joking, aren't you?' said Jen.

'I'm bloody well not. It's a feat of pure poetry, Jen, a nut-cracking climax to our comic opera. Now, get the rest of this down and call up our press team to see who can help with the media management.'

Jason Hatch, having run round a ledge 50 feet up, stood for the next five hours beside the Queen's balcony with the world's media watching. I'd be lying if I said I wasn't thoroughly delighted, if slightly overcome with a belligerent arrogance that even I found rather nauseating.

'Beneath this cunningly constructed vision of handsomeness,' I told Jenny, 'lies a man with a penchant for inspired thinking and killer copy.'

'Fuck off, Matt. You're going to go down for all of this one day.'

'They'll have to catch me first, Jen,' I crowed.

'Or knobble you,' she said. 'They're going to fucking get you, Matt.'

'I'll live with it,' I told her, wrapped in the cocoon of publicity. 'This will knock the fucking stuffing out of them.'

The next call turned out to be one of our Scouser members. They'd nicknamed me 'Fat Boy Spin' as a result of the coverage. I nipped over to the *Daily Mail* newsroom and caught Channel 4 news. It was the main headline and presenter Jon Snow was struggling to keep a straight face as he described the incongruous juxtaposition of one of the world's most iconic superheroes perched on one of the world's most iconic buildings.

Initially the good coverage outweighed the bad. OK, there was a bit of rough and tumble on *Newsnight* that evening when Kirsty Wark attacked me with her jabbing left finger, and followed up with a verbal right hook.

'Shouldn't you be concerned about national security? Isn't what you did irresponsible? What if it had been al-Qaeda?' she growled.

I paused for a moment, caught off guard by the ferociousness of her opening gambit and the bizarre image of Bin Laden in a Batman cozzie. But to me a nation of fatherless children was pretty irresponsible. And what did national security matter when you had no personal security, when you couldn't even see your own kids, let alone protect them? But, feeling weary and tired, I batted the ball over to the other talking head who had been wheeled in opposite me.

'Listen, I'm just here to get as much publicity for the cause as I can. It's my job. If you want to ask somebody about national security, why don't you ask the man sitting beside you? You did, after all, introduce him as an expert on such matters.'

The following day we all gathered in London to wait for Jason's release. In twenty-four hours we received over three thousand emails from across the world. The response was euphoric:

I've just turned on the TV. FANTASTIC, BRILLIANT. I am an F4J member, I'm not well off but please increase my subscription by 100 per cent. I haven't felt like this inside since Jonny Wilkinson kicked the final goal when we won the World Cup last year.

Hi, My name is Gillian and I am a single mum from East Yorkshire. Just a quick line in support of your latest protest . . . absolutely brilliant! I don't quite know how you get it all organised, but you certainly made the news in a spectacular way. The TV coverage is causing quite a stir and is for the majority in your favour. EXCELLENT. Unfortunately my son and I are on the other side of the coin, having been in dispute with the CSA for the past six years trying to get a few quid from my ex husband to help us manage . . . but he couldn't care less about us. I hope you ALL succeed in your efforts. Your children are so lucky to have your love and in the future I'm sure they will know how much you have tried for them.

Superheroes, Super Dads, Super Guys . . . SUPER PEOPLE
Keep up the publicity . . . it WILL WORK
All the best,
Gillian
PS If you ever need a WONDERWOMAN, I am volunteering first!!!!

Go for it, Fathers 4 Justice. We love the outfit. Good luck with your campaign.
Barry F., Swindon

Hi All, I don't have any kids myself . . . yet ! I'd hate to have to go through what some fathers have, almost off putting enough to get started in the first place. I don't want to even think about the pain caused by not being able to see/visit/care for my child. Good luck to everyone, please keep up the pressure, I'm sure it's working.
Regards, Stephen *future father – perhaps*

I'm sitting at home in Dubai UAE watching Sky news, F4J is doing a fantastic job highlighting the difficulties fathers face in the UK, I too faced the same situation in the UK and decided enough was enough and left. Hopefully you could bring a change to the Law and I could return to the UK and get access to my son. Keep up the good work.
Regards, Brett

Bro, it's Dave. I was in Pepper's Bar in Ibiza yesterday telling some chap what you got up to, you know, dressing up and causing mayhem. Anyway he starts pointing at the TV behind me and says 'what like that?' and fuck me if you ain't at it again on Buck House. Nice one bro! I've dined out on it all night and had a load of free beers! Anyway here's a joke from the Balearics: 'So Batman came up to me and he hit me over the head with a vase & he went,

'T'PAU!' I said 'Don't you mean KERPOW?' He said, 'No, I've got china in my hand.'

Cheers, your brother

Hi F4J, my name's Rupert and I'd like to make an offer to buy Jason's Batman costume or at least some sweaty socks.

Not everybody shared our collective joy though. One solicitor even likened us to terrorists.

Dear Sir, Another day, another puerile piece of adolescent attention-seeking. The stunt at Buckingham Palace has done nothing but further cripple your once-legitimate cause. How can you consider yourselves representatives of a mature, responsible masculinity when you stoop to such witless posturing? Yours etc.

Andy M.

Hi, It's all very well and fine staging VERY silly protests in VERY silly costumes at various locations in the capital but the one thing that many men need to learn – to treat their children and wives with more respect. Many men treat their wives very badly, failing to show any loyalty – in which case, they should expect to have their children withdrawn from them. Many children are better off without their cheating fathers. If a child has been withdrawn from a man there is good reason.

Danny T.

If your 'activists' displayed the same level of egotism in their married lives, it's no wonder that they went belly up.

George E.

I sent the boys to pick Jason up from Charing Cross Police Station where he had spent the night and we retired to the back of a coffee shop in the Charing Cross Hotel before moving on to a press conference outside the Palace. That evening we enjoyed a celebratory champagne and vindaloo at my local curryhouse.

Over the next twenty-four hours the world's media descended on my place in Suffolk. Colombians, Russians, Japanese, Finish, Koreans, French, Italians, Germans – the list was endless. *Nuts* magazine sent a Queen lookalike to Kimsings for a staged break-in.

Even clients started calling up. The Mr Armani of Ice Cream, Frank

Frederick, rang to ask why I hadn't given Batman a Flake '99 to hold when he was up on the balcony. It was a great idea, I told him, but stopping to buy an ice cream for Batman en route hadn't been top of our list of priorities.

Batman@the Palace hit every front page. The *Sun's* headline read 'Holey Security Batman', while the *Daily Mirror* ran with 'Batma'am'. Sir John Stevens, Head of Scotland Yard, told the press that Hatch had been just eighteen seconds from being shot.

In the all-out media frenzy that followed, tabloid hacks ripped into Jason's private life. His ex-girlfriend Gemma sold her story to the *News of the World* for £25,000. We made the cover of *Time Magazine* that week, but given the cesspit of shit that was engulfing us, it was hard to feel enthused.

For the first time, Jason's rictus grin headed southwards. The porcupine-scalped painter and decorator was shell-shocked when he opened the papers to find his nocturnal shenanigans had been unzipped. We'd asked him before-hand, 'What skeletons are in your cupboard, mate?' I didn't expect him to be squeaky clean, but it turned out that some of his activities were beyond the pale. Some papers were alleging that he had also threatened to kill his ex – an off the cuff remark I suspected at the time might have been made in the heat of the moment – he wouldn't be the first to say something like that in the heat of separation.

With everybody still ensconced at Kimsings, I took the opportunity to have a quiet word with him. 'Look, Jase, you're going to have to clean up your act. I'm no beacon of morality and I've pursued a few liaisons dangereuses in my time, but for fuck's sake, rein in that libido of yours. You've had your fifteen minutes of fame, now you're having fifteen minutes of shame and it's affecting the campaign.'

In an ideal world we would have handpicked squeaky-clean protestors for these demos, but people were hardly queuing up for the privilege of being shot. And therein lay the Achilles heel of the entire operation. Instead of campaigning for a cause – our 'Blueprint for Family Law' with its vision of an open justice system and equal parenting – we were perceived as cam-paigning for our own cases. While the likes of Greenpeace were showered in plaudits, we were showered in excrement. Every skeleton in a member's closet would be dragged out and used to smear thousands of mostly good, loving parents. You wouldn't find the media going through the recycling bins of Greenpeace activists to check that they were recycling their waste correctly, yet on several occasions I found individuals foraging through my household waste in the hope of finding dirt.

As our profile grew, our reputation seemed to plummet as the balance of media coverage shifted significantly into the red. It was easy for the press to caricature Batman as 'Bad-man'. We were being demonised for our efforts while single mums were being canonised.

'But, Matt,' said a frustrated Ron Davies one evening, 'we must try and secure more favourable press.'

I tried to explain that the backlash was inevitable. My research had shown that acts of subversion or revolution always resulted in the instigators and the campaigns they ran being smeared. There wasn't a campaign that hadn't had the dirty tricks treatment, from the Suffragettes to Martin Luther King.

'Shit happens, Ron. This is our shit and we have to wear it. It isn't pleasant and it isn't comfortable. But it's what we do.'

Despite the smear campaign, we still appeared to enjoy massive public support. Poll after poll gave us a 70 to 80 per cent support rating among the general public.

A week after the Buck Palace escapade, in a BBC interview Michael Portillo said, 'Every time one of these Fathers 4 Justice protestors climbs a building people think more deeply about the rights of fathers when they separate.'

More significantly, we received numerous letters of encouragement like this one from 16-year-old Leanne:

Reading about your fathers' rights action makes me think even more negatively of the government . . . fathers play just as important a part as mothers. I don't expect anything to come out of this but I wanted to express my anger from my point of view, whose father she has lost contact with and knows how big the need for a father a child wants and needs is. I just hope things change.

BAD BLOOD

With all the publicity I should have been on top of the world. But it soon began to feel that the world was on top of me.

It turned out there was a flipside to press coverage: press intrusion. Shortly after the Batman debacle, the *Daily Mirror* offered Sophie £25,000 to dish the dirt on me. When she refused, they turned on the rest of the group instead, running a series of hatchet jobs on members' private lives. It turned out that they had infiltrated F4J, and for some time they had been recording private conversations using directional parabolic microphones.

Back in Suffolk, I got a call that left me wondering whether I was the victim of a wind-up or something more sinister.

'Is that Matt?'

'Who's calling?'

'I can't say who I am, but Granada TV tried to recruit me yesterday to infiltrate your organisation. I work in security, but I've turned their money down as I agree with your campaign. See, I've got kids too. I know the system's fucked. Good luck and watch your back. . .'

The phone went dead. Taking the warning seriously, I issued private warnings to senior F4J figures that somebody might be planning to run a major hatchet job on us.

Within the hour I received what was to be the first of several threats.

'Matt O'Connor?'

'Who's calling?' I asked nervously, increasingly wary of calls to my mobile.

'Shouldn't you be taking care of your family?'

'Sorry?'

'You've got a nice family, a nice job. Wouldn't want to risk all that. Things happen, people can get caught up in this sort of thing. Think about it. Think about what you could lose. You would do well to step back from this.'

Then he hung up, leaving me staring blankly out of the office window.

'You all right?' said Jen, concerned. 'You're a bit uncharacteristically quiet.'

'I've just had two calls. One to say that Granada are trying to infiltrate F4J, the other was a threat, I think.'

'A threat? What sort of threat?'

'I don't know. It was sort of vague but implied. You know, the choice of words, intonation in the guy's voice, that sort of thing.'

'Shouldn't you call the police?'

'Oh yeah, that's a great fucking idea. I'm sure after catching them with their trousers round their ankles in Parliament and then rubbing their noses in it at Buck Palace, the boys in blue will be really concerned about my personal safety. They're probably the ones making the calls.'

'Don't be stupid, Matt. They wouldn't do that.'

'No? Someone would. Someone will. Who knows who it might be? Mad dads? Monarchists? MI5? You don't piss off that many people without there being a consequence to our actions. I'm head honcho. They know damn well if they bring me down, the whole show comes crashing down.'

'So what do you think is going to happen?'

'You don't want to know.'

I called Sophie. 'Hi, darling, you and the boys OK?'

'Of course we are. Do you want to speak to the boys?'

'Nah, it's OK, just wanted to make sure you're all right. I'll speak to them later.'

'Is something wrong?'

'No, nothing you have to worry about. It's just me. Take care and tell them I'll call back later.'

But it didn't end there. I received a series of threatening emails, including one fantasising about me putting a gun in my mouth and blowing my head off, and another threatening to 'execute' me.

We were also receiving some alarming emails and phone calls from militant dads threatening to firebomb CAFCASS or commit suicide by blowing their brains out in front of Tony Blair. It was troubling stuff and the worst of it got passed straight to the Yard. Our campaign had always been about non-violent direct action; we wouldn't have been acting responsibly if we'd sat on the information.

Every book you'll ever read about protest groups and campaigns will tell you the same thing: Watch your back. Setting off internal divisions and running dirty tricks campaigns against anyone who takes on the state is an age-old tactic.

I thought more and more about what had befallen activist groups like the Black Panthers in the 1960s. A short-lived American civil rights group – once described by FBI director J. Edgar Hoover as 'the greatest threat to the internal security of the country' – the Black Panthers had indulged in inflammatory talk of a 'revolutionary war'. In reality, their actions had been little more than street theatre, but this hadn't prevented the FBI ordering field agents to take 'all measures necessary' to crush the group by a process of infiltration, provocation and disinformation. Once embedded deep within the organisation as respected and trusted activists, the FBI's counter-intelligence operatives would set about causing seismic internal dissent.

The first evidence of a split within F4J came at our coordinators conference at the Stretton Hall Hotel in Shropshire that autumn. While everyone bathed in the reflected glory of the Buck House job, it had become apparent to me that we were at our most vulnerable. The more arrogant we became, the more complacent we were in covering our backs. Dizzy on a euphoric high, we allowed the first cracks in our previously 'tighter than a duck's arse' ranks to appear. At such times it's vital to take swift, decisive action, but by now the size of the organisation had mushroomed beyond even my dictatorial control.

After the powder-bombing of Tony Blair and now Buck Palace, the situation was primed for any agent provocateurs to explode like Chinese fireworks. Because they had been in the organisation for some time and won the trust of their colleagues, they were in a position to exploit the internal jealousies and resentments that pepper organisations such as ours.

One malevolent coordinator broke ranks and launched a blistering attack on one of our management team. With gobs of spittle hanging from his chin, he proceeded to rip into his colleague. I pulled the meeting immediately, but unfortunately a BBC documentary crew had caught the whole thing on film.

'I want him shot now,' I raged afterwards. 'I'm going to string him up by his fucking bollocks from the nearest lamppost, the fucking cunt. How dare he? He isn't even a father, for fuck sake. Just who is he?'

Jason, Burchy and Cox all looked on bewildered.

Trying to calm the situation, Burchy argued, 'Look, if we get rid of him now, it's going to cause a major split.'

'But if we leave him there to fester, what happens when he goes off again? He is a malign influence and dangerous with it. Any threat to F4J should be dealt with forcefully. He's like a fucking cancer. And like cancer, if it ain't cut out straight away, it will fucking eat us alive.'

But in the end I was talked into reconciliation, even though I knew, I just knew, that this would be the beginning of the end for Fathers 4 Justice. By failing to act, we had signed our own death warrant.

Jenny was critical of the fathers for allowing the situation to deteriorate. 'You're becoming a glorified zookeeper, Matthew, with all this in-fighting. Fathers 4 Justice is becoming a bunch of fucking pirates.'

'I don't know about zookeeper, more like playground assistant. I can't run a fucking show like this. How can I campaign when I'm spending my entire time shit shovelling?'

Contaminated by infiltration and poisoned by a bitter cocktail of malice and resentment, the group began to fall apart. Where once we had shared the common goal of fighting injustice, it seemed we were now intent on fighting each other.

Our predilection for penetrating national 'insecurity' had been profoundly embarrassing for the authorities. They had raised the F4J security level from miffed to peeved and then to national nuisance. Now, using internal dissent, they were able to orchestrate our demise.

A few disgruntled ex-members began to sell their stories about me to the *News of the World*. Very thoughtfully, the paper called me twenty-two times in a single afternoon, asking to hear my side of the story.

I told them I'd rather eat my own testicles.

I was portrayed as a reckless drunk who was intent on sleeping his way through the boudoirs of femme fatales drawn from our relatives' support group, the Purplehearts. Worse, it was claimed that I'd defrauded the organisation of tens of thousands of pounds, ripping off desperate dads.

The paper ran interviews with ex-members about plans to kidnap Dame Elizabeth Butler-Sloss's pooch and a proposal for a drive-by shooting of Children and Families Minister Lord Filkin with a paint-ball gun. It didn't require a massive leap of the imagination to see where this train of thought was going.

I jokingly responded that I had indeed once participated in a threesome with Batman and Spiderman, luxuriating in a post-coital hot-tub filled with Cristal champagne. Afterwards, I'd nipped over to the Côte d'Azur in my private jet for a spot of lunch before heading off in my Aston Martin DB5 to spunk the membership fees in the casinos of Monaco.

Complete bollocks, of course, but still people remained suspicious. What was I doing, running a campaign for fathers denied access, when my own case had been satisfactorily resolved? There had to be an ulterior motive, they reasoned.

Sophie begged me to stop the campaign. As a primary school teacher, she'd had to endure questions from parents wanting to know why I was still campaigning when I could see the boys all I wanted. Now even she was wondering whether I was driven by a genuine motivation to change the law, or an ego-fuelled cocktail of anger and vengeance.

'I'm doing it for them, Sophie,' I said, looking at the boys. 'And all those other poor bloody kids caught up in this nightmare.'

'Are you, Matthew?' she asked, in a voice steeped with disbelief.

'Well, I'm hardly doing it for me, am I? Let's face it, I could have had a great life again, gone round the world, but I chose this. If one child gets to see their father or one grandparent gets to see their grandchildren, then it's all worth it.'

Sophie shot me a despairing look. 'Is it? At what price, Matthew? You're just so bloody frustratingly reckless.'

'You say reckless like it's a bad thing.'

'It is when it impacts on all of us. We didn't choose this campaign, Matthew, but we're all being dragged kicking and screaming into it. You're not trained to be a counsellor and you've totally underestimated the emotional toll it would take on the rest of us. You can't carry on dealing with desperate dads and suicide calls, life-and-death moments at the end of the phone. You're not cut out for it.'

But I couldn't just drop it and walk away. It was as if I was being driven by some powerful force. The flipside to my creativity is a self-destructive streak. Though the struggle between the two often seems set to consume me, the reality is that one could not exist without the other. And so I carried on, my business suffering as I juggled clients' demands with the F4J campaign; two full-time jobs on four hours' sleep a night, fuelled by industrial quantities of coffee and Red Bull.

I was wracked with guilt because my workload was preventing me from seeing the boys as much as I should. The irony tugged constantly at my conscience. But what would happen if nothing had changed by the time they became dads? Would they too end up at the mercy of the family courts?

The negative cost of F4J was by now in danger of outweighing any positive gain. My ego was being massaged one minute and pummelled brutally into submission the next. Instead of working on the next campaign, I was spending my time shit-shovelling. And while I was being accused of bleeding dads dry, I was ploughing money hand over fist into F4J to cover demo and travel expenses, plus rising admin costs. The flood of enquiries post-Batman had sent the office phones – manned by a staff of two, Jen and Julie – into meltdown, and then there were the thousands of letters and emails to deal with.

When my accountant, Tony, came in to crunch the numbers, he was appalled. 'It's a black hole for your hard-earned cash, Matt. The only person you've defrauded is yourself – to the tune of tens of thousands of quid. End it now for your own sake and concentrate on your design business.'

If only I could have walked away.

Day in, day out, we were sinking deeper into the mire. Some members seemed drunk on the oxygen of publicity, tangling fiction and reality in their polyester tights. Even more disturbingly, a criminal subculture was emerging. We found evidence that membership funds were being siphoned off at local level and some individuals were collecting money from an unsuspecting public while posing as F4J charity-chuggers at stations across London. Allegations of racism, misogyny and violence were levelled at one of our local groups, and then counterfeit F4J groups began springing up across the world, pirating our intellectual property and yet, to my intense annoyance and frustration, managing to register the trademark as their own.

As the nutters poured out of the woodwork, it dawned on me that I had created a Frankenstein's monster of a fathers' group – a monster I could no longer control. It came to a head one day when a tearful Jenny reported that she'd been threatened by one woman-hating caller, while another misogynist sent a vile and offensive email:

> *We should kill them all, the fucking feminazi bitches . . . the Taliban have got the right idea . . . put them on football pitches and stone the bitches to death.*

LAUGH? I NEARLY DIED

Inevitably the cumulative pressures exacted their price and I was rushed to hospital suffering from a suspected heart attack. My blood pressure was taken three times by a disbelieving nurse. Never one to do things by half measures, I'd achieved a reading beyond the maximum for severe hypertension.

For several hours, as I lay in my hospital bed wired up to an ECG machine, I ran through the events and pressures that had put me there.

Geldof once told me he'd received seventy bin-liners full of mail from desperate dads asking for help. He gave up after just the sixth letter because the pain was too much. Yet here I was, two years on, thousands of letters, emails and telephone calls later. It wouldn't have been so bad, but the enquiries came from all over the bloody planet. From Bromley to Bogotá, Margate to Moscow, a tsunami of humanity surged towards us as we tried to hoover up an ocean of broken people who washed up into the tiny office at Kimsings.

It was overwhelming, dealing with so many people in despair, but then my spirits would be lifted by the breathtaking heroism displayed by some of the fathers who turned to us. Even those who were to betray me deserved recognition for their efforts. What I was going through was as much a crisis of faith as a suspected coronary failure. What was my motivation? What was the motivation of our members? Was it all about vengeance and retribution? Sure, if the tables had been turned and prejudices in the system were skewed in their favour, most fathers would have taken advantage, just as the mothers were doing. That was why our 'Blueprint For Family Law' was so important, with its strategy to reduce conflict by promoting early intervention and mandatory mediation. Retribution never entered into it.

And what about our members? Were the peccadilloes of our members any more unhealthy than those of the average politician? When it comes to racism, sexism, violence and alcoholism, I suspect the behaviour of members of the House of Commons to be infinitely more extreme and depraved than that of our members, but still the criticism and sniping continued unabated. According to some commentators we were all feckless, failed fathers, hell-bent on wreaking vengeance on our ex-partners. To others we were thrill-seeking extreme sports enthusiasts. One paper rather pathetically described me as an attention-seeker, as if it were a crime.

'Well, I wouldn't be very good at my job,' I said to Jenny, post Buckingham Palace, 'if I wasn't getting attention for the cause I campaign for would I? It's what I fucking do.'

Whilst I was the first to acknowledge that not all our dads would have been whiter than white, why was it that if you wanted to see your children after separation, you needed to have been spin dried twice over in Persil and have spent six-months flagellating yourself in barbed wire underpants on the floor of a Tibetan monastery?

If you wanted sainthood, I argued, go find Bono or Bob Geldof. Most of us aren't going to be beatified or canonised and anyone who has lived is going to carry some kind of skeleton-filled baggage with them. It reminded me of the slurs levelled against Dr Martin Luther King that the civil rights movement he fronted was full of communists. King responded by saying that there were 'as many communists in this freedom movement as there were Eskimos in Florida'. I took some comfort in the fact that at least the establishment was attacking us. It might have been unpleasant, but as Jenny pointed out, it signified the impact we had made on the debate.

'I guess you're right Jen,' I told her. 'The cops hate me. The judges hate me. The solicitors hate me. The press hate me – even the splitters in the movement hate me – I must be doing something right.'

In the early days of Fathers 4 Justice we'd been desperate for journalists to cover the campaign. Now I was desperate to keep them out. Throw in a few plainclothes coppers and the odd suspiciously parked van and paranoia started to set in. At least, I told myself it was paranoia. One day, shortly after leaving an F4J meeting in the City, I thought I spotted a couple of Bishopsgate-based plain-clothes police officers on my tail. When I made a sudden run for it, they followed me into the Papermill. After sinking a few jars with Jo, the manager, I got on the phone to Bob Geldof to ask his advice. By this time I was tired, disorientated and befuddled, but his words were sober and forthright. 'Get the fuck out now, get the fuck out of the pub, Matt, and don't let them catch you in there.' I knew I was in trouble when Bob Geldof started telling me to get out of the bar.

My response to the mire of depression was to drink. Alcohol had become my Kryptonite. My penchant for vertical living, whether heading straight up through the roof or crashing back down into the basement, had finally pummelled me into submission. As a spiritual advisor, Sir Jack of Daniels left a lot to be desired; the escape provided by his anaesthetic proved short-lived and my subsequent re-entry into the real world was to be unspeakably painful.

The following morning my brother David found me on the sofa and, when several sadistically sharp prods with a broomstick failed to rouse me, he summoned an ambulance.

'Christ,' said Jen when she arrived on the scene. 'He smells worse than a dead sheep.'

'According to Homer,' said Dave, unhelpfully quoting chunks of Greek mythology, 'he's caught between Scylla and Charybdis.'

'What's that?' asked Jenny.

'They're two monsters in the world of Odysseus. The closer he moves in one direction, say towards the campaign, he's damned; and if he drifts towards depression he's also damned. He's literally caught between a rock and a hard place.'

'You all right, mate?' said a sympathetic voice, somehow penetrating the fog of the living room.

It turned out to be an ambulanceman with a face like a Methodist preacher but the voice of an angel.

'Am I still on this fucking planet?' I slurred.

In October, a few days after Channel 4 screened *Dad's Army: The Men Who Stormed the Palace* as part of a double bill with *Geldof On Fathers*, I did the fashionable thing and went into rehab to uncork.

As it turned out my spell at the centre I visited lasted just three days because everybody else was chain-smoking, smuggling in booze and drugs and engaging in group sex in the upstairs bedrooms. No wonder rehab was so expensive, I thought.

You went in with one addiction.

And left with four.

There were also the modelling fees. A tall, elegant South African lady had admitted me when I arrived and it turned out that she was to be my doctor.

I'll admit it wasn't my finest hour. Triple glazed eyes and breath like Father Jack's week old underpants.

'What's happened to you?' she asked.

'To purloin the words of Tommy Cooper, I've been on a whisky diet.'

'Whisky diet?'

'That's right. I've lost three days already'.

I was later resuscitated on an invigorating tonic of elderflower cordial, which turned out, rather ironically, to be the most expensive bar bill of my entire life.

As I lay back on the couch she wired me up to a variety of drips and began a series of blood tests for a toxicology report. About an hour later she returned carrying a five-foot roll of paper.

'I'm sorry it's taken a bit longer than I expected but we had to run the tests twice because the results were quite extreme. However we have now finished our toxicology and it's quite serious.' The results were delivered with a reassuringly soft and seductive patter and a fake sincerity worthy of an Oscar.

'Technically Mr O'Connor,' she said, 'you should be dead.'

Apparently, I discovered, if you suddenly stop drinking, your body can go into seizure and suffer a sudden cardiac arrest or even a stroke as a consequence.

'I know if I had a choice I'd plump for an old fashioned heart attack over a stroke any day,' I told her. 'Nobody likes a vegetable.'

'Can I ask you, Mr O'Connor, if you are suffering from or have been diagnosed with depression?'

'Well, I think it's fair to say that I'm desperately unhappy.'

'Would you say you had a drink problem?'

'I'd describe it more as a life problem. I understand that people react differently to being under pressure.'

'Perhaps then,' she told me, 'the alcohol is merely a symptom of a deeper psychological malaise.' And with that she left. I stared up at the ceiling and tried to make sense of everything that had happened over the last few years.

When I got back to Suffolk my favourite ex-wife called. We cracked a few jokes about my condition. She said it served me right for getting involved in too many hand-to-hand combats.

'Don't tell me,' I quipped when she tracked me down, 'rehab is for quitters.'

'Why didn't you tell me you'd gone into rehab?' she asked.

'Well it's embarrassing and let's face it, it's all so fucking passé. Everybody who's anybody is in fucking rehab these days. To be honest I feel like such a dick, but I do think I've got issues around reoccurring depression, maybe even bi-polar disorder.'

'Your life's no joke Matt, it's like Vietnam,' she said, 'I know you have a reputation to live down to, but don't take it to the grave. You must stop fighting Quixotic battles and trying to do the honourable thing in spite of yourself. Look at the damage you are doing. You'll kill yourself. You've fought the law and the law won. Give up!'

'Christ's sake Sophie, show some mercy and compassion.' My head was beginning to thump and the conversation was starting to take a sanctimonious, holier-than-thou tone. Over the last few years an underlying current of resentment would occasionally spike the surface of our relationship. Such slips though, were, on the whole, mercifully short lived.

'I'm in recovery,' I said, pleading for understanding. 'I'd been in that place for three days and the RAC still hadn't bloody turned up'.

There was a moment's pause and then we both collapsed laughing.

It transpired that she had had builders around to do some work on the family home. She asked them to paint the front door Cadbury mauve but got Fathers 4 Justice purple instead.

'Everywhere I go, I can't escape it,' she laughed in her throaty Castilian rasp. Given my current predicament and talk of Cadbury's, now seemed like a good time to mention the fact that I was undergoing a character assassination by some executives at one of my other design clients as a result of our high-profile campaign. I'd survived a few shots from behind a grassy knoll before but one woman there had taken a serious dislike to Fathers 4 Justice and my involvement with it. In short there had been discussions about my compatibility with their company, given my profile and involvement with the campaign.

'Well, things could be worse,' I mumbled to Sophie, knowing that this news might ignite her Latino temperament as maintenance might be affected.

'What could be worse than you continually breaching national security, having half the national papers in the country trying to run hatchets on you and your own people sticking the knife in?'

'Well I could lose one of my clients, possibly more, which would leave me in a spot of bother'.

'What sort of bother?'

'Well, financial – but I'm sure I'll get out of it as I have before, it's just that this time round the odds are rather stacked against me and my reputation as a gentleman of culture and creative ability has been besmirched by my little campaign. If I lose the account I'm up the proverbial shit creek without a paddle.' The problem is, I told her, I didn't think about an exit strategy when I started the campaign. I knew how I got here, but I didn't know how to get the fuck out. Sophie took it all in her stride and I breathed a sigh of relief that I hadn't been verbally mangled by her. In fact our little chat had been rather entertaining and my spirits were raised, though as a pioneer of the reverse hangover, my head was feeling worse rather than better and the jokes were wearing thin.

I began to feel angry and ashamed. Worst still I suffered a spate of nightmares, which seemed to have been unlocked in my subconscious. The memories of the courts and the fear of losing the boys never to see them again began to haunt me and at times I was so frightened I didn't want to close my eyes. I was even scared of dying, of going to sleep and never waking up again. The cumulative effects of the last four years were continuing to pile up in a mental road crash.

When Big Ron called, though, normal service was resumed.

'Can't you develop something sexier,' he said, 'like an overnight coke habit?'

'Nice to see that we're still trading in jokes, Ron, instead of throwing punches.'

Once I'd plugged back into the real world the collective view seemed to be that I needed to delegate work out to other people to relieve the pressure on me and the only person with time on his hands was Jason Hatch. Unfortunately it became apparent that Jason might be a little out of his depth as our UK Operations Manager and as I loosened my grip on the organisation, so the problems escalated.

In the meantime there were a series of contretemps with hostile parties. On 30 October 2004 Alan Beith, Chair of the Parliamentary Select Committee, wrote to inform me that as a result of our 'ungentlemanly conduct' F4J would not be invited to give evidence. This would, in effect, deny members of the largest equal-parenting group in the country the opportunity to submit their testimony. Only when Bob Geldof threatened to withdraw in protest did Beith relent and allow us to present our case.

On 3 November I got into a major ding-dong with a fierce-looking Fiona Bruce during an interview for BBC's *Real Story* programme after she made what felt to me like a disingenuous attempt to beat F4J with the domestic violence stick. As we filmed outside Parliament, Bruce was so hostile it was all I could do to stop myself from tipping her into the Thames to cool off.

'Fiona,' I said, trying to placate her, 'please give me a break and let's have an intelligent debate about the issues, not some Salem witchhunt against dads. Unless, of course, you have convicted Fathers 4 Justice already as a bunch of wife-beating, dog-kicking, bush-lurking misogynists.'

Which, of course, she had. A month before, she'd written a piece for *Marie Claire* magazine, headlined 'Cause Célèbre', about a friend who had suffered domestic violence. Fathers 4 Justice made a convenient whipping boy. For Bruce and others like her, Dad had become a dirty word.

And on the subject of causes célèbre . . .

'Kate Winslet!' shrieked Jenny. 'I've got a journalist from the *Mail* on the phone, says her ex-husband Jim Threapleton has joined us. That's news to me because, if he has, he hasn't coughed up his membership fee.'

'Are you sure she isn't pulling your leg?'

'No. She says that he's got access problems with his 4-year-old daughter Mia. Apparently she's in the States a lot with Mum.'

The next day the *Daily Mail* ran a full-page article with the headline: 'Kate's ex joins Batman and the Fathers4Justice' and you couldn't help but think that some of the coverage was getting a bit hysterical.

16

OPERATION CUFF JUSTICE

On 19 November 2004, pressing on with the campaign, we launched 'Operation Cuff Justice', which involved livening up a family law conference at the Lowry Hotel in Manchester with a citizen's arrest on Children's Minister, Margaret Hodge.

The boys had booked a room at the hotel the night before in order to evade any security that would be in place the following morning. Jolly called me just as it was about to happen and I listened in as he walked up to Hodge and announced, 'You're under arrest,' clamping a pair of Ann Summers fluffy leopardskin handcuffs on her.

Apparently Jason had seven shades of shit kicked out of him in the fracas that followed. It took an hour before Jol could be separated from the Minister with a pair of bolt-cutters. The picture made the front cover of the *Evening Standard* under headline 'Protestor Handcuffs Himself to Minister.'

Jolly called me once he was out of nick. 'Bugger me, what a palaver.'

'What happened in the station?'

'Big song and dance about the cuffs.'

'So what's the outcome?'

'No idea, but they mentioned "kidnap and unlawful imprisonment" in passing.'

'What, for the courts keeping children from their fathers?'

'I wish! No, for holding hands with her for forty-five minutes.'

'Christ, you could get damages yourself – mental cruelty and traumatic stress disorder, for starters!'

I called Jo Phillips, Bob Geldof's right-hand woman, to gauge her reaction. To my surprise, it turned out that Bob was delighted, having woken to the news in New York that morning. He described Hodge in terms that, even by his standards, were fairly forceful.

A few days later and Home Secretary David Blunkett had launched an astonishing access bid to see his 2-year-old son, William, after an affair with American-born publisher Kimberly Quinn. It made a change, after all the adverse publicity F4J had been getting, to see a government minister on the receiving end. It was alleged that Quinn was denying him access on the grounds that she disputed paternity, and Blunkett now found himself, as Home Secretary, rather ironically in the same position as many members of Fathers 4 Justice.

In his subsequent resignation statement made on 15 December 2004, after he was accused of fast-tracking a visa for Quinn's nanny, Blunkett said, 'I believe these issues would never have been raised had I not decided in September that I could not walk away from my youngest son. I could not live with myself or believe I had done the best for him in the long term if I had abandoned my relationship with him. I only sought continued access to him through the courts, as I made clear two weeks ago, because all other avenues had been denied me.'

Naturally, we thought Blunkett would raise the issue of the family courts, especially as it was rumoured that he was only to be allowed to see his 'little lad', as he called him in news interviews, for just two supervised hours a month. Blunkett, however, bottled it. Rather than pursue the right course of action, he didn't want to let himself slip any further down the greasy political pole he had spent his entire career climbing, by aligning himself with Fathers 4 Justice. In doing so he let us down, himself down, and perhaps most importantly, he let his son down.

That week Tim Lott wrote in the *Evening Standard*, 'I am happy to confess that I am a fan of Fathers 4 Justice, who have cheekily invited David Blunkett to join them in order to help with his fight for paternity rights over Kimberley Quinn's children.'

Mark Lawson wrote in the *Guardian*, on 4 December 2004, 'Yet events until now have so defied the conventional wisdom of politics that almost any outcome must be considered possible: from Blunkett becoming Britain's first blind, single-father prime minister, to the former home secretary spending a third Blair term hurling condoms filled with purple powder from the public gallery of the Commons while wearing a Fathers 4 Justice T-shirt.'

At least the continuing furore over the Blunkett affair was proving manna from heaven for F4J, with Fleet Street cartoonists creating festive skits based on the premise of Blunkett joining Fathers 4 Justice.

I was still on a learning curve, though, as far as the media were concerned. On a pilot for a new current-affairs-based programme, Morgan & Platell, I was taken in by the good cop, bad cop routine interview technique of Piers Morgan and Amanda Platell. Platell looked like a pussycat but the claws came out halfway through. I decided it was time I started playing these journalists at their own game. Next time I was to be interviewed, I would to dig a little dirt beforehand as an insurance policy in case things turned nasty.

Shortly afterwards I was invited back to do the show for real in the wake of the David Blunkett affair. On 4 December I was invited for another flame-grilling on Morgan & Platell. As always, Piers Morgan seems like a genuinely top bloke, but then I am a lousy judge of character. Amanda Platell was limbering up for her bad-cop routine when I caught up with her.

'Hi, Amanda, you're looking very glammed up. Expecting anybody special on the show today?'

'No, it's only you today, Matt,' she said, giving me a saccharine smile.

'Well, go gently with me this time round. Remember, I'm just a good, clean-living Catholic boy.'

'I've just been doing my homework, Matthew.'

'So have I, Amanda, so perhaps you might not want to pursue some of your more aggressive lines of questioning – especially those that delve into personal morality.'

For once, her steely glint faded. But beyond hinting that I knew something about her, I chose to keep things in my back pocket for insurance purposes in case things turned sour.

In the end the interview went well. I managed to bat most of the balls out of the ground, ending on a crescendo with a volley of quips about the Blunkett affair that regrettably found their way to the cutting room floor for libel reasons.

After the programme I was interviewed by *Third Sector* magazine, a journal for voluntary organisations. Journalist Indira Das-Gupta dubbed me 'Father Chaos', but concluded that, love us or hate us, there was no denying that Fathers 4 Justice had had a phenomenal year. While declining to fill her in on the gory details of the last twelve months, I explained that F4J was very much a work in progress.

'What matters,' I said, 'is that we are moving in the right direction.'

'But, Matt, you must admit that the group has come to enjoy the sort of recognition that charities take years to achieve?'

'I don't think the word "enjoy" is appropriate. Though there have been vertiginous highs, those have been counterbalanced by some fairly serious troughs. It's true, we have stolen the headlines, if only because we have broken the mould as to what voluntary groups can do. The problem is that if you are beholden to your paymasters then you are hamstrung as to how far you can go. We aren't beholden to anyone. We have never and would never accept one penny of government silver.'

'Do you think that perhaps you might be over-exposed?' she asked with a wry smile. 'The *Observer* warned recently that Fathers 4 Justice was in danger of combusting under the weight of its own publicity. Public opinion is going to turn against you.'

'I think we can dismiss that opinion, can't we? The wise thing is to stop when we are in danger of becoming an irritation to the public. If and when that day comes, I'll act accordingly. In the meantime, every opinion poll I've seen shows us surfing a wave of 75 per cent public support. Show me a political party that gets that! What political commentators and the public think are two very different things.'

In another example of shameless exhibitionism I agreed to demean myself by donning the trademark Father Christmas outfit for a few happy snaps to accompany the feature.

'I look such a twat, don't I?' I challenged her. 'How many of your charities have people stupid enough to get involved in this malarkey?'

'Not many, I'll admit.'

'It's all bloody showbiz anyhow. Can't be any worse than what our ecumenical leaders are wearing this season.'

As I slung the sack over my shoulder, she wrapped up the interview with a parting shot. 'You seem under pressure, Matt. You said that you have had tip-offs about undercover journalists trying to infiltrate the group. How long will you pursue this campaign?'

'Until either I keel over or we change the law. Inevitably, what goes up must come down. I know, or at least I think I know, what's going to happen next. It's all there in the history books. Every lesson for people like me has already been laid out for us to read. Even though the future is clouded, I reckon we are going to hit some pretty major turbulence in the next year.'

With that we concluded the interview. She asked if I wanted to go out for a drink, but I opted instead to return to camp and evaluate the coming year's campaign and the possibility of serious trouble ahead.

On Saturday 4 December Morgan & Platell was broadcast to favourable reviews. The programme had been cleverly edited as becomes a firing-squad style interview, but considering it was a heavyweight political show with big hitters such as John Reid, George Osborne and George Galloway guesting, I didn't think I performed too badly and we got a steady slew of complimentary emails at HQ.

Dear Matt,
I just wanted to offer my support to your organisation. I find myself in the same position as so many people you deal with every day. I'm watching my

boyfriend struggle to see his children and feel ashamed of all women who play this extremely cruel and spiteful game. Every day that goes by, I pray to God that things change. Every time I hear 'fathers 4 justice' . . . I smile and hope! Well done to every one of you!!! Keep on fighting!
   Ruth I.

Dear Fathers-4-Justice
I just watched Matt O'Connor on the television programme Morgan and Platell. Most people have seen or heard of the F4J campaign efforts but I hadn't heard Matt himself talking about his experience or the fundamentals of the campaign. I am writing to you to say how much I enjoyed listening to Matt argue his case. His facts and references were well put, he was articulate and fluent and obviously a great ambassador for the campaign. It's just as well he hasn't been shot as you would have lost a great power source. Well done Matt. I hope you succeed.
   David H.

TRAFFIC JAM

By Christmas 2004 it was time for a change of tactic where Scotland Yard was concerned, too. Fond as I had become of Adrian Laurie over the years we'd been liaising with the Operational Planning Department, when negotiations for our forthcoming Christmas demo broke down I decided to try a new approach. Disinformation.

I put out a press release announcing that F4J, having obtained a substantial quantity of raspberry jam, were planning to spread it on the M25 as part of our latest stunt, 'Traffic Jam'. For a few hours, we toyed with the idea of actually going through with it, even contacting Chivers Hartley, the jam people, to research what would be involved in such an escapade. It turned out that jam is delivered in plastic pillows which in turn could be emptied into plastic drums which in turn could be emptied on to the M25 from the back of a van. Vehicles behind the van would hold traffic back and activists would place cones around said jam to prevent them driving into it. In the end, we rejected the idea and opted to stick to the disinformation tactic.

The bellicose Nick Ferrari from LBC Radio took the bait. I agreed to a phone interview on his morning show, which kicked off with Nick asking what we had planned.

'It's like this, Nick: we've got two tons of jam and we're going to use it.'
'Where exactly, Matt?'

'Wherever it will create the biggest jam.'

Over the next few hours we fielded hundreds of calls from concerned travellers asking for further details. The Metropolitan Police Authority leapt into action, authorising additional patrol cars and stationing road-cleaning equipment at every junction on the M25. The reported cost was £250,000 – all for something that was never going to happen.

The following morning, Nick Ferrari called again.

'You bottled it, didn't you, Matt?' he said.

'No, Nick,' I replied. 'We couldn't get a knife big enough to spread the stuff on with.'

DING-DONG MERRILY ON HIGH

Christmas was wrecked by an ill-considered nocturnal gallop to Sandringham where our posse of twenty Santas, armed with a 'Ding Dong Merrily on High' David Blunkett banner, were to scale the roof of the church in time for the Queen's regular Christmas Service. Things began to go horribly wrong from the moment the boys turned up at my country pile, around 11 p.m. on Christmas Eve, the worse for wear after imbibing too much festive cheer.

'At ease, gents,' I said, picking my way through the bodies scattered across the floor of my lounge.

''Ello, Matt, fancy a sweeg?' cried one chap, staggering to his feet and waving a bottle of Bell's in my direction.

'Nah, I don't drink that standard-blend stuff. Besides, you need to be in tip-top condition for a few hours' time.'

'Easa goin' be a lucky eefa weea git up onda churchy wiffou gittin shot.'

All I could think as I surveyed the bunch of turkeys laid out in front of me, was that I'd given up a cosy Christmas shacked up with my then girlfriend Giselle for this. Given my 'Fathers 4 Justice' lifestyle it was about as conducive to romance as chestnut stuffing was to festive fowl. I wasn't best pleased.

At about 2.30 a.m. Jolly rolled up, umming and ahhing about whether or not he should join in the festivities. He had two crazed canines in tow. 'Mind looking after these two, Matt, if we get nicked?'

'How could I resist? After all, I have slept with them both before.'

'When was that?'

'When we had that coordinators conference at the City Inn hotel in Bristol and I woke up in the morning with a pair of dog's bollocks nuzzled in my face. Remember?'

'So what's the plan?'

'Well, we seem to have a few too many people for a change, some of whom don't look as if they can get vertical, let alone scale a church.' I went on to outline the plan in detail, but Jol looked far from convinced. 'I agree, it's a tough one. It's pitch black and you're in the middle of woods being patrolled by MI5. That's why nobody should stick a Santa suit on until you find the thing.'

'But we don't have time for that, Matt. We'll need to run as soon as we find it. Haven't we got any combat gear so we could blend in a bit more?'

'What do you think? Course we fucking haven't. You could go cunningly disguised as a Christmas Tree with a fairy on your bonce, a bulb in your gob and a fucking great plug up your arse. I'm sure that will have them convinced.'

Somehow we roused the sozzled Santas and, having issued them with specific instructions, I followed in my Mini, directing them from a mile away. But it was as black as black could be, nothing but indefinable woodland cloaked in darkness and no identifiable landmarks. They were still driving around the estate looking for the church when the vans were lit up by the headlights of a fleet of black MI5 Range Rovers. Some guys made a run for the church, only to be met with armed police and a pack of snarling Alsatians.

I finally caught up with coordinator John Levis in the main car park at about 8 a.m.

'Matt, it's all gone tits up. I didn't see much, but they got hammered.'

I decided to waft around to the church entrance, but it was being watched. A officer immediately approached me. 'Morning, sir.'

'Felicitations to you.'

'Here for the Queen then, sir?'

'In a manner of speaking.'

More quickly than you could say 'Christmas crackers', eleven of the boys had been hauled off to spend Christmas Day residing in the cells at King's Lynn police station on no charge other than some spurious claim that a dozen bad Santas had been found loitering with intent in the woods next to Sandringham.

Dejected, I returned to the ranch to share Christmas dinner with Jol's dogs.

THE FATHERS 4 JUSTICE CELL SURVIVAL GUIDE

OK, so you've been nicked on a job and you're settling in for your first night, care of Her Majesty's minimalist hotel chain. If you haven't worked this one out already, the first thing I look for in overnight accommodation is a mini-bar. Sadly these rooms are strictly 'no thrills'. But don't worry, after all, what's the worst that can happen? Generally, it's room service. Or lack of it. The menu doesn't exactly scream Michelin stars. For a start, there's the fresh-off-the-pavement microwaved doggy-doo that passes as police standard-issue Chilli Con Carne. Come back, McDonalds, all is forgiven! At least the tea is highly quaffable. Enjoy!

The management like to soften you up with what I'd call 'tough love' and a rough-and-ready bedside manner. Generally the cells are equipped with a plastic-covered foam mattress and no pillows or Egyptian linen. This is minimalist with a capital 'M'. Your room will also be wired, so if you end up sharing a cell with a colleague, don't chat about the day's events. If you are clever, you might get away with the old F4J trick of slipping your mobile between your arse cheeks or concealing your SIM cards in your socks. However, if they catch you gassing on your mobley and blowing kisses to your girlfriend, you might end up with an Abu Ghraib-style strip-search and a stint sewing mailbags for the rest of the week.

The general rules are:

1. Dispose of any incriminating evidence before you are booked in. Eat and swallow any paper trail PDQ.
2. The custody 'suite' is NOT like a hotel suite. It's where you give your name and details.
3. The only interview you should give is a 'no comment' interview. We don't like 'squealers', so just remember to remain strong and silent and not slip into a bout of verbal dysentery. Every copper will tell you how they agree with you and sympathise. At York police station a detective inspector said his daughter had been sitting in the choir when I gave my sermon and she'd told him how it was. If I'd said, 'Thanks, it wasn't too bad, if I say so myself,' I would have admitted to being there. They're only pandering to your ego to get you to spill the beans.
4. Don't be bullied. When one of them threatened to strip search me to look for DNA that would prove I was in York Minster, I told him to go forth and multiply.
5. Final rule-of-thumb guide – whatever the policeman says, if in doubt, do the opposite. The Bill tell major porkies. Period.

F4J AND THE FBI

On 4 January 2005 Jol and Jason set off for New York on a five-day reconnaissance mission. I had hoped to travel with them, but work commitments forced me to pull out at the last minute. The plan was to hook up with our US coordinator, Jamil Jabr, and pull off an Anglo-American stunt with Batman and Captain America on the Brooklyn Bridge. The risks involved were considerable, but after conducting copious amounts of research we thought we should give it a go.

After a meeting with Susan Dominus, a senior journalist from the *New York Times* who had contacted me with a view to writing a substantial piece about Fathers 4 Justice, the boys called in a panic. Susan told them she thought they were being tailed by the FBI. It sounded to me as if they were looking for an excuse to chicken out and do a tourist jaunt around New York. After paying out several thousand pounds of F4J funds to finance the trip, that just wasn't an option as far as I was concerned.

'What's the story, Jol? Are you seriously telling me you think the FBI are on your tail?'

'That's what Susan thinks and, I'll admit, a couple of people at the hotel do look familiar. Jason was held at John F. Kennedy airport by the authorities for several hours on the way through and he was interviewed by the police – they were also asking where you were.'

'Well, tell them they'll have a long fucking wait for me to arrive Stateside. I just can't believe that you've already got the FBI with you. Are you sure you're not pulling my fucking leg, Jolly?'

'Honest, Matt. We hadn't noticed, but Susan's here – do you want to speak to her?'

'I'd better, I guess.'

Jolly put Susan on. 'Well, Matt, this is the United States. They don't miss a trick, especially if you arrive through JFK airport. At least you know your reputation goes before you. I can't see Jolly or Jason doing anything if that is the case; they'll be on them in seconds.'

I paused for a moment before deciding that there was only one way of finding out for certain. The boys would have to do a runner.

'Right, Jolly, I want the pair of you to exit the lobby at the same time and then split, one of you goes one way, the other belts up the other side of the street. Run like hell and see what happens, but for fuck's sake don't do anything stupid.'

'All right, Matt, I'll speak to Jason.' Jolly sounded worryingly relaxed, which, to be fair, is his modus operandi, but this was New York post 9/11 and we had no idea how the cops or FBI would react.

The boys made their way out of the lobby, leaving a nervy Jamil with Susan Dominus. Just a few feet outside they peeled off in different directions, sprinting up the pavements adjacent to the hotel only for carloads of FBI officers to spill out on to the street.

'OK, boys, easy does it. You going somewhere?' an FBI agent asked Jolly. 'We've got people everywhere, so you're not going anywhere without us.'

'What people?' said Jolly, in his unflappable West Country accent.

'Three cars, nine guys on my team and a back-up team of five in case we lose you. You're the biggest security threat to New York City at this time.'

'Fuck me,' Jolly said, recoiling in disbelief. 'Wait till Matt hears this.'

'Look,' the man approached Jolly, resting a hand on his shoulder while pulling a picture of Jolly from his pocket. 'We've got pictures of you, Jason, Matt, everyone, so don't think you're going to be climbing any bridges in this city. In the meantime, you're going back in a few days, let us show you a good time in New York.'

Jolly returned to the hotel lobby and called me.

'All right, Matt?'

'Fuck it, Jol, what happened?'

'Well, I thought they looked familiar. Apparently they have a room next to us in the hotel with listening equipment, the full works. They even know about that banner artwork you sent to the bureau in Manhattan.'

'Didn't you notice them? I mean, if they've been with you the whole fucking time...'

'It's not something you run into much, down in Devon.'

'What did they say?'

'They said that Fathers 4 Justice were the biggest security threat to New York City at this time.'

'You what? Fathers 4 Justice? Fuck off!'

'No, Matt, I'm being serious. These guys aren't fucking around, we've got a whole squad with us, the full works, it's like something out of a movie. You'd love it.'

'Fuck me gently, who'd have thought it?'

'It seems, Matt, that they want to be our tour guides for the next few days, show us round and everything.'

I sank back into my chair, genuinely stupefied by the level of surveillance we were now under. 'At least it's comforting to know that the police keep a close eye on us even when we're outside our own country.'

'So what's the plan now, Matt?'

'Well, it's a fucking expensive vacation. At least check out the Brooklyn Bridge, get some happy snaps and email them back to me. If these guys are stuck to you, what else can you do? Jack fucking shit.'

And so Fathers 4 Justice left the hotel in a cab, followed by top *New York Times* journalist Susan Dominus and three carloads of FBI agents. It all sounded surreal, even by our madcap standards: a cortège of cars rolling round the streets of New York City. All we were missing was a police helicopter.

The FBI even offered to escort the boys to various downtown nightclubs, passing them off as royalty in a bid to prevent them from donning capes and scaling the Brooklyn Bridge.

The entire enterprise had been a shocking waste of valuable resources. There was no denying that our plans had been well and truly scuppered by the Federal Bureau of Investigations.

BIG BOTHER

On the boys' return, Jason shot up to Suffolk and we immediately got stuck into another plan: our first attempt at live agitprop direct action on national television. The target was Channel 4 and Endemol's *Celebrity Big Brother*. We wanted to reach the young men who watched the programme, some of whom would be fathers themselves, and make them aware that they had little or no rights in law to see their children. The plan was to get into the ferociously guarded compound with a small army of about twenty activists, deliver food to the contestants, and place a banner with a picture of Home Secretary David Blunkett dressed as Batman on the roof. On the night, though, it became clear that somebody had leaked the plan to the authorities.

While I had toyed with the idea of activists dropping into the house using powermotor parachutes, in the end we opted for old-fashioned ladders and sheer courage. Once they were over the perimeter fence, however, the plan quickly fell apart. Fireworks placed as a decoy device at the main entrance instead lit up half of Borehamwood, bathing our activists in a pyrotechnical glow. Within seconds ex-SAS men who were patrolling the site with rottweilers began picking off the boys as they trod their way across a muddy no man's land towards the internal fence where the Big Brother house and garden were. Minutes later a police helicopter was mobilised, scanning the ground using a thermal-imaging device.

I called Jason on his mobile as he lay concealed under a bush.

'They've nicked my fucking ladder,' he whispered angrily. 'They can't take that. I even got it back after Buck Palace. How can I get up on the bloody wall now?'

'Where are you?'

'Face down in shit and shrubbery,' he panted, 'with a pack of man-eating rottweilers sniffing around. Can't we do something easier next time round, like *Celebrity Love Island*? This makes Buck House look easy.'

The next day Jason reported in from St Alban's police station. The body count totalled fifteen arrests. The *Sun* newspaper reported that *Big Brother* chiefs had hired more ex-SAS security men amid fears we would hijack the show's finale.

The following week I discovered that I had been nominated for the Great Briton Awards 2005. What sweet irony! Not only had I been shortlisted among the twenty candidates, but the ceremony was to take place in that cathedral of cruelty, the Royal Courts of Justice. On the night, Coxy, Burchy and Jason joined me, hoping to absorb as much hospitality as they could throw at us, like the social sponges we are.

'God forbid you win,' said Burchy. 'It'll be, "Oh shit, Oh fuck, O'Connor!"'

In the end the richly deserving Jane Tomlinson claimed the award for best campaigner, but we spent an enjoyable evening, highly enriched by the sight of my ugly mug projected on to the wall of the great hall.

'Now that's what I call justice,' I quipped. 'Never thought I'd see the day when there would be a 30-foot picture of me in the Royal Courts!'

A few weeks later, and we picked up another nomination, this time, for the second year running, for the Channel 4 Political Awards. Amanda Platell, who had been former Conservative leader William Hague's ill-fated spin doctor, sidled up to me, an intoxicating blur of fragrance and friendliness with a blow-torch smile that could melt an ice cap at the other end of the world. We exchanged pleasantries for a few minutes before she sidled off, her glass of bubbly held at a suitably un-conservative angle.

With the award bashes out of the way, it was time to get back to the nitty gritty. Since starting F4J I'd chewed up 120,000 miles of tarmac in my Mini, trying to build support in a never-ending tour of duty across the country. This time, it was Southampton, where our South Coast team had been going great guns. Despite my reservations about one of our coordinators, it seemed he had done a great job in motivating people and getting the all-important bums on seats. The meeting was rammed with supporters, including one attractive woman who was furiously scribbling notes on a pad. She looked like a journalist and stood out like a pork pie at a Jewish wedding. Eventually my curiosity got the better of me and I approached. At first I took her to be a bit stand offish, but she was wearing a smouldering, full-bodied pout that would make a lollypop happy. That on its own was enough to win me over. She told me her name was Nadine Taylor, and she was going through a messy divorce. She'd come to the meeting looking for advice, or to check out the other side of the story. Either way, I set my people the task of checking her out to make sure she was bona fide.

A few days later I attended a debate at the Oxford Union. My fellow speaker was campaigner Peter Tatchell, a man I'd long admired. Quiet and unassuming, yet with a steely look of determination in his eye, Peter was an impressive presence. I felt humbled both by the man and his achievements.

Campaign colleague Richard Castle, a.k.a. 'the Fat Italian', had come as my guest, but he somewhat undermined my good work by getting entangled with another generously proportioned female guest who was a member of the League Against Cruel Sports – though you'd never have thought so from the way she was devouring Richard. A Chianti-veined purveyor of 'vino collapso', Richard looked like the long-lost love child of John Travolta and Danny de Vito, but lurking beneath his well-fed exterior lay a man who had been poisoned by contact denial and sucked into the courts by a tractor beam of conflict and secrecy. His daughter Jennifer had been taken to Forres near Inverness some four years earlier. Despite shelling out over £40,000 in child maintenance in that time, neither Richard nor his 71-year-old mother had seen the girl since.

My second guest was Susan Dominus, who had flown over to interview Jason and me for the *New York Times* Sunday magazine cover story and was only too delighted to tag along to Oxford. That weekend she joined me at a coordinators conference at F4J supporter Charlie Baker's Stretton Hall Hotel. CAFCASS chief executive Anthony Douglas was also in attendance.

Unlike our previous conference, this meeting of minds ran smoothly enough – unsurprisingly, given the threat of immediate expulsion for anyone who broke ranks. Douglas was a revelation at conference and a stark contrast to his predecessor, an implacably hostile civil servant called Jonathan Tross. Tross had presided over CAFCASS at a time when a House of Commons Constitutional Affairs Select Committee condemned the organisation, commenting: 'CAFCASS's failure to establish even a minimum training and professional development strand appears to be one of their more serious shortcomings ... in the absence of data, the identification of what might be best for any particular child in any particular case is fraught with difficulty.' Tross was suspended, then dismissed, the Chairman resigned and the entire board was sacked by the government. The arrival of Douglas signalled a new dawn for an organisation that was in meltdown.

A man in his late forties with a tidy crop of greying hair, Douglas was a calm, softly spoken man who carefully marshalled his words, though he had a disconcerting tendency to lapse into mumbo-jumbo psycho-babble. We managed to establish a rapprochement between our two organisations, agreeing several key points that they would work on, including a new case-recording system and a move away from time-consuming Section 7 reports to briefer, more focused report writing and early interventions. More significantly, they would agree that Shared Parenting would become the starting point in all residence and contact disputes. Even 'Parental Alienation', where a child is turned by the parent with care against the other parent, would be recognised.

Over lunch, we engaged in a frank discussion of our differences.

'You see, Anthony, I think you apply the public law thinking that involves social workers, where children are often in danger, and apply it to private law cases that involve families in breakdown. Do you think that colours your view? Having been a Director of Social Services yourself?'

Douglas paused for a moment before delivering a considered and insightful answer.

'I was adopted,' he said, 'and it's very much shaped my thinking and who I am. The thing is, there are casualties when families break down. Children want their parents to be together and sometimes the biggest issue is how to keep siblings together. One might go one way, one the other, but I don't accept that how we work in private law cases is affected by our experiences in public law. It is a very difficult and personally draining area to work in. These cases are very hard to resolve, but it's also incredibly rewarding when we do get it right.'

'But don't you accept,' I ask him, 'that if we have a clearly defined law, a presumption of shared parenting on the statute book, combined with early interventions and mandatory mediation, most of your work would evaporate overnight? Instead of writing endless reports you would have trained, skilled mediators banging heads together and resolving these issues constructively for the benefit of children, rather than having their parents slug it out to the point where they become emotionally and economically bankrupt.'

'But, Matthew, it's like this ...' he stared hard into my eyes, craning his neck towards me. 'We both know there is big money in conflict. Our mark of success would be if cases are resolved in six months and the parents have found peace instead of conflict and moved on, but it isn't like that. The average length of cases is between four and five years.'

'And look at the damage that is doing.'

'I know, but there is resistance to your campaign of change, not least from civil servants who are trying to veto the reforms that Harriet Harman is looking to introduce. I don't think you can look at your campaign in a matter of three or five years, but over twenty-five years. There isn't any political will at the moment, despite all your efforts. All we are dealing with is the symptoms, not the causes.'

I was taken aback by his frankness. 'Looks like we're in for a long-distance marathon then, rather than a sprint for justice. I hate long-distance running, Anthony. I really hate it.'

If a senior figure in the family justice system was that damning, what must the rest of the family law professionals working at the coal face be thinking?

'Look, Anthony,' I said, 'we've given CAFCASS a right hammering in the last few years, and to some extent we've been quite right to do that, but I can't escape the impression that all is not well at your end – if I'm reading between the lines correctly. You have my word that we'll create a "green zone" around CAFCASS and won't engage in any further direct action for the foreseeable future, unless you guys renege on your commitment to shared parenting. I'd much rather you plug us into the loop while we go fry some bigger fish.'

'Thanks, Matt, I appreciate that.'

'It's the right thing to do, to give you some space, but I'll probably get crucified for doing a deal with the devil. Sometimes, though, we need to make political and tactical decisions.'

'Is there a danger of a split in the organisation?'

'There's always a danger of us doing the splits. I don't know how much longer I can carry everybody along. We've already had rumblings here and there, but if there are problems we'll let you know. You have to laugh about it, though.'

'Why's that?'

'I'm not sure who has the worst job. You trying to carry your organisation, or me trying to carry mine.'

That evening a crowd of us headed off for a raucous joint birthday party for Jason and me at a grimy French restaurant in Shrewsbury. My girlfriend Giselle had come along for the ride, albeit she made it clear that scrapes and japes didn't make for great dates and that our relationship was in terminal decline. Over the last few years, maintaining any kind of friendship with the opposite sex was hampered by my life less ordinary and the closest thing I was getting to a personal relationship were the dulcet tones of the lovely Jane – the speaking voice on my Mini's sat nav. However, Giselle was phenomenal fun and all weekend she had effortlessly oozed cosmopolitan chic, and New York-based Dominus and her husband, who joined us for the soirée, were smitten with her.

'Any girl who rolls up at the ranch from London with a bottle of Laurent Perrier rosé champagne in an ice bucket in her car is fine by me, Susan,' I laughed, as the merriment overwhelmed any semblance of dining-room etiquette.

Birthday celebrations aside, there was another more serious reason for the soirée. We were in the process of planning another protest, this time at Downing Street. Yet again the plan was mind-numbingly simple. Jason would hire a van, pick up activists Pete Chipping and Andy James en route, and drive to London, rolling up on to the pavement outside the Foreign and Commonwealth Office just 100 yards from Downing Street. Dressed in reflective jackets, they would place a ladder against the side of the building and climb to a ledge 50 feet up which would take them round into Downing Street, where they would strip off their workmen's attire to reveal superhero cozzies.

'Piece of piss, Matt. Should run smoother than a baby's bottom. How do you think it will play?' asked Jason.

'Well, I think we'll have exhausted every last drop of PR out of this campaign theme with this one, so I want to ditch the superheroes and work up some fresh ideas.'

Jason looked disappointed, but every campaign has a use-by date, and this one had long since expired.

That Monday morning as I walked down Whitehall I saw a rolling road-block, where police had set up mobile stopping points in different parts of Whitehall. Each roadblock remained for some ten or fifteen minutes before being moved to another section. I warned Hatchy to hang fire for an hour until it cleared, then parked up with Giselle and Susan Dominus at the coffee shop of the Charing Cross Thistle Hotel, a venue that had become a favourite of ours after the Buckingham Palace protest. Susan asked whether I thought it was odd that I didn't come from a conventional campaigning background.

'Well, I did, at least when I was younger,' I said.

'But most leaders of social movements hail from the ranks of unions, sweatshops and churches. You were a brand designer for hip restaurants and food products,' she pointed out.

'I guess so, but I never lost the fire in my belly, it's just that the family courts ignited my passion again.' Giselle was sitting opposite me, looking très chic again, this time in oversized sunglasses under a broad hat.

'I'm not sure I can put up with this much longer, Matt,' she told me when Susan broke away to take a call from New York. 'It's very exciting, but I want stability and I'm not sure I'm going to find much of that where you are standing.' I smiled back at her, knowing that she was dead right. It was no life, being attached to some lunatic with a death-wish penchant for breaching national security. We were in the process of discussing the end of our relationship when my phone crackled into life. It was Jason.

'I'm up,' he said, and then the phone went dead.

I grabbed the girls and we piled into a cab as police sirens filled the air. The police hadn't realised anything out of the ordinary was going on until a crowd of tourists queuing at the gate of Downing Street started cheering the protestors. Apparently somebody shouted, 'They're behind you!' and in authentic pantomime tradition a copper turned round, muttered the words 'Oh shit', then radioed for assistance.

A cluster of boys in school blazers waved up to the men and Hatchy gave a typically theatrical flourish when he put on his mask and twirled his cape. Beneath him, six or seven teenage girls, also waving wildly, started screaming and blowing him kisses. Jason being Jason, he couldn't resist blowing a few back.

As I stood quietly on the other side of the road from Downing Street, orchestrating the press, it was clear to me that we had exhausted the PR value in this campaign theme. Within ten minutes I felt a tap on my shoulder and turned to see Adrian and Andy from Scotland Yard.

'Fancy meeting you here, Matt,' said Andy Sharp with more than a hint of sarcasm.

'Guys!' I exclaim. 'So this is what it takes to get you out of the office.'

'What's happening then, Matt?' asks Andy.

'Well, I was just walking through London on this delightful Monday afternoon and I happened to come across a triumvirate of superheroes positioned on the corner of Downing Street. I thought it looked jolly spectacular.'

'Matt, come on,' said Adrian. 'This has your fingerprints all over it. I bet you've been busy down here orchestrating this.'

'You may say that, Adrian, but I couldn't possibly comment,' I retorted, doing my best House of Cards impression. 'I'm just the song-and-dance man.'

Most of the nationals ran the story the next day, with the *Daily Mail* dedicating the whole of page three, under the headline 'They made a nonsense of Commons security and fools of the Palace guards ... now they've done it again in the PM's front yard'.

Sadly the demo also marked the end of my short-but-sweet relationship with Giselle.

'Your universe moves too fast for anyone else to keep up, Matt,' she told me. For once, I couldn't argue.

THE UNIVERSITY OF ADVERSITY

Our occasional victories were now being played out against an unsavoury back-drop as the campaign for equal parenting descended into madness and mayhem. 'Inside Fathers 4 Justice: Racism, Sexism, Violence' screamed the front-page headline on the front of the *Portsmouth Evening News* in early 2005, in an article that made a series of serious allegations against two of our South Coast coordinators. In one instance we subsequently discovered that one of them had been pocketing membership fees collected in cash at meetings. It was a shocker. A thousand-volt jolt straight to the heart of F4J that shook me to my jowls. The man was suspended immediately and eventually turfed out, but not before he'd lobbed a few threats in my direction.

'I've killed sixteen people, Matt, don't fuck with me,' he warned, claiming to be an ex-mercenary.

When I drove down to Southampton with Jason Hatch and Barrister Michael Cox to take charge of the local group's next meeting there was a collective sense of foreboding that something wasn't right. A man-mountain whom I'll call 'Mark', although that's not his real name, was circling the bar menacingly. As bald as bald could be, he looked half-man, half-walrus. Another guy was wandering around so shit-faced it was a miracle he was still standing. The man, who was known to suffer from serious mental health problems, had been plied with alcohol all afternoon by Mark, who we later discovered was an agent provocateur and thug hired by a major television company.

About halfway through the meeting I had to leave to head back to Suffolk. I had a sense that something might kick off, but even so I was shocked to get a call saying that both Jason Hatch and Michael Cox had been assaulted by the man Mark had been buying drinks for. Remarkably, Mark just stood back and watched from a distance until the man was restrained and ejected from the meeting. It was the first time there had ever been any violence at an F4J meeting. We were certain it had been orchestrated, but by whom? Our ex-coordinator? The television company? Or somebody else?

It wasn't all bad news, however. An Oxford graduate had turned up, offering to help out by conducting more meticulous and thorough research than we'd been able to. An affable chap, Nick Langford was softly spoken with something of the author Truman Capote about him. An incisive thinker with a razor-sharp mind, Nick quickly began to make substantial contributions to the philosophical substance and direction of the campaign. Whereas I am a big-picture man, Nick was able to examine the minutiae and expand it into easily understandable facts without the waffle.

That Saturday, finding myself loveless once more, I agreed to meet up with Nadine Taylor for lunch at Hakkasan, a hip, sophisticated restaurant ensconced in a Tottenham Court Road basement. At the time, I remember thinking I'd seen more meat on a butcher's pencil, but then lord knows what she made of the slab of Irish beef sitting opposite her.

We got off to a somewhat tense start, picking through the details of her separation and the various contact problems she was experiencing with her ex-husband, none of which made for stimulating table talk. Once we'd circumnavigated the case, I told her that we'd do what we could to assist. After all, we were in the business of promoting equal parenting. I made it clear that, if she wanted our help, it was a philosophy she would have to subscribe to.

'So what exactly is the problem with contact?' I asked bluntly, midway through a course of sublime melt-in-your-mouth roast duck.

'It goes back to when I left him. I panicked when I discovered he had applied for sole residency of my daughter. He's never forgiven me for leaving,' she whispered.

'But he has contact, right?'

'Yes, he does, but he doesn't want shared residence, he wants sole residency.'

Fearing lunch might be overwhelmed with a distasteful mix of bitterness and rancour, I changed the conversation quickly.

'Great eh?' I said to her. 'Between the two of us, we have enough excess baggage to ground a 747.' Nadine started to laugh and I decided to switch subjects on to something a bit brighter.

'Didn't your mummy tell you, you shouldn't go out with strangers?' I quipped.

'But I know who you are.'

'Do you?'

'I hear you break the law a lot,' she said brightly.

'It's become something of a vocation for me.'

'But you seem very cautious,' she continued. 'Suspicious actually if you don't mind me saying.'

'Having a reputation to live down to makes me cautious. Well, let's just say I'm not very trusting. My faith in people has been shaken over the last few years.' Nadine smiled at me, a smile that spread like an electric charge across her face.

'You look like somebody has just plugged you back into life,' I tell her. 'Your face just lit up.'

'Maybe it's a trick of the darkness,' she said.

Whatever, I thought. As we spent the rest of the day carousing my favourite London watering holes I had an unnerving feeling that I was falling under her spell. It was the start of a relationship that was to have a profound effect on me and the destination of Fathers 4 Justice.

The *Daily Mail* got wind of our liaison and wanted to run a feature, which I stupidly agreed to do. With typical *Mail* disdain they poured scorn on our relationship, dismissing Nadine as a pitiful creature with a vulnerable demeanour, while describing yours truly as a 24/7 fully paid-up alky with psychopathic tendencies.

Someone must have taken the allegations seriously. In late March I got a call from a mysterious American asking if Fathers 4 Justice were available for hire.

'What, like the A Team?' I asked facetiously.

'I need you to do a job,' he drawled. 'How much would you charge to disrupt the wedding of Charles and Camilla?'

I thanked him for his inquiry but made it clear that F4J was not for hire.

FROM HELLRAISER TO HOMEMAKER

On Friday 20 May, I was in the office being interviewed by a freelance journalist about my views on abortion. It seemed an odd request but I said that, in principle, I was against it. The next call I got was from Nadine. There was a disconcerting pause before she broke down, sobbing uncontrollably.

'What's wrong, darling?' I asked.

'I think I'm, I'm ... pregnant,' she whimpered.

'What? How? When? Where?' I could feel the blood draining from my face.

'Brighton ...' she said.

'What? That weekend in Brighton?'

So now we had another souvenir to go with the 'Kiss Me Quick' hat and stick of Brighton rock.

I'd only been going out with Nadine for a few months. But I never expected to end up with a subscription to CBeebies, watching repeats of the

Tellytubbies I'd watched first time round with my two eldest boys. Or being knee-high in shitty nappies again. Even so, once over the shock, we were both happy and relaxed about the news.

'Don't forget, darling,' I told her, 'at least you'll be one of the few people who can claim to have slept with Father Christmas.'

I called my brother, who was instantly unsympathetic.

'I'm surprised your sperm wasn't swimming backwards after the year you've had,' he remarked. 'Anyway she doesn't need another child when she's got you.'

But for the first time in five years I began to feel grounded. It felt as if I was slowly emerging from a tunnel of darkness and that this slow-burning love of home would leave me feeling comforted and sheltered, rather than exposed and burnt. I succumbed at last to the gravitational pull of normality and the spiritual nourishment of nights in enjoying pan-fried fillet steak and pommes frites, washed down with elderflower cordial, in time to crash and snore by 9 p.m. Nadine wasn't always impressed with the aftermath.

'Christ, Matt,' she said to me one night, 'you don't half make a lot of mess when you cook.'

'Wherever I go I tend to make a lot of mess, I'm afraid,' I responded, asking for her tender forgiveness. 'Besides, this is saintly behaviour for me. I don't smoke, gamble, or philander, and I barely drink – rumour has it the beatification is in the post. But I have developed a worrying taste for Chupa Chup lollypops. Do you think that qualifies as an addiction?'

'Only if your teeth fall out,' she said reassuringly.

Still uncertain of my ground, I probed carefully to check that she knew what she might be letting herself in for, taking me on as her partner. But Nadine soon reassured me that everything would be fine, and Archie's birth in December 2005 proved her right.

MAY CONTAIN TRACES OF NUTS

At the beginning of May, I took off for the States with Nadine. With Susan Dominus's F4J story due to appear on the cover of the *New York Times* magazine that coming weekend, it seemed the perfect time to hook up with our US coordinator, Jamil Jabr, and thrash out a US strategy for the group. Even though we'd been forced to abandon our previous mission to New York, we had continued to plot ways of exploiting the phenomenal potential for the group in the States. I had identified a series of possible sites for 'benign' protests including the Golden Gate Bridge and the Hollywood Sign, which we were going to scale and cover the letters 'Hollyw' with a banner in the same type style so that the sign would read 'Fatherhood'. I'd also worked up a Pythonesque idea for an epic journey on horseback from New York to San Francisco dressed as Knights of the Round Table, a display of eccentric British expeditionary spirit that would be sure to go down well with the American public.

I had no concerns whatsoever about leaving Jabr to run the show. He had signed all his agreements in the presence of a notary and seemed totally at ease and on message, although the boys had reported back in January that he'd turned Shrek green when the topic of civil disobedience came up.

For some reason, Jamil was unable to meet us in New York, so he suggested that we fly to Minneapolis and St Paul instead. We were only planning to spend a few days in the 'Twin Cities', yet for the first day or so we were left kicking our heels. I thought perhaps Jabr was leaving us to recover from jetlag and catch some of the sights. Sunday morning arrived, as did the *New York Times* magazine with us on the cover. Susan Dominus's story centred on Fathers 4 Justice with passing references to various other US fathers' groups. I thought it odd that there was no mention of our US coordinator. That afternoon, some of the US contingent finally showed up – to take us for an afternoon out on the lakes, fishing. All very convivial, but we hadn't flown all that way to fish and we were due to leave the following day.

On the Monday morning, I finally understood that all was not well and that our trip and US operation had been compromised. Nadine and I sat quietly listening to Jamil unravel everything we had spent the last six months planning.

'You know, guys, I had the FBI round here, and you know, it's worrying,' he said. An American Palestinian, Jamil had been an enthusiastic advocate of Fathers 4 Justice, but now he was backpedalling faster than Lance Armstrong in reverse. 'It's just so dangerous . . . we thought what we might do, Matt, is set up a not-for-profit charitable organisation in the United States that provided pastoral care.'

By now Nadine's hands were clasping mine like a pair of clamps and she was whispering that I should count to ten before speaking. There was an uncomfortable silence in the room while I followed her instructions.

'Jamil . . .' I said finally, then paused again, fearing a sudden and cata-strophic explosion. 'Jamil, we have flown all this way at our own expense. We flew activists out here in January. Did you not think to tell us before we left? This is not what we agreed. It's not what you signed up to. You know the drill. If you want to start up another self-help group then that's fine and dandy, but F4J is a direct-action group, not a moniker for you to stick on

David Blunkett Father Christmas Demo, 18 December 2004
(Photo by Johnny Green/PA Archive/PA Photos)

From left to right: Daniel, Matt and Alexander at Kimsings, 2002
(Photo by Matt O'Connor)

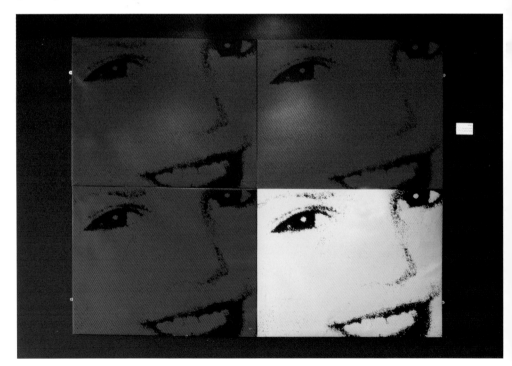

Daniel 'Smile' Canvas, 2001
(Design and photo by Matt O'Connor)

Matt at Santa Demo, 2004
(Photo by Garry Clarkson)

Our inaugural Father Christmas demo, 17 December 2002
(Photo by Bruce Head)

'Heartbreak Hotel': Elvis Valentine's Day protest, 14 February 2003
(Photo by Michael Stephens/PA Archive/PA Photos)

'Dangerous Decorating': Sarah Ashford and Shaun O'Connell painting the door of CAFCASS, Ipswich, 5 February 2003
(Photo by Bruce Head)

'Purple-handed' Matt gets arrested after painting the door of CAFCASS, 5 February 2003
(Photo by Bruce Head)

'Black Friday': F4J storm the Principal Registry of the Family Division, 13 June 2003
(PA/PA Archive/PA Photos)

'Men in Black' on Black Friday, on the battle bus, 13 June 2003
(Photo by Garry Clarkson)

Rosy and Jolly Stanesby, 'Wild, Wild West Tour', Summer 2003
(Photo by Garry Clarkson)

Batman and Robin (Eddie and Jolly) on the roof of the Royal Courts of Justice, 21 October 2003
(Photo by Chris Young/PA Archive/PA Photos)

'Tanks a lot': Matt and tank on 'Rising' demo, 22 October 2003
(Matt O'Connor)

Right: 'Spiderman' in close-up,
4 November 2003 (Photo by
Matthew Fearn/PA Archive/PA Photos)

Below: 'Spiderman' aka Dave
Chick, catches London in his web,
4 November 2003 (Photo by Graeme
Robertson/Getty Images)

'The Funpowder Plot' – flour power for dads. 19 May 2004
(PA/PA Archive/PA Photos)

Eleven frame composite: left to right from top left
1) Tony Blair answers question from Michael Howard; 2) first missile (visible above wooden seat
back in space between TB and John Prescott); 3) JP watches missile hit seat behind TB;
4) TB and JP look up to see where missile came from; 5) second missile (above and to left of TB);
6), 7), 8) second missile hits TB on back; 9) TB looks at notes on despatch box;
10) Speaker suspends the house; 11) MP leave the chamber

Day of the Dad demo, 18 June 2004
(Photo by Peter Macdiarmid/Reuters)

Monks (left) on the roof of St Pauls, 25 March 2005
(Photo by Michael Stephens/PA Archive/PA Photos)

'Unholy Fathers' cause mayhem at
York Minster, 11 July 2004
(Photo by John Giles/PA Archive/
PA Photos)

'Unholy Fathers' on scaffolding outside York Minster, 11 July 2004
(Photo by John Giles/PA Archive/PA Photos)
*Fathers 4 Justice protest about the Church's failure to take the lead in lobbying the Government
over fathers who have no legal access to their children, at York Minster, where they disrupted
the traditional Sunday service of the Church of England's General Synod*

Batman at the Palace, I – Superheroes scale the palace with just a window-cleaning ladder (PA/PA Archive/ PA Photos)

Batman at the Palace, II
(Photo by Scott Barbour/Getty Images)

Batman at the Palace, III
(Photo by Michael Stephens/PA Archive/PA Photos)

Batman at the Palace, IV: guarding the stable door
(Photo by Scott Barbour/Getty Images)

Father Time: Guy Harrison does it again, this time on the Palace of Westminster, 27 September 2005
(Photo by Sergio Dionisio/AP/PA Photos)

Downing Street protest: Park and ride, climb
ladder and scale Foreign Office into
Downing Street
(Photos by Scott Barbour/Staff; Getty Images)

Stephen Fletcher protests on top of the Tyne Bridge, 11 February 2005
(Photos by Owen Humphreys/PA Archive/PA Photos)

Every father is a superhero to his child
(Photo by Garry Clarkson)

something completely different. It's like sticking a Ferrari badge on the front of a fucking milk float. And of all the weekends, we have the fucking cover of the fucking *New York* fucking *Times* magazine and you start selling me some spineless bullshit. You'll wreck everything!'

'But, Matt, we could do some things ...' Jamil was clearly very tense, looking nervously to his colleagues for support, but they remained mute.

'Yes, really smart. Did you not see what happened to Greenpeace here? The reason for having an offshore operation was so that the organisation was protected. You do one piece of direct action in the US now with your fucked-up charitable vehicle and any individuals affected will sue you, the state government will sue you and the federal government will sue you. I think I've said all I've got to say. Anything else is a waste of your time and mine.'

And there, in a small weatherboard house in St Paul's Minnesota, my dreams for a US launch had been scuppered by undoubtedly well-intentioned but misguided campaigners. Worse still, they had applied to register the name, design identity and intellectual property I had created for the campaign at the US Patent Office without my consent or knowledge. In effect, all my work had been pirated.

Back in the UK it was election time. Some of our members were unhappy; though we had spent thousands of pounds on campaign materials, they felt we should have put some candidates up for election on an equal-parenting ticket. To my mind it would have been folly, an absurd waste of money, trying to fight the well-oiled election machines of the major parties without significant funding and on a single-issue ticket that would have left us dead in the water and bereft of £500 deposits all over the country.

We had considered the possibility of knocking out TV transmitters across the country on the evening of the election in a deliberate act of agitprop so the results would not be easily broadcast. And there had been talk of storming the Labour Party HQ, but that plan had to be shelved when it became apparent that they had pretty much moved out of their offices in Queen Anne's Gate. I chewed over the idea of disrupting the election by any means necessary, but in the end ruled against it because I feared the state's response would be to crush F4J. It seemed a time for sensible stewardship rather than rash daredevil protests.

At the end of May, Jason and I flew to Holland to meet Andy Work, our International Coordinator. Andy's outer calm was a Kevlar-thin veneer concealing a cauldron of nervous energy. He introduced us to the Dutch team, and we sat in with them, planning demos and succumbing to the allure of the Banana Bar and other less savoury establishments in Amsterdam.

The mood changed dramatically the next day. Two of our members were accused of duping a Gloucestershire pensioner out of £500 after promising to publicise her fight over an undisclosed medical condition. Apparently she had approached one of them and his sidekick, asking them to help publicise her problems, but the men were no Max Cliffords. Promises that the money would be paid back went unfulfilled, so in the interests of easing my conscience and trying to salvage what little reputation we had left, I paid her back from my own personal money. We had no choice but to take action: both were kicked out. It came at the worst possible time for the organisation.

At the time I made my views explicitly clear in an interview with Simon Hattenstone in the *Guardian*: 'What I find really morally abhorrent is when people start stealing shit, when people start taking money off pensioners, and when people are racist and misogynist. Then you go, "You know what? Fucking take it". Honestly, if I thought the whole organisation was like that . . .'

'I can't believe what the man's done,' I told Jolly. 'He's like some Walter Mitty type with petty criminal tendencies. Worse still, we put him in a top position and paid him a salary. It was a cataclysmic mistake on my part.'

'But how were you to know, Matt?' reasoned Jolly. 'He's a lovely bloke, but the bugger is also a liability. The problem is, he could do some serious damage. How much stuff has he got of Fathers 4 Justice at the moment?'

'Jen's tallied it up to about £20,000, including banners, exhibition stands and merchandise. I doubt we'll see any of it back.'

And we don't. Despite going through the motions with the police, they couldn't care less about helping a bunch of outlaw fathers secure the return of their stolen property. I had to write it off as an expensive lesson. Both my assistant and right-hand-'man' Jenny and I felt bitterly let down. Jenny had worked tirelessly for a campaign for which she felt sympathy, but given she didn't even like kids she went beyond the call of duty in every respect. Unlike others, she never got paid a penny for the work she did – everything she did was on a voluntary basis. The men concerned, by contrast, had been paid a good salary and had been well looked after but had repaid our generosity with contempt.

At the same time concerns were raised about other members who were suspected of pocketing membership fees. I had returned from Holland specifically to meet with two Bristol coordinators, but they cancelled at the last minute.

Then, on 5 June 2005, we hit major turbulence when a handful of individuals conspired to hijack the group. The planned meeting with the two

Bristol coordinators had been deliberately cancelled to avoid us resolving further allegations they had been making against Jason Hatch. By now we had become infected by the malevolent leprosy that had been spreading throughout the organisation during the last few months. I decided to take swift, unforgiving action against anyone who so much as mooted their support for any possible splinter group. The same individuals were later to fly us into the middle of a kidnap plot that would bring about the demise of F4J. A few left of their own volition and we purged the organisation of others whose commitment was questionable. It felt to me as if there was malice aforethought at play; somebody was attempting to bring the organisation down.

Jenny was in no doubt that we were doing the right thing. 'Matt, they're stunted fucking oompa-loompas who don't deserve their kids.'

'You can't say that, Jenny.'

'But is it any surprise they have problems getting on with their exes if this is how they treat you? I know the campaign for equality is right, but these people don't deserve justice.'

'It's as I said, Jen, as I said. Somebody is stirring the pot of shit and trying to flush my work down the fucking khazi along with the rest of those festering turds.'

I spoke to a few colleagues and decided that, rather than continuing as a glorified playground assistant, trying to keep all factions happy, I should concentrate on campaigning. The splinter group summoned me to a meeting, the tail trying to wag the dog, but I told them to fuck off. In my mind it was clear that there were agents provocateurs in their midst, hell-bent on wrecking Fathers 4 Justice.

With less than a fortnight to go to our Fathers' Day demo, which that year had a 'McDads' theme, I decide to pull the plug. I wasn't going to waste somewhere between £3,000–£5,000 on a demo in the current climate. There were several heated exchanges with people who were upset at being turfed out and I sent out an email reiterating my position:

As the founder of Fathers 4 Justice I am committed to seeing this project through to its conclusion using the methodology and structure that has served us well over the last few years. While I understand that we all get frustrated from time to time, anyone who wants to break their agreements or go against the spirit of the organisation I set up should leave forthwith if they do not agree now with what they originally signed up to. I for one however will not be diverted from our objectives or our way of working by a minority of individuals. Any division will serve only to play into the hands of our opponents and I'd ask everybody to consider whether it is right to embark on a period of conflict where individuals will be fighting each other rather than fighting injustice. Judge me by what I have done, not who you think I am. I would ask you that you think hard about what you want to do. I hope you arrive at the conclusion that there is only one credible force for change. That's the Fathers 4 Justice I started, the one I run and the one that will change the law.

Matt O'Connor, 6 June 2005

DEMON DADS

'It's mind-blowing,' Jolly railed down the phone. 'It makes me want to scream sometimes.'

'What's wrong?' I asked.

'Rosie's school have said that the children aren't allowed to make Fathers' Day cards. They made Mothers' Day cards, but they say that because so many kids don't have fathers it could be a bit controversial if they make up cards for Fathers' Day.'

But the story was true. 'Dad' had become a dirty word.

We had hoped we could do something to support a mentoring charity called Chance UK who were working with children from fatherless families who were at risk of becoming young offenders or engaging in anti-social behaviour. We had planned an event for Fathers' Day to raise funds to support their excellent work but our efforts came a cropper early on.

'You can't mention fathers,' their chief executive, Gracia McGrath, told us.

'Why, if 85 to 90 per cent of your cases involve boys who don't have fathers and are at risk of offending?' I asked.

'Because some people will see it as being offensive.'

'Who would find that offensive?' I said, gobsmacked.

'Our clients, the single mums who come to us for help.'

'But by your own admission it's the truth: these boys are fatherless. What else would you describe them as being?'

'Children without positive male role models,' she stated glibly.

'Isn't it going to be a bit difficult to organise a Fathers' Day event without using the word "Father"?' Gracia had no answer. 'Shall I rename it "Positive Male Role Models' Day" then? Would that help?'

Even better, I remarked later to Glen Poole, who had helped set up the meeting, why not create a new group to counterbalance this mumbo jumbo?

'What about SPERM?' he suggested. 'The Society for the Promotion of Equal Rights for Men. It's got a certain premature ring to it.'

'Next thing,' I retorted, 'you'll be saying we should set up our own Sperm

Bank with a current account that goes against the flow, a savings account for those who need to make a withdrawal, and a deposit account for those who have a penchant for philanthropy and don't mind the CSA chasing them. What it really comes down to, though, is getting young men to vote with their loins in the first place.'

EQUAL OPPORTUNITIES

The Equal Opportunities Commission is working to eliminate sex discrimination in Britain today. If women and men had equal chances in life, things would be different ... we deal with sex discrimination and inequality related to gender. Women. Men. Different. Equal.

Equal Opportunities website

No matter how much government-backed quangos like the Equal Opportunities Commission try and sugar the pill of discrimination, it's still something many fathers have to swallow day in day out in the family courts. About as much use as the United Nations when it comes to gender conflict, the Equal Opportunities Commission have spent the last four years with their heads neck-deep in ignorance of the inequalities and injustices of the family courts.

Other children's organisations such as the NSPCC and the Children's Society have also found a political blind-spot when it comes to the abuse of children in the family courts. Not only have they ignored the effect prolonged court conflicts have on young children and their families, but they have perpetuated the myth that all fathers pose some sort of risk to their children after separation. Yet figures from the NSPCC show that children are at greater risk of abuse from their mothers than from their fathers. Their report, *Child Maltreatment in the Family, 2002*, showed that 65 per cent of total child abuse (neglect, sexual, emotional and physical) is committed by mothers and that 8 per cent of child abuse is committed by fathers.

We live in an age where boys grow up with women, are taught by women, and then told by women who are there to help them that they must use the term 'male role model' as opposed to the word father. It's bollocks! If that is the professional advice being dispensed, what hope is there for our children? Instead of healing fractured families, they're making the damage worse.

No matter what the legal fraternity, CAFCASS, the voluntary sector, or family law professionals would have you believe, as a man you have a 3 per cent chance of getting residence of your child and a 40 per cent chance of losing all contact with your children within two years of separation.

As a man, if you are angry in court you are perceived to be violent.

If you say you love your children, this is seen as unhealthy in the extreme.

If you stay calm, you clearly don't give a shit so why would you want to see them?

For thousands of years, being a dad was a respectable occupation. You were the hunter, provider and protector of your family, a testosterone-charged pillar of the community. Now you've been given your P45 and made redundant, superfluous to requirements. And the more the position of fathers is undermined, the less respect their children show society.

Men don't make good or easy victims. Men are supposed to be all powerful, yet contemporary society demonises and denigrates men, ridiculing them in adverts, greetings cards and TV programmes like 'Bring Your Husband to Heel'. Yet all many men want – for both themselves and for women – whether in the workplace or in the home, is an old-fashioned principle called equality.

In one report, it was found that there was 'no systemic bias against fathers in court proceedings' and that 'most couples made their own arrangements without resorting to court.' The government argued this report made it clear that just 10 per cent of separating couples resorted to court – this '1 in 10' figure becoming something of an urban myth. The figure derived from the Blackwell and Dawes report of 2003* which was a sample of just 961 parents for whom contact *was already working and not in dispute*, of whom about 11 per cent had court-ordered contact at the time they were questioned.

But to expand upon this sleight of hand, another report argued that only a tiny minority of contact orders were 'no contact' orders. They completely ignored the fact that many fathers *already* issued with an order for contact were permitted no contact whatsoever because the order was being flouted, or that these contact orders only allowed for either supervised contact (in a contact centre) or indirect contact (sending a Birthday or Christmas card once a year). These hardly constituted grounds for a meaningful relationship with your children.

Either way, by her own admission, Harriet Harman, Minister of State for Constitutional Affairs admitted in 2007 that a staggering 70 per cent of children entering the court system simply shouldn't be there, but because

---

* Blackwell & F. Dawes, Non Resident Parental Contact Report, from the National Statistics Omnibus Survey, October 2003, commissioned by the Department for Constitutional Affairs.

there was no transparency and no accountability, there were no reliable figures that anyone could source, hence the government could spin them any way it wished. However, from whichever perspective you approached the issue, the inarguable fact was that fatherlessness and family breakdown were massive and rapidly growing social calamities.

The court welfare service CAFCASS is itself dominated by the trade union NAPO, whose equal rights committee had no male members:

After a lively internal debate it was resolved in 1989 that this committee would be a women-only group because it was agreed that women working in NAPO needed to progress together through continuing barriers between women, in terms of sexual orientation, race and disability in order to challenge effectively the male oppression of women.

Their bizarrely named Anti-Sexism policy stated:

There is potential for collusion in home making and peacemaking by the women without ensuring that men share equally in these roles. Family Court work is an important opportunity to build on the strengths and the expansion of women's roles.

So their equality is achieved by ensuring that men do not share equally.

Increasingly, these Punch-and-Judy sex wars have been played out in the courtrooms of the family justice system. It's a curious if unpalatable truth that children bring out the very best and very worst of their parents, especially after separation. I've spent years examining family law and from every angle it's an unedifying spectacle. Combatants take sides and increasingly bitter accusations are made.

If all else fails, an accusation of domestic violence, for instance, will be enough to ensure that a father will never see his kids again. While Mum can bring home the next Ian Huntley, Peter Sutcliffe or Ian Brady, Dad is made to sweat. According to the Home Office definition, Domestic Violence now includes:

Any violence between current and former partners in an intimate relationship, wherever the violence occurs. The violence may include physical, sexual, emotional and financial abuse.

So just about any kind of argument about contact, money, fidelity – anything – could be technically construed as domestic violence. And while nobody doubts that this is a serious crime, by watering down the definition so much, it diverts valuable resources from those at most risk.

On 16 August 2005 a team of six dads from F4J made a presentation to the twenty-two strong board of CAFCASS – something that would have been unthinkable just a few years ago. The invitation itself meant that love us or hate us, you couldn't ignore us and that our campaign was weighted with gravitas in these circles at least. Using a PowerPoint presentation and overhead projector, I conducted a comprehensive demolition of CAFCASS, its administration, its competence and its inadequacies. I exposed the claim that CAFCASS act in the child's 'best interests' as a wicked deceit used to deflect criticism of the system. In reality, it was a claim they could not substantiate as CAFCASS had not kept any records on the outcomes for children. That said, at the time I still retained confidence that their Chief Executive, Anthony Douglas, who had been present, would honour the agreement reached earlier in the year about shared parenting and early interventions.

Meanwhile the shenanigans at the CSA continued to run and run. On 3 September the government rolled out the usual lame reforms, blithely ignoring the link between contact and the payment of child support. You can't have one without the other. Child support should mean that you provide both emotional and financial support to your children, but dads were being reduced to little more than cash cows. Politicians were using fathers as scapegoats for the culture of maladministration and incompetence that ran across all areas of family law. The entire family justice system was in need of radical reform.

A little less than three weeks later, an F4J member who for a number of reasons we had become increasingingly suspicious of, travelled up to see me in Suffolk. He spent about fifteen minutes with me, asking me leading questions, most of which I refused to answer on the grounds that he could be an undercover reporter – which, as it turned out, he was.

'It'll be interesting to see where this turns up,' I remarked to barrister Michael Cox.

We found out soon enough.

TRIALS AND TRIBULATIONS

On 27 September 2005 Guy Harrison, in yet another high-profile protest, scaled the Palace of Westminster in a shining display of brass-balled audacity on his daughter's birthday. The Met were oblivious to his presence as he perilously scaled an apex of the roof of Westminster Hall to his roost, some

120 feet above Parliament Square. This was at my insistence – I wanted photos of the event to include Big Ben in the background. It took a little old lady to raise the alarm with the prophetic words, 'Is that man supposed to be on the roof?' At that very moment I was calling Scotland Yard's Gold Room to let them know that it was a Fathers 4 Justice protestor on the roof of Parliament and not an errant Brazilian.

It immediately became clear that one of the two hundred plus CCTV cameras around Parliament had picked up Glen and myself orchestrating events from St Stephen's Green.

'Fuck, Matt,' exclaimed Glen, faced with a wall of coppers marching towards us. 'You don't exactly blend in wearing that pinstripe effort,' he said, eyeing my beefy frame swaddled in charcoal black with thick chalk lines, 'You must have the most dangerous suits in Britain.'

With that we split and I took up temporary residence at nearby Westminster Abbey, where I was castigated by the Dean for doing an interview on a mobile phone while kneeling down in one of the pews.

'Sorry, I'm really sorry,' I said, asking for forgiveness rather than permission. 'I just hope our man gets down off the roof safely.'

'He isn't on our roof, is he?' the Dean rasped with concern.

'Not exactly. He's on the roof of the Houses of Parliament and I'm praying for divine intervention that he gets down in one piece.' He shot me a daggers look and I made further apologies before stepping outside, where I almost collided with Guy's girlfriend Emily.

'What are you doing skulking around the grounds of Westminster Abbey, Em?'

'Lying low, actually.'

'Well, be careful,' I said. 'I know what this lot are like, they'll nick you over nothing. By the time they see the CCTV footage of you two entering Parliament, they'll have your card marked.' And sure enough, about an hour later, Emily was lifted by the Bill and taken to Charing Cross Police Station where she was interviewed.

She called me two hours later, remarkably composed for a girl with no experience in these sort of high jinks, her only fear being that her parents might find out she'd been arrested.

Guy trundled down off the roof at about 9 p.m. As ever, the element of surprise had been integral to the demo's success. The Met are inclined to go totally OTT when it's all too late – on this occasion an 'all access Merlin rope team' were dispatched in a helicopter to pluck Guy to safety.

The subsequent trial was an utter sham. The previous year, Greenpeace protestors had scaled Big Ben and got off scot free, but for us charges were always de rigueur. This time they charged him with causing a public nuisance, a summary offence tried by jury in a Crown Court. The maximum tariff? Five years in the clink.

The last day of the trial slid from the sublime to the ridiculous. A human wall of Met flesh prevented public access to the court to hear the verdict. Only after making representations were just four people allowed in.

'They don't even have this at terrorist trials,' Guy quipped as he strode into the glass cage where defendants must sit through the laboured and laborious legal arguments.

'Fuck that,' I told him, 'I've only been here a few days and I'm already losing the will to live. I'm sure I've got some grass growing at home that I can sit down and watch rather then listen to this attack of verbal diarrhoea.'

In his summing up, the judge had described how Harrison, the man who powder-bombed the Prime Minister, had gained access to the House of Commons by strolling in as if he were just another visitor checking out the current exhibition on another 'Guy'. Guy Fawkes, to be precise. There he made his way through a toilet window, down a drainpipe, climbed up some scaffolding on to the roof, then scaled the masonry apex of the roof.

The prosecution spent several bum-numbing, tedious days arguing that the 'nuisance' aspect of the offence arose because Mr Harrison might have 'bounced' if he had fallen and could have hit a member of the public in doing so, despite being at least a 100 feet away from the road. 'It might have rained and got slippery,' said another police officer. But it didn't. Or, even more bizarrely, 'He could have fallen on to the main Commons roofs.'

'What?' I whispered to Emily. 'A 50-foot horizontal fall?' They must think he really was a superhero.

The jury were equally unimpressed with the prosecution case and Guy was found not guilty by a unanimous verdict.

Naturally everybody was ecstatic. Yet again a jury trial had demonstrated that members of the public were not prepared to convict Fathers 4 Justice activists for protests that involved peaceful, humorous acts of non-violent direct action.

There were numerous trials over that period for a veritable melting pot of offences. There was the time when Dave Pyke, aka Robin at Buckingham Palace, was charged for being in possession of a knife. Rather ironically this was the only charge to be made as Jason Hatch astonishingly hadn't broken the law by climbing on to Buckingham Palace. In desperation Pyke became their token scalp. He never made it up the ladder on to the ledge at Buckingham Palace, after police threatened to shoot him.

At the subsequent trial East End Eddie or Edward Goreki, as he was known to our friends in the law enforcement community, was asked to give evidence about the carrying of knives by protestors as the Crown Prosecution Service pursued a knuckleheaded line of questioning about how 'dangerous' we all were. In Ed's case, he was being quizzed about the use of knives during his sojourn on the roof of the Royal Courts of Justice in 2003 whilst dressed as Batman.

Said Eddie, 'Wi all carry knives like. I 'ad mine in my utility belt.'

'What sort of knives?' probed a gleeful looking prosecutor, hoping that Eddie was about to spill the beans on some kind of F4J knife culture.

'A pocket knife to cut cords on banners, otherwise,' he said grimacing, staring into mid space, 'we might still be attached to the motor vehicle when it drove off, like.'

'Were you in possession of any other knives Mr Gorecki?'

'Yeah, I had a butta knife,'

'What did you use that for?'

'Spreading butta, like.'

'Where?'

'On mi bread. I woz famished up on that bloody roof.'

In another trial, over a year after the London and Clifton Suspension Bridge protests, half a dozen activists were brought to trial at Southwark Crown Court on charges of conspiracy to cause a public nuisance. Houses were raided, doors smashed down and computers and files taken from the properties of those involved. But the trial concluded with a hung jury. The judge, knowing the jury was divided, strongly recommended to the Crown Prosecution Service that the case be dropped. Instead, at the behest of Dru Sharpling, the Chief Crown Prosecutor for London, they pressed ahead with a re-trial in October of that year at Kingston Crown Court. The result? A unanimous not guilty verdict and a cost to the tax payer of over £1.5 million for both trials.

In October the Child Contact and Inter-Country Adoption Bill began its passage through the House of Lords and House of Commons. Inevitably it turned out to be more of a token gesture, designed to steal the wind from our sails, than a genuine attempt at reform. We had come within a whisker of achieving our key objective in the Lords – a legal presumption to contact – but Lib Dem peers had the frighteners put on them by the NSPCC, who argued that it was a charter for dangerous dads to abuse their kids – using grossly distorted propaganda to advance their arguments.

Much to our surprise, our old friend Judge Munby popped out of the woodwork to attack the family law system. In a judgment made after a father abandoned a five-year battle to maintain contact with his 7-year-old daughter, he stated, 'We failed them. The system failed them. . . we need to act. And we need to act now.' It was an astonishing admission. Perhaps, however slowly, our campaign was winning hearts and minds and shaping people's thinking.

Just as things were starting to turn around, I nearly walked straight into a honey-trap. I was having a night on the razz in London when a pretty blonde woman threw herself at me at a hotel bar. Mindful of advice I'd received in the early days of the campaign warning me that scantily clad birds who act as if they're overcome with lust for you are probably up to foul play, I avoided her like a Thai chicken with avian flu. Yet still she persisted with a line of suggestive banter peppered with questions about Fathers 4 Justice.

'Listen,' I told her, 'I'm not averse to social intercourse, but it isn't going any further than that. I used to be a man of earthly pleasures but now I'm specialising in personal suffering. I haven't even told you who I am yet somehow you know I head up a fathers' campaign group. Can I respectfully suggest that you totter off back to your bosses and tell them next time they try setting me up, they should send me something dark and dusky like a brunette.'

The following morning, still at the hotel, I got one of those calls when your legs turn to jelly and the ground around you starts to sink. Fast.

'Hello, Mr O'Connor, it's Adam Leary. I'm a producer/director from the Granada *Tonight* programme.'

'How can I help?'

'We have been investigating Fathers 4 Justice since October last year. We wanted to offer you a right to respond to the allegations we are making in the programmes.'

'Programmes? You mean there is more than one?'

'Yes, there are two programmes that will be broadcast in the same week on ITV1.'

I paused for a few seconds as my brain tried to process the information.

'Mr O'Connor? Are you still there?'

'Yes, I am, sorry.'

'Do you want to respond?'

'Well, I guess you know you've made it when you get not one but two hatchets on prime-time telly in the same week. Thank God nobody watches ITV1 any more.'

Granada must have been desperate to interview me. Later that same day I received a call from Philip Reay-Smith at ITN News. He said he wanted to run a story about Fathers 4 Justice off the back of the Guy Harrison protest. Back at the office, Jenny smelled a rat.

'Don't you think it's a bit odd, them popping out of the woodwork on the same day as Granada?' she said. 'It is the same network, after all. Perhaps they need something on you that they haven't been able to film undercover?'

'Christ knows, Jen. The more I see the less I know. People think I'm suffering from heightened paranoia, but can anybody blame me? Media stitch-ups, backstabbing and dodgy birds throwing themselves at me, it's all getting rather bizarre.'

'But it's obvious, Matt, somebody, somewhere has it in for you. The question is, where will it end?'

Foolishly I agreed to go along with the ITN interview and see what transpired. We agreed the areas that would be covered and we met up so that they could film us doing some reconnaissance work. All the pieces of the puzzle suddenly fell into place when Reay-Smith pulled a fast one during the interview.

'So what about your drinking, Mr O'Connor? Don't you think people should know about that?'

'Well, this is a surprise. Where did that one come from – Granada TV? Don't tell me: they didn't they have any footage they could smear me with, so they send you along to do their dirty work as a precursor to their programme.'

'It's a fair question. . .'

'No it isn't, it's a private matter. But seeing as you ask, I am on record, talking openly about every aspect of my life. You'll know I'm a morally fragmented agent of justice and I'm sure you've Googled me and have got the articles you need, so if you don't mind I'll refer you back to those. I've discussed it at length in them and I'm not going to discuss it again.'

'Have you ever been unfaithful to your partner?'

'Have you?'

'I'm not the one who's agreed to an interview.'

'And I didn't agree to be interviewed about my private life. But again, for the record, the answer is an emphatic no, but I'm sure you know that already.' With that I removed my mike and walked off in disgust.

A couple of days later we held our 'Bedlam' demo in London as part of a campaign to ensure that overnight staying contact is the minimum recommended by CAFCASS and the family courts. Reay-Smith showed up, along with a team from Granada, and he approached Nadine for an interview.

'Nadine, how do you feel about Matt doing all this?'

'I fully support him, otherwise I wouldn't be doing it with him. It's a bit of a silly question, if you don't mind me saying.'

'But how do you cope with his drinking?'

Nadine looked at him and laughed. 'Are you trying to stitch him up?' she asked incredulously as the line of questioning became transparent. Thanking her for her time, Reay-Smith drifted off to join the rest of the demo.

By now I was convinced that the programme-makers had no damning footage of me, which came as a relief, but I was furious with the man from ITN. If this was meant to be a hatchet job, it was a ham-fisted attempt. On reflection, it was also apparent that if we hadn't cancelled our 'McDad' demo in June the programme would have run on Fathers' Day. They needed something to hang the programme from and Guy Harrison's roof-top protest at Parliament and our Bedlam demo gave them the hook they needed.

The next day Granada were back on the blower again. I argued that it would be impossible for me to comment on allegations levelled in a programme I hadn't seen.

'We have given you a statement which addresses the points in your letter,' I told them. 'We have asked for a transcript, which you have refused to provide, and I have offered to do a live interview with Trevor McDonald or one of your journalists after the programme has been broadcast. If you don't want to avail yourself of one of these offers then fine, but don't think I'm stupid enough to give you an interview which will be edited to make me look like a complete cunt. I do that job well enough on my own, thank you very much.'

'But what do you have to say about your plans to knock out TV transmitters across the UK on the night of the last election?'

'Listen pal, there is witness evidence to suggest an undercover man from one of the major television companies plied a mentally ill father full of alcohol for an entire afternoon before inciting him to commit an act of violence at one of our meetings. It's lucky I'm committed to non-violent direct action. If he's cretinous enough to arrive encased in a 3-foot-thick winter leather jacket in the middle of summer – and cretinous enough to swallow our tactical deployment of red herrings then I'm delighted. And if you're daft enough to broadcast it to the last three people left watching ITV1, then I'll be even happier.'

On 7 November Nadine and I settled down with Michael Cox and his wife Beth to watch the first of the two Granada *Tonight* programmes about the evils of F4J. In a perverse way, I was flattered. Two programmes on prime-time TV in one week, and they had gone to the trouble of producing snazzy comic-book graphics. For the most part, both programmes focused either on ex-members or people who had nothing to do with the organisation. Amazingly, I came out of it remarkably unscathed.

'I was expecting plenty of Matt O'Connor in a horizontal position,' I said sarcastically. 'So on this occasion I'll admit that I'm just a tad disappointed that I didn't really feature.'

'But that's why they were desperate to get something on you,' said Michael. 'Yet again, Mr O'Connor, you've sidestepped a bullet.'

'But for how much longer?' I asked. 'How much longer can we parry these strikes? We can't keep going round this hamster wheel of controversy without public support heading south. Sooner or later, Mike, these fuckers will catch up with me with a hatchet that I won't be able to extricate myself from, and that's what worries me. Something feels terribly wrong.'

On 16 November I'd been invited to give a speech at Southampton Solent University by one of the senior lecturers there, Carol Cummings-Osmond. It was one of a series of talks I was doing across the country and, to be frank, after the last few weeks I was looking forward to having a break doing something I enjoyed. In fact, I was glad to be anywhere.

Support came from an unexpected quarter in the shape of female students expressing admiration for our efforts. A whinger from the legal department started to heckle me about the cost of our protests and the disruption they caused. I explained that in 2000, in a report produced by the Family Matters Institute, the cost of family breakdown was estimated at £30 billion and that kids without dads caused crime. One in four teenagers was now a criminal, and the cost to the country of young offending had reached £10 billion according to the Office of National Statistics. Our protests, I told him, were designed to highlight these facts, and were very small beer in cost comparison.

THE ARCHBISHOP OF PORK

On 22 December Jenny and I traipsed up to Bishopthorpe Palace, the generously proportioned pad of John Tucker Mugabi Sentamu, the Archbishop of York. Sentamu initially came across as an all-round good egg with an eye for a publicity stunt himself, whether it be African drummers and dancers at his inauguration, camping out in York Minster in an act of solidarity with those caught in the crossfire of the Israel/Lebanon conflict, or simply dunking parishioners in an inflatable Argos swimming pool at Easter. He also had a penchant for wearing the most colourful threads in Christendom. We were treated to tea and invited to take a pew in a large room overlooked by portraits of the previous incumbents at York Minster. I expressed our gratitude for his time, but right from the off he was pretty pugnacious and began to offload his sermon on me. It became apparent that this so-called radical man of the cloth was singing from the same hymn sheet as the rest of the church.

'Mr O'Connor, I find the antics of Fathers 4 Justice are a hindrance to progress on this issue.'

'What progress is that then?'

'For there to be sensible discussion, you must stop these theatrical stunts.'

'But with the greatest respect, Archbishop, if it wasn't for our protests I doubt whether you'd be seeing us at all. Perhaps it might be better if we set the matter of Fathers 4 Justice to one side and focused on the issue of family breakdown.' I thought this would divert his train of thought, but no, Sentamu was on a one-man mission to chastise me for the campaign.

'But this dressing up is so unnecessary. If you give up your stunts then we can engage in dialogue.' He shot me what I suspected was a deeply insincere smile from the corner of the sofa where his diminutive frame was parked. Reading his hostile body language and listening to the tone of his voice, I concluded that the only reason he had agreed to see us was because we had him by the short and curlies over F4J protests planned for Christmas services nationwide.

'Well, Archbishop, there is the small matter of the Church not actually debating family breakdown for over sixteen years at General Synod meetings. In fact, you seem to have debated everything from global warming to Guantanamo Bay, but not the one issue that directly affects your parishioners. Isn't this a little odd? Dare I also say your criticism of us sounds a little overripe, coming from a man of God who has a predisposition for a little showbiz himself?'

But Sentamu sailed over the questions and instead carried on with his monologue.

'Mr O'Connor, you may be aware that the Conservatives once practised a policy called "back to basics" which was seen as a direct criticism of single mothers, and that we in the Church have to be mindful of that. Any interest in this issue is difficult, especially if we were seen to apportion blame to single mothers.'

'Are you telling me then that the Church of England is apologising for its patriarchal past?'

'What I am saying, Mr O'Connor, is that if you give up your stunts then I will help you.'

'In what way?'

'When I return to the House of Lords at the end of January next year I will consult with the Law Lords about this matter and get back to you, providing of course you don't do anything in the meantime.'

'I'm sorry you are placing conditions on your involvement in trying to help the millions of children and parents caught in the crossfire of family breakdown. And I'm not talking about just anybody either, I'm talking about the congregation in your Church, your flock. I've already asked you to set the matter of Fathers 4 Justice to one side, but what we really need is for somebody like you to act and to speak out on this matter – will you do that for me? If you do, then we'll agree to your request.'

'Mr O'Connor, I'm afraid I'm out of time, but thank you for coming.'

'Can I just ask one final question, Archbishop? Wasn't Jesus Christ a pioneer of direct action? Didn't he turn over the tables in the temple?' The Archbishop's face turned to molten pumice stone. 'You could have preached a public message of equality and unity for families – that's what you would have done if you were a man of God.'

And there, standing in the Archbishop's palace on the banks of the River Ouse, I wondered whether, if faced with a second coming, the Archbishop would only support Christ if he 'gave up the stunts'. What happened to unconditional love? Were conditional offers of help compatible with Christian teachings?

By the beginning of February it was clear that the Archbishop hadn't fulfilled his promise to raise this issue in the House of Lords, so I sent him a final email.

Dear John,

I'm both surprised and disappointed that we appear unable to find any common ground. In particular I am very surprised that despite repeated assurances that you would raise the important matter of family breakdown in the House of Lords you have failed to do so in breach of your promise to me.

I can't help but feel this has been a cynically orchestrated exercise on your part in attempting to divert us away from plans to disrupt Christmas services across the UK which you were aware of. There may also be other more personal reasons you have for not acting. Is it because I stood in your pulpit once and gave a sermon? Is it because you used to be a High Court Judge in Uganda? Is it because you think men dressing up in tights offends your Christian sensibilities? Because, if it is, then let he who is without a silly costume cast the first stone. Or is it because you simply don't care? You are without doubt a case of the same product, wrapped in different packaging.

Yours sincerely
Matthew O'Connor

Sentamu emailed me back and suggested I read Dale Carnegie's legendary book, *How To Win Friends and Influence People*. Odd that, I thought. What sort of Archbishop would tell you to read a book on salesmanship and not the Bible? But this wasn't to be the end of the matter. At a subsequent event we took a plate load of pork pies to hand out outside York Minster with an 'Archbishop of Pork – Not, In The Name Of The Father' poster as part of a photo opportunity. Our natural-born protestor Jolly had driven me up.

'So what's all this about? Sounds like a feud to me.'

'I think he's reneged on his promise but I intend to hold him to it. Did you know he was a High Court Judge in Uganda and his sidekick and spokesman is one Arun Arora who – you guessed it – used to be a solicitor?'

That afternoon Arora calls me up to ask if it's true that I've called the Archbishop of York the Archbishop of Pork.

'Yes it is true. He made a promise to act and we intend to cash that in, be it now, or in the future. As far as I am concerned he told us a porkie.'

'I should remind you that the Archbishop has made it clear to you face-to-face and in email communication that he will not engage with your group whilst any pranks are on-going.'

'Sorry, I must have missed something – when did he engage? All he needs to do is make his position clear with regard to fatherlessness and family breakdown – surely that can't be much of a task for the second highest clergyman in the Church of England?'

A terse Arora bristled. 'The Archbishop has survived being threatened by one dictator, he won't be dictated to by another.' I was speechless. The Archbishop of York was likening me to a brutal African dictator because I was asking him to clarify his position with regard to fathers and family breakdown.

'And Mr O'Connor, if you do not withdraw your threat of violence or action I see little point in continuing our conversation.'

I turned to Jolly, 'Fuck me, did you hear that Jol? I talk about a pastoral symphony of protest and he keeps banging on about violence. What violence? What am I going to do? Mug him with a pork pie?'

I was incandescent with rage but kept a lid on my emotions. It was clear this discourse was at an end and we were only fishing a shoal of religious red herrings as they attempted to deflect any direct criticism of the Archbishop in the local media.

KIDNAP

Just after Christmas 2005 I heard through the grapevine that several people on the periphery of the movement had either been visited or called by SO13, the Anti-Terrorist Unit at Scotland Yard, warning them that if they pulled any 'stunts' they would be shot dead. It just didn't add up. I called Jolly, who always had his finger on the pulse where grass roots were concerned, but nothing was on our radar. We could only surmise that something had been said at the last demo attended by non-members.

It was really bugging me that I didn't know what was going on, so on 8 January 2006 I emailed Andy Sharp in the Yard's Operational Planning Department.

Hi Andy,

Further to our conversation last week I have now been contacted by a freelance journalist about the following. I am not sure where he got this from but he appears to be looking to run yet another hatchet on us using some 'terrorist' labelling. This is what we know to date:

1. Several individuals who are not members of F4J but may be part of splinter groups or seen as being linked to the group, have been visited at their homes by plainclothes police from Scotland Yard purporting to be from the Anti Terrorist Unit SO13. Others have been visited by plainclothes police who refused to say which department they were from.

2. One F4J member, Jolly Stanesby, has also been visited.

3. These 'visits' have occurred at the end of last week and over the Christmas period.

4. As we understand it the inquiries related to the possible use of firearms and the issuing of a warning saying that activists WOULD be shot on sight if they attempted any stunts in 'sensitive areas'. The officers also asked the individuals concerned whether there was any 'information they would like to share' as well as a slight mocking concern for the lower numbers in attendance at our recent demo – though we could argue that might be down to the OTT policing and constant intrusion of your intel people taking pics of pregnant women and pensioners which most find pretty distasteful.

5. *The officer's information we have gathered is one telephone number 070170 17730 for an officer who refused to be identified but allegedly was from Scotland Yard and another officer called PC Steve Higgins No 186584, tel no 077986 17611. To help them explain their actions I put their details on our web site.*

6. *As you know we share information concerning anything that goes beyond our mandate of peaceful non-violent direct action. I won't go into details but you will understand that there exists a spirit of cooperation. If you had any concerns we would have hoped these would have been made directly to us so we could assist with your inquiries. The fact that you haven't done this troubles me enormously.*

7. *If this is now a one-way street and we ourselves are not made aware of concerns Scotland Yard may have, especially given the gravity of any suggestion about the use of firearms or involvement of SO13, then that puts this relationship in jeopardy and is inflaming what was a stable situation.*

8. *Further, if you can't provide us with the information we are asking for (what the nature of the inquiries are about at the very least) then we will withdraw with immediate effect from cooperating with the Met Police, period.*
Regards
Matt

On receiving the email, Andy called me.

'What's fucking going on, Andy? This is worrying me. We've never had any shit like this before. I mean SO13, the Anti-Terrorist Unit?'

'I don't know, Matt. I've asked the powers that be upstairs and we've been told to keep our noses out in no uncertain terms.'

'But if I don't know what's going on, what can I do? It feels like I'm being deliberately kept in the dark here. Has somebody indicated they are going to be doing a protest in Whitehall?'

'Nobody has told us if they are. I guess it could be a splinter group.'

'It doesn't add up. Those guys don't have the necessary skills, apart from talking about it. I'm just worried though, especially when people are getting threatening phone calls. Was something picked up at the last demo?'

'Like I say, Matt, we know as much as you, I'm afraid.'

It was the last we heard from Scotland Yard until nine days later.

KIDNAP

I couldn't have predicted the manner of my demise that rain-lashed January night. The guile and cunning they deployed. The twisting scalpel blade of spin slicing through what credibility we had left, severing the Lycra-clad legs from the 'Men in Tights' and thus putting an end to the most notorious campaign group of recent political history.

The state-sponsored character assassination involved a 5-year-old-boy, Scotland Yard, Special Branch, MI5, the *Sun* and the dark-art masters of the New Labour spin machine. In other circumstances, I would have been flattered. Instead I was busy working through the ramifications.

This was our Dunkirk moment.

If we carried on, the group would have been decimated by the state and all its agents who were conspiring our downfall. The organisation had been infiltrated by undercover journalists and police, and a welter of hatchets had been deposited between my shoulder blades over the last twelve months. The rest of my reputation had been bludgeoned into oblivion by sanctimonious truncheons of newsprint, and life was beginning to resemble some awful TV reality hybrid, a cross between *EastEnders*, *Big Brother* and *24*.

In the Dunkirk spirit, I decided the best course of action would be to paddle back across our metaphorical channel and regroup to fight another day.

It was about 10.20 p.m. on 17 January 2006. After working on a client project for twenty-four hours straight I had crashed out in my living room, assorted files clutched to my chest and a mug of warm milk on the table beside me. The damp wood on the fire had begun to spit gobs of flame out on to the cold oak floor. I put the television on to catch the back end of the Ten O'Clock News and lay prostrate across the sofa, hugging a cushion to my stomach for comfort.

The phone began to ring.

And ring.

First one line, then both, out of kilter, discordant. There was a moment's pause and then they both fired up again. The bells, I thought. I felt like Quasimodo.

Experience had taught me it could be one of three things at that time of night. One, a mad dad. Two, a suicide call. Three, the press, responding to something that had just happened. I waited for the phones to stop then picked one up, expecting the message service.

'Matt? Is that you, Matt?' said the voice.

'Who is this?' I replied curtly.

'It's Michael Crick, from BBC's *Newsnight*.'

'Michael, fuck's sake, it's nearly half past ten at night, give it a break and call me tomorrow.'

There was a stunned pause. 'You don't know, do you?' Michael said, his words weighted with implication.

'Don't know what?'

'You're on the front page of tomorrow's *Sun*. They are reporting that Fathers 4 Justice plotted to kidnap Leo Blair, the Prime Minister's 5-year-old son.'

The news was like a bomb going off in my head. I collapsed back into the sofa, shell-shocked, and then rang Nadine.

'It's clever,' I told her. 'Very, very clever.'

'Why's that?' she asked.

'You know what, the fucking *Sun* haven't even called me yet to get my comment on the story. Why? Because they know I'd scupper it. Now it's being presented to me as a fait accompli on national TV, where it's leading all the news stories. Both *Newsnight* and the ITN News are running it and we're sitting here at eleven o'clock at night and we're dead in the fucking water with the world's news media about to descend on us.'

'What are you going to do?'

'I don't know. I've been expecting this for such a long time now, the final coup de grâce, that there just seems an inevitably about this. It's a stitch-up, a brilliant fucking stitch-up, the bullet I couldn't side step. I just wish you were here, darling.'

'Hang in there, Matt,' she pleaded. 'You have to follow your instinct on this. There's nothing anyone can say to you now, you have to manage this the way you see fit.'

'What about the others?'

'But, Matt, you're the one who's carrying the can for this. Who's sitting in the hot seat? You are. Time and time again you defend your corner. Just promise me you'll come out fighting.'

'Darling, I don't know how to do anything else.'

I closed my eyes for a few moments peace before stepping out into the storm of phones ringing relentlessly in the office. I gave my first live interview for ITN at 3 a.m. from my house via a satellite truck. Straight after, I plunged into a cold bath and then into a waiting car for GMTV. The next few hours were spent breathlessly running from studio to studio. I had a pre-arranged meeting with Harbour Pictures and a possible director for a film about my life story at the Electric Club in Notting Hill, but even there ITN tracked me down for another live slot on the lunchtime news. From the outset, in every interview, I made our position clear.

'We are in the business of reuniting children with their fathers, not separating them.'

I was knackered and my head was spinning, trying to calculate what to do next, but the fatigue was impossible to overcome. I decided to trust gut instinct.

As the media circus intensified, the odds against F4J were looking insurmountable. Like David against Goliath, I was taking on a giant. There was no way I could absorb the firepower of New Labour's spin machine *and* fight running battles with backstabbers at the same time. Besides, with all the skulduggery, political occult and intrigue, the day's events were beginning to resemble some dark fable from the pages of a John Le Carré novel.

CHECKMATE

In a surreal twist, journalist Sarah Womack of the *Daily Telegraph* called to let me know that some disgruntled dads had accused me of concocting the entire Leo Blair story myself to provide me with an escape route from F4J. But one father, a little-known ex-member of Families Need Fathers, was first to jump on the post-kidnap bandwagon, and it wasn't long before he had sunk his nose into the trough of controversy. A man with more ambition than ability, he had hovered on the periphery of the fathers' movement, dipping in, but mostly out of the campaign, living vicariously through the actions of others more courageous than him.

Despite the fact that he'd never been a member of Fathers 4 Justice, this man had been involved in a splinter group apparently named after the provisional wing of the IRA but with about as much clout as Super Ted. Scenting a story and the opportunity to make some capital, he suddenly started appearing in the media, a bit like the TV character Mr Ben. When he jumped on the F4J bandwagon, I jokingly told Nadine that he would soon be claiming F4J was all his idea in the first place. Which he promptly did. Another Alpha male desperate to be top dog. Me, I just wanted to get the fuck out. Pronto.

The government's cynical use of the Prime Minister's 5-year-old son as a tool to bring down F4J really began to rankle, not least because the media had acquiesced before in suppressing news coverage in order to protect the privacy of Tony Blair's family. So who sanctioned the use of the Prime Minister's youngest son to be splashed all over Britain's biggest selling national newspaper and every TV channel? Who would want to even risk giving anyone ideas about kidnapping their children? The same thought had occurred to Tony Booth, Cherie Blair's father. In a letter to the *Guardian* newspaper the following day, Booth wrote:

As Leo Blair's grandfather, I find it utterly unbelievable, actually unforgivable, that the Sun *newspaper would endanger the personal safety of my five-year-old grandson by not only publishing details of the alleged kidnap plot, but also splashing this little boy's photograph across its front pages. There can be no excuse for this action.*

I recall, at the end of last year, the discretion exercised by that same newspaper over the contretemps between its editor, Rebekah Wade, and her partner, Ross Kemp. Then the only issue was of the personal dignity of a pair of adults, not the personal security of an innocent child. Shame on you Wade and your unthinking cohorts.

Tony Booth, Blacklion, Ireland

Guy Harrison was abroad. When we spoke it was clear he was less than impressed with the unfolding drama and my tactics in dealing with it.

On the train back from London, I discussed folding the entire enterprise with Nadine.

'First the in-fighting, then *Granada Tonight*, then the *Screws of the World* and now this. What's next? Better to take an early retirement and live to fight another day. I need to destroy this campaign in order to save it – I'd rather abandon it now, than abandon all hope.'

'But will people see it that way?' says Nadine. 'This is their life-raft, Matt. F4J is their only hope. Without that they are lost.'

'There will be those who understand and accept it, those that despair, and then there's the mob that wanted me gone from the moment I started. At least they should be pleased. Besides, give it a few months and see if the splinter groups fill the vacuum. If they don't, which I suspect, we'll re-group and reinvent ourselves. But Fathers 4 Justice in its current form simply isn't tenable as a campaigning force for change.'

One of the many members of the 'Matt O'Connor Fan Club' – please form an orderly queue, you'll have an opportunity to insert a blade between shoulder blades shortly – sent me a typically cunty email:

You have proven yourself to be the spineless fraudster that I have known you were for a long time . . . you are one of sickest individuals I have ever met.

'Isn't that nice, Jenny? Recognition and accolades already and I've barely departed, but don't you think this is a bit odd coming from a man who wanted me gone years ago and blackmailed us for money before he returned a £900 banner?'

All-round good egg, journalist Phil Doherty from North East paper the *Sunday Sun*, let me know that he'd interviewed a former MI5 officer about the alleged kidnap plot and the prognosis wasn't good.

'Fathers 4 Justice have been set up, Matt, and the plan is to bring you down personally.'

It was time to beat a retreat, at least until things had died down. Better to go out in a blaze of glory than as a damp squib. I scheduled an interview with Channel 4 News, live from Winchester Cathedral. I stopped taking calls from F4J in case they talked me out of it. By 7 p.m. I'd been up over forty-eight hours.

As obituaries go, I got an OK ride on Channel 4, but it was clear the events of the last three years were about to pull me under. As we walked back through the grounds of the cathedral, a woman lurched towards me and grabbed me by the arm. It was Samantha Simmons from Sky News. They'd spent hours driving round in their satellite truck, trying to track me down. But tonight just wasn't her night. As they wired me up for the interview I could hear my arch nemesis at the other end, babbling over the headphones. 'It ain't happening,' I told Samantha. 'I'm out of here.' As Nadine and I walked back up the cobbled street, Samantha was clutching my arm and pleading, ' Matt, please, Matt, you must do this, please.'

'No,' I told her. 'This party's over.'

The sound of multiple phones ringing was coming from Archie's pram as we returned to the car. I took the batteries out and threw them in the back of the car. We stopped for a Chinese meal in Romsey. I took one sniff of a chilled glass of Sauvignon Blanc and passed out.

BYE BYE, BATMAN – HELLO, WONDER WOMAN

I had little sympathy for the dads in superhero suits – until yesterday

MARK LAWSON

The demise of F4J was front-page news. The *Telegraph* ran it as their main cover story, as did the *Sun* and most other nationals. People started saying complimentary things about Fathers 4 Justice. All of a sudden we were going to be missed. The obituaries were generous, even flattering. People call you a cunt while you are alive and then, all of a sudden, when you shuffle off the mortal coil, you become the people's friend.

The *Sun's* letters page ran the headline 'Fanatics have ruined cause':

Extremists on the fringe of Fathers 4 Justice plotted to kidnap Tony Blair's son Leo but were foiled by police, who warned they would be shot. F4J chief Matt O'Connor has scrapped the group and many readers are sad the campaign has been destroyed by radicals.

What a pity Fathers 4 Justice have had to disband because of the actions of extremists. Children need to see both parents so I hope the access issue doesn't die with the group. The welfare and happiness of our kids is too important.

Alison, Newcastle upon Tyne

Fathers 4 Justice have given inspiration, advice and support to me and thousands of fathers in the same position – fighting through the courts to gain access to their children. I have battled for eighteen months to see my two kids after my ex-wife met a guy on the internet and disappeared with them. It is terrible that F4J has closed because of four men in Santa outfits. I hope Matt O'Connor continues to help dads.

Darren, Porthcawl, South Wales

What a shame that extremists attached themselves to Fathers 4 Justice. The

campaign is a worthy one and I hope the public understand this plot was hatched by a lunatic fringe.
  Nik, Southampton

I was horrified that extremists planned to kidnap Tony Blair's son Leo. But it is a tragedy that this has led Matt O'Connor to scrap Fathers 4 Justice. This well-meaning organisation should not be stopped by a small number of militants.
  Jack, Great Yarmouth, Norfolk

Extremists wanted to further the rights of shut-out fathers. Instead they've set the agenda back ten years. It's sad but right that Matt O'Connor is disbanding Fathers 4 Justice. No organisation can afford to provide oxygen for lunacy.
  Chris, Nottingham

The would-be kidnappers are a disgrace to any father who is genuinely trying to gain access to his child.
  Sue, Scunthorpe, Lincs

I called Glen to ask his opinion. It was a bit belated, though. I hadn't consulted anybody about this beforehand, and I was aware there would be some severely pissed-off people out there.

'It's genius, Matt, sheer bloody genius. It must be great living in Matt-land, taking a negative story like that and turning it into a victory by claiming you had no choice to finish it. It's bollocks. Glorious, clever, unashamed bollocks,' said Glen admiringly.

For a few moments I thought it was divine providence, but he was seriously wide of the mark in his summary. His comments perhaps said as much about his approach as it did about mine. Where Glen moved from project to project, I wasn't really prepared to walk away from F4J. My decision was a pragmatic and tactical one rather than a statement of surrender. I was intent on finishing what I'd started. Every fibre in my body had been dedicated to what was now a glorious failure. I felt beaten, but I knew that the conditions that had led to the creation of Fathers 4 Justice were still prevalent and, if anything, on the increase. Mothball it, I thought, retool it, sans baggage, and make it a leaner, meaner fighting machine. In the meantime, sit back and see what the provisional wing of the father's movement could do.

The Times said that when historians look back on British Society at the start of the third millennium they would accord a small but important chapter to the men in tights. The phrase 'fathers' rights' had entered the political lexicon as a result of our Lycra-clad efforts.

Some commentators complained that fathers still needed justice and that I had been too hasty. Others, from Lorraine Kelly in the *Sun* to the *Telegraph* leader column, agreed that I had done the right thing.

The kidnap plot even popped up across the water in an episode of the US TV show *Saturday Night Live* when they ran a sketch featuring a news reader delivering the following bulletin:

Fathers 4 Justice announced today that they would be disbanding following a failed plot to kidnap the British Prime Minister's son, Leo Blair. Apparently the fathers involved in the plot forgot that it was their turn and failed to pick the child up on time.

At the time it seemed that, if we had achieved nothing else, Fathers 4 Justice had brought about a climate change, opening up the family justice system to public scrutiny and challenging the status quo with its gutsy if provocative campaigning style.

Predictably, the lame-duck dads' groups were lining up to celebrate our demise and to trample on what was left of our reputation. The 'El Presidente' of one two-bit organisation went so far as to describe my decision as a 'huge relief'.

However, many emails and letters of encouragement poured in, urging me to reconsider abandoning the campaign.

Dear Matt,
   I really have so much respect for you to start such an organisation. You have inspired thousands of people including myself.
   Simon S., Student

Dear Sirs,
I am trying to contact Matt O'Connor. I am a practising Catholic who, maybe, has a different angle on this situation. In my diary it says this, 'Defeat is only a temporary situation, giving up is what makes it permanent.' God does not want Matt to give up. Children have a right: the right to be loved and cared for by the father God gave them.
   Regards
   Steve

'Sounds like somebody has been talking to God on the big white telephone,' said Jenny.

'I'll take encouragement from any source at this moment in time,' I replied.

My longstanding *fidus Achates* and campaign colleague Andy Neil, left me surprised and deeply touched when he emailed our forum to say that if he hadn't met me, he'd have killed himself.

None of this was enough to dampen the *News of the World*'s desire to dance on my grave. Having dusted off a previous hatchet, they were lining up for a second bite of my testicles. Some disaffected expelled members chipped in the odd bucketload of bullshit in an apparent effort to raise funds for a floundering splinter group they had set up.

Journalist Jane Atkinson emailed me a copy of the article. Some of the stories were so outrageous that if the paper had bothered to check its facts they would have known they had been sold a right load of porkies. Jenny, Nadine and I agreed that the best comment was no comment. If they went ahead and published, we would sue the fuckers.

Later I went to meet my MP at his constituency surgery to discuss my concerns about family law. An unwitting Mark Oaten asked what I thought about the Fathers 4 Justice campaign. 'It got things moving,' I said, 'when politicians were turning an expedient blind eye to fatherlessness and its social consequences.' He admitted it was a remarkable campaign, but said that MPs couldn't be seen to capitulate to that sort of pressure. If they did, all the other pressure groups would be at it.

Honouring prior commitments, I did a handful of public turns.

An impossibly intelligent Will Self dropped in to interview me for *GQ* magazine. Having swum in the deep end of the addiction pool, Self had transformed himself into a beacon of health. That is, apart from his habitual fag habit and the misanthropic grave-digger look he had fashioned for his exterior.

The interview was for an article timed to coincide with the launch of his new tome, *The Book of Dave*. With barely disguised relish, he revealed that it was based on me. I'm at a loss as to how a story about a racist, misogynistic, homophobic cab driver could be based on somebody who was in the anti-apartheid movement, whose mother is a feminist and was an admirer of campaigner Peter Tatchell. At least he was honest, admitting that the exploit-ative nature of his trade can seem amoral. He hadn't wanted to research me too much; instead he'd constructed his fable around the caricature he saw in his mind's eye. Journalists don't like facts that won't bend to fit a story.

Despite being likened to a maddened East End cabbie, I found Self to be an admirable chap steeped in a humanity accumulated while climbing the face of some pretty monstrous demons. Perched at the breakfast bar in my new house, overlooking the River Itchen, Self inhaled deeply before drawling out a line of questions.

'So why did you bring Fathers 4 Justice to a close, given the *Sun's* story stank to high heaven?'

'I was the guy who gave birth to the thing, so I had the right to kill it off,' I said.

'That's a fairly apposite choice of parental imagery for somebody who, more than any other, has put fathers' rights on the British political agenda.'

'It's a long story Will, but I really hated the thing with a fucking passion – and everything it had become.'

'Well, your critics concede you have done the right thing.'

'I'm not sure that's the reaction I wanted.'

'Don't you think though that the story ran at a time when Blair needed a sympathy injection and the CSA was in its death throes? What better way of reaffirming the Prime Minister as daddy-of-us-all than exposing – and then crushing – a threat to his own kid? All the story needed to get going was one crank of the Downing Street spin machine and a compliant police source.'

'It's a beautiful piece of work by the government,' I agreed admiringly, 'very clever.'

'Do you not think you're a bit of a conundrum? There's the considerate man of reason trying to contain the excesses of your followers, who'd resolved his own issues and now has a new partner and baby son, and then there is this feisty, combative man who takes no prisoners. Blair, the Archbishop of York and Tory grandee Bill Cash have all come under your lash.'

'I don't like bullshitters and I don't like backstabbers. I take no prisoners and I leave no survivors. That's my modus operandi. That's how I work.'

'In that case, you may feel differently about me when you have a look at your own fictional portrayal.'

'I'm in a reflective and generous mood at the moment, so don't worry too much. Besides, I don't doubt I'll have an opportunity to respond with an appropriate gesture, if that's necessary.'

Over the coming months various journalists traipsed in and out of the 'not-your-run-of-the' Millhouse in Twyford, known in my social circle as the 'Twyford Zone', for post-coital F4J interviews and to discuss plans for a new libertarian campaign group called 'Agents For Change'. In the old days I'd have given my right arm for this sort of thing, but now . . . now, I was almost past caring.

Foolishly, I agreed to one final interview with the *Independent* before ducking out of the spotlight for a while.

I started off by abusing journalists. All of them. Not the greatest start to an interview, even by my standards, but then this was to be my final word on Fathers 4 Justice for some considerable period of time. As gob-in-chief I'd been shooting my mouth off enough and I figured most people would be glad of the break. It's common practice among professional journalists to agree areas which are *off* limits and *on* limits. Off limits were my private life, where possible, and my client work. Some of my clients had been, not unnaturally, uncomfortable with the campaigning side of my work. So far as I was concerned, there was little difference between selling ice cream or selling a campaign and ideology I passionately believed in. Nevertheless, I didn't want to hack them off and for that reason they had remained unnamed during the four years of my F4J involvement.

Bless Deborah Ross from the *Independent* then. She was the perfect assassin for my final interview. Up she rolled, a petite ball of good-natured banter, and we agreed the demarcation lines. However, within minutes of the interview getting under way, it was clear that she had an agenda. Already tired after flying back from a product launch at the Royal Highland Show in Edinburgh, I was in no mood for her prodding and goading with the odd, 'Men in tights, pah!' sort of dismissive comment. Finally I snapped.

'You think it's all some big joke. Funny fucking ha-ha. Grown men in tights who can't be taken seriously.'

'You don't seriously expect me to believe that judges stop kids seeing their fathers for no good reason?' she retorted.

'No, of course not. Why else would we do what we do? We're just doing it for adolescent kicks. I've got nothing better to do with my life than go out and engage in a bit of mischief making. Other people like nothing better than the thrill of being shot at . . .'

'But the courts don't want to wipe fathers out of children's lives. There must be a jolly good reason before they —'

I thumped my fist on the table. 'You don't get it, do you? You live cocooned in your own world of blissful ignorance. The fact that you can't see it, because we have secret courts, doesn't mean it isn't happening. There has been an awful misunderstanding. You think because I have a sense of humour I think it's all a bit of a joke. But it isn't. It's my defence mechanism. Humour is my mask, my way of coping with people topping themselves, people clinging by their fingertips to the edge of humanity. I wanted to open your eyes, but you've come here with your own agenda.'

Ross looks at me with wide-eyed astonishment. 'You swear a lot, don't you. If I was your mother I'd wash your mouth out.'

'And if I was your son Miss Ross, I'd clean your ears out, because I don't think you are hearing a word I am saying.' I got off the stool and stepped towards the door.

'What would you do, Miss Ross, if somebody came along and took your child away?' She looked right at me, her mane of tightly curled mousy hair framing her face, eyes cold and taut. 'This interview is over.' I tell her.

'I can't make you out,' she replied, adopting a conciliatory tone. 'You're neither one thing nor the other. Why can't you be straight up and down like Will Young? He was an easy interview.'

'He's hardly straight, is he? I'm not a pop star and this isn't fucking *Pop Idol*.'

The article was an unmitigated disaster when it appeared the following week, not least because for the first time a journalist had broken the verbal understanding that my clients would not be mentioned. 'Elsanta taste like shit compared to these,' she quoted me as saying, referring to a variety of strawberry sold by one of my clients – who subsequently called me to discuss that 'interesting' interview.

In the post-interview fallout, the girls ordered me to take time out until September, but it wasn't to be. The failure of the splinter groups to fill the vacuum left by Fathers 4 Justice or provide any credible alternative troubled me greatly. In the end, Jenny inadvertently encouraged me to step back up to the campaign.

'That bunch of eunuchs couldn't get anything organised, they're all so busy clubbing each other over their heads with their man-bags. They must be the first group in the history of direct action to be suffering from campaign erectile dysfunction – the inability to get anything or anyone up.'

We got wind that the government was considering opening up the family courts and decided we must capitalise on this opportunity. This was unfinished business.

One afternoon in April, Jolly called. 'That Gandhi thing you always quote?'

'Yeah.'

'First they ignore you, then they laugh at you, then they fight you, then you win? Well, they ignored us, then we played it for laughs. Then they fought us and tried stitching us up in the *Sun*. Surely that means that the next stage is winning?' Jol sounds expectant and excited.

'Have you been drinking from the fountain of optimism again, Jol?' I asked wearily. 'I don't know what to think any more.'

Inwardly I was reconciling myself to the reality that, whatever I did, however I felt, this mission seemed to have my name sewn into the very fibre of the campaign.

'Perhaps we should find out,' said Jol. 'You're the ideas man, Matt.'

'Well, the one thing I do know is that a well-toned imagination will always save the day.'

The group was repositioned with more beef and less bollocks and a critical emphasis on helping young offenders from fatherless families, and families, and mothers. Not least because mothers like Trupti Patel, Angela Cannings and the late Sally Clark have also suffered terrible injustices at the hands of the family courts.

Aiming to broaden our franchise, we decided to challenge the cartoonish representation of our organisation, which had, rather ironically, been run by women since its inception – a fact that didn't receive any airtime because it didn't fit the perceived stereotypical wisdom about F4J.

SHAMBOLLOCKS: THE CHILD SUPPORT FIASCO

'Without rights there cannot be any incumbent duties.'

MARY WOLLESTONECRAFT, AUTHOR, PHILOSOPHER & FEMINIST 1759–1797

'I don't know what to do,' the dismembered voice said despairingly. 'They're after me for £14,000 in arrears, they've fucked my second relationship 'cos my girlfriend can't deal with this shit, and I've lost my home, my wife, my child. One month they took so much out from my salary they left me with two hundred quid to live on, pay my mortgage everything. I'm on the brink, I just feel so suicidal. I've got nothing left to live for.'

This was just one of several hundred calls I received over four years relating to the issue of child support. While it wasn't one of the main focuses for Fathers 4 Justice at that time, it was an issue that stole vast tracts of time from the core campaign. Anyone who wanted to see an exercise in incompetence need look no further than the universally loathed Child Support Agency. Sitting-duck dads were easy targets, waiting to be fleeced. The CSA plundered the most vulnerable to the brink of suicide while 'dodgy' dads escaped paying a single penny, leaving many families in dire financial straits. It was too much like hard work for the minions in the Department for Work and Pensions to pursue somebody who was self-employed or working in the black economy. Likewise those muppet mums who denied all contact for no good reason yet still expected their pound of flesh. And with the CSA's help, they got it.

The primary piece of legislation that formed the basis for the activities of the Child Support Agency was openly discriminatory on gender lines. This was because the mother had automatic 'Parental Responsibility' (PR), while the father only had automatic PR if he was married to the mother. The mother therefore became the parent with care and was therefore automatically in receipt of Child Benefit.

The Social Security Contributions and Benefits Act 1992 specified that between a husband and wife 'the wife shall be entitled' and that between parents 'the mother shall be entitled'. The father was deliberately labelled as the 'parent without care' or 'non-resident parent' after separation by the legislation, with no contingency for a shared parenting arrangement. Far from being a choice for fathers, the absence of fathers (after separation) was demanded by the 1991 Child Support Act. It became, effectively, not a description, but a prescription.

To many fair-minded people, Child Support should have meant both financial *and* emotional support on a level footing with the other parent, sharing rights *and* responsibilities. Like bread without the butter, divorcing child support from contact or parenting time was impossible in the real world. The two were inextricably linked.

In effect, the consequence of this ill-written and discriminatory piece of legislation was that Child Support had become a tax on fatherhood. What we describe in more colourful parlance as a 'punitive penis tax', based not on equality, but on gender. Worse still, the intellectual response of Ministers was to dump the blame for the integral failings of the CSA on fathers, in a pathetic attempt to absolve themselves of their own incompetence by scapegoating dads in the media.

'Don't tax my tadger!' shouted our barrister, the savvy Michael Cox, at one meeting to discuss the CSA. In fact Coxy had more reason that most to protest. All his life he had lived within the law and now as a barrister, worked within the legal system. As a man of law, he was such a noble and rare find that, in the immortal words of Basil Fawlty, we ought to have had him stuffed. However the father of five from Hythe near Southampton was now preparing to go to prison rather than pay the Child Support Agency. He was prepared to go even further. If incarcerated, he would go on hunger strike.

Michael complained that the CSA treated him as the 'absent' parent or 'parent without care,' except he wasn't absent and looked after his children 50 per cent of the time.

'Are you sure you are prepared to go through with this?' I asked him during a break, 'I mean prison, it could be a rough ride.'

'It's bloody offensive, Matt, I'm not absent – nobody pays me when the kids are with me so why should I pay the state for the other 50 per cent of the time? If the buggers think I'm going to cough up all this money they allege is outstanding, then stuff them. The boy's mother already receives all the child benefit and family tax credits. I get nothing because I'm a man, and father to my children.'

The CSA had been beset by all manner of catastrophes and condemnations. The agency itself cost £200 million more to run than it collected. For every £1 it obtained, about 25 pence went to the Department for Work and Pensions. Half of the alleged £3.5 billion owed by so-called absent fathers was owed to the Treasury, not to the children.

Last year CSA staff were paid the princely sum of £25 million in bonuses for *failing* to collect £3.5 billion in unpaid maintenance leaving a record 1.4 million families trapped in the system. Now the government planned to introduce a new child support agency which was based on exactly the same principles as the CSA: motivating as many parents (read dads) to pay maintenance for their children.

In other words, the government's myopic approach was focused on recouping benefits from the only people who could genuinely lift their children and their families out of the benefit trap without any need for state intervention. If only the state would allow them to play their role as parents. So much for joined up government.

The government were also at one stage thought to be considering introducing the mandatory naming of the father on the birth certificate to make him financially responsible. If the father was made financially responsible, then the state must also allow dads the right to be emotionally responsible.

As the feminist Mary Wollstonecraft argued at the turn of the century, rights and responsibilities are indivisible, one cannot exist without the other.

THE JAILING OF MICHAEL COX

'An individual who breaks a law that conscience tells him is unjust, and who willingly accepts the penalty of prison in order to arouse the conscience of the community over its injustice, is in reality expressing the highest respect for the law.'

DR MARTIN LUTHER KING, JNR.

Just weeks after our refusenik barrister Michael Cox baited the suits at CSA by defying a court order to start making child support payments, he found himself in front of a coterie of magistrates at Southampton Magistrates Court.

The bottom line for the CSA was that Cox had, over ten years, ran up a bill of some £42,000 in unpaid child support and that he was on some sort of 'crusade' against the Child Support Agency. It was payback time – either

Mike coughed up or he would be banged up – care of Her Majesty's already overcrowded Prison Service.

From the outset, the omens did not look favourable. The CSA sharks were to demonstrate a previously unsurpassed level of emotional brutality. Having publicly signalled that they were to come down on 'dodgy dads' like a 'ton of bricks', the naming and shaming of fathers on the CSA site (with their ex-partners' permission) had scented the waters. Cox's case was to send them into a feeding frenzy.

His scalp was infinitely more valuable than that of the average 'deadbeat' dad. Firstly, he was a man of law, who was prepared to break the law to uphold a principle. Secondly, he was a high-profile F4J figure. His incarceration and subsequent scapegoating would send a clear signal to other itinerant fathers who defied the CSA and the government. If it could happen to a barrister and member of F4J – it could happen to you.

But the case wasn't as cut and dried as the propaganda made out. Michael Cox's ex-wife had written to the court pleading with them not to lock him up as it would force her to stop work and resort to benefits. Mike's boys, Elliott (16) and twins Matthew and Daniel (13), were also desperate that their dad wasn't sent down.

Cox himself saw it in black and white terms. He looked after his boys 50 per cent of the time. He clothed them, fed them, took them on holidays and provided a roof over their heads. He didn't receive any child benefit for the time they were with him, so why should he have to pay the government for the other 50 per cent of the time?

Why did the CSA say he was an 'absent father' when quite clearly he wasn't? Why did the state treat the mother as the carer, and the father as nothing more than a financial provider? Michael wasn't on a 'crusade' as the CSA said – he was on a quest for equality. He was a man of modest means. He drove a mashed up Renault that had a hole in the footwell and the bumper held on by tie-clips. Every penny he earned went on his family.

For son Matthew, who had come to court on that fateful day, the trauma of the thought of his father going to jail was too much for him. He had to act. He had to do something. The magistrates had decided to hold Coxy's committal to prison in closed court. As I got up close and personal with security, wedging the door open with sheer brute force as the guard clamped my torso against its metal frame, Matthew slipped through and burst into court to shout, 'Don't jail my dad! Don't send him to prison! I love my dad!' In tears, the boy was ushered from the court back into the waiting area where the rest of us, neutered once more by the closed doors of a secret court, stood, helpless and frustrated.

'Don't worry, Matty,' I said as I wrapped my arms around his shoulder, 'I'm sure he'll be alright.'

Famous. Last. Words.

When the bench retired, the few press who had been allowed in told me that it was inevitable he'd be sent down. The clerk of the court had told the magistrates that their decision was not to rule on the 'children's bests interests' as the Child Support Agency had already considered their 'interests'. The matter for the bench was whether Mr Cox had broken the terms of the court order and that if he had, he should be committed to jail, unless there was good reason to the contrary. This, they were told, was according to the CSA, 'in the child's best interests'. Trouble was, nobody ever asked the kids. It was hard to think of anything that could be in their worst interests.

Michael was sentenced to forty-two days' imprisonment starting immediately. With a clunk and a click he was cuffed and sent straight down. Outside we were overcome with emotion. His son Matty was crushed by the news.

'I don't want him to go to jail! He's my *dad*. I love him!' I thought Michael could have avoided the outcome quite easily, simply by paying something. Anything. But he wouldn't sacrifice his principles. He'd rather surrender his liberty instead to make the point that he wanted to be treated as an exact equal to the mother in the eyes of the law. Not a walking wallet. He was now a prisoner of his own choice. A prisoner of conscience.

Outside the court, I confronted the prosecution barrister. 'I'm proud,' I told him. 'Michael Cox could have spent this day on his knees begging you for mercy, but he stood on his feet for his principles and for his children. He's got more guts than you and me both. Pass my thanks on to your management. You have just re-ignited the flame of Fathers 4 Justice.'*

FAMILY LAW LOTTO: NEXT TIME IT COULD BE YOU

As I considered the repositioning of the group, I hooked up with Glen for a brainstorming session. We wanted to explore different types of protest that would involve women and curb my Rabelaisian excess. First up on the drawing board was a 'naked truth' protest in Trafalgar Square, or 'Trafalgar Bare', as Glen liked to call it.

'It's got to be tasteful though, Glen. Could be a bit fruity.' I cautioned.

'I know' said Glen, 'what about this as an idea for a stage show: "Talking

---

* Mr Cox was released on bail by a judge at Bristol Crown Court on 5 July. At the time of writing he is planning to challenge the decision to commit him to prison.

Bollocks" our answer to the *Vagina Monologues*.' We laughed at the absurdity of the ideas but each of them contained nuggets of pure campaign gold.

We also took a long hard look at Nelson's Column, which had scaffolding erected around its base.

'Why don't we fit old Nelson up in a giant condom?' I said to Glen. 'Or paint the old bugger a nice shade of purple? Even better, I've got a contact in Canada who can produce a Judicial Toilet Paper with a picture of the President of the Family Division on it. We could deposit them in courtroom toilets across the country with the slogan 'Wipe out family law injustice'.

In the end we opted for a protest with balls, but using somebody else's rather than our own. We needed an injection of new blood and some momentum to rebuild the campaign. My first objective was to engage in a little piece of public service broadcasting, our own infomercial on BBC1, prime-time, no less. It needed to be a live show, one with a big audience and as dull as dishwater. The only unimaginative drivel that met that criteria was the BBC's National Lottery Jet Set Show. I worked up a plan and deliberately didn't tell anyone what was involved until I met up with the team of six activists in a hotel room in Paddington. This operation was going to be tight.

'Right, guys and girls, are you feeling lucky tonight?'

'What's the plan, Matt?' asked John Levis.

'The National Lottery. Jolly has already been on a recon, so we know the seating plan and the format of the programme. We are 90 per cent certain that it goes out live with no time delay. The plan is really simple: Jol and Darryl, you head over the barriers and down on to the stage floor. John, Ray and Nadine, head down the stairs to the front and around on to the stage. The pincer movement should do the trick. Remember to take off your tops so the T-shirts are visible, and then it's showtime.'

'Is that it, Matt?' said Darryl, his face etched with nervousness.

'That's it, mate. That's all you need to do. Nadine, if you get a chance, remember to give Eamonn Holmes a big smacker on the side of the cheek, depositing as much lipstick as possible. OK? Let's rock and roll.'

With that everybody was piling into cabs and heading off to the BBC, their 'Family Law Lotto: Next Time It Could Be You' T-shirts hidden underneath their everyday attire.

At about 7.45 p.m. 10 million people tuned in to see not just the Lotto draw, but a classic example of agitprop infinitely more entertaining than the show it replaced. Gobsmacked host Eamonn Holmes was left bemused and skulking behind his female co-host as the programme was taken off air, leaving the 'voice of the balls' Alan Dedicoat floundering, clutching at words to fill the time while viewers stared at a screen grab of the National Lottery Jet Set logo.

This time the protest was headed up not by a dad but a mother, my partner Nadine. Not everything went to plan, though. Darryl failed to make an appearance after jumping a barrier and landing on a couple of TV cameras. Jol made it up, but was brought down near the podium where the presenter starts the lottery. Ray Barry made a brief appearance before being bundled off, but then Nadine arrived to take centre stage. Within seconds my mobile went.

'Dad! Dad! I've just seen Nadine on the telly,' screamed my 9-year-old son Alexander. 'I was just watching the TV and it was really boring and then I could hear shouting and I thought, who's that? And then Nadine went on TV in front of the screen and I could hear more shouting and it was really funny. I want to see more rugby tackling on the lottery, Dad.'

Guy Harrison and Darryl Westell spent most of the following day doing interviews and touring newsrooms.

'The lottery is a metaphor,' argued Guy in one interview, 'for what can happen to any parent, mother or father and their children at the hands of the secret family courts.'

The following day we received considerable coverage in the Sunday papers and the website took hundreds of hits and membership inquiries.

Dear Sirs,
Thank you for coming back. I never doubted that you wouldn't but you've given me renewed hope once more that this iniquitous law will change.
David D., London

Well done Fathers 4 Justice,
I'm still feeling proud of you, well done to you all. Thank you for highlighting such an important issue for British law. The nation is entitled to be made aware of what goes on in the Family courts. There is so much illegal behaviour and children are suffering. It has to stop.
Mrs Angela F., Cheshire

But the sweet turned sour when Monday's *Daily Mail* ran a hatchet on Nadine under the headline 'Hypocrite of lottery demo fathers' rights protestor won't let her ex-husband see their little girl.'

In the article, journalist Dan Newling produced a piece that was so wildly inaccurate that it wouldn't have been out of place being broadcast on Jackanory. And later, Guy had some warming words for me post the Lottery demo when we had lunch at the Hotel du Vin in Winchester.

'You know Matt, now that you've kick started things again, if you carry on, they'll assassinate you,'

'Don't be fucking stupid Guy,'

'It's true. You keep making yourself a pain in the arse of the establishment and they could take you out … car crash, induced heart attack and then whoosh, kaput – you're gone…'

'Cheers, mate. And people think I'm paranoid enough already!'

Whilst I didn't subscribe to what most people would view as a pretty outlandish theory, as I eyed my salmon sandwich with heightened suspicion, it did occur to me that historically, people who 'tried to do the right thing' tended to get knocked off in mysterious circumstances. I could only think of what Churchill had said. That I would never surrender, and that if they came to get me, they'd have to drag me out by my boots.

MOTHER TONGUE

The overriding principle of our campaign was not 'justice for fathers', but 'fathers for justice'. I'd seen many mothers lose their children in the family courts for no good reason and, despite the fact they were in a minority, the pain and suffering inflicted on them was unspeakably cruel, with the added burden of the social stigma society attached to mothers not seeing their children.

I had also seen the way my mother had been treated by my father, and I knew that there had to be a better way through personal relationships than engaging in a life of perpetual conflict.

'I don't know what else I can do,' I told Nadine one day when she broke down in tears on the sofa in despair at her ongoing case.

'I don't think it's ever going to end,' she sobbed. 'I can't face it, Matt. I simply can't face any more of this.'

'Well, there is one positive,' I said. 'At least I can now speak authoritatively on all aspects of family law, having experienced both sides of the story.'

We held each other tightly, but the effect of proceedings placed an intolerable pressure on our relationship because I really, really didn't want to be involved in anything that would drag me back into the gladiatorial court system. Nadine's experience released all the painful memories that had been ring-fenced in my mind for the last four years. Once again, I was living the nightmare, not just for myself, but for a partner I deeply loved and cared for, and our family.

SPY GAMES

Off the back of the Lotto demo, F4J resurfaced on the radar of the security services. Suddenly everywhere we went in the UK our company car was being stopped by the police. Apparently we were now one of eighty cars tagged as a 'security risk' in the UK. Unfortunately on each occasion it was the long-suffering Jenny that was stopped. At the Royal Highland Show in Edinburgh we were organising an exhibition for a client when Jen was pulled over by half-a-dozen armed cops and an unnamed plainclothes Royal Protection Officer. They turned the car inside out in a hunt for superhero costumes which they seemed to believe we had buried away in boxes full of strawberry paraphernalia for the exhibition stand.

'But I can't stand kids!' Jen protested to the Royal Protection Officer.

'Where is Mr O'Connor?'

'At the stand. You should be speaking to him if you have any questions.'

Taking her advice, he called me. 'Mr O'Connor?'

'Yes.'

'I'm a Royal Protection Officer. I've pulled one of your colleagues over and searched her car. Can I ask what you are doing at the show?'

'It's heart-warming to know I'm so well protected, but I'm with clients on a stand. By all means pop by for a strawberry and a chat, but if you think I'm up to something you're seriously mistaken. I never mix business with the pleasure of campaigning.' Still he persisted in trying to discuss matters relating to national security. 'Look, mate, I'm on fruit duty today. I despair with police surveillance because you guys inevitably roll up at the wrong place at the wrong time with the wrong end of the wrong stick. I don't know about police intelligence, because so far I haven't seen any.'

'Can I take your date of birth, then, to verify who you are before I go?' he asked.

'Excuse me? Are you on some kind of medication? I don't even know your name and yet you are asking me for my date of birth? You've just spent fifteen minutes discussing national security with me, yet from what you say you need to verify who I am. I could have been anyone. If I am who you think I am, I'm sure my date of birth will be well known to you.' And with that the conversation came to an abrupt end.

The following morning at the hotel Jenny told me she thought the car had been broken into. Mysteriously, nothing has been taken.

'What do you mean, somebody has been in the car?' I asked, standing in the car park looking at 'Roxy' the company wheels. 'She looks fine to me.'

'But look, Matt, the rubber sealant on the driver's window has been pushed in and there are flecks of green paint inside the car. All the paperwork has been taken off the passenger seat where I'd left it and put in the back, but nothing is missing. Nothing. Do you think it's anything to do with yesterday?'

'I guess it's possible the car has been bugged and had a tracking device fitted. It could be spooks, Jen, but then that's an occupational hazard.'

'Well, they won't get much from our conversations – all we do is argue like an old married couple.'

'There is only one way of finding out. I've been bloody followed, covertly filmed and recorded over the last few years and I'm beginning to get a tad cheesed off. We'll need to get a counter-intelligence investigator in to sweep everything. The car, the house, everything. It's seriously overdue, but I need to review all our security arrangements.'

I called Adrian Laurie at the Yard to pick his brains about what had happened.

'What do you expect, Matt? They've all got your picture anyway.'

'What do you mean? Who's "they"?' I asked.

'Every police station in the UK has a copy of your picture.'

Fucking great, I thought, I'm an outlaw. Bloody Billy the Kid, Ned Kelly and now Matt O'Connor. Probably some wobbly shot of my tower of chins blown up to A3 size. Let's hope they didn't get me confused with Shrek or a gay Johnny Vegas.

I called in a retired counter-intelligence officer to conduct an electronic debugging sweep of the property and the car, as well as to discuss future vetting and security procedures for Fathers 4 Justice. He told me that the electronic eavesdropping and industrial espionage industry was worth millions of pounds a year and that, with advancements in modern technology, spy games have never been easier.

According to the spying watchdog, the Interceptions and Communications Commissioner, in the last year alone 439,000 requests were made to monitor people's telephone calls, emails and post. These applications were made to 795 separate bodies including MI5, MI6, GCHQ, 52 police forces, 475 local authorities and 108 other organisations.

That's in addition to the fact that 20 per cent of the world's CCTV cameras are in London and that the UK has the world's largest DNA database. In my dealings with the police and state over the last few years I concluded that Britain was living in a state of national insecurity which was rather ironic given that national security was relatively straightforward to breach.

Within minutes the sweep had started and he was on to the external phone line supply which enters the property from underground via an external box. His inspection revealed that the insulation rubber on the cables had been stripped back to give access to the inner metal core, which in turn had given access to the telephone line. In short it looked like the landline had been tapped at some point in the recent past but the rest of the property and the car were clean.

'That isn't to say that it wasn't bugged yesterday, Matthew,' he said. 'The problem we have is that bugs can be easily placed and removed, depending on what risk you are perceived to pose. The higher your profile, the bigger the risk, the more likely it will be that you will be under some kind of surveillance.'

THE DENOUEMENT: HOW MUCH FATHER TO GO?

'It's been a black Christmas,' Richard Castle told me at the end of 2006. 'I don't know if I'll ever escape this. I've been stripped of everything but my love for my daughter.' He cut a broken figure, his life fractured by separation, but I'd exhausted my rhetoric and stock of ideas when it came to saving people. Despite paying over £40,000 in child support since 1998, neither he nor his mum had seen his daughter in nine years. His 72-year-old mother was in frail health and suffering from diabetes, asthma, anaemia and arthritis, and had given up hope of ever seeing her granddaughter again.

'Hang in there, mate,' I told him, searching deep in my soul for some kind of answer. 'You are going to be a father again. We're going to get your daughter back, I never give up on anyone.' Everything I had strived for and fashioned still hadn't been realised for the parents abandoned by society at the coalface of the court system. Had I, as my ex-wife had said, fought the law, and the law had won?

Even the eternal optimists were struck low.

'Family courts?' said a strangely muted Big Ron Davis. 'It should read "Welcome to hell". Having the option of either going back into court or not seeing your kids is like being given a choice between cholera and the plague,' he told me. He had moved heaven and earth to see his children, yet his case had fossilised in a never-ending spiral of hearings.

Even those who'd thought they had escaped the clutches of the court system still found themselves being reeled back in. Ray Barry, Gary Burch and Jolly Stanesby, to name but a handful, had all flicked the trip switch back to a dislocated parallel universe of misery. All still there, fighting to see their children. I couldn't help but feel that I had failed them all. A glorious failure, but a failure nonetheless. When we had taken our foot off the accelerator of direct action, the government had eased off on its response. There was, I concluded, only one language they understood. The language of revolt. Of sedition.

'It's the loss of hope that crushes you, Matt,' said Big Ron. 'Every time I go back into that emotional Abu Ghraib, they pick away at the scabs so you never heal. I think it could be the end of us if we don't achieve something tangible soon.'

'I'm really sorry, mate,' I told him. 'I wish I could have done more, but I won't give up, you have my word on that. This isn't the end of Fathers 4 Justice. It's the beginning, Ron. This is only just the beginning.'

'Why don't we make St Jude our campaign icon then?' Ron asked. 'He is the patron saint of lost causes, after all.'

'Well, I'm praying for a happy ending, Ron, even if nobody else is.'

We cracked a few jokes and the atmosphere grew a bit rosier, but piecing together the fragments of their shattered lives was no easy task when those fragments were still raining down like shards of glass around them. The human psyche can only take so much punishment before it's choked to extinction.

And if it was true that David Blunkett, the former Home Secretary, was only permitted to spend two supervised hours of contact a month with his son, what hope was there for the rest of us? Even the patron saint of good causes, Sir Bob Geldof, had been put through the mangle trying to get to see his kids. So what about the ordinary man on the street? The judges blame the law, the lawyers blame the parents and the parents blame each other, and in the absence of open courts and clear, fair and just legislation that promotes equal parenting, this destructive pattern is printed on every case that enters the family justice system.

But the government knew exactly what it was doing. It looked at opening the door to family justice by a few inches, but it did so with major qualifications. It will become a criminal offence for your case to be discussed in public. The only journalists allowed in would be accredited, court-approved hacks, mouthpieces for the courts. It was a token gesture, designed to appease the angry masses of dispossessed parents, to coerce the unwilling to conform, and to solicit the submission of those too frightened to speak out.

Those who were brave enough to shake off the threat of such sanctions would remind others of what we have forgotten: that the strength of our society depends on the strength of our families.

And I was still living the nightmare. Nadine's case continued to rumble on with unpleasant side-effects. She had to be hospitalised after a series of panic attacks and I was concerned that there might be a more serious underlying reason for the problems. With a legal aid bill in excess of £100,000, I finally told her to ditch her legal team. Because my involvement as the founder of Fathers 4 Justice had seemed likely to prejudice her case, we had persisted in using solicitors until, in the face of her ex's implacable hostility, their role in proceedings became redundant. Now I would go into court with her as a McKenzie friend, a friend or associate allowed in to assist a person who isn't legally represented.

You would think that after four years of campaigning, Fathers 4 Justice could celebrate some kind of victory. But the only battles we won were the moral victories and a critical battle for survival against all the odds. If there was a legacy that could be attributed to this insane venture, it was the fact that our withering attacks had all but destroyed the credibility of the secret courts.

Before 2002 nobody talked about family breakdown or the secret family courts; now the nation was aware of a fundamental injustice at the heart of the family law system. But our legacy extended beyond that. Fathers 4 Justice became part of the national fabric of popular culture, spoofed by comedy acts ranging from Rowan Atkinson on Comic Relief to Catherine Tate's 'Gingers 4 Justice', as well as TV adverts for Vodafone and various cartoons. There was Fathers 4 Justice Lego and 'Fathers 4 Justice' the song, written by a punk band called the Malloys. Even Scotland Yard, rather bizarrely, covertly got in on the unofficial merchandise act when a commemorative metal badge was produced depicting Batman standing astride Buckingham Palace with the date of our protest '13th September 2004' and Roman letters and numerals that read 'S.O.XIV' – an abbreviation for Special Operations 14 at Scotland Yard – the Royal Protection unit. When the impact of a campaign enters the mainstream vocabulary of a culture then you know you have made a seismic impact in terms of awareness.

In an effort to tackle the problem from the children up, rather than the fathers down, I eventually followed through with my commitment to set up a campaign to tackle fatherlessness and family breakdown. After climbing into the public's consciousness by scaling Britain's landmarks dressed as superheroes, the F4J inspired 'Future Heroes Project' would be a social initiative run by kids, for kids, funding projects that would help make Britain a better place to grow up. The Future Heroes Project would also aim to help children develop self-respect, build better relationships and take positive risks.

The project was catapulted into existence through my sheer exasperation and desperation at the ongoing ambivalence of political and religious leaders who did plenty of anguished hand-wringing about family breakdown, but little else. My credo about how, rather than acting in the 'child's best interests', the government, church and children's groups were failing our kids, was subsequently leant extra gravitas.

In early 2007 UNICEF published a report that put Britain bottom of twenty-one first world industrialised countries when it came to child welfare. In short, the report said, Britain was the worst place in the industrialised world in which to grow up – and this after ten years of Labour government.

The report analysed forty indicators of child well-being in twenty-one developed countries for the years 2000 to 2003. It identified the UK as a nation of broken families producing a generation of children that were unhappy, unhealthy and putting themselves at risk. The epitaph to the report read, 'The true measure of a nation's standing is how well it attends to its children – their health and safety, their material security, their education and socialisation and their sense of being loved, valued and included in the families and societies into which they are born.'

Evidence, if further evidence were needed, that the 'child's best interests principle' was a discredited and wicked deceit.

In tandem with this I was also working up concepts for a separate political vehicle for future activities. All these ideas and options were gestating in exactly the same way that the embryonic idea for Fathers 4 Justice had vacillated in my thoughts between 2000 and 2002. These gave me a range of differing solutions on how we could best effect change should our current strategy fail to deliver the results we required.

But these initiatives required funding and support, and, at that time, the detritus of family breakdown continued to swamp our office, overwhelming my best endeavours and frustrating future plans. Inevitably, the malevolent spectre of the threat of violence was never far away. In the last four years I'd dealt with firebombs, suicides, a father threatening to blow his brains out in front of Tony Blair, the Leo Blair kidnap plot, and a whole raft of unpleasant situations I never wanted to find myself in. And here again, history repeated itself. As I travelled on a bus from Winchester to Romsey to see my partner, I received a call on my mobile. The man at the other end of the line seemed composed, his thoughts collected and his rationale understandable, up to a critical point.

'It's not working, is it?' he said.

'What isn't?'

'What have you achieved? Very little. You've lined your pockets, helped yourself, but have you helped anyone else?'

'I'm sorry, but I object to that. You have no idea what I've been through.'

'Have you sold out then? I mean, have you given up on direct action?'

'I'll never give up. Ever. Not until we establish a fair, just, open and equitable system of family law.'

'You know what,' he said, his voice clouded by despair, 'I've lost everything: my kids, my wife, my house. I wasn't unfaithful. But she fucked around on me, she dumped me and then went off to live in another man's house, with my kids. Know how that makes you feel, do you?'

'I've a pretty good idea.'

'I want to frighten people, I want them to know what it's like to lose the people you love the most, for them to know that what they do isn't acceptable.'

'How? You won't win hearts and minds by scaring people.'

'Armed struggle, it's what Nelson Mandela believed in, it's the only way forward: a fathers' jihad. You probably know yourself deep down that people need to die before anything will change.'

'Only if somebody got shot on a peaceful protest, and God knows we've been close enough to that on several occasions. Violence is the language of people who can't argue their case. We can.'

'But no one's listening to you, Matt O'Connor. I'll plant something that will make them listen.'

'Mate, there's no future in that sort of talk for any of us —.' But the phone had gone dead. I rested my head against the window as the bus rattled along the country lanes of Hampshire. Deep down in my gut I knew that the call was genuine. You develop a sense for these things. The people who pose a real threat are not the drunken, mad dads, but those that are keeping it together and focused while inside they're crippled by a bitterness that has been incubating a deep-seated hatred of the system.

Back in 2003 I'd said that it was only a matter of time before an angry dad went out, got a gun and took out a judge. Now those prophetic words were coming back to haunt me. Despite passing information on to the Yard, our relationship with them had become increasingly strained since the Leo Blair kidnap story, when the anti-terrorist unit, Special Operations Unit 13, were suspected of being involved in leaking the 'plot' to the press. Now, our relationship with the police was to come to a sudden and dramatic end.

'You couldn't write this shit,' said Jolly a few days later. 'I've just had a letter from Scotland Yard which contains a veiled threat from the buggers.'

The call had come through from Jol at seven o'clock one morning, reviving ugly memories of the Leo Blair kidnap plot.

'Not again,' I said despairingly. 'What is it now?'

'I think they are worried about the State Opening of Parliament, Matt. It says our personal safety could be at risk.'

We'd had conversations earlier in the year about the ceremony and what could and couldn't be done, including handcuffing a protestor in a Homer Simpson mask to the Queen's carriage, but it was something we'd already ruled out. Either police intelligence had got the wrong end of the stick or they were trying to stitch us up once again. Twenty minutes later and a letter from the Yard dropped through my letterbox.

Dear Mr O'Connor

I am writing to you as a person believed to be a member or supporter of the group known as Fathers for Justice. At a recent Trooping the Colour ceremony, members of this group crossed police lines and attempted to disrupt the event.

There are, in the near future, a number of other ceremonial events in Central London that you have historically targeted as opportunities to raise publicity for your group. These imminent events include the State Opening of Parliament on 15 November 2006... you should clearly understand that any attempt to breach these cordons would place your personal safety at risk.

Yours sincerely

Commander Bob Broadhurst, Scotland Yard

Never in the history of Fathers 4 Justice had there been a showdown like the one at Scotland Yard which followed this letter. It had gone out not just to a handful of F4J members, but also to people who either belonged to splinter groups or had nothing to do with our campaign. The entire enterprise had the disconcertingly familiar overtones of the Leo Blair kidnap plot about it. With one simple phone call to me, the Yard could have established whether anything was in the offing, but they chose instead to label all manner of people as 'members or supporters' of Fathers 4 Justice. The Met were fully aware that this wasn't the case since they already had close tabs on the various splinter groups.

To my mind it seemed like a deliberate attempt to lump the dark underbelly of the movement in with the official group and thereby tar Fathers 4 Justice by association. I was incandescent.

Not only had the letter laid down a challenge to radical, extreme elements to attend the State Opening, but I was being warned off from entering London that day, the implication being that I would be arrested if I did. In telephone conversations with the Yard I was told that my personal safety and that of other activists could not be guaranteed. In other words, we could be shot. Given their trigger-happy ways, who was I to argue?

I needed to know what was happening in the event that the Yard leaked a story about this to the press. Having barely slept over the last couple of days I began to feel physically sick, fearing that a lone activist might get shot in the event they interpreted the provocative tone of the letter to be an open invitation to launch a protest at the State Opening.

'But we wouldn't do that,' countered Commander Bob Broadhurst, the blank-faced beanpole of a copper responsible for all major ceremonies in the capital.

I'd come to the Yard for an urgent con-flab with Nadine and Archie both in tow. It made for a surreal meeting as we sat in an office festooned with pictures of Broadhurst's family.

'What do you mean, you wouldn't do that? Course you would, you already have. Leo Blair kidnap plot, anyone? Or did that just mysteriously leak into the ether by mistake?'

'I can't comment on that.'

'Well, I can. It was leaked from the Yard to the *Sun*, who, it's my guess, must have secured the tacit approval of the Blairs before the story was published, as they never let anyone publish anything about their kids. Did you guys fucking investigate it? Did you fuck! I might look stupid, but don't insult my intelligence by playing dumb. We all know the game and we know how you play it.'

'Mr O'Connor, I find your language unnecessary.' Broadhurst was beginning to look flushed. Six of his colleagues, including Adrian Laurie, had joined us. All of them seemed to be staring blankly at the table top or out the window. None of his arguments were washing with me.

'I think it's unnecessary to get stitched up by one of your colleagues, but it happened. I find it unnecessary to be threatened with being shot or arrested if I enter the capital on a certain day. You wonder why I'm pissed off? It's because I don't believe you when you say that the letter you sent was a mistake. I've been there before. If any of this gets published, there will be consequences and it won't be the disbanding of Fathers 4 Justice again.'

Broadhurst swallowed hard and leaned towards me. 'Mr O'Connor, you'll be aware that two of your associates breached a cordon at the Trooping of the Colour in June. One of them got within twenty feet of the Queen and the Duke of Edinburgh. I had a call on the day to say that two protestors had been arrested. Initially, I thought nothing of it, until I saw the footage and it was clear that Mr Jolly Stanesby could quite easily have climbed into the carriage. For some reason he stopped within twenty feet of the vehicle. If he had carried on, you'd be talking to somebody else today.'

I resisted the urge to give a flippant reply along the lines of 'What, like a proper policeman?' It was clear that he had a difficult job to do and I didn't envy him. But I also had a job to do, and my job was to secure as much publicity for the cause as possible.

The Trooping of the Colour incident had indeed been sanctioned by me, but more as part of our testing and probing strategy. Jolly rightly pulled back at the last minute. Those last twenty feet were the difference between global headlines and no headlines, our leading activist cadging a lift up the Mall with Her Maj. I endeavoured to explain our strategy to the Commander.

'Look, I understand your position, but our strategy is an open book. It's no secret that we have an ideas bank of protests, that we consider everything and anything that involves peaceful non-violent direct action. We also try and keep it funny, though you guys won't see it that way, especially if you are made to look stupid. But all it takes is one call from you to me. It's a cat-and-mouse game, but if you suspect something then, generally, we won't do it. If somebody like Adrian Laurie calls me and says, "Look, Matt, you've been rumbled," then we'll pull it. I'm sure you understand why we do this.'

'No, not really, I don't understand why you can't use conventional routes.'

'Other groups have ploughed the conventional route for thirty years and jack shit has happened. All we're doing is pointing out that family law is a burning issue and we're sounding the alarm. Stick a million people on the streets for the anti-war demo and what happens? Jack shit happens. If I'd been running that gig, I'd have had them sit down for the entire day on the streets of London and, I tell you what, the result would have been very different.'

'I'm glad you weren't in charge of that.'

'But my point is that this government was born of civil disobedience. It unapologetically carried a social message about equality. To my mind, Fathers 4 Justice is cast from that same mould, but ultimately this isn't an issue like animal rights or fox hunting. This is an issue that touches every family in the country and then dumps the effluent on your doorstep in the shape of young offenders. You're a family man, Mr Broadhurst, do you have children?'

'Yes, I have.'

'So what would you do if you were walking down a high street on a Saturday afternoon and somebody snatched your child from you?'

'It's a silly question.'

'No it's not. You're a police officer, it happens, right? So answer the question.' But Broadhurst wouldn't, he was embarrassed at being put on the spot in front of his colleagues.

'Just answer the question, it's only hypothetical. . .'

'I'd respond.'

'How?'

'Physically.'

'You'd be violent?'

'Probably.'

I slammed my hand down hard on the table, dispensing with any last vestiges of etiquette and releasing a concentrated dose of rage.

'And that's my fucking point. How have we responded? We have responded in Lycra, in Father Christmas outfits, we have responded peacefully, but your response is to threaten visiting violence on us. Imagine dead dads on the streets at Christmas. A dead fucking Father Christmas outside Parliament. Why? Because you don't know how to deal with people like me, and in lieu of conversation with your puppet-masters you seek resolution with a truncheon or a bullet. So pass this back up your food chain. We have hundreds of new people joining us, the family courts are recruitment centres for Fathers 4 Justice. You've had fuck-all convictions of F4J activists because juries understand we act with a higher moral authority, an authority that's above the bastardised justice they call family law. Your role is to contain us, but you can't contain an idea. If I had to take a bullet for this cause, if nothing changes, then I'd be prepared to do it – that is the unstoppable force you face. But God help us all, Mr Broadhurst, if you respond with violence.'

As I got up to leave, I looked at Archie, who was grimacing with a face that read 'Shit O'Clock'. He let out a satisfying sigh of relief as the aroma of exploded nappy permeated the room. We bid our adieus and made for the door.

'That's my boy,' I said, then turned to Adrian, 'I think Archie has just articulated how I really felt.'

Adrian gave me a warm smile, 'Just remember, stay away from the splinter groups, stay out of trouble and take care of yourself. There are a lot of people out there trying to bring you down to their level.'

'Do you know what I really think, Adrian, about our fucked up little democracy here?' I looked down at Archie in his pram and thought about everything I had seen over the last five years, the thousands of parents the government had abandoned, the suicide calls, a world soaked in unrelenting misery and despair. 'I think Guy Fawkes had the right idea.'

And with that I spun 180 degrees on my heels and marched out the door with Nadine and Archie.

In an effort to disperse my anger, I excused myself for half an hour and headed off to the nearest watering hole, the Feathers pub in the Broadway outside the Yard. Pulling up a stool at the bar, I scanned the hypnotic crystal receptacles on the back bar.

'What's your poison?' a grizzled couldn't-give-a-fuck barman asked.

'I need a large one. A fucking large one. Get me a soda water, splash of Elderflower, twist of lime and a big bag of fucking nuts.'

'Looks like you need something stronger.'

'Nah, my strength has been tested already and I'm past the breaking point.'

'What's that mate?'

'I run a campaign group, Fathers 4 Justice, you know, Men in Tights, all that sort of shit. Guys fighting to see their kids.'

'Well, cheers to Fathers 4 Justice then. Guess every day must be Fathers' Day for you?'

'Guess so, hence I'm off the sauce when I'm on the job – you've got to be able to see your enemies coming. Not only that, blood's thicker than water and warmer than whisky. I need time to reflect on things with a clear head and go away and dream it all up again.'

EPILOGUE

LIFEBLOOD

It's started. I was answering a call of nature in Brighton Family Court when Archie got into trouble with a judge, just like his old man. We were at a hearing for Big Ron when the clerk of the court came out to remonstrate with Nadine. Apparently Archie was making gurgling sounds that the judge found 'unsettling'.

'But it's a public area and there aren't any available rooms to take him to,' argued Nadine.

'Can you leave the building?' asked the clerk. 'His Honour doesn't like children being around as it makes him twitchy.'

'But he isn't even 12-months old yet. Isn't this supposed to be a family court, or don't you allow families in a family court?'

'I'm afraid I'm just following the judge's instructions.'

'Is there a problem?' I asked on my return. When Nadine explained the situation to me, I was not impressed. 'Look, we aren't going anywhere unless the judge wants to use the court tipstaff to physically eject a one-year-old in a pram on to the street. And if he does I'll make sure every local paper is there to get pictures. He's only making the odd warbling sound. He's a happy gurgler – is that a crime? Besides, if you think he's bad now, just wait till he starts walking.'

'He's definitely following in his father's footsteps, going everywhere he's not supposed to,' said Nadine on the way home. 'I've even caught him leafing through the lingerie pages in the Next catalogue on three occasions.'

Poor Archie. How that boy has lived in his first twelve months. From his birth through to the Leo Blair kidnap plot, press interviews, meetings with film directors, countless photo shoots, depositing a multi-coloured yawn over the sofa in CAFCASS Southampton and being thrown out of court, not to mention filling his nappy in a meeting with a senior commander at Scotland Yard. He has shat, belched and farted his way through said events with barely an eyebrow raised, although I must admit the odd buttock cheek has been raised in anger on occasion. How great must it be to be one year old?

Shortly after the meeting at Scotland Yard I received another menacing call but I didn't think it was connected. One thing I have deduced from my numerous meetings there is that internal communications are very fractured at the Yard, with every department adopting a fiercely protective, territorial approach to the sharing of information and activities, especially covert operations. Still the cool, calm assured voice, the inflection and the manner of delivery was not that of an angry, outraged father. I don't know who he is or who he represents, but deep down in my gut I know that it's been the same people the whole way along.

'Matt O'Connor?' He sounds somewhere in his thirties. Softly spoken but assured.

'Yes.'

'You don't take a hint, do you?'

'Excuse me?'

'Are you slow?' he asks.

'Sorry, what the fuck is this about?' I was bristling with frustration until it dawned on me what the call was about.

'Most people would have got the message by now. But you, you're still plotting and planning. You're sailing close to sedition and, in an age of terrorism, where your fellow citizens are dying at the hands of Islamic extremists, you and your family could find yourselves caught up in something very messy.'

The casual reference to my family was enough to ignite my defences.

'Haven't I had this conversation before with you or one of your colleagues? It's not rocket science, pal, I'll back off when somebody in government gets our message. In the meantime, you can ambush me, throw shit at me, hijack our group, crucify me in the press, do whatever you fucking want to do, because I'm past fucking caring. You want sedition? I'll give you fucking sedition – all fucking singing, all fucking dancing. I can close London off in two hours and make you people look like you couldn't run a train set, let alone national security. And if you ever, ever mention my family again, you cunt, I'll fucking make your life so un-fucking-bearable you'll wish you'd never heard my name, because whatever, however, I'll be there pushing and pushing and pushing for what I believe in. If you think you can take me, you bring it on, big boy, you bring it on because I will not yield!'

With that I jabbed at the off button on the phone screaming, 'Cunts! You fucking cunts!' And in the white-hot heat of fury I hurled my mobile across the office. Such was the force of impact when it hit the wall that it hung, embedded momentarily, before dropping to the floor in two pieces. I placed my head in my hands and began to sob. Fuck it, I thought. That's the seventeenth mobile phone I've lost or broken in the duration of this campaign. Jenny's going to absolutely fucking kill me.

Daniel and Alexander spent a chunk of the year at my new house, part of an old mill overlooking the River Itchen just outside Winchester. They make an irrepressible pairing. Alexander, now 9, cut a mischievous figure with his spiky straw-blond hair and tungsten-blue eyes. An effortless poser, he knows all the right moves, seducing everyone with his mock-rock charm and flamboyant turns.

'Dad, if I get into trouble at school and think it's unjust,' asks Alex, 'can I climb on the school roof dressed as Spiderman?'

'Er, no, son, that's not how it works.'

Where Alexander thinks in broad brushstrokes, Daniel is more thoughtful, pondering a raft of different issues. A tall, lean, olive-skinned boy, Dan, being the older of the two, has always been the one to either drop me in it by asking me the square root of some ridiculous number on a crowded train and then teasing me that I don't know the answer, or asking me the most probing questions.

In April 2007, just before his eleventh birthday, he bluntly asked me why I started Fathers 4 Justice. Initially, I struggled to find an explanation. Then, as I realised how quickly he was growing up and that I was a paterfamilias to a rebellious brood of boys, I told him that it might not be so long before he became a father and explained that I wouldn't wish the experience our family went through on anyone, let alone for us to go through it again. But the most important lesson, I told him, is to learn the 'F' word when relationships break down.

'Daaaad! Curb your profanity!' he berated me, sounding remarkably like his mother.

'No, Daniel,' I told him, 'not that word. The "F" word I'm talking about is forgiveness. Never forget how to forgive. And remember, you will always be 50 per cent Mum and 50 per cent Dad.'

'But what about Fathers 4 Justice, Dad? What's going to happen there?'

'I can't tell you what happens next.'

'But, Dad, you can tell me, I'm your son.'

'Well, I've told you about the rock, now comes the roll.'

'Dad,' said Alexander, chipping in, 'with Fathers 4 Justice, well, my friends want to know why you are afraid of heights when, you know, your people climb cranes and stuff?'

'That's because I'm the ground man, Alex, the ground man.'

As we walked out of the house on to the strip of grass overlooking the millstream, I gathered them round me.

'Listen, boys, we need to have a grown-up chat, man to man, like. I haven't been around for you as much as I should have been over the last few years, what with the campaign and all that, but sometimes adults have difficult choices to make.'

'We understand, Dad. You have to do what you do because that's who you are. You're doing it for us, aren't you?' said Daniel.

'Well, that's all that matters, no matter what anyone else says. Because if I didn't make a stand, who else is there? I've been trying to tell a story about fathers these last few years and I think I've been failing. I've been telling it really badly and I'm not sure how it's all going to end, but the one thing I do know is that I'm proud of you boys for hanging in there, working hard at school as well as keeping your old man routed to terra firma. The only sort of thing that has made the emptiness bearable over these last few years is being with you guys.' With that, Daniel wrapped his tanned arms around my torso and leaned up to kiss me on the cheek.

'You see, boys, adults often squander relationships with those that we love the most. I'm sorry if I've let you down in the past. Sometimes we need to fall so we can learn to climb back up again. It helps put life into clear focus. Nearly losing you, what was most precious to me, changed me. Hopefully I'm a better dad now.'

'Mum still thinks you're mad,' said Alexander. They exchanged knowing smiles before roaring with laughter. Alex started waving his hands around in the air like a whirling dervish before rolling on to his side.

'She thinks you're bonkers!' he said, laughing uncontrollably,

'And no offence, Dad,' said Daniel pointing at my mane of hair, 'You're not only bonkers, but me and Alex think that when you get older, you are going to be a slaphead.'

'Cheers guys,' I say despairingly as my two offspring continue their barracking

'Don't worry, even if you were bald, you'd still do a good job, Dad.' Daniel grabs Alex by his arm, lifting him up, and they stagger towards me in a fit of hysterics.

'You know, boys, you've just reminded me of something I'd nearly forgotten.'

'What's that, Dad?'

'Governments can't argue with the sound of laughter.'

Our arms entwined tightly in a scrum-like cuddle, heads down, and for a moment we all look seriously at each other.

'Mum's right, I am bonkers, but I'm doing it for you because my history will be your future one day. Always remember boys, Daddy loves you. Daddy will always love you.'

And as we hugged, bathed in the warmth of a glorious spring day, I clung tightly to both of them in the knowledge that the only real love is the unconditional love we have for our children. It's one love that's too precious to destroy.

'Human salvation lies in the hands of the creatively maladjusted.'

Dr Martin Luther-King Jnr

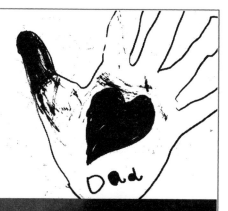

FATHERS4JUSTICE™

OPENING THE DOOR ON CLOSED COURTS FAMILY JUSTICE ON TRIAL

FATHERS4JUSTICE™

PRODUCED BY NICK LANGFORD AND FATHERS 4 JUSTICE

NOTE: Appendices are from the F4J website (www.fathers-4-justice.org) and are reproduced here in facsimile.

INTRODUCTION

reading your fathers rights reaction makes me think even more negatively of the government and the way it works today... Fathers play just an important part as mothers. i dont expect anything to come out of this but i had to express my anger from a 16 year old girls point of view, whos own father she has lost contact with and knows how big the need for a father or father figure a child wants and needs. i just hope things change

Leanne Miller, aged 16, responding to the Fathers 4 Justice demonstration at Buckingham Palace, 17 September 2004[1]

MYTH BUSTING

1. The Family Courts and the government are working in the child's "best interests."

   Neither the courts nor the government have kept any records on the outcomes for the hundreds of thousands of children whose futures have been determined by court judgements. They do not even monitor whether ordered contact is taking place. Orders are made in ignorance in a knowledge vacuum and are a muddle of supposition, bigotry and habit in which every child effectively becomes the subject of an experiment. There is thus no evidence or longitudinal research to prove that positive outcomes have resulted. In fact the evidence suggests the opposite: there appears to be a direct correlation between the explosion in young offending and the epidemic of fatherlessness.

   Further, the adversarial nature of the courts engenders maximum parental conflict which is emotionally destructive to children and economically devastating for families, forcing many onto benefits. Again, there is a woeful lack of evidence to demonstrate how protracted family court proceedings impact on children.

2. Open Courts will damage children.

   There is not a shred of empirical evidence to support this claim. Instead it is based on supposition and speculation. Are we to believe that children in other jurisdictions, where open justice operates, are being 'damaged' (In Florida, for example, where a transparent, accountable and open justice system operates)?

   Closed courts were introduced in the 60's not to protect children's interests but to protect adults' privacy.

3. The justice system relies on sound evidence in order to make judgements, yet throughout the Family Courts, and in both of these two critical examples, none exists.

---

[1] http://www.downingstreetsays.org/archives/000890.html

OPENING THE DOOR ON CLOSED COURTS

Public confidence in the just operation of the Family Courts has evaporated following the four year campaign by Fathers Justice exposing injustice in the handling of *private* law cases – parents fighting each other. Increasingly the press has taken up the challenge and widened the debate to include *public* law cases – parents fighting the social services – which include children taken away from their parents, and forced adoption.

Peripeteia, the point of crisis, has been reached. To do nothing, to repeat the bland reassurances of the past, is no long an option. Equally, to open the Courts to public scrutiny and reveal the mendacity within is unthinkable for the governme and judiciary. Some sort of compromise is required; something which will create the illusion of candour, restore public confidence, and neutralise the campaigners for change.

A ready-made solution has come from New Zealand, where a new system allowing accredited journalists into the courts pioneered in July 2005 as part of the Care of Children Act 2004. Britain's Lord Chancellor, Lord Falconer, travelled to N Zealand to see for himself:

> "One of the things I am very keen to see while I am here is the arrangements you make for letting people com and watch what is going on in family courts..."

> "We've had in England and Wales a large number of cases in which, particularly fathers, have alleged that the system has not been fair to them."

> "The press coming in means nobody can say it's being done behind closed doors." [2]

This document examines the proposed solution in the light of what really goes on behind the closed doors of the Family Courts.

---

[2] http://www.nznewsuk.co.uk/news/?ID=3984&StartRow=1

WHAT IS WRONG WITH FAMILY LAW?

On 23 March 2001 District Judge Hearne, sitting at Walsall County Court, had to make a key decision concerning a child's welfare. The child had alleged to the police that he was being abused by his mother, and that he wanted to live instead with his father. The mother said that the allegation was untrue, and that the matter should end there. The father wanted a psychologist to investigate the truthfulness of the allegation. As he listened in exasperation to the arguments from both sides in court, Judge Hearne took a coin from his pocket, tossed it, asked the father to call, and told the father he had lost the toss. Although a psychologist was appointed, he was not instructed to assess the allegation, and the child was eventually sent back to live with his mother.

"We estimate that over 1million people every year now find themselves in the family courts."

Harriet Harman, speech to National Family and Parenting Institute, 5 October 2006[3]

Let's be absolutely blunt: there are only two options for providing child care post divorce or separation.

The first, favoured by family courts worldwide, is to grant custody to one parent only, designated the 'resident parent' or 'parent with care,' and usually the mother (English legislation uses the word 'mother'). With custody goes all effective responsibility for the child, and the right to make unilateral decisions regarding his education, religious upbringing, medical care, etc. The other parent, usually the father, is designated the 'contact' or 'non-resident' parent or, disgracefully, the 'absent parent.' He must then effectively apply to the resident parent for consent to have any contact with his own child; although he too has parental responsibility in theory, in practice it is far more difficult for him to exercise it. This leads to the stereotype of the lone mother on income support with young children and the absent father with significant income.

"60% of fathers have little or no meaningful relationship with their children post separation."

Former President of the High Court Family Division, Dame Elizabeth Butler-Sloss[4]

This option has two advantages. Firstly, it doesn't work, which means that the non-resident parent is locked into an endless cycle of litigation, seeking so-called 'contact orders,' which more often than not are violated, and then seeking enforcement, which usually results in further orders offering progressively less contact. This arrangement keeps the family courts in business and gives the lawyers involved a guaranteed income, and to a lesser extent, the parasitical agencies which collect around lawyers, such as CAFCASS.

Secondly, it provides funding for the child support industry, because as long as one parent is considered to be 'absent' they must pay the other parent money (this is what they mean by 'support') for the care of the child. This is assessed on the

---

[3] http://www.harrietharman.labour.co.uk/ViewPage.cfm?Page=19950

[4] Speech: the Paul Sieghart Memorial Lecture at the British Institute of Human Rights, King's College London, 3 April 2003 http://www.dca.gov.uk/judicial/speeches/dbs030403.htm

basis that mothers have the right to bring up children while fathers have the responsibility to pay for children, and thus th 'absent' parent becomes responsible not just for his share of support but for all of the child's costs. Needless to say, not of this money ends up benefiting the child, for every £1 taken by the Child Support Agency, about 25p goes to the Department for Work and Pensions – effectively this is a tax on fatherhood. Actually this has minimum impact (about 0.5 on the total benefits spend.[5]

The second option is shared parenting, in which the father and mother are treated as equal parents with balanced rights a shared responsibility, and financial arrangements are based on a symmetrical, gender neutral, formula. This solution isn ideal – the ideal is two loving, married parents – but it results in vastly reduced litigation, and a reduction in any need for money to change hands; it is thus unpopular within the legal and child-support industries – which would collapse, and unpopular to governments which cannot impose the tax on fatherhood. Despite the vociferous claims of opponents, equ responsibilities and rights are not the same as equal time and financial contributions, which are clearly not always practic Nor, as is also often claimed, does shared parenting result in obliging children to live with abusive parents (i.e., in their bigoted world, fathers), it is perfectly possible to protect children from abuse by investigating allegations properly – something that does not happen at present. Awarding an Shared Residence Order in 2004, Lord Justice Wall said,

> *This case has been about control throughout. Mrs A. sought to control the children, with seriously adve consequences for the family. She failed. Control is not what this family needs. What it needs is co-operation. making a shared residence order the court is making that point. These parents have joint and equal pare responsibility. The residence of the children is shared between them. These facts need to be recognised b; order for shared residence[6].*

Family breakdown can be managed; the escalating failure to achieve this has resulted in massive family misery, and devastating consequences for the children concerned who have as an upshot a vastly increased likelihood of poverty, p health, academic failure and involvement in alcohol and drug abuse, unintended pregnancies and violent crime.

The government holds up as exemplars those parents who resolve parenting arrangements without going to court. The majority of these parents achieve an effective arrangement of shared parenting. Why is it, therefore, that the system the government likes to see imposed when parents cannot agree between themselves and need help is the precise opposit and one which involves the removal of one parent?

---

[5] Independent think-tank Child Support Analysis

[6] *A v A (Shared Residence)* [2004] para. 126

SOME BASIC FACTS AND BACKGROUND

STATISTICS

- This graph shows the increase since 1970 in the numbers of children who are affected by the separation of their parents:[7]

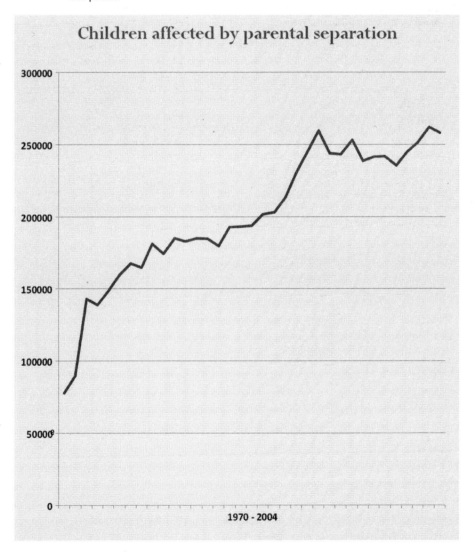

Children affected by parental separation

1970 - 2004

---

[7] The Office for National Statistics (ONS)

- Last year (2005) there were about 645,000 births in England and Wales.[8]

- 43% were to unmarried mothers.

- This graph shows the increase since 1950 in the percentage of illegitimate births:

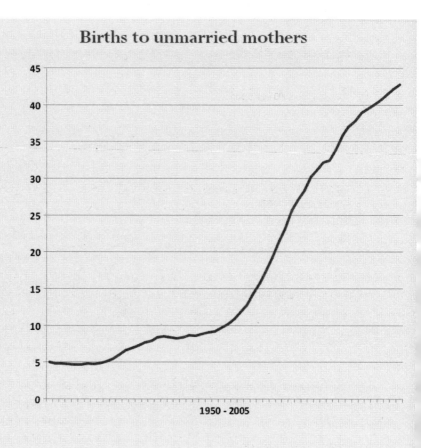

Births to unmarried mothers

1950 - 2005

- **It is out of control.**

---

[8] ONS

- 3 million children, more than a quarter of the total, now live in households headed by a single mother.[9]

- Last year the Family Courts issued 60,000 Contact Orders,[10]

- and 30,000 Residence Orders.[11]

- There were 100,000 applications.[12]

- In 2004 there were 120,000 applications and 78,000 Contact Orders.[13]

- The rise in the number of births outside marriage means fewer fathers have Parental Responsibility (PR)[14] and are able to apply for contact.

- And the cost of an application rose in the period from £90 to £120 and then to £175.[15]

- Since the year 2000 375,000 Court Orders for Contact have been made.[16]

- An astonishing 97% of non-resident parents are fathers.[17]

- Fewer than 2% of resident parents defaulting on Contact Orders face any consequence.[18]

---

[9] ONS

[10] Judicial Statistics, England and Wales 2005.

[11] Ibid

[12] Ibid.

[13] Judicial Statistics, England and Wales 2004.

[14] PR is described in the 1989 Children Act as *"All the rights, duties, powers, responsibilities and authority which by law a parent of a child has in relation to a child and his property."*

[15] In the Lords on 16 March 2006 Lord Goodhart expressed his concern that these "fees are now so high that they constitute a real bar to access to justice."

[16] Judicial Statistics.

[17] Kielty, S., *Similarities and differences in the experiences of non-resident mothers and non-resident fathers*, International Journal of Law, Policy and the Family, University of East Anglia, 2006.

[18] Harriet Harman in written answer to John Hemming, Hansard, 4 July 2006, http://www.publications.parliament.uk/pa/cm200506/cmhansrd/cm060704/text/60704w1420.htm#06070491000037

- In 2004 an estimated 66.5% of separating parents applied to the Family Courts for contact.[19]

- Between 75% and 86% of these were fathers.[20]

- Many children will lose all meaningful contact with the non-resident parent – estimates range from 15% to 28% up to 40% within two years,[22] to as high as 60% overall.[23]

- An estimated 100 children a day lose all or significant contact with a parent; a total of more than 300,000 sinc Labour came to power.

---

[19] The average age of a child at divorce is 7 so the average child affected by divorce in 2004 would have been born in 1997. In that the percentage of births within marriage was about 63%. In 2004 there were 83,809 divorces involving children, so if that represents of all separations, there were another 31,009 separations of non married couples, and therefore a total of 114,818 separations involv children. There were 76,426 applications for contact (we'll ignore applications for residence and other orders) in 2004, so the percen of separating couples going to court over contact was 66.5%.

[20] University of Oxford Family Policy Briefing 3, Child Contact with Non-Resident Parents, Joan Hunt & Ceridwen Roberts, January 2

[21] Blackwell, A. and Dawes, F., Non-Resident Parental Contact, based on data from the National Statistics Omnibus Survey for the Department for Constitutional Affairs, October 2003.

[22] Bradshaw and Millar, 1991.

[23] Former President of the Family Division, Dame Elizabeth Butler-Sloss: the Paul Sieghart Memorial Lecture at the British Institute c Human Rights, King's College London, 3 April 2003   http://www.dca.gov.uk/judicial/speeches/dbs030403.htm

APPENDIX I

THE INTENTIONS OF PARLIAMENT, EUROPEAN LAW AND THE UN

"The Children Act 1989 rests on the belief that children are generally best looked after within the family, with both parents playing a full part and without resort to legal proceedings... and seeks to encourage both parents to continue to share in their children's upbringing, even after separation or divorce."

Consultation document, Lord Chancellor's Department, March 1998, p 13, para. 42.[24]

"The Children Bill, which emphasises the importance of both mothers and fathers in child-rearing, will end the inhuman, callous and cruel practice of divorcing a child from one of his or her loyal and devoted parents."

Sir Raymond Powell (Labour, Ogmore) during Commons debate, 27 April 1989.[25]

"The underlying philosophy of the Children Act is that parents have a shared responsibility for the upbringing of their children even after the parents' relationship has broken down. This reflects the Government's belief that children generally benefit from a continuing relationship with both parents."

Rt. Hon. The Lord Irvine of Lairg, 8 May 1999.

"Every child has the right to a decent start in life, whether their parents live together or apart. All children have the right to the emotional and financial support of both their parents, wherever they live... Non-resident parents have a vital place in their children's lives. We want to encourage their involvement with their children, even when they cannot live together."

Rt. Hon. Harriet Harman, Secretary of State for Social Security, 1999

"Everyone has the right to respect for his private and family life."

The European Convention on Human Rights, Article 8.

"Spouses shall enjoy equality of rights and responsibilities of a private law character between them, and in their relations with their children, as to marriage, during marriage and in the event of its dissolution."

The European Convention on Human Rights, Protocol 7, Article 5. **The UK has neither signed nor ratified this Protocol.**

"Parents have common responsibilities for the upbringing and development of the child. Parents or, as the case may be, legal guardians, have the primary responsibility for the upbringing and development of the child."

The UN Convention on the Rights of the Child, Article 18.

---

[24] The Procedures for the Determination of Paternity and on the Law on Parental Responsibility for Unmarried Fathers, http://www.dca.gov.uk/consult/general/patfr.htm#part16

[25] Hansard: http://www.publications.parliament.uk/pa/cm198889/cmhansrd/1989-04-27/Debate-7.html

THE SINGLE PARENT EPIDEMIC

> *Mr. Justice Munby ordered the end of all direct contact between a father and his three children while noting that the mother "wished the children could have contact with the father. She said there was no need for all this litigation. The children should see the father."*

- The teenage pregnancy rate in the UK is the highest in the developed world, 4 times higher than the West European average,[26] and 6 times higher than the rate in Holland.[27]

- Half of these pregnancies end in abortion. In 2002 there were 3,514 abortions carried out on girls under the ag[...] 16.[28]

- The other half of these pregnancies results in by far the highest rate of single mothers in Europe: one in 4 child[...] 3.2 million, now lives with a single mother, and single mothers as a social group have increased by 250,000 u[...] New Labour, increasing by 17% in England and 24% in Scotland. Britain will soon overtake the United States[...]

- In 2005 43% of births were to unmarried mothers, and in some cities the figure is over 50%.

Why?

- Beverley Hughes, the children and families minister, says there is nothing further the government can do, that[...] up to the parents.[29]

The state actively promotes single motherhood with additional benefits and tax advantages, preferential access to coun[...] housing and other resources:

- In her study *The Effect of Benefits on Single Motherhood in Europe*[30] Libertad Gonzalez has clearly demonstr[...] that there is a simple relationship: as benefits rise, so does single motherhood.

- UK benefits to single mothers were the highest in Europe in 2001.[31] Benefits paid to a single mother increase[...] 75% between 1994 and 2001.[32]

---

[26] *Teenage mothers: housing and household change*, Oxford Brookes University, http://www.brookes.ac.uk/schools/social/population-household-change/10_allen.html!

[27] *Teenage Pregnancy*, a Social Exclusion Unit Report, June 1999.

[28] Melanie Johnson, House of Commons, 8 March 2004.

[29] E.g. interview with the Guardian, 26 May 2005, http://society.guardian.co.uk/children/story/0,1074,1492434,00.html

[30] Libertad Gonzalez, *The Effect of Benefits on Single Motherhood in Europe*, Department of Economics and Business, Universitat Pompeu Fabra, Barcelona, Spain, March 2006, http://www.econ.upf.edu/~gonzalez/.

[31] Libertad Gonzalez, *The Effect of Benefits on Single Motherhood in Europe*.

[32] Frank Field.

- One study showed 5% of teenage mothers living in council housing before the birth of their children; within a year of giving birth a third were in council housing with another third on waiting lists.[33]

- The same study found half were living on their own with their babies, with barely more than half still in contact with the fathers.[34]

- A married couple on average pay of £24,000 with one earner, a mortgage and two children is only £1 a week better off than a lone parent household living entirely on benefits.[35]

The state promotes marriage break-up:

- A couple on average earnings of £460 per week for the husband and £250 for the wife would be £170 per week better off if they separated (January 2005).[36]

- An average married couple with two children pay £5,000 more in tax than they receive in benefits. If they split up the two single households would get £7,000 more in benefits than they pay in tax.[37]

- Existing policies concentrate on assisting single mothers either with aborting their children or with funding them once born, not with preventing conception, despite the government's pledge to reduce teenage conception by 50% by 2010 from 1998 levels.[38]

---

[33] *Teenage mothers: housing and household change*, Oxford Brookes University, http://www.brookes.ac.uk/schools/social/population-and-household-change/10_allen.html!

[34] Ibid.

[35] Kirby, J., *The Price of Parenthood*, Centre for Policy Studies, January 2005, http://www.cps.org.uk/cpsfile.asp?id=387 (summary only).

[36] Rowthorn, R.,

[37] Kirby, J., *The Price of Parenthood*, Centre for Policy Studies, January 2005, http://www.cps.org.uk/cpsfile.asp?id=387 (summary only).

[38] Social Exclusion Unit report on Teenage Pregnancy, launched by Tony Blair, June 1999.

THE SOCIAL COSTS OF FAMILY BREAKDOWN

Mr. Justice Wilson, acting against what he called "the deep wishes and feelings of three intelligent, articulate children," ordered the end of all direct contact with their father. Upheld on appeal by Butler-Sloss, LJ.

FAMILY BREAKDOWN DAMAGES THE ECONOMY

In 2000 the Lords and Commons Family and Child Protection Group commissioned a report from the Family Matters Institute into the social and economic costs of family breakdown.[39]

- It estimated a direct cost per annum of £15 billion and rising.

- And an indirect cost of double that.

  o This includes £8.5 billion welfare support

  o Legal Aid – £452 million in 2004-05

  o the Child Support Agency – about £200 million more than it recovers

  o special needs schools (disproportionately used by children from broken families), and child psychology services

  o some of the costs of the criminal justice system, remand centres and prisons

  o lost productivity and work disruption

  o plus additional costs of health due to family breakdown.

- The immediate cost of an intact family breaking down is between £4,000 and £12,000 each year in additional benefits and lost taxes.[40]

- If a woman has 2 children she can receive more than £11,000 a year in benefits.[41]

---

[39] *Family Matters*, report by the Family Matters Institute, 2000, http://www.familymatters.org.uk/cfb.html.

[40] Robert Rowthorn, Professor of Economics at the University of Cambridge, in his Foreword to *The Price of Parenthood*, by Jill Kirby, Centre for Policy Studies, January 2005.

[41] Ibid.

FAMILY BREAKDOWN CAUSES CRIME

- 70% of young offenders identified by Youth Offending Teams come from lone-parent families.[42]

- 48.5% of secondary school pupils have broken the law.[43]

- One in four teenagers is now a criminal,[44]

- Britain has the highest level of hooliganism in Europe.[45]

- The cost to the country of youth offending is £13 billion every year.[46]

- Boys from lone-parent homes are twice as likely as those from two-birth-parent families to be incarcerated by the time they reached their early 30s.[47]

- A study of boys aged between 12 and 16 from a deprived area of south London compared those at a secure unit for unmanageable adolescents with those having no criminal convictions. 80% of the 'good boys' were close to their biological fathers compared with only 4% of the 'bad boys.' The research showed step fathers to be an additional risk factor.[48]

- Children aged 11 to 16 years were 25% more likely to have offended in the last year if they lived in lone-parent families.[49]

- Prisoners are far more likely to have been taken into care as children.[50]

- Prisoners are most likely to reform when they have a secure family to return to.[51]

---

[42]Review 2001/2002: *Building on Success*, Youth Justice Board, London: The Stationery Office (July 2002).

[43] Beinart, S., Anderson, B., Lee, S. and Utting, D., *Youth at risk? A national survey of risk factors, protective factors and problem behaviour among young people in England, Scotland and Wales*, Joseph Rowntree Foundation, April 2002.

[44] Donnellan, C., *Dealing with crime*, Independence Educational Publishers, April 2004.

[45] Study by Prof Gloria Laycock, of the Jill Dando Institute, University College London, commissioned by security company ADT, May 2005, http://www.telegraph.co.uk/news/main.jhtml?xml=/news/2006/05/09/nyobs09.xml&sSheet=/news

[46] Figure from July 2006; the social and economic cost of crime is estimated at £60B a year for England and Wales according to the Home Office Research Study 217 published in 2000. Young people aged 10 -17 make up 22% of the people who commit crime and are therefore responsible for 22% of the cost of crime which computes to £13B a year.

[47]Harper, C. and McLanahan, S. (August 1998), *Father absence and youth incarceration*, San Francisco: paper

presented at the annual meetings of the American Sociological Association, http://www.aboutdads.org/reports/Father_Absence_and_Youth_Incarceration.pdf

[48]Research carried out by Dr Jenny Taylor for the South London and Maudsley NHS trust.

[49] Youth Survey 2001: Research Study Conducted for the Youth Justice Board (January–March 2001),

www.youth-justice-board.gov.uk/policy/YJBREP _published_report_2001.pdf, p. 9.

[50] Ibid.

[51] Ditchfield, J., *Family ties and recidivism*, Home Office Research Bulletin 36, 1994.

THE PERSONAL COSTS OF FAMILY BREAKDOWN

> In one incident outside Court 32 on the 23rd January 2003, Honourable Mr. Justice Singer was loudly heard saying to a child, "If you don't go with your mum, I'll put you in a place where you can't see your mother or your father - how do you like that?"

FAMILY BREAKDOWN CAUSES POVERTY

- The 2001 Report by the Taskforce on Tackling Overindebtedness (sic) found relationship breakdown to be a m cause of financial difficulties.[52]

- The median financial loss to the family of divorce and custody disputes is £50,000 (in 1996), and this usually involves the loss of the family home.[53]

- One in two lone parent households are on income support compared with one in 30 couple households.[54]

- Lone parents have twice the risk of persistently low incomes.[55] [56]

- Lone parents are 8 times as likely to be out of work.[57]

- Lone parents are more than 12 times as likely to be receiving income support.[58]

- The UK has the highest proportion of children living in workless households in Europe.[59]

---

[52] Consumer Affairs Directorate

[53] *The Emperor's New Clothes: Divorce Process and Consequence*, the Cheltenham Group, 1996.

[54] Lyon N., Barnes M., & Sweiry D. (2006) *Families with children in Britain: Findings from the 2004 Families and Children Study* (FAC Department for Work and Pensions Research Report No 340.

[55] Ibid.

[56] *Households Below Average Income 1994/95-2000/01*, Department for Work and Pensions, London: The Stationery Office (2002).

[57] *Work and Worklessness among Households*, Office for National Statistics, London: The Stationery Office, Autumn 2001.

[58] *Family Resources Survey, Great Britain, 2000–01*, Office for National Statistics, London: The Stationery Office, May 2002.

[59] Palmer G., Carr J., & Kenway P., 2005 *Monitoring poverty and social exclusion*, Joseph Rowntree Foundation, 2005.

FAMILY BREAKDOWN CAUSES ILL HEALTH

- Adolescents from lone-parent families engage in greater and earlier sexual activity.[60]

- British teenagers are the most sexually active in Europe.[61]

- Children of lone parents are twice as likely to have mental health problems.[62]

- Children of lone parents are two to three times as likely to develop schizophrenia.[63]

- Britain has the highest level of self-harming in Europe.[64]

- Children of lone parents are twice as likely to smoke, drink heavily or take drugs. [65]

- Children of lone parents are five times more likely to suffer physical and emotional abuse.[66]

- Children of lone parents are 100 times more likely to suffer fatal abuse.[67]

---

[60] Carol W. Metzler, et al. *The Social Context for Risky Sexual Behavior Among Adolescents*, JOURNAL OF BEHAVIORAL MEDICINE *17*, 1994.

[61] Institute for Public Policy Research, October 2006, http://www.ippr.org/pressreleases/

[62] Meltzer, H., *et al.*, *Mental Health of Children and Adolescents in Great Britain*, London: The Stationery Office, 2000.

[63] Study by Dr Craig Morgan of Kings College, London, reported in the Guardian, 22 November 2006, http://society.guardian.co.uk/socialcare/story/0,,1953959,00.html.

[64] Catherine McLoughlin, et al., *Truth Hurts*, Camelot Foundation and Mental Health Foundation, March 2006, http://observer.guardian.co.uk/uk_news/story/0,,1739832,00.html

[65] Sweeting, H., West, P., and Richards, M., *Teenage family life, lifestyles and life chances: Associations with family structure, conflict with parents and joint family activity*, International Journal of Law, Policy and the Family, 1998.

[66] Cawson, P., *Child Maltreatment in the Family*, London: NSPCC, 2002.

[67] Daly, M. and Wilson, M., *Homicide*, New York: Aldine de Gruyter, 1988.

WHAT THE POLITICIANS SAY:

> *Mister Justice Johnson: ordered a father declared a vexatious litigant for seeking more than one overnight stay per fortnight with his 5-year old son. Upheld on appeal by LJ Thorpe.*

"Let's try and understand what's gone wrong in these children's lives ... often it's young people who are brought up in car when they should be in loving homes."

David Camero

"You don't have to be an expert on crime to know its causes are woven into the very fabric of our society. Family breakdo leaving kids without a stable framework in which to grow up."

Tony Bla

"The single biggest social problem in our society may be the growing absence of fathers from their children's homes, because it contributes to so many other social problems."

President Bill Clintc

"What would you do? Would you give in? Imagine you thought he was next door in another house. Would you break th door down and risk upsetting the people inside and perhaps getting arrested. Would you do that as a decent dad? Of course you would," and he nodded. I said, "because you would do anything for your kids, even if it meant you sometime overstepping the mark?" and he said, "yes, I would." I told him he was no different to me and I was no different to him.

Paul Watson, Fathers 4 Justice North East Co-ordinator, in conversation with the Prime Minister, Tony Bl

---

[68] BBC Breakfast interview, 10 July 2006, http://news.bbc.co.uk/1/hi/uk_politics/5163798.stm

[69] Speech to the Peel Institute, 26 January 2001, http://www.number10.gov.uk/output/Page1577.asp

[70] President Clinton, 1995, quoted by Stephen Baskerville, PhD, in *The Politics of Fatherhood*, 8 December 2002.

[71] Posted on Fathers 4 Justice internet forum.

THE THREE GREAT LIES

> *Judge Goldstein, after a father filed a complaint against him, ordered all contact between that father and his children stopped for three years. Overturned on appeal by Butler-Sloss LJ, who described the judge's behaviour as "outrageous."*

There are many lies told by the enemies of the family, but these three are told more often than most.

29 CHILDREN HAVE BEEN MURDERED DURING CONTACT WITH THEIR FATHERS

- In their report, Twenty Nine Child Homicides,[72] Women's Aid attempted to show that the courts routinely order contact in circumstances known to be unsafe. They said that 29 children in 13 families had been killed during contact (and one during residence) over the 10 year period from 1994 to 2004. Shockingly, they claimed that 5 of these children had been murdered merely so that the father could "take revenge" on the mother.

...AND THE TRUTH

- In 2006 Judge Nicholas Wall undertook a review[73] of these claims; he found that:

  - 18 of the 29 children had never been subject to any court proceeding,[74]

  - in only 5 of these cases had the children been killed during court-ordered contact,[75]

  - in only 3 cases could it be argued that the court could have made a different judgement.[76]

  - He concluded: "*I am in no doubt that all the contact orders in the cases concerned were made in good faith and that the judges did their best conscientiously to apply section 1 of the Children Act 1989.*"[77]

- Women's Aid have subsequently revised their claim down to 11 deaths.[78]

---

[72] Saunders, H., *Twenty-Nine Child Homicides: lessons still to be learnt on domestic violence and child protection*, Women's Aid, 2004.

[73] Wall, N., *A report to the President of the Family Division on the publication by the Women's Aid Federation of England entitled* **Twenty-Nine Child Homicides: lessons still to be learned on domestic violence and child protection** *with particular reference to the five cases in which there was judicial involvement*, March 2006, http://www.judiciary.gov.uk/docs/report_childhomicides.pdf

[74] Ibid., Paragraph 8.2

[75] Ibid., Paragraph 1.2

[76] Ibid., Paragraph 8.4

[77] Ibid., Paragraph 8.7

[78] Aitkenhead, D., *The Sins of the Fathers*, published in the Guardian, 8 May 2006, http://www.guardian.co.uk/g2/story/0,,1770011,00.html

- Women's Aid and the NSPCC have long lobbied that contact orders are unsafe and that courts routinely ignore fifth item of the welfare checklist, "*any harm which he has suffered or is at risk of suffering.*"[79]: they state, "*that t. Act fails children as family courts continue to grant contact orders in situations where a child is in potential dang from a parent or step-parent. In recent years 19 children have been killed following contact arrangements.*"[80]

- There is, however, little evidence to support their claims, and the only studies they quote are their own:

- Failure to Protect,[81] for example, made the claim that 18 children had been ordered to have contact with father: who had been convicted of schedule one offences.

  o The survey was not based on verifiable statistics but on the replies of the self-selected residents of 178 women's refuges. None of the figures given can be supported by independent, objective evidence.

  o *Unreasonable Fears*[82] claimed 76% of children were abused during contact, and was presented as evider to the DCA Select Committee.[83]

  o Again, this was a study of 130 self-selected women who claimed to have been abused, and is not therefo representative of women generally, nor are the findings independently verifiable.

...AND SOME OTHER FACTS

- Each year in the UK, for the last 28 years, an average of 79 children are murdered, giving an approximate tota 790 in the decade covered. Only 5 of these 790 (0.6%) were killed by fathers during court-ordered contact.

- During the period covered by the Women's Aid report 45 mothers were convicted of infanticide.

- During the period covered by the Women's Aid report 555,399 Contact Orders were made.

- In the 6-year period 1995/96 to 2000/01, a total of 296 children were murdered by their biological parents, 16C fathers and 136 by mothers. In addition, a total of 56 children were killed by their step-parents, 54 by stepfathe and two by stepmothers.[84]

- Where the victims are under one year of age, mothers are the suspects in 47% of cases.[85]

- A study by Southampton University showed that 80% of child murderers were family members of whom 55% w mentally ill.[86]

---

[79] Children Act 1989, Part I, 1 (3) (e).

[80] http://www.nspcc.org.uk/home/informationresources/nspccandwomensaidarchive.htm

[81] *Failure to Protect? Domestic violence and the experiences of abused women and children in the family courts*, Women's Aid Foundation, November 2003.

[82] Radford, L., et al., *Unreasonable Fears? Child Contact in the Context of Domestic Violence : A Survey of Mothers' Perceptions of F* Women's Aid Foundation, 1999.

[83] http://www.publications.parliament.uk/pa/cm200405/cmselect/cmconst/116/116we27.htm

[84] Letter from Home Office dated 2 May 2002 in response to enquiry by Mr V Ward.

[85] Wilczynski and Morris, 1993.

[86] Pritchard, Colin and Bagley, Christopher, *Suicide and murder in child murders and child sex abusers*. Journal of Forensic Psychiatr 2001 (Vol. 12, pp269-286).

- Figures from the NSPCC show that children are at greater risk of abuse from their mothers than from their fathers. Child Maltreatment in the UK, 2000, showed 49% of children abused in the home were abused by their mothers and 40% by their fathers.[87]

- A second report, Child Maltreatment in the Family, 2002, showed that 65% of total child abuse (neglect, sexual, emotional and physical) is committed by mothers and that 8% of child abuse is committed by fathers.[88]

- Women's Aid and the NSPCC are politically very powerful organisations; their campaigning has skewed thinking on these issues and the outcome of individual cases. The very few genuine cases they are able to uncover that support their thesis proves that court-ordered contact is actually very safe. Their obsession with safety however means that other clauses of the welfare check list are given less prominence, with the result that orders are not always practical or enforceable.

ONLY 0.8% OF FATHERS ARE DENIED CONTACT

- It is often claimed that the parents who campaign for the reform of the Family Courts are only those fathers who receive Orders for No Contact. For example, Harry Fletcher, Assistant general Secretary of NAPO said, "*the finding that there is no systemic bias against fathers in court proceedings is most welcome. Research shows that only 0.8% of fathers are actually refused contact.*"[89]

- These orders are rare and account for some 1 to 2% of orders year to year. They are made in cases where a parent has been shown to pose a substantial risk to the child, and about a third of the orders are in fact made against mothers.

...AND THE TRUTH

- This is a deliberately misleading confusion between the rare Orders for No Contact and the relatively common loss of contact through parental obstruction.

- Most of the supporters of equal parenting groups are in receipt of Contact Orders. They join either because these orders are not being honoured or enforced, or because the level of contact they represent is insufficient for maintaining a meaningful relationship.

- So-called 'indirect' contact, particularly – which may specify the occasional sending of a postcard or letter, for example – delivers a level of communication between parent and child which is entirely inadequate for sustaining any sort of relationship; but it enables the Courts to avoid Orders of No Contact.

- A casual glance at 0.8% of Family Court orders is no basis for an evaluation of alleged bias.

---

[87] Cawson, p., Wattam, C., Brooker, S., and Kelly, G., *Child maltreatment in the United Kingdom: a study of the prevalence of child abuse and neglect*, November 2000, NSPCC.

[88] Cawson, P., *Child maltreatment in the family: the experience of a national sample of young people*, February 2002, NSPCC.

[89] Press release, 2 March 2005, http://www.napo2.org.uk/cafcass/archives/2005/03/family_courts_-.html

"ONLY 10% OF SEPARATING COUPLES RESORT TO THE COURTS"

- This figure is regularly wheeled out by the Government. Sadly it is also repeated by opposition parties. Lord Adonis, for example, said, "*About 90 per cent of separating parents make provision for bringing up their children including contact arrangements, without recourse to the courts.*" [90]

...AND THE TRUTH

- The figure derives from the Blackwell and Dawes report of 2003[91] which was actually a sample of 961 parents **whom contact was working**, of whom about 10% (actually nearer 11) had court-ordered contact at the time they were questioned.[92]

- The true figure is about 55% most years,[93] and as noted above, was 66.5% in 2004.

- The 10% figure actually shows how inadequate the courts are: where contact works 90% of parents get there on their own, without the help of the courts, but where contact does not work the courts are usually unable to make significant difference.

---

[90] Hansard, 29 June 2005, http://www.publications.parliament.uk/pa/ld200405/ldhansrd/pdvn/lds05/text/50629-04.htm

[91] Blackwell, A. and Dawes, F., *Non-Resident Parental Contact*, based on data from the National Statistics Omnibus Survey for the Department for Constitutional Affairs, October 2003.

[92] 649 parents had residence and 312 were non-resident; 26 were both. Between them they had responsibility for 1,506 children. 13% children whose non-resident parent was the respondent and 9% of children whose resident parent responded had their contact arrangements ordered by court. A further 5% and 6% respectively had contact arrangements negotiated by a mediator or lawyer.

[93] In 2000 it was 54%, in 2001 57.5%, in 2002 53% and in 2003 55%. Figures calculated from ONS and Judicial published statistics.

THE 1989 CHILDREN ACT: INTENTION AND REALITY

> *Judge Catlin: a) when a mother refused to obey an order for shared residence, he ordered the cessation of all contact between a father and his two sons in response to unsubstantiated charges of abuse; b) at a subsequent hearing 12 months later, when all charges of abuse had been dismissed by the investigating officer, he ordered 1 hour of contact between father and son per month.*

The 1989 Children Act was introduced to Parliament on 27 April 1989 by David Mellor, the Health Minister, with a great sense of optimism and achievement; he said,

> *"We have high ambitions for this Bill. We hope and believe that it will bring order, integration, relevance and a better balance to the law -- a better balance not just between the rights and responsibilities of individuals and agencies, but, most vitally, between the need to protect children and the need to enable parents to challenge intervention in the upbringing of their children."*

The Act became law on 14 October 1991. It has failed to live up to expectations. The Act is weakly written and poorly represents the will of Parliament.

THE BASIC PRINCIPLES

- The first principle of the 1989 Children Act is *"that the child's welfare shall be the court's paramount consideration."*[94] This is the so-called *paramountcy principle*, and it is slavishly reiterated.

- Concomitant with this principle is the Welfare Checklist, also referred to as The Voice of the Child, which is a list of the sort of things to be considered when a Section 8 order is made or changed.[95]

  - Unfortunately this principle is not defined within the Act; thus it lies open to interpretation by anyone with an axe to grind and becomes a meaningless mantra. It also excludes other equally important principles such as the presumption of contact.[96]

---

[94] Children Act 1989, Part I, Section 1, http://www.opsi.gov.uk/acts/acts1989/Ukpga_19890041_en_1.htm

[95] Children Act 1989, Part I, Section 3: (a) the ascertainable wishes and feelings of the child concerned (considered in the light of his age and understanding); (b) his physical, emotional and educational needs; (c) the likely effect on him of any change in his circumstances; (d) his age, sex, background and any characteristics of his which the court considers relevant; (e) any harm which he has suffered or is at risk of suffering; (f) how capable each of his parents, and any other person in relation to whom the court considers the question to be relevant, is of meeting his needs; (g) the range of powers available to the court under this Act in the proceedings in question.

[96] For example as described in Teresa May's Early Day Motion 128 of May 2005: "That this House believes that separated parents should each have a legal presumption of contact with their children, so that both parents can continue to parent

their children and children are able to benefit from being parented by both their parents, as well as from contact with any grandparents and extended family members able and willing to play a role in their upbringing; and urges the Government to

- The second principle is that, "*In any proceedings in which any question with respect to the upbringing of a chil arises, the court shall have regard to the general principle that any delay in determining the question is likely t prejudice the welfare of the child.*"[97]

- Giving evidence to the Select Committee on Constitutional Affairs, Dame Elizabeth Butler-Sloss emphatically denied that tactical delay takes place, the legal profession was equally forceful.[98]

  o The reality is that, for many reasons, delay is the norm and there are often periods of many months betwe hearings while reports are prepared by CAFCASS or while applicants wait for times when all parties, solicitors, barristers and others can attend court. Many cases drag on for years.

  o The Select Committee concluded, "*Given the strong animosity between the parties which is common in contested family cases, we find it hard to believe that tactical delay is not sometimes used to the advanta of resident parents.*"[99]

  o The Courts are predisposed to preserving the status quo ante; given that contact applications are made w contact is obstructed, the status quo is taken to be the state in which the child has obstructed contact rat than the normal satisfactory contact which existed before. The longer this state can continue, the more li it is that the Court will preserve it.

- The third principle is the No Order Principle, "*Where a court is considering whether or not to make one or mor orders under this Act with respect to a child, it shall not make the order or any of the orders unless it considers doing so would be better for the child than making no order at all.*"

  o The purpose of this principle was to reduce the number of orders the courts were making, which were at very high level before 1989. The graph shows the dramatic effect that this principle had immediately, an inexorable increase of orders subsequently.[100]

---

replace the legal term 'contact' with 'parenting time' and to ensure that parenting time orders can be and are made and enforced by th courts, save where a child's safety would be at risk."

[97] Children Act 1989, Part 1, Section 1 (2).

[98] Select Committee on Constitutional Affairs, Fourth Report,
http://www.publications.parliament.uk/pa/cm200405/cmselect/cmconst/116/11606.htm#a7

[99] Ibid.

[100] The graph shows orders for Custody and Access prior to the 1989 Act and orders for Residence and Contact after it.

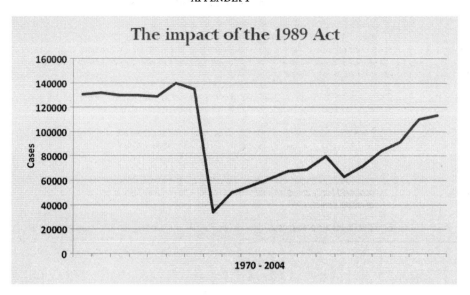

The impact of the 1989 Act

THE COURT

- The Act created the new concept of "The Court", which comprised Magistrates Courts, County Courts and the High Court. The new orders available under the Act could be made at any level within "The Court." This meant that proceedings could be transferred with greater ease, and that one no longer had to select a particular court for a particular remedy.

  o The result is the complete absence of judicial continuity, and the consequent failure of judges fully to understand a case until it has appeared before them on a number of occasions.[101]

PARENTAL RESPONSIBILITY

- The Act created another new concept, that of "Parental Responsibility" (PR), which could be conferred by a separate Order. Previously it had been included under the heading of Custody Orders. It is defined as, "*all the rights, duties, powers, responsibilities and authority which by law a parent of a child has in relation to the child and his property.*"[102] The idea was that schools, doctors and others should treat the non-resident parent on an equal footing with the resident parent.

---

[101] Conversation with former family Court judge Ian Starforth Hill.

[102] 1989 Children Act, Section 3 (1).

o   The reality is that a non-resident parent is treated at best as a second-rate parent and at worst as no parent at all. The huge increase in illegitimacy has resulted in fewer fathers having PR. Unmarried fathers do not have PR automatically and if their child's mother is not in agreement they must make an application to the court; only a few thousand such orders are made each year.

SECTION 8 ORDERS

Orders made under Section 8 of the 1989 Children Act can be for Residence, Contact, Prohibited Steps and Specific Issue. In introducing the new Orders, David Mellor said,

> *"New orders are introduced to reflect our emphasis on encouraging parents to participate fully in the child's upbringing."*

RESIDENCE ORDERS

- These orders determine with whom the child is to live and replace the old Custody Orders. They were designed have sufficient flexibility to allow for various shared care arrangements. Under the new Act residence and parental responsibility were treated as entirely separate concepts so that non-resident parents could continue to have an involved role in their child's upbringing. Giving one parent residence would not take away PR from the other.

  o   The reality is that Residence is still awarded overwhelmingly to mothers, and that non-resident parents are still effectively relegated to second-rate parents. Only 3% of non-resident parents are mothers.[103]

  o   Shared parenting was to have been the central plank of the Act, made manifest in orders for Shared Residence. In practice such orders are very rare, and the Labour Government has reinterpreted these or to enable them only where mutual consent is possible.

  o   When Peter Luff (Conservative, Mid Worcestershire) raised a question in the Commons about the number SRO's since 1989, the Government's answer was the stock one of, "*I am sorry to have to tell you that this information is not available and could be obtained only at disproportionate cost.*" [104]

CONTACT ORDERS

- Contact Orders replace the old Access Orders; the intention was that these orders should be viewed from the perspective of the child rather than of the parent. It is *"an order requiring the person with whom a child lives,*

---

[103] Kielty, S., *Similarities and differences in the experiences of non-resident mothers and non-resident fathers*, International Journal of Law, Policy and the Family, University of East Anglia, 2006.

[104] http://www.publications.parliament.uk/pa/cm199495/cmhansrd/1995-06-29/Writtens-1.html

to live, to allow the child to visit or stay with the person named in the order, or for that person and the child otherwise to have contact with each other."[105]

o   Like the child's *welfare*, *contact* is not defined. Contact can be either direct or indirect, thus contact regularly means, for example, that a parent can send his child no more than one letter a month – which the resident parent need not acknowledge, or even that a parent may receive a photograph of his child every 6 months. That is still classed as 'contact.' Incidentally, 'direct' contact includes telephone conversations.

o   By the time he goes to court, a father is already, as defined by the 1991 Child Support Act and not withstanding changes to the terminology since, designated 'the absent parent.' The 1989 Children Act now adds the designation, 'non resident parent,' further excluding him from his family. Because he has been unable to resolve the issue of contact without going to court he is automatically considered dysfunctional; he is also, by definition, absent. His application for contact is therefore considered somewhat perverse.

o   The minimum level of contact necessary to maintain a meaningful relationship has been defined as not less than one third of the child's non-school time.[106] This translates into every other weekend and half of school holidays. Any Court which orders contact of less than this is guilty of destroying that child's relationship with his parent.

o   The effect of the Act has actually been to increase the proportion of applications for contact. Before the Act orders for Custody and Access were roughly equal, but since the Act Contact Orders have increased to 2.6 times the number of Residence Orders:

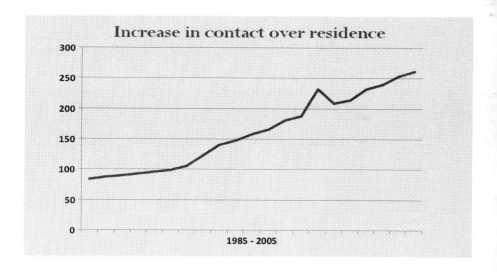

o   Solicitors recommend that fathers apply for Contact rather than Residence on the grounds that they are more likely to be awarded it; the problem is that innocently applying for a Contact Order holds the implied request to be treated as a contact parent, a non-resident parent, an absent parent, a second rate parent.[107]

---

[105] Children Act 1989, Part II, 8 (1).

[106] Recommendation by academics such as Professor Michael Lamb of the University of Cambridge.

[107] Fathers 4 Justice recommends application for a Shared Residence Order as the only acceptable starting point.

o   These Orders are routinely flouted by resident parents, and so do not achieve their objective of facilitating sustaining proper relationships between children and their non-residential parents. A study by the Cheltenham Group for Families Need Fathers found non-compliance in 60% of contact orders and some degree of obstruction in 80%.[108]

o   A study by the DSS showed that 40% of mothers admit obstructing contact as a way of punishing their form partners.[109]

o   Judges are unable and unwilling to enforce Contact Orders[110]. They do not use the sanctions available to them, such as simply transferring residence or imposing custodial sentences.[111] Courts will regularly imprison mothers for condoning truancy but not for the greater crime of preventing paternal contact.[112] Ye the same government department, the DfES is responsible for both.

o   Lord Justice Ormerod summarises the judicial view, *"There is no doubt and it should be clearly understood...throughout the legal profession that an application to commit for breach of orders relating to access (and I limit my comments to breaches of orders relating to access) are inevitably futile and should be made. The damage which they cause is appalling..."[113]*

o   Over successive hearings, often over a period of years, the level of contact specified in the Orders is stea eroded.[114]

PROHIBITED STEPS AND SPECIFIC ISSUES ORDERS

•   "A prohibited steps order" means an order that no step which could be taken by a parent in meeting his parent responsibility for a child, and which is of a kind specified in the order, shall be taken by any person without the consent of the court;[115]

•   "A specific issue order" means an order giving directions for the purpose of determining a specific question wh has arisen, or which may arise, in connection with any aspect of parental responsibility for a child.[116]

THE PRESUMPTION OF CONTACT

---

[108] *The Emperor's New Clothes: Divorce Process and Consequence*, the Cheltenham Group, 1996.

[109] *Children First: a new approach to child support*, DSS 1998.

[110](F v M [2004] EWHC 727; A v A[2004] EWHC 142=20 (FAM); C v C[2004] EWCA Civ 512); C v C [2004])

[111] The proposed Child Contact and Adoption Bill makes certain sanctions available to courts such as curfews and unpaid work requirements and compensation for financial loss, http://www.dfes.gov.uk/childrensneeds/pdf/Adoption%20Bill.pdf

[112] No information is recorded on how many prison sentences are imposed for obstructing contact, http://www.publications.parliament.uk/pa/cm200506/cmhansrd/cm060704/text/60704w1420.htm#06070491000037, in the only notabl recent case a mother in Devon was jailed for three months, http://www.telegraph.co.uk/news/main.jhtml?xml=/news/2004/02/22/nkidz22.xml&sSheet=/news/2004/02/22/ixhome.html.

[113] Churchard v. Churchard [1984] FLR 635.

[114] This includes the absurd principle of 'indirect' contact – letters and email – phone calls are regarded as 'direct.'

[115] Children Act 1989, Part II, 8 (1).

[116] Ibid.

- Equal parenting organisations want a 'presumption of contact' to be introduced into family law. The Conservatives have also adopted this principle, for example through Early Day Motion 128, launched by Theresa May on 18 May 2005, which says,

PARENTING TIME PRESUMPTION

That this House believes that separated parents should each have a legal presumption of contact with their children, so that both parents can continue to parent their children and children are able to benefit from being parented by both their parents, as well as from contact with any grandparents and extended family members able and willing to play a role in their upbringing; and urges the Government to replace the legal term 'contact' with 'parenting time' and to ensure that parenting time orders can be and are made and enforced by the courts, save where a child's safety would be at risk.

- The Government has consistently resisted such a presumption; Vera Baird expresses their opposition most clearly:

  "In a situation in which it is not the child but the parents who are battling, the parents are obviously expressing what one might conjure up as the right of the child to have contact with dad, but it is dad who is fighting for that right, so it is his right. Once one makes that the presumption, the welfare of the child cannot be paramount, so the presumption must be ousted in some other way. In that case, one must bring to the surface the danger to the child in order to rebut."[117]

- The answer to this is simple: the child self-evidently cannot make an application to the court himself; as the law stands only an adult with PR can do so, and that adult is usually 'dad.' Once the child has separate legal representation, an issue subject to current debate, the application becomes the child's and not the father's.

- Organisations such as Women's Aid dismiss the demand for a 'presumption of contact' to be added to the 1989 Children Act by claiming that there is already such a presumption.

- There is no such presumption. At least not in Private Law.

- In Public Law the case is different. Section 34 of the Act, which deals with children taken into care by a local authority, states:

  34.—*(1) Where a child is in the care of a local authority, the authority shall (subject to the provisions of this section) allow the child reasonable contact with—*

  (a) his parents;

  (b) any guardian of his;

  (c) where there was a residence order in force with respect to the child immediately before the care order was made, the person in whose favour the order was made; and

  (d) where, immediately before the care order was made, a person had care of the child by virtue of an order made in the exercise of the High Court's inherent jurisdiction with respect to children, that person.

- The government has so far failed to implement section 11 (4) of the 1996 Family Law Act[118] which affirms:

[117] Hansard, Commons debate, 2 March 2006, Column 467, http://www.publications.parliament.uk/pa/cm200506/cmhansrd/cm060302/debtext/60302-25.htm

[118] The Family Law Act 1996, http://www.opsi.gov.uk/acts/acts1996/c1996027.htm#11.

(c) the general principle that, in the absence of evidence to the contrary, the welfare of the child will be best served by–

> *(i) his having regular contact with those who have parental responsibility for him and with other members of his family; and*
>
> *(ii) the maintenance of as good a continuing relationship with his parents as possible.*

OTHER CONCERNS

> *Judge Milligan, to a parent who had been unsuccessfully trying to see his child for 2 years: "This is a father who needs, in my judgment, to think long and hard about his whole approach to this question of contact and to ask himself sincerely whether in fact he seeks to promote it for his own interests dressed up as the child's interests."*

SECRECY

- The Family Courts operate in secret, closed to the media and to the public, closed to scrutiny and accountability. Justice cannot possibly thrive in an environment of secrecy.

- Within this protected environment the judges have developed a "virtual new legislation," promoting concepts not included in the parliamentary legislation such as equality and non-discrimination, and usurping the role of Parliament.[119]

- *"It is now plain that the incorporation of the European Convention on Human Rights into our domestic law will subject the entire legal system to a fundamental process of review and, wherever necessary, reform by the judiciary."*[120]

FALSE ALLEGATIONS

- False allegations are allowed, even encouraged,[121] in the Family Courts and go unchallenged. Allegations of domestic violence, of physical and even sexual abuse can be made which profoundly influence the nature of the orders made, and yet opportunities for exploring or countering these allegations are denied.

- It is apparently perfectly acceptable to make a false allegation within family proceedings, and indeed this practice is extremely widespread. Conduct which in any other circumstances would be considered a serious crime, is routinely dismissed as being understandable at an emotionally-charged time: a response to the 'distress' of the proceedings.

- By the same token, a mother who implacably stops contact between child and father is treated as someone who is upset and needs time to 'cool off', rather than someone who is failing to put the needs of the child first. Fathers are told to put these allegations behind them.[122]

---

[119] See *Institutional Injustice: the Family Courts at Work*, 2005, by Martin Mears, former President of the Law Society.

[120] Lord Hope, quoted in *Institutional Injustice: the Family Courts at Work*.

[121] There is ample evidence for this; a false allegation is referred to by solicitors as the 'magic bullet.'

- Serious allegations are made of a degree which should be dealt with under the criminal law "beyond reasona doubt" standard of evidence, and not under the civil law "balance of probability" standard.

- This enables extremely effective false allegations to be made, encouraged by solicitors and by CAFCASS.[123]

- When children are genuinely considered to be at risk the case should be reported to the child protection autho and proper process followed – not dealt with in the kangaroo Family Courts merely on the basis of probabiliti

PARENTAL ALIENATION

- The term Parental Alienation Syndrome (PAS) was coined by psychiatrist Dr Richard Gardner in the early 1980's.[124] The expression fell foul of the medical and psychiatric community because the word 'syndrome' w one they preferred to confer themselves. In fact, though PAS is not included in DSM-IV (the Diagnostic and Statistical Manual of mental disorders) it is being considered for inclusion in DSM-V, to be published in 2011

- PAS describes the behaviours of children who have been poisoned or alienated through constant denigratio one parent against the other, in a manner common in contact disputes. Indeed, PAS is almost unique to cor disputes.

- Since the 1989 Children Act PAS has become a very effective strategy for gaining custody, because the Act greater consideration of the 'child's wishes.' In PAS cases the 'child's wishes' are not in fact his but the wish the alienating parent. A parent who prevents contact can avoid the charge of contempt by maintaining that t child does not wish to see the other parent; a Court Welfare Officer will then investigate and confirm this, the will take the 'child's wishes' into consideration and stop contact. Contact may well not resume until the child enough to make decisions independently of the alienating parent.

- It is vital that proposed measures to increase the role a child plays in the court process should take account alienation.

- The syndrome is recognised by Courts but NAPO (the National Association of Probation Offers, which is the which dominates CAFCASS) has no official policy on it and it is rarely considered as a factor in the reports CAFCASS prepares for the Courts.

---

[122] In the case of A v A [2004] EWHC 142 (FAM) Lord Justice Wall stated, *"It would be hoped that father might have been able now this matter on one side. It seems that he is not yet able to do so... the father would inevitably feel intensely bruised and battered by allegations of sexual impropriety...despite his understandable sense of outrage at the allegations he had really learnt nothing from tř whole process."*

[123] Resident parents who have subsequently regretted their actions have often admitted that they were encouraged to make false allegations.

[124] The Late Richard Gardner was a member of the Department of Child Psychiatry, College of Physicians and Surgeons, Columbia University, New York.

CAFCASS

> *In the case of 'G' (A Child) [2003] EWCA Civ 489 in Northampton County Court., HHJ Mitchell recognised that prior to any contact mother 'went to pieces', and so ordered a* **five-year bar** *on further contact proceedings concerning a* **two-year-old** *child, on the basis that "everyone needed some peace and a breathing space."*

- The Children and Family Court Advisory and Support Service (CAFCASS) was established on April Fools' Day 2001 under the Criminal Justice and Court Services Act with a brief to safeguard and promote the welfare of children involved in family court proceedings.

- The new body was cobbled together from 117 pre-existing agencies and was initially rushed into existence and poorly funded. There were delays in appointing the board, disputes with practitioners, tensions between members of the management team, and financial irregularities.[125]

- Despite the 'no delay' principle of the 1989 Act, delay in appointing a guardian increased from 24 hours pre-CAFCASS to 5 weeks post-CAFCASS. Fewer cases were handled, standards of recruitment declined, and there was a lack of training or professional development. The existing system of appraisal and performance management disappeared. Six million pounds was provided for a case management IT system, but the project was halted.[126]

- From its inception it failed to in its duty to promote the welfare of children through unfairly denying children contact with absent parents (usually fathers). In 2003 Lord Falconer dismissed the entire board and responsibility for appointments was transferred from the Lord Chancellor's Department to the Minister for Children.

- Perhaps the greatest criticism of CAFCASS is their attitude towards fathers. It is little known that the guidelines for the writing of CAFCASS reports were drawn up by NAPO (National Association of Probation Officers), the union to which many CAFCASS practitioners belong (the other union is NAGALRO). Their 'Equal Rights' committee, from which men are excluded,[127] drew up the now notorious NAPO 'Anti-Sexism Policy which includes these statements:

  > *The structuring of society has been based on patriarchal assumptions in which, through the process of paternity, there is male control over women, children and the family as an institution. These assumptions extend through all social relations into the institutions of capitalism, the education system, the health services, the criminal justice system and the welfare state. Patriarchy has been the back drop (sic) against which all women have been subordinated and ignored.[128]*

  > *There is potential for collusion in home making and peacemaking by the women without ensuring that men share equally in these roles. Family Court work is an important opportunity to build on the strengths and the expansion of women's roles.[129]*

---

[125] Third Report by Committee on the Lord Chancellor's Department, http://www.parliament.the-stationery-office.co.uk/pa/cm200203/cmselect/cmlcd/614/61402.htm

[126] Ibid.

[127] "After a lively internal debate it was resolved in 1989 that this committee would be a women only group because it was agreed that women working in NAPO needed to progress together through continuing barriers between women, in terms of sexual orientation, race and disability in order to challenge effectively the male oppression of women." NAPO Anti Sexism Policy, 1996.

[128] NAPO Anti Sexism Policy, 1996.

[129] Ibid.

- In August 2006 Her Majesty's Inspectorate of Court Administration (HMICA) published a damning report on CAFCASS.[130] They said:

  - *CAFCASS has not produced for practitioners guidance on the standards expected of them, what the focu the work should be, how the work should be planned or how the work should be carried out. Consequen practitioners often work in very individual ways. Many interviews are not organised well and much information is gathered which is not relevant to the task.*

  - *There are often vital issues of whether domestic violence has occurred and what the effect on the childre has been. This part of the assessment is of particular significance when the dispute is regarding where th child should live or what contact, if any, the child should have with specific adults. However, currently practitioners usually assess domestic violence unsatisfactorily.*

  - *Practitioners often rely for their recommendations on their individual views and experience. CAFCASS ha little research regarding the effectiveness of its work or the value of particular recommendations. Practitio pay insufficient attention to the 'no Order principle'; this requires that Orders should only be made where doing so would be better for the child than making no Order at all.*

  - *Reports are often over-lengthy and include a substantial amount of historical information, which is not alw relevant to the dispute. Where, as is often the case, the adults have conflicting views, practitioners freque report these without evaluating the information.*

  - *Arrangements in CAFCASS to ensure accountability remain unacceptably weak. Managers have insuffic knowledge of the actual practice of practitioners and whether reports are reliably based on sound assessments. There are significant amounts of waste in practitioners' work because of inefficient methoo*

As with much child care, there has been no evaluation of CAFCASS interventions as outcomes are not recorded. Recommendations are therefore made to the Courts in a knowledge and evidence vacuum, and every child becomes th subject of "an uncontrolled experiment."[131]

---

[130] *An inspection undertaken between October 2005 and March 2006 of the Children and Family Court Advisory and Support Service (CAFCASS) concerning private law front-line practice*, HMICA, August 2006, http://www.hmica.gov.uk/files/Private_law_front-line_.p

[131] Mike Stein, Co-director of the Social Work Research and Development Unit at the University of York.

THE CSA

> *I didn't fully understand what had happened. But I understood that my father had gone away and was never coming back. I knew I wouldn't see him again and, after all these years, I still miss him. If it wasn't for the CSA my Dad would be alive and I wouldn't have grown up without a father.*
>
> *Stacy McKay, aged 18, talking about the suicide of her father, Jim, 30 July 2006[132]*

Every day, we hear increasingly about 'Deadbeat Dads' and 'Feckless Fathers' - those despicable low-life characters who won't even support their own children. Every day, we hear about some heroic politician who has decided to 'get tough' on them by introducing a draconian new regulation or measure. Most recently, this has taken the form of proposing that the immense uncollected debts to the Child Support Agency (CSA) be recovered by private debt-collection agencies who will then be allowed to cream off a percentage. With these debts now at an alleged £3.5 billion, this is an attractive proposition. What we have never heard amongst all this bluster is anyone asking the very simple question, 'Why don't fathers pay?'

There is now such a degree of insidious misandry in society that the casual assumption can be made about fathers that they are merely irresponsible and negligent, without any sense that this view is deeply bigoted. The easy alliterative stereotype of the 'feckless father' or 'dead-beat dad' blinds commentators to the reality.

So let us consider some of the *real* reasons for non-payment. They are not necessarily legally justifiable reasons, and they are not necessarily very noble, but they need to be grasped and tackled, not disregarded, and with them must be acknowledged the very profound resentment and grievances which exist amongst a large proportion of men in our society.

CHILD BENEFIT

The problems for a father begin with the fact that Child Benefit is almost always paid to the child's mother; indeed, this is one area in which the legislation itself is gender biased. This is largely because only the mother has automatic Parental Responsibility (PR) for the child, while a father has PR only if he is married to the mother, and can otherwise usually only acquire PR if the mother wishes it. While parents remain together this slight bias is entirely insignificant, but as soon as they separate, there arise many difficulties. In those few cases in which the father is paid Child Benefit it is the mother who suffers these consequences.

THE CHILD SUPPORT AGENCY (CSA)

The 1991 Child Support Act designates the parent in receipt of Child Benefit the 'Parent With Care' (PWC), the other parent was designated the 'Absent Parent,' also known since the 2000 reform as the Non-Resident Parent (NRP). This distinction, written into the legislation, is hugely significant: the casual prejudice of most commentators, presented with the adjective

---

[132] Sunday Telegraph, 30 July 2006.

'absent,' assume that this absence is voluntary and deliberate; that it describes fathers who walk out on their families, le their partners, abandon their children: 'feckless fathers,' 'dead-beat dads.' They are ignorant of the fact that 'absence demanded by the Act, and becomes, effectively, not a *description* but a *prescription*.

It is understandable that responsible fathers, fully intending to remain very *present* in their children's lives and to pla responsible and committed role, and equally ignorant of the wording of the Act, are enormously resentful at being descr as 'absent,' or consider that the term and therefore the legislation do not apply to them.

Many couples when they divorce or separate intend to share the care and upbringing of their children more or less equ between them. The intervention of the CSA makes this practicably impossible.

THREE AND A HALF BILLION POUNDS

The estimate of how much Child Support the CSA has failed to recover has increased recently to £3.5 billion. Would cynical to see a political motive in this: a way to further demonise fathers in order to make the Government's proposal pursue non-paying fathers with bailiffs more palatable to the public? Some of these estimates are based, not on figures, but on surveys of single mothers which are then scaled up.

No sensible father will allow himself to fall into the hands of the CSA. If he has any sense he will make maintena contributions to the mother and hope that she will not set the CSA onto him. Many fathers refuse to cooperate with the but continue to make payments direct to their former partners. Obviously the CSA will not take these contributions consideration and will continue to pursue payment; to prevent loss of contact fathers have been known to pay twice.

One should view the £3.5 billion figure with extreme circumspection.

THE FIRST REASON FOR NON-PAYMENT: EXCESSIVE ASSESSMENT

Many fathers claim that they simply cannot afford to pay Child Support.

The CSA operates two systems of assessment: the Old and the New. The New System is designed to suit the C notoriously ineffective computer system. It allows only four variables for the calculation of contributions: the numbe qualifying children, the time the children spend with their father, the father's assessable income, and the number of children in his new household. Under this system he pays 15% of his income for one child, 20% for two and 25% for t or more. There are some variations and exceptions to this basic formula. About a quarter of assessed cases are unde New System.

The Old System allows for a much greater number of variables, such as the distance of the journey to work. Unde father can pay as much as 33% of his income for a single child. Three quarters of cases are still dealt with under the System.

Neither system considers the income of the mother, or allows for the cost of pursuing court applications for contact. Ne system acknowledges that both parents can be both PWC and NRP at different times. Assessments are regularly pur and unsupportable for any length of time. Fathers deliberately change jobs to evade the system, they take lower paid to minimise contributions, become self-employed the better to hide earnings, or sign on unemployed. The result of t that half of CSA assessments are for a token £5 per week, not really a good return on the massive bureaucratic Sometimes fathers take their own lives; the CSA is held to be responsible for a very considerable number of suicides. of this helps children, and has earned the CSA a reputation for merely redistributing poverty. Why is this?

Both systems contain fundamental flaws which vastly reduce the willingness of men to pay. Firstly, the basic assessment is based on the economic dynamic of the married family, in which the mother is the primary care-giver and the father is the primary wage earner. The CSA assessments hold that the father is fully responsible financially for the child. This is not only hopelessly anachronistic, the economic dynamic of separated families is very different; applying this false principle results in a reductio ad absurdam with the mother doing all the child care and the father doing all the paying. This is not about good parenting.

Under the CSA system the Child Support contributions lessen as the time the children spend with their father increases. Thus a father who looks after his children fulltime will pay nothing to the mother, but neither will she pay anything to him. If the childcare is shared equally the father will still pay half of his maximum assessment to the mother.

In an age in which women constitute half of the workforce and fathers undertake eight times more childcare than their own fathers, it is surely right to share the financial burden just as much as the childcare. If the childcare is shared equally, all other things being equal, there should be no need for any money to change hands, or for the CSA to be involved at all. In some absurd cases where each parent receives Child Benefit for one child, equal sums of money are exchanged via the CSA between the parents. The administrative cost is borne by the taxpayer.

The second flaw is the rather strange feature of the CSA that they only consider childcare which takes place at night. Fathers' contributions are only reduced according to the number of nights per week their children stay with them, any childcare which takes place during the daytime is discounted. This is particularly prejudicial to fathers for two reasons: firstly, fathers often have no suitable accommodation for their children to stay at night, and have to return their children in the evenings. Secondly, the Family Courts habitually make orders which do not include overnight staying contact.

The effect of these and other factors is that there is enormous financial advantage in becoming the Resident Parent, and that many contact disputes are therefore about money, and not about children.

THE SECOND REASON FOR NON-PAYMENT: LOSS OF CONTACT

The second reason why fathers do not make Child Support contributions is the most significant and the most simple: they are being prevented by their former partners and by the Family Courts from having proper contact with their children and from playing an equal role in the care and upbringing of their children, which can not be fulfilled simply by signing a monthly cheque.

It is an often quoted principle of the Family Courts that there should be no link between Child Support and contact: a mother who is receiving no or inadequate contributions from the father should not prevent contact. After all it is not the child's fault. Unfortunately the CSA ignores this important principle: they make a clear connection between the two. If a mother refuses contact she will, in theory if not in practice, receive higher contributions; there is therefore a financial incentive, offered to her by the CSA and the child support legislation, to prevent contact. This is criminal. The CSA bases its assessments on actual levels of contact rather than those levels ordered by the Courts. **If this principle was simply reversed, it would have the two effects of increasing contact and increasing willingness to pay, and would be enormously beneficial to the children concerned.**

THE THIRD REASON FOR NON-PAYMENT: THE GOVERNMENT'S ANTI FAMILY POLICY

The CSA is based on the fundamental principle that individuals require the state to administer things for them; yet it is healthier if people are left to make these arrangements themselves. It is also designed around children and their moth living on benefits, and is far from ideal for other types of family. The main beneficiary in these cases is the treasury and the child.

It should also be apparent by now that many existing structures designed to determine a child's welfare and finan provision after divorce are profoundly prejudicial to men. While fathers remain married they are rarely exposed to consequences of this prejudice, but as soon as they separate or divorce, they find themselves stripped of their child home and assets, and obliged to perform for many long years like the organ grinder's monkey to the tune of the Fa Courts. They believe that the 'no fault' divorce, the tax and benefits systems, the very favourable treatment of sin mothers, the CSA's system of assessment, and that the Family Courts almost invariably award Residence to the mothe make divorce an extremely attractive proposition for women. They consider that if the State wishes to exclude them f the lives of their children, and take on many of the functions traditionally performed by fathers, the State should also take the financial responsibility. This responsibility and his nurturing, parenting responsibilities should be protected by the S as indivisible, not divided up and auctioned off. A responsible state would enforce continuing contact even more fore than financial support.

PROPOSALS FOR CHANGE

This year saw two reports on the CSA by The Independent Case Examiner and the National Audit Office, and two studie reform, the first by Chief Executive Stephen Geraghty, which was not released to the public, and the second by Sir D Henshaw, former chief executive of Liverpool City Council. This report recommended a scaled down version of the which would target the most hardened non-payers and the largest debts. Penalties would be harsher and include seizure of passports, curfews, electronic tagging and community service. In July 2006 Work and Pensions secretary Hutton announced a 'fresh start' for the agency, however any substantial change will require new primary legislation there is no sign of this on the political horizon.

THE BOTTOM LINE

> *District Judge Hindley: dismissed a father's application to phone his 7 yr old daughter on Christmas morning calling it "too disruptive - she would be opening her Christmas presents."*

- The simple truth is that the Family Courts do not actually work! They do not fulfill the task given to them by Parliament to perform. Where parents are highly conflicted they do not facilitate contact, and where it takes place and works effectively it does so only when the Courts have had no involvement.[133]

- Disputes over residence and contact are often substitutes for other conflicts; the introduction of the 'no fault' concept into divorce law and the abrogation by the CSA of parents' rights to sue over maintenance make this the one issue over which parents can take each other to court. Thus in effect the court system channels parents into a parenting contest from which only one can emerge victorious.[134]

- The best that research has been able to show is that the Courts don't necessarily make matters worse.[135]

- Other research shows that the court process exacerbates rather than resolves disputes.[136] It isn't much of a claim for a multi million pound industry.

- Post separation parenting works where parents are able to co-operate and put aside their differences. It follows that public money should be put towards enabling co-operation and conciliation rather than into a process which is adversarial and encourages animosity.

---

[133] Trinder, L., Beek, M., and Connolly, J., *Making contact: How parents and children negotiate and experience contact after divorce*, Joseph Rowntree Foundation, October 2002, York Publishing Services, 64 Hallfield Road, Layerthorpe, York YO31 7ZQ

[134] See Smart, C., May, V., Wade, A., and Furniss, C., *Residence and Contact Disputes in Court*, University of Leeds, June 2005, DCA Research Series 4/05.

[135]

[136] Trinder, L., Connolly, J., Kellett, J. and Notley, C., *A Profile of Applicants and Respondents in Contact Cases in Essex*, Department for Constitutional Affairs, 2005.

WHERE ARE WE NOW?

THE BAD NEWS...

> *District Judge Kenworthy-Browne: A child of 3 "will have developed no Christmas associations with the father, and even if he has spent Christmases at the father's home, he will not remember them. As such, he will not expect increased contact with his father over the holidays."*

- The Green Paper, Parental Separation: Children's Needs and Parents' Responsibilities was followed by the Children (Contact) and Adoption Bill and finally by the Children and Adoption Act 2006[137] which received R Assent in June. However the Act has not yet been implemented and there is no timetable for doing so.[138] Funding which will be necessary for implementation is not yet in place. CAFCASS are not expected to incor the Act into their practice until April 2007.

  o There is no provision in the Act for early resolution, and the Act achieves little more than tweaking. The some new powers for enforcement, monitoring contact and compensation for financial loss due to obst contact.

- There will be nothing in the Queen's speech on the 15th of this month.

- On 24 July the Work and Pensions Secretary John Hutton announced new proposals[139] to ensure that fathe responsibility for their children – the underlying assumption being that at present they do not. One of the op considered was "changing the law on registration of births to encourage or require joint registration." Such a measure should also confer the right to have meaningful contact with his child.

IF THE FATHER IS NAMED ON THE BIRTH CERTIFICATE,

AND HE IS MADE TO BE RESPONSIBLE FINANCIALLY,

THEN HE MUST ALSO BE RESPONSIBLE EMOTIONALLY.

- It now seems extremely unlikely that the Early Interventions project, or anything like it, will be resurrected in foreseeable future.

---

[137] http://www.opsi.gov.uk/ACTS/acts2006/ukpga_20060020_en.pdf

[138] Written answer provided by Lord Adonis to Baroness Anelay of St Johns, 24 July 2006, Hansard, http://www.publications.parliament.uk/pa/ld199900/ldhansrd/pdvn/lds06/text/60724w0246.htm#06072416000063

[139] Press release, 24 July 2006, http://www.dwp.gov.uk/mediacentre/pressreleases/2006/jul/cphs032-240706.asp

- New court forms, C1[140] and C1A[141] introduce additional bureaucracy and delay, contrary to the aims of the 1989 Act. They also include a presumption of domestic violence (DV) and a definition of DV which includes ordinary behaviour; they actively encourage every separating parent to make allegations. They carry the capacity to stop contact or to establish DV litigation as a prequel to contact litigation.

- The Government's approach to family breakdown can be gleaned from recent statements:

  "Existing research suggests that while stable, two-parent families tend to be associated with favourable outcomes for children, factors such as work status, income, and family conflict and disharmony, are likely to be more influential than family structure alone.

  "The House of Commons Education and Skills Committee took oral evidence on this topic from four expert witnesses on 12 July 2006. The witnesses agreed that family structure was a relatively unimportant factor in predicting children's outcomes compared with other factors such as poverty." – Education Minister Lord Adonis[142]

- In the area of In-Vitro Fertilisation the Government has clearly expressed its view that a father is unnecessary, allowing the creation of ever more fatherless children and signaling its approval of children-as-commodities; designer babies will not be far behind:

  "We are minded to retain a duty in terms of the welfare of the child being taken into account, but we are thinking there is probably less of a case for a retention in law to the reference for a father.

  "That does not mean fathers are not important. What's important is that the children are going to be, as far as we know, part of a loving family. We are considering whether the need for a father is something we need to have." – Health Minister Caroline Flint,[143]

- Despite the overwhelming evidence that marriage provides the most stable environment in which a child can prosper, the Government is still advocating alternative, short-lived, relationships as no less valid; an argument it justifies through the use of crude stereotypes:

  "We also have to recognise that the modern family is not always a married family. Marriage can provide stability, but it's not for everyone.

  "Our focus should not be on whether people marry or not, it should be on the welfare of the child, and the quality of the upbringing." – Education Secretary Alan Johnson[144]

- The average marriage, however, lasts about 11.6 years (2005) while the average cohabitation lasts about 2 years. A child stands a much better chance of his parents remaining together for the duration of his childhood, therefore, if he can contrive to be born to married parents.

---

[140] http://www.hmcourts-service.gov.uk/courtfinder/forms/c1_1205.pdf

[141] http://www.hmcourts-service.gov.uk/courtfinder/forms/c1a_0105.pdf

[142] Written answer to Lord Northbourne, 24 Julky 2006, Hansard, http://www.publications.parliament.uk/pa/ld199900/ldhansrd/pdvn/lds06/text/60724w0246.htm#06072416000063

[143] Evidence given to Commons Science and Technology Committee, 12 July 2006.

[144] Speech to National Family and Parenting Institute, 25 July 2006.

...AND THE GOOD

> *Mr. Justice Munby sentenced a father to four months in prison for giving his children Christmas presents (a bike, a camera and a walkman) during a scheduled contact meeting. Upheld on appeal by Thorpe LJ and Butler-Sloss LJ.*

- In September 2006, however, the Work and Pensions Minister John Hutton contradicted established Labour tradition – and amazed the equal parenting community – by endorsing the two-parent family; he said it is,

    "*undoubtedly the case that children have a better prospect of making the most of their lives if they are brought up in a household where there are two caring, loving parents... My approach is this - that the r stage of welfare reform has actually got to put the family at centre-stage, because it's the families in this country that provide the most care and most welfare.*"[145]

- Following pressure from and talks with Fathers-4-Justice, CAFCASS agreed the following:

    o   In October they would introduce a new Case Recording system; at the time of writing this is in place in 6 of 10 regions.

    o   There would be a steady move away from standard Section 7 reports towards briefer, more focused rep writing and earlier intervention (this is driven to some extent by a cash shortage within CAFCASS).

    o   The starting point in residence and contact disputes would be Shared Parenting.

    o   They will be launching a new initiative called the Respect Agenda, which will include measures to stop c parent denigrating the other.

    o   Parental Alienation would be recognised but not as a syndrome.

    o   NAPO, now led by Siân Griffiths and no longer by Harry Fletcher, has tacitly accepted the changes prop by Anthony Douglas.

- The HMICA report[146] made the following recommendations, that CAFCASS should:

    1.   *Clarify its functions in private law proceedings and the associated range of practitioner roles.*

    2.   *Publish national standards and supporting private law practice guidance.*

    3.   *Develop and implement a strategy (the Performance Framework) to deliver agreed changes in front-line practice.*

    4.   *Take further steps to ensure quality assurance is effectively undertaken in local area teams and local accountability is improved.*

---

[145] John Hutton, interview on Radio 4's Today programme, 15 September 2006, http://news.bbc.co.uk/1/hi/uk_politics/5349000.stm

[146] An inspection undertaken between October 2005 and March 2006 of the Children and Family Court Advisory and Support service (CAFCASS) concerning private law front-line practice, HM Inspectorate of Court Administration, August 2006, http://www.hmica.gov.uk/files/Private_law_front-line_.pdf

5. *Develop and implement a strategy the Knowledge, Learning and Development Strategy) to address the assessed training needs of staff undertaking private law work.*

6. *Continue to work with relevant organisations, Judiciary and Departments to agree and implement protocols covering new referrals to CAFCASS*

7. *Develop a framework to help assess how effectively its work with families contributes to improved outcomes for children, as defined in Every Child Matters.*

8. *Develop a longer term research strategy with a clear child focus outcome, in partnership with other family justice agencies, relevant organisations and Departments.*

- All these recommendations are to be enacted by April 2007.

THE DCA CONSULTATION

> *In the case of 'G' (A Child) [2003] EWCA Civ 489 in Northampton County Court., HHJ Mitchell recognised that prior to any contact mother 'went to pieces', and so ordered a **five-year bar** on further contact proceedings concerning a **two-year-old** child, on the basis that "everyone needed some peace and a breathing space."*

Following the Clayton[147] case, in September 2006 the Department for Constitutional Affairs (DCA) launched a consulta on the issues of separate representation of children and the opening up of the Family Courts to the public and to the pr The consultation invited contributions from interested parties, set up two internet forums for adults and children to post comments and culminated in a conference held in London on 30 October 2006 organised by Care and Health.[148] The government's view was represented by the Minister of State at the Department of Constitutional Affairs, Harriet Harmar of the judiciary by Lord Justice Wall and that of those members of the public whose lives have been wrecked by the far courts, by Tammy, some of whose comments opened this document.

THE CONSULTATION PAPER

The DCA published a consultation paper on the Separate Representation of Children[149] on 1 September 2006. This considers extending the right to representation by a CAFCASS guardian and solicitor that children in public law cases to children in private law. As things stand such representation is often only ordered after many months or even years c litigation. By this time great damage has already been done to the child's relationship with the non-resident parent.

Research commissioned from the University of Cardiff[150] showed that such representation was most beneficial in intrac cases but could impose too much responsibility and stress on the child if it thought the judge's decision would be base entirely on their view. The report said that children can feel confused and manipulated by their parents, "*repeating unfounded allegations or simply reciting the parent's view to the guardian.*"[151]

The Cardiff recommendations went further, covering for example the need for expedition and early assessment and th necessity that CAFCASS guardians are properly trained and trustworthy, with an aptitude to gain children's confidence report emphasizes appropriate keeping of documentation and judicial continuity.

---

[147] Clayton v. Clayton [2006] EWCA Civ 878, Para. 77. The practical consequence which flows from this judgment is that henceforth be appropriate for every tribunal, when making what it believes to be a final order in proceedings under the 1989 Act, to consider whe or not there is an outstanding welfare issue which needs to be addressed by a continuing order for anonymity. This will, I think, be a discipline for parties, judges, and family practitioners alike. If there is no outstanding welfare issue, then it is likely that the penal consequences of s.97 of the 1989 Act will cease to have any effect, and the parties will be able to put into the public domain any mat relating to themselves and their children which they wish to publish, provided that the publication does not offend against s.12 AJA 1

[148] Care and Health: http://www.careandhealth.com/Pages/Event.aspx?EventID=281bb443-0cce-4ae4-a575-375ec7c2a7e3

[149] http://www.dca.gov.uk/consult/separate_representation/cp2006.pdf

[150] Douglas, G., Murch, M., Miles, C., and Scanlan, L., *Research into the Operation of Rule 9.5 of the Family Proceedings Rules 199 Final Report to the Department for Constitutional Affairs*, Cardiff Law School, 2006 http://www.dca.gov.uk/family/familyprocrules_research.pdf

[151] Ibid., page 11

The researchers recommend that there should always be separate representation before enforcement under the Children and Adoption Act and that the guardian should ensure protection of the child from adverse repercussions following an enforcement order.

THE INTERNET FORUMS

The DCA set up two internet forums on which it invited contributions to the debate, one for adults[152] and one for children.[153] Responses were carefully steered in desired directions and heavily censored. Public confidence was clearly low and the consultation itself was widely viewed as a PR exercise; the adult forum netted about 200 responses, and the children's only about 30, some of which were manifestly from adults.

THE JUDGE: LORD JUSTICE WALL'S SPEECH

Lord Justice Wall's overlong and confused speech illustrates the dilemma the government and Family Court judiciary is in: he tries on the one hand to profess himself in favour of open justice and press freedom, but is quite clearly alarmed by the idea that press or public – for whom he has equal contempt – should have any routine right of access to Family cases.

He outlines the justification for open justice:

- to enable informed and proper public scrutiny of the administration of justice;

- to facilitate informed public knowledge, understanding and discussion of the important social, medical and ethical issues which are litigated in the family justice system;

- to facilitate the dissemination of information useful to other professions and organisations in the multi-disciplinary working of family law

He acknowledges that the public should have access to other courts, "The actions of public authorities directly related to matters such as arrest, detention and the collection of evidence must all be open to public scrutiny." Why should the actions of public authorities directly related to matters such as care orders, forced adoption, denial of parental contact, etc, be any different? There are, he says, two reasons:

- the presence of the public would be likely to inhibit the parties and their witnesses.

- provided there is the opportunity for responsible media reporting of the proceedings, the public's presence serves no purpose in the public interest.

With all due respect m'lud, that is only one reason – which would apply equally to all other courts, the second is only an opinion, and 'responsible' in this context means playing by the rules imposed by the court. The real reason lies in his distrust of the public, "it is to guard against the public's sometimes prurient curiosity that I am opposed to opening up family proceedings to members of the public."

He would grant entry, therefore, only to the press. He begins by describing a carefully controlled system in which the press would have access only on the basis of "clear ground rules about what they can and cannot report." In more sensitive cases they would be issued with carefully vetted 'anonymised' press releases.

But the expectation that the press would be content with that is naïve: the press deal in the personal, not the general. Wall extends the contempt he has for the public to the press, "I remain permanently dispirited about the way in which the media seize on family disputes involving the rich or those otherwise perceived as celebrities."

He describes the coverage by the Daily Mail of a case - *Re H (Freeing Orders: Publicity)* [2005] EWCA Civ 1325 - as "*highly tendentious, and illicitly obtained... The message from the newspaper was that local authorities, aided and abetted by a secretive judiciary, were implementing a covert policy of social engineering by removing children from the care of their*

---

worthy and God-fearing parents on the specious ground that the parents concerned were not sufficiently intelligent to care for them."

Wall says that his principal aim is to prevent tendentious or sensationalist reporting and suggests the judiciary should "meet the press half way and ensure that when it takes the view that an issue ought to be reported, the issue in question is presented to the press in a way in which the press can properly use it." Thus revealing that he wants to control both which cases are covered and how they are presented to the public.

The Daily Mail, however, defended itself, "We thought then – and we still do – that the court's decision was cruelly wrong."

On the same day the Mail's columnist, Melanie Philips, wrote that the report, "brought to light the hitherto unrecognised scandal of social workers routinely removing children from their families on account of nothing more than the presumed impact upon them of their parents' low IQ."[155] She went on,

> Incidentally, the Press reporting of this case made clear that only the mother had a low IQ; the father was mistakenly classified as such by social services.

> This error was itself only brought to light by the "tendentious and illicit" reporting of this case.

> Is it not more than a little worrying, therefore, that a Lord Justice of Appeal, threatening to fetter Press freedom because of "distorted" reporting, himself misreported the media and also failed to note the sloppiness of the social workers' false description of the father in the case?

On the same day Mr. Justice Munby ordered that gagging orders on a remarkably similar case should be lifted,

> It is a fundamental and long established principle of our legal system... that justice is administered in public. Legal proceedings should be conducted in public and should be fully and freely reported.

> If the media are to be permitted access to the forthcoming hearing that access cannot properly be confined to the particular organs of the media who are before me. It is not for a judge to licence the media, preferring one over another.

Two days later Munby ruled that the couple, Mark and Nicola Webster, could take their fourth child, Brandon, home. Next year they may seek an application to reopen the care hearings which took their three other children.[156]

Like the Daily Mail in the other case, the BBC programme Real Story had fought a legal battle to report this case. It is manifestly in the public interest that where there has been a clear miscarriage of justice or where a miscarriage of justice has been alleged such cases should be open to public scrutiny. In the case of the Websters they wanted their case publicised and the press wanted to report on it; in the vast majority of cases the press would not wish to do so, which is why access to the public and not just to the press must be allowed. The timing of Munby's ruling, coming so close on Lord Justice Wall's speech, shows his attempt to gag the press for what it is.

No member of the judiciary or government has yet been able to answer the fundamental question: what harm has ever been shown to have befallen a child because his identity has been revealed in court? Any perceived harm is pure speculation; indeed, Wall himself points to the benefits such publicity can sometimes have.

[154] Daily Mail, Comment, 1 November 2006

[155] Melanie Philips, Daily Mail, 1 November 2006,
http://www.dailymail.co.uk/pages/live/articles/columnists/columnists.html?in_article_id=413829&in_page_id=1772&in_author_id=256

[156] The Guardian, Judge says couple accused of abuse can have their youngest child back, 4 November 2006,
http://society.guardian.co.uk/children/story/0,,1939342,00.html

THE MINISTER: HARRIET HARMAN'S SPEECH

Harriet Harman has already established her anti-father credentials in her 1990 Pamphlet, the Family Way, and in previous speeches which are available on her website. Her opening sets the tone:

> Taking a child from its mother and placing it for adoption changes lives - and changes them irrevocably. That decision will affect, for the rest of their lives, the child, the child's mother (and sometimes father).[157]

Questioned from the floor by F4J's Ray Barry on her evident bias against fathers, she replied unconvincingly that male on female violence is more likely to result in death and that in her book "it's the body count that matters."

Her speech is platitudinous - "Public policy cannot make men and women happy together in their relationships," or "Everyone agrees that it's better for children when adults can agree about their care." There is little here of substance, and her few proposals can be summarised briefly.

- To use the legal aid system to encourage mediation.

If this means withholding legal aid until parents have agreed to mediation, it comes close to the compulsory mediation demanded by F4J – it is unlikely though that she means to go that far. In this context Harman refers to the Children and Adoption Act 2006[158] which should have been implemented by now, and its requirement for applicants to consider mediation. In fact the Act enables a court to make a direction for a 'contact activity,' which include ,

11A (5)   (a) programmes classes and counselling or guidance sessions of a kind that –

(i)   may assist a person as regards establishing, maintaining or improving contact with a child;

(ii)   may, by addressing a person's violent behaviour, enable or facilitate contact with a child;

(b) sessions in which information or advice is given as regards making or operating arrangements for contact with a child, including making arrangements by means of mediation.

The Act specifically excludes compulsory mediation,

(6) No individual may be required by a contact activity direction –

(b) to take part in mediation.

Either she needs to read the Act more closely, or she recognizes its weakness and intends to use the legal aid system to compensate.

- Solicitors as a source of mediation.

Significant levels of mediation – which will only happen where there is a degree of compulsion or coercion – will result in fewer cases going to court and a drop in custom for solicitors. This proposal to train solicitors (at whose expense?) as mediators is a concession to that profession. Solicitors have not welcomed the proposals for changes in Legal Aid funding, and some have gone on strike in protest.

- Involving children

The one person absent from the court room is the child himself; Harman quotes Adam, "Listen to the child. It's not about the parents, it's about the children."

---

[157] Harriet Harman, speech to Care and Health Conference, Listening to children: in open and accountable family courts, 30 October 2006

[158] Children and Adoption Act 2006, http://www.opsi.gov.uk/acts/acts2006/20060020.htm

This is simplistic and ignores issues such as alienation, but clearly children should be involved in matters which can affe
their lives profoundly. Harman raises the question but does not answer it; she mentions the children's forum on the DC/
consultation, but the take-up of that initiative was very poor. This is what children really think, and see also Tammy's
contribution to the Conference, below:

> reading your fathers rights reaction makes me think even more negatively of the government and the way it w
> today... Fathers play just an important part as mothers. i dont expect anything to come out of this but i had to
> express my anger from a 16 year old girls point of view, whos own father she has lost contact with and knows
> big the need for a father or father figure a child wants and needs. i just hope things change

> Leanne Miller, aged 16, responding to the Fathers 4 Justice demonstration at Buckingham Palace, 17 Septer
> 20■

Protecting privacy in an open family court system

The consultation process is driven not by a concern for greater justice, but by the awareness that public confidence in th
system is ebbing. Harman identifies three areas of concern: failure to facilitate contact, failure to protect, and enforced
adoption. The problem for her is one of PR: "*How can we ensure that the important work of the family courts is underst*
and valued?" Shame on the public for not valuing this work.

The solution is the same as that prescribed by wall: "*Allowing the press in, and others in on application to the court. But*
reporting restrictions which guarantee anonymity. And we need to ensure that we have tough penalties for those who
overstep the mark." Penalties which would include the removal of accreditation from journalists who publish reports dee
unacceptable. She also plans to wait and see what conclusions New Zealand comes to when they review their new sy:
next year and then follow this with a new Family Justice Bill. Melanie Phillips again:

> Permitting only an approved reporting of proceedings would open the way to the Press being forced to censo
> itself in order to keep on the right side of the judges – thus producing a truly distorted picture with a likely coll■
> altogether of public confidence.[160]

---

[159] http://www.downingstreetsays.org/archives/000890.html

[160] Melanie Philips, Daily Mail, 1 November 2006,
http://www.dailymail.co.uk/pages/live/articles/columnists/columnists.html?in_article_id=413829&in_page_id=1772&in_author_id=256■

THE VICTIM: TAMMY'S SPEECH

Tammy Coulter's story[161] is shocking and emotive and deserves to be read in its entirety; what follows are merely the highlights:

> I am a young adopted adult; I was taken from my mum nearly 17 years ago on a false allegation, I was seven months old.

> I was a child who was wrongfully removed from the care of my mother and most of all I have had the rights taken away from me to have enjoyed the right to a family life with my natural family.

> All my mum wanted was to fight for me, she attended many family courts, which were held in secret and she was not allowed to talk about our case or me to anyone.

> The judge who heard my case made his decision on the basis that social services had delayed my case for over two and a half years. On reading his decision to my mum (he stated) "Miss Coulter if I return your daughter home to you, you will be a stranger to her" and on that decision I was freed for adoption and my whole future was completely changed... however my foster parents and my adoptive parents were also strangers.

> Finding out that you are adopted is one of the worst feelings in the world because you feel that all your identity you have known of yourself is a lie; for example your whole childhood and personality.

> I know I am not the only person to have gone through the hell of secrecy in family courts and hope to have expressed the way in which they will feel and are feeling at my age.

In some ways Tammy was lucky, she found her birth mother again and now lives with her and the brother and sister who were later born to her mother.

Tammy condemns the decisions in family Courts which are founded on opinions and not on facts, and are made by unqualified personnel She shows that the routine removal of children from families is the most damaging solution and recommends instead greater support for families where low IQ, depression or domestic violence is an issue; she says,

> (The) slow integration of a child back with its natural family should be paramount and decisions to take away the child should be the last resort.

[161] Speech by Tammy Coulter, In the best interest of the child, delivered to the Care and Health Conference, 30 October 2006, http://www.fassit.co.uk/opening_up_family_courts.htm

With acknowledgements to FASSIT, the Families Anti-Social Services Inquiry Team

OPEN JUSTICE: THE NEW ZEALAND EXPERIENCE

The arrangement for open justice currently being considered by the government has already been running for 16 months a very similar form in New Zealand. The arrangement itself was enabled by but not defined in the Care of Children Act 2004; details were agreed between the Ministry of Justice and the Newspapers Publishers Association: any organisation applying for accreditation of an employee must have a code of professional standards, a complaints procedure and a mechanism for dealing with complaints. Accredited employees must identify themselves to the Court which will have a lis approved journalists. The journalist will then be given a pass for that day in the form of a sticker. Journalists may not identify the children, the parents, other parties such as supporters, witnesses or 'speakers on cultural issues.' Penalties f breaching the reporting restrictions are up to a 3 month prison sentence or $2,000 fine for individuals and up to a $10,00 for companies.

The response of the media to attend hearings was not overwhelming. In the first 12 months after the Act there were 40 requests to attend, which resulted in only 12 instances when a journalist was recorded as attending, 20 instances when journalist attended, and 8 where media attendance was not recorded.[162]

Journalists who have sat through hearings have not found them particularly news-worthy and have not witnessed the bia and prejudice they have hoped for. It is not good use of a journalist's time to sit, possibly for days, through such a hearir

Peter Boshier, who heads the NZ Family Courts, has complained bitterly in a recent and much reported speech[163] that th style of media reporting is still antagonistic to the Courts, and still unbalanced, with assertions made by litigants which cannot be challenged. For example, the media present the views of the fathers in cases, but not those of the mothers or children. Reporters have the right now to read the Courts' judgements, but very rarely do so.

For their part, organisations campaigning in New Zealand for equal parenting believe nothing has changed; they quote c Family Court judge, Judge Inglis, as saying himself that the system is biased against fathers. They demand shared parenting as a starting point; a far higher standard of evidence when allegations are made; legislation to prevent a paren taking their child out of the family home. They want judges to be better trained, and to follow the law rather than make it

Campaigning against the Family Courts has increased since the Care of Children Act, with an emphasis on targeting individuals' homes – they call this 'bothering.' In May, Jim Bagnall, Children and Family spokesperson for the Republic o New Zealand Party, advocated the complete abolition of the Family Court. He said that family lawyers encourage false allegations of abuse with impunity, and that they make thousands from alienating children from their fathers. He would replace the Court with a mediation service based on equality.[164]

---

[162] NZ Ministry of Justice

[163] E.g. Peter Boshier, Principal Family Court Judge

[164] 5 May 2006, http://republicans.org.nz/?p=61#more-61

FINAL WORD

THREE WAYS TO REBUILD PUBLIC CONFIDENCE IN A DISCREDITED FAMILY JUSTICE SYSTEM

Early Interventions & Mandatory Mediation:

Before couples seek legal recourse, the government must recognise that ALL couples should be bound to enter into mandatory mediation, with appropriately trained mediators.

Presumption of Contact & Shared Parenting:

The best parent is both parents. The starting point after separation should be to maintain where possible what the status quo was before separation. Children currently have no right in law to see their parents. The principle of shared parenting creates a level playing field where conflict can be reduced, as opposed to the current 'winner takes all' scenario which generates maximum conflict.

Open Justice:

The current family justice system has been publicly discredited by organisations such as Fathers 4 Justice. Only a fully open, transparent and accountable system of justice can restore public confidence. The various half-measures currently being floated by the government will only serve to fuel public unease and distrust of a secret system. There is not a shred of empirical evidence to support the claim that open justice could 'damage' children.

If the government is genuinely nervous of the consequences to children, why not submit open justice to a limited trial, and monitor the results?

APPENDICES

APPENDIX I: THE IMPORTANCE OF FATHERS

The nature of the relationship between a father and his child is a very special one for which there is no substitute. Most fathers, and their children, know this intuitively, but there has been much recent research to confirm this. Here are some the key points recent researchers have made about the importance of the father-child relationship:

- Infants form close attachments to their fathers (bonding) as readily and deeply as, and at the same time as mothers.'[165]

- Fathers are as excited as mothers over their newborns, and bond to them at the same time and pace. Fat hold and rock more than mothers, and equal mothers in talking, kissing and imitating.[166]

- In general, girls who have a warm relationship with their father and feel accepted by them are more likely to comfortable and confident when relating to the opposite sex. . . . During the teen years and later, a girl who not had a rewarding relationship with her father is apt to feel insecure around males. She may feel unattracti a woman, doubt that any man could love her for herself, and distrust men in general.[167]

- Even at five months, the boys who have more contact with their father are more sociable with a stranger.[168]

- When fathers are away for long periods of time, as in the case of sailors at sea, their boys are less popular classmates and do not enjoy friendships as much as do boys who have more contact with their fathers.[169]

- Fathers do more physical play. When two-and-a-half-year-olds want to play, more than two thirds of the time will choose their father over their mother.[170]

- A lot of physical father play corresponds to better, deeper friendships with peers among children. Children self control, how to manage and express their emotions and recognize others' cues.[171]

---

[165] *Role of the Father*, Michael Lamb, pp. 1 - 63; Michael Lamb, *Father-Infant and Mother-Infant Interaction in the First Year of Life*, C Development, Vol. 48 (1977), pp. 167 - 181.

[166] Greenberg & Morris, *Engrossment: The Newborn's Impact upon the Father*, American Journal of Orthopsychiatry, Vol. 44 (1974), 526; Parke & O'Leary, *Father-Mother-Infant Interaction in the Newborn Period*, in *The Developing Individual in a Changing World*, Vol Riegal & Meacham, eds. (The Hague: Mounton, 1976), pp. 653 - 663.

[167] Richard Warshack, *The Custody Revolution*, p. 44 - 45.

[168] Milton Kotelchuck, *The Infant's Relationship to the Father: Experimental Evidence*, Lamb, ed., Role of the Father, pp. 329 - 344.

[169] Richard Warshack, *The Custody Revolution*, p. 41.

[170] Clarke-Stewart, *And Daddy Makes Three: The Father's Impact on Mother and Young Child*, Child Development Vol. 49 (1978), pp - 478.

[171] MacDonald & Parke, *Bridging the Gap: Parent-Child Play Interaction and Peer Interactive Competence*, Child Development vol. 5 (1985), pp1265 - 1277; Youngblade & Belsky, *Parent-Child Antecedent of 5-Year-Olds' Close Friendships: A Longitudinal Analysis*,

- Girls whose fathers play with them a lot tend to be more popular with peers and more assertive in their interpersonal relationships throughout their lives.[172]

- Men and women who have had warm paternal relationships have better, longer marriages and engage in more recreation.[173]

- It has been suggested that a father's pheromones delay the onset of puberty in girls, possibly as an incest-avoidance mechanism.[174] Experiments on laboratory animals has confirmed this. Exposure to the pheromones of unrelated males can cause premature puberty.[175] Research has shown that girls are reaching puberty 18 months earlier than their mothers and 2 years earlier than their grandmothers.[176] Precocious puberty is associated with depression, promiscuity, teenage pregnancy and academic failure.

- The presence of a father is also necessary for the normal sexual development of their sons; fatherlessness has been implicated in gender identity disorder. One study found that of the less disturbed males, 54% were fatherless; of the most profoundly disturbed, 100% were fatherless, and 75% had no father substitute or male role model.[177] The age at which a boy loses his father is significant, and in the study 80% who had no father had lost their fathers by the age of 5.

Developmental Psychology Vol. 28 (1992), pp. 700 - 713; Snarey, *How Fathers Care for the Next Generation,* Cambridge, MA: Harvard University Press, pp. 35 - 36; Gottman, *The Heart of Parenting,* New York: Simon & Schuster, 1997, p. 171.

[172] Parke et al, *Family-Peer Systems: In Search of the Linkages,* Kreppner & Lerner, eds,. *Family Systems and Life Span Development* (Hillsdale, NJ: Erlbaum, 1989), pp. 65 - 92. As cited in Parke & Brott *Throwaway Dads* (Boston: Houghton Mifflin Co., 1999).

[173] Franz, McClelland, & Weinberger, "Childhood Antecedents of Conventional Social Accomplishments in Midlife Adults: A 36-Year Prospective Study," *Journal of Personality and Social Psychology* Vol. 60 (1991), pp. 586 - 595.

[174] Ellis, B., McFadyen-Ketchum, S., Dodge, K., Pettit, G., and Bates, J., Journal of Personality and Social Psychology, Vanderbilt University, Nashville, Tennessee, 2000.

[175] Child Development, March/April 2001.

[176] *Precocious Puberty,* research by Psychologist Dr Aric Sigman, commissioned by Clearasil.

[177] G. Rekers. Journal of Family and Culture, 2, No. 3 (Autumn, 1986), p. 8-31.

APPENDIX II: THE EARLY INTERVENTIONS PROJECT

- The priority in all cases is to prevent them reaching the point of intractability and implacable hostility. It was in recognition of this simple fact that the Government set up the New Approaches to Contact (NATC) Early Interventions (EI) project.

- This initiative was to be run jointly by the Departments for Constitutional Affairs and for Education and Skills. It was headed by Oliver Cyriax, a former solicitor. Based on eight years of protracted research and discussion, including analysis of functioning and successful schemes such as the Norwegian system and the 'Florida model,'[178] it culminated in an international conference on March 27, 2002, chaired by Dame Margaret Booth, the distinguished former High Court family judge; she said, "*this is the way forward … it would be incomprehensib* *the pilot project did not receive official sanction from the DfES and the Department for Constitutional Affairs.*"

- It was submitted to the DCA on 8 October 2003; on the 21st it was recommended by Lord Filkin, the DCA Minis on Newsnight, and on the 23rd was recommended to the Commons by Margaret Hodge.

- The two core elements of the project were:

  o Programmes to educate separated parents in how to act in the best interests of their children consis of written-down Parenting Plans, conveyed to parents before the first hearing.

  o The mediation would be compulsory; as Judge John Lenderman of Florida said, "*I'm totally convinced mediation should be mandatory. Every judge that I've talked to around the United States says mandatory mediation is the way to go.*"

- The project aimed to ensure that children continued to have "generous, frequent and continuous contact" with parents following divorce: "*Most parents, judges, experts and professionals already agree. An ideal model of alternate weekends, half the holidays and midweek visits is hardly controversial.*"[179]

- The project was endorsed by the Department for Constitutional Affairs Minister, the President of the Family Division, the High Court judiciary, the Family Law Bar Association, the chairman of the Solicitors Family Law Association, the Coalition for Equal Parenting, Fathers Direct, Families Need Fathers and the leading child development experts.

- It is very likely that the scheme, if enacted, would have been very effective in resolving contact disputes before they reached the Family Courts.

---

[178] These schemes were first referred to in the Law Commission working Paper 96 of 1986 in Footnotes 161 and 178.

[179] *Contact: a question of time*, Oliver Cyriax, article in the Times, Law Section, 22 June 2004.

THE DARK RIVAL

- The scheme was passed in January 2004 for implementation to a 'Design Team'[180] of civil servants established by Margaret Hodge at the DfES. They first met on 17 March, the members of the team were not briefed, on 25 May they rejected the proposals without discussion.[181]

- Instead, the leader of the team, a civil servant called Bruce Clark, introduced his own scheme, called Family Resolutions, while pretending to be working on the EI scheme. In forming his new scheme he appears to have been aided by CAFCASS, indeed Family Resolution was the name of an old CAFCASS project.[182] Mr. Clark comes from a family protection background and is primarily known as the man who drew up the now discredited Munchausen's guidelines.

- Under Mr. Clark's scheme the priority was not continuing contact by protection from 'harm.' Any application for increased contact would trigger an investigation and risk assessment. Where the quality of contact was deemed to be satisfactory there would be no need to increase it; where it was considered bad there would be no more contact; where the quality was indeterminate there would be a cessation of contact while the case was deferred.[183]

- Oliver Cyriax described it as, "*a green light to withhold any increase even where - as often happens - contact is just two hours a fortnight. Applications for more access can be dismissed because the alleged 'quality' of the applicant's existing contact is good - and hence sufficient - or bad, and thus too much.*"[184]

- In brief, the Family Resolutions project was the opposite of the project announced by the Government in the Green Paper; the opposite of the project announced the previous year in Family law; the opposite of the project submitted to Government; and the opposite of the project which had across-the-board professional support.[185]

- The ministries, and Parliament, were consistently misled as to the nature of this new scheme, and fooled into thinking that it was really the original, but under a different name.

---

[180] Mavis Maclean, DCA, Chair, Paul Ahearn, DfES, Steve Bagnall, Relate, Bruce Clark, DfES, District Judge Crichton, Brian Kirby, CAFCASS, John Miller, Court Service, a Project Manager, a Convenor.

[181] *Contact: a question of time*, Oliver Cyriax, article in the Times, Law Section, 22 June 2004..

[182] See Celia Conrad's evidence to the DCA Select Committee, 20 April 2005, http://www.publications.parliament.uk/pa/cm200405/cmselect/cmconst/116/116we19.htm

[183] Interpretation by Families Link International, http://www.familieslink.co.uk/pages/sp_government_interventions.htm.

[184] *Contact: a question of time*, Oliver Cyriax, article in the Times, Law Section, 22 June 2004.

[185] Article by Mavis Maclean in the September 2004 issue of Family Law.

PILOT

- On 21 July 2004 the Government launched a Green Paper, Parental Separation: Children's Needs and Paren Responsibilities. In Paragraph 68 it states that "*the development of the Family Resolutions Pilot Project [FRP has been informed by the earlier work of an ad hoc group which presented its early intervention proposals to government in Autumn 2003.*" This was not the case; the FRPP was not the same as the EI project.

- In September a Pilot Project was launched, which ran until August 2005. It was run in Brighton, inner Londor Sunderland and aimed to attract 1000 participating couples.

EVALUATION

- An evaluation of the Family Resolutions Pilot Project was published in March 2006 by the University of East Anglia's Centre for Research.[186] It found that only 62 couples had been referred by the courts to the pilots, th only 29 completed the programme, and that 18 dropped out before even starting.

- District Judge Crichton gave as the reasons for this failure the lack of readiness, poor sales pitch and a suspi amongst potential clients that it was merely more of the same.[187] But one of the principal areas where the Fa Resolutions Project differed from the EI scheme was the lack of compulsion, which could not be introduced w enacting additional primary legislation; Judge Crichton:

  > I do not see a difficulty in saying to people, "If you want access to a judge in a courtroom, which is a ve expensive facility and not necessarily the best facility to try to resolve your problems, you have first of a try one of a range of options to see if we can find another solution to your problem", but because we co not do that we got very significantly less (sic) people into the project than we had hoped for.[188]

- The official report concluded, "*The pilot was a mixed success, with some of the innovative elements, particul the group work stage, showing real promise, although referrals and completions were clearly disappointing. pilot has not produced a clear blue print for the future development of services, but it has provided a number important pointers for future developments within the family justice system and beyond. In particular, the pilo underlined the potential of interventions designed to help parents focus on the needs of children and to supp effective co-parenting.*"[189]

---

[186] Trinder, L., Kellett, J., Connolly, J. and Notley, C., *Evaluation of the Family Resolutions Pilot Project*, DfES Research Report No. http://www.dfes.gov.uk/research/data/uploadfiles/RR720.pdf.

[187] Quoted in the Sixth Report of the Select Committee on Constitutional Affairs, http://www.publications.parliament.uk/pa/cm200506/cmselect/cmconst/1086/108606.htm.

[189] Trinder, L., Kellett, J., Connolly, J. and Notley, C., *Evaluation of the Family Resolutions Pilot Project*, DfES Research Report No. http://www.dfes.gov.uk/research/data/uploadfiles/RR720.pdf.

APPENDIX III: THE FALSIFICATION OF DOMESTIC VIOLENCE

- The last century has seen enormous cultural change in the way that society regards women and an corresponding increase in gender empowerment for women. It is therefore tragic that a small extremist element has drowned out more rational and moderate voices and dominated much of the debate about the family, and has done enormous damage to the role of men within family relationships. This mischief has been achieved largely through the misrepresentation of and a fixation with the problem of domestic violence.

- In their book *Sweet Freedom* Anna Coote and Beatrix Campbell wrote that "*they saw domestic violence as an expression of the power that men wielded over women, in a society where female dependence was built into the structure of everyday life.*"[190]

- Dobash and Dobash maintained, "*Men who assault their wives are actually living up to cultural prescriptions that are cherished in Western society—aggressiveness, male dominance and female subordination— and they are using physical force as a means to enforce that dominance.*"[191]

- For these extremists wife-battering formed part of normal marital relations: a cultural construct which had cultural approval. The arena in which this violence took place was the family, and the family was therefore an institution seen as hostile to women's interests. In the refuges in which these women worked men were not allowed to visit, nor were they allowed to sit on any of the committees of those refuges affiliated to the National Federation of Women's Aid. Many of these refuges excluded boys over twelve.

- The intimate or domestic violence (DV) paradigm has developed from neo-Marxist feminism in which the familiar Marxist terms of bourgeoisie and proletariat are replaced by men and women and in which the male dominance and subjugation of women is achieved not through economic means but through violence. Female violence is dismissed as defensive.[192]

- Not until the mid 1990s did the British Crime Survey record male victims of domestic violence. Subsequent research[193] showing levels of female violence equivalent to male levels was met with scepticism:[194] it didn't fit the paradigm. Most research concentrated exclusively on male violence: it was believed that a greater good of women's rights and the protection of women should prevail over scientific accuracy and objectivity. Data inconsistent with the paradigm were dismissed, ignored, or explained away.

- The irony was that all data used to shore up the paradigm came from those countries (the US, Canada, Britain and New Zealand) in which gender empowerment for women was greatest. Research shows clearly that society does

---

[190]*Sweet Freedom*, Campbell, B. and Coote, A., Virago 1982.

[191]Dobash, R. E., & Dobash, R. P. (1979). *Violence against wives: A case against the patriarchy*. New York, Free

Press.

[192]E.g. Bograd, M. (1988). *Feminist perspectives on wife abuse: An introduction*. In M. Bograd, & K. Yllo (Eds.), *Feminist perspectives on wife abuse*. Beverly Hills7 Sage.

[193]E.g. Stets, J., & Straus, M. (1992). *Gender differences in reporting marital violence. Physical violence in American*

families (pp. 151–166). New Brunswick, NJ, Transaction Publishers; Stets, J., & Straus, M. (1992). *The marriage license as a hitting license. Physical violence in American families* (pp. 227–244). New Brunswick, NJ, Transaction Publishers; Straus, M. A., & Gelles, R. J. (1992), *How violent are American families?* In M. A. Straus, & R. J. Gelles (Eds.); *Physical violence in American families* (pp. 95–108). New Brunswick, NJ, Transaction Publishers; Straus, M. A., Gelles, R., & Steinmetz, S. (1980), *Behind closed doors: Violence in the American family*. New York, Anchor Books.

[194] E.g. Dobash, R. P., Dobash, R. E., Wilson, M., & Daly, M. (1992). *The myth of sexual symmetry in marital violence.*

Social Problems, 39(1), 71–91; Jaffe, P., Lemon, N., & Poisson, S. E. (2003). *Child custody and domestic violence: A call for safety and accountability*. Thousand Oaks, Sage.

not in fact condone spousal abuse.[195] Intimate violence is not specific to men and cannot be explained on the basis of gender or gender roles.[196]

- More scientific accounts attribute violence to *"psychopathology, anxious attachment, angry temperament, arou alcohol abuse, skills deficits, head injuries, biochemical correlates, attitudes, feelings of powerlessness, lack o resources, stress, and family of origin."*[197]

- Some research, indeed, shows that rates of female violence are higher than for males,[198] and particularly amo women below the age of 30. Martin S. Feibert compiled no fewer than 364 studies *"which demonstrate that women are as physically aggressive, or more aggressive, than men in their relationships with their spouses or male partners. The aggregate sample size in the reviewed studies exceeds 170,000."*[199]

- There is also no evidence to suggest that violence in lesbian relationships is any less than in heterosexual one Some studies suggest that the incidence is comparable,[200] while others suggest that levels of violence may be higher.[201]

- Government victim surveys in the UK,[202] the US[203] and Canada[204] consistently reverse these findings due to a variety of factors: methodological bias, presentation to respondents as surveys on violence towards women,[205] reliance on police figures[206], male under-reporting[207] and lower female arrest rates.[208]

---

[195]Simon, T. R., Anderson, M., Thompson, M. P., Crosby, A. E., Shelley, G., & Sacks, J. J. (2001). *Attitudinal acceptance of intimate partner violence among U.S. adults. Violence and Victims*, 16(2), 115–126.

[196]Dutton, D. G. (1994). *Patriarchy and wife assault: The ecological fallacy.* Violence and Victims, 9(2), 125–140.

[197]Holtzworth-Munroe, A., Bates, L., Smutzler, N., & Sandin, E. (1997). *A brief review of the research on husband violence. Aggression and Violent Behavior*, 1, 65–99.

[198]Kessler, R. C., Molnar, B. E., Feurer, I. D., & Appelbaum, M. (2001). *Patterns and mental health predictors of domestic violence in the United States: Results from the national comorbidity survey.* International Journal of Law and Psychiatry, 24, 487–508.

[199]References examining assaults by women on their spouses or male partners: an annotated bibliography, Martin S. Fiebert, Department of Psychology, California State University, Long Beach, 2005,

http://www.csulb.edu/~mfiebert/assault.htm.

[200] Island, I. and Letellier, P., *The Scourge of Domestic Violence*, Gay Book # 9, San Fransisco, CA, Rainbow Ventures Inc, Winter 1

[201] Gwat-Yong Lie and S. Gentlewarrier, *Intimate Violence in Lesbian Relationships: Discussion of Survey Findings and Practice Implications*, 15 Journal of Social Service Research 46, The Haworth Press, 1991; Ristock, J., *And Justice for All?...The Social Conte Legal Responses to Abuse in Lesbian Relationships*, 7 Canadian Journal of Women and the Law 420, 1994.

[202]Walby, S., & Allen, J. (2004). 2001 British Crime Survey. London, Home Office.

[203] Bensley, L., Macdonald, S., Van Eenwyk, J., Simmons, K. W., & Ruggles, D. (2000, July 7). *Prevalence of intimate partner violence and injury*—Washington, 1998. Washington State Department of Health.

[204] Statistics Canada (2000). *Family violence in Canada: A statistical profile.* Ottawa, Canadian Centre for Justice Statistics.

[205] Archer, J. (2000b). *Sex differences in physical aggression to partners: A reply to Frieze (2000), O'Leary (2000), White, Smith, Koss, and Figueredo (2000).* Psychological Bulletin, 126, 697–702.

[206] Malloy, K. A., McCloskey, K. A., Grigsby, N., & Gardner, D. (2003). *Women's use of violence within intimate relationships.* Journal of Aggression, Maltreatment, and Trauma, 6(2), 37–59.

- Relying on their own figures, governments incorporate the feminist paradigm of domestic violence into their thinking and policy.

- Together with Patricia Hewitt and Harriet Harman, now senior members of the Government, Anna Coote produced a pamphlet entitled *The Family Way*.[209] They wrote, "*It cannot therefore be assumed that men are bound to be an asset to family life, or that the presence of fathers in families is necessarily a means to social harmony and cohesion.*"[210]

- This type of feminism is nothing to do with equality, it is founded on the hatred of men, and seeks to establish superiority and to strip men of their rights. Nevertheless, and despite 30 years of feminism, these same feminists still seek to portray themselves and their sisters as victims.

- To understand an alternative view of domestic violence it is instructive to read what the former feminist and founder of Women's Aid, Erin Pizzey, has said about it.

ERIN PIZZEY'S THEORY OF INTIMATE VIOLENCE

- The first shelter for female victims of domestic violence in Britain[211] was established by the poet and playwright Erin Pizzey in Goldhawk Road, Chiswick, West London in 1971.

- She also opened a refuge for men in North London but it closed for lack of support and funding[212].

- Pizzey found "*that of the first hundred women who came into the refuge, sixty-two were as violent or, in some cases, more violent than the men they left behind.*"[213]

- She developed a theory to account for this that DV was a learned pattern of behaviour in early childhood, "Some children who are exposed to violence at the hands of their primary carers, usually their mothers and fathers, internalise the abusive behaviour and thereafter use violence and abuse as a strategy for survival."[214]

---

[207] Stets, J., & Straus, M. (1992). *Gender differences in reporting marital violence. Physical violence in American families* (pp. 151–166). New Brunswick, NJ7 Transaction Publishers.

[208] Brown, G. (2004). *Gender as a factor in the response of the law-enforcement system to violence against partners.* Sexuality and Culture, 8, 1–87.

[209] *The Family Way: A New Approach to Policy Making* (Social Policy Paper), Coote, A, Hewitt, P. and Harman, H., Institute of Public Policy Research, 1990.

[210] Ibid.

[211] A shelter called Haven House had been set up in California in 1964 for the victims of violent alcoholics,

[212] Pizzey, E., *Domestic Violence is not a Gender Issue*, on-line essay, October 2005, http://www.fathersforlife.org/pizzey/DV_is_not_a_gender_issue.htm

[213] Ibid.

[214] Ibid.

- Pizzey speaks of the 'family terrorist,' "*a woman or a man (but for the purposes of this work, I refer only to wom*
who, pathologically motivated (by unresolved tendencies from a problematical childhood), and pathologically
insensitive to the feelings of other family members, obsessionally seeks through unbounded action to achieve
destructive (and, therefore, pathological) goal with regard to other family members... Such individuals, spurred
by deep feelings of vengefulness, vindictiveness, and animosity, behave in a manner that is singularly destruct
destructive to themselves as well as to some or all of the other family members... The family well may be
characterized as violent, incestuous, dysfunctional, and unhappy, but it is the terrorist or tyrant who is primarily
responsible for initiating conflict, imposing histrionic outbursts upon otherwise calm situations, or (more subtly
invisibly) quietly manipulating other family members into uproar through guilt, cunning taunts, and barely
perceptive provocations."[215]

- Pizzey's controversial position alienated her from the feminist movement which she accused of becoming
politicised. She received abusive phone calls, bomb scares and death threats from the very women who deny
female violence can exist. The family dog was killed. In 1982 she left England to live in New Mexico. Today t
organisation she founded refuses her entry and has erased her name from its official history.[216]

- The refuge she founded has become hijacked by extremist feminism, the triumph of which, Pizzey believes, ha
enabled violent, abusive women "*to sexually abuse, batter and intimidate their children and their husbands*" wi
the full support of a politically correct state.[217] "*They took their aggressive, bullying and intimidating behavior w*
them. Talking with the men who were accused of abusing their women, I was aware of this movement with its
and extravagant claims against men had fuelled the flames of insecurity and anger in men. I watched horror
stricken, as in home after home, I saw boys denied not only their access to their fathers, but also access to all
was normal and masculine in their lives."[218]

THE NATURE OF PAEDOPHILIA

- Conventional wisdom, and certainly the extremists within the feminist movement, would have it that all
paedophiles are men and therefore that all risk to children of sexual abuse comes only from men; that women
cannot be paedophiles. Queen Victoria famously believed that women could not be homosexual. The truth is
different.

  o Between 1963 and 1965 the most notorious of female paedophiles, Myra Hindley, together with Ian Brad
  abducted, tortured and murdered 5 children. Only Hindley's voice on a recording she made of the assau
  on Lesley Ann Downey persuaded the jury of her participation.

  o Rosemary West was the wife of Fred West and a bisexual with a preference for women, she enjoyed ext
  bondage and sadomasochism even more than her husband. In 1994 the Wests were charged with mult
  murders, Rosemary with 10 and her husband with 12. Among her victims were her daughter Heather ar
  stepdaughter Charmaine. Prior to murdering them, the couple sadistically tortured their victims.

  o Marie Thérèse Kouao was the great-aunt of Victoria Climbié whom she murdered, with her boyfriend Ca
  Manning, on 25 February 2000. The pathologist noted 128 separate injuries on Victoria's body.

---

[215] Pizzey, E., *Working with Violent Women*, September 1997, http://www.fathersforlife.org/pizzey/terror.htm

[216] Wendy McElroy, *Feminists Deny Truth on Domestic Violence*, Fox News, May 2006,
http://www.foxnews.com/story/0,2933,197550,00.html

[217] Pizzey, E., *How Women were Taught to Hate Men*, http://www.fathersforlife.org/pizzey/how_women_were_taught_to_hate_men.h

[218] Ibid

○ In the French city of Angers in March 2005 27 women were accused of raping and assaulting at least 45 children aged from 6 months to 12 years. 65 adults were accused altogether and 62 convicted after a trial that lasted 93 days. Many of the accused had themselves been abused as children.

• In 1997 the BBC produced a Panorama documentary called the Sexual Abuse by Women of Children and Teenagers.[219] It showed how reluctant society is to accept the sexual abuse of children by women. A survey by the charity Kidscape showed that 86% of children describing abuse by a woman were not believed.

• In truth there is no reason why most paedophiles should be men or why just as many women should not seek sexual gratification with children. Under-reporting and a blatantly separatist feminist agenda in organisations such as the NSPCC or ChildLine have led to serious misrepresentation. Sue Hutchinson, who runs the telephone counselling line SAFE, says, "*At least half of my callers say that the female abuser was more violent and humiliating. The problem is that very few people with a normal upbringing can handle the idea that a woman, who is supposed to be a nurturer can do this.*"[220]

---

[219] Full transcript available at http://www.menweb.org/panofull.htm.

[220] Quoted here http://www.paedosexualitaet.de/women/abuseByWomen.html

APPENDIX IV: MARK HARRIS' JUDGEMENT

Note: Mark Harris had a Contact Order in place for *unsupervised* contact during the period these 'crimes' took place; the mother in the case breached this order by failing to facilitate contact, but with absolute impunity.[221]

By orders dated the 3rd day of July 1998 as subsequently varied on 18 September 1998, 25 November 1998, 20 January 1999, 11 March 1999 and 7 February 2000 (SEE ATTACHED HERETO)

Upon the application by the Petitioner by notice of Motion dated 18th October 2000.

AND UPON HEARING Counsel for the Petitioner, Counsel for the respondent and Counsel for the Official Solicitor

AND UPON READING the affidavit of Peter Stewart Smith sworn on 12 October 2000, Charles Oliver 12 October 2000, "The mother" sworn on 13 October 2000, "The mother's boyfriend" sworn 13 October 2000, Lianne Verna Katibeh sworn 16 October 2000, Mark Dean Harris sworn on 8 December 2000 and "the mother" sworn on 4 January 2001.

And the respondent accepting that a copy of the said orders and said summons have been served upon the Respondent Mark Dean Harris,

AND having taken the oral evidence of "the mother", "the mother's boyfriend", Lianne Verna Katibeh, and Mark Dean Harris,

AND UPON it appearing to the satisfaction of the Court that the said Mark Dean Harris has been guilty of contempt of Court namely that;

1) On 2 April 2000 **he approached the children** (eldest), (middle) and (youngest) outside Chaplins superstore Plymouth and talked to them there by breaching paragraph (h) of the order,

2) Shortly before 20 April **he sent to the mother through the post a cheque for £900** post dated to 29 April 2000, with a note stating that the Cheque could be cashed if (the eldest) attended the next session of contact and
continued to attend contact, thereby breaching paragraphs (d) and (i) of the order,

3) On April 25 2000 **he did enter (road A) in a car seeking contact or communication with the children a driving past the mother** thereby breaching paragraphs (a) (d) and (h) of the order,

4) On 26 April 2000 **he did hand birthday presents to (middle) and (youngest) during the session of contact and without the presents first having been approved by Plymouth City Council** thereby breaching paragraph (h) of the order,

5) On 27 June 2000 he **left a note for (the youngest) in one of her school books after attending an eveni at (her school) to discuss her work** and without the note first having been approved by Plymouth City Council thereby breaching paragraph (h) of the order,

---

[221] Judgement copied

6) On 7 August 2000 **he entered (road A) , Plymouth, in a car** seeking contact or communication with the children and driving past waving to the mother and the children thereby breaching paragraphs (a) (d) & (h) of the order,

7) On 24 August 2000 he entered (road A) in a car seeking contact or communication with the children and driving past the mother and the children thereby breaching paragraphs (a) (d) and (h) of the order,

8) Shortly before 30 August 2000 **he sent or caused to be sent through the post to (the eldest) an article** from "Families Need Fathers" and without the article first having been approved by Plymouth City Council thereby breaching paragraph (h) of the order,

9) On 5 October 2000 he entered (road A) in a car seeking contact or communication with the children thereby breaching paragraphs (a) and (h) of the order,

10) On 7 October 2000 **he approached (the eldest) in New George Street, Plymouth and spoke to her** thereby breaching paragraph (h) of the order.

It is ordered that;

(1) **for each of his said contempts 1 and 10 above the Contemnor Mark Dean Harris do pay a fine of £250 each** (total £500) to be paid within 12 months from today,

(2) for **each** of his said contempts 2,4,5. and 8 above the Contemnor Mark Dean Harris **do stand committed to Her Majesty's Prison at Pentonville for a period of 4 months** or until he shall be sooner discharged by due course of Law (these sentences to run concurrently with each other)

(3) for **each** of his said contempts 3,6,7 and 9 above the Contemnor Mark Dean Harris do stand committed to Her Majesty's Prison at Pentonville **for a period of 6 months** or until he shall be sooner discharged by due course of law (the sentences to run concurrently with each other but consecutively to the sentences in (2) above

AND the Contemnor Mark Dean Harris can apply to the Judge to purge his contempt and ask for release,

And it is further ordered that any application for the release of the said Mark Dean Harris from custody shall be made to a Judge,

And it is further ordered that there be no order for costs, save that there be detailed assessment of the publicly funded costs of the assisted parties,

DATED 23 MARCH 2001.

A BLUEPRINT

FOR FAMILY LAW IN THE 21ST CENTURY: THE CASE FOR URGENT, RADICAL REFORM

A BLUEPRINT FOR FAMILY LAW IN THE 21ST CENTURY
THE CASE FOR URGENT, RADICAL REFORM

BY MATTHEW O'CONNOR
WITH GARY BURCH & MICHAEL COX

ALL PHOTOGRAPHY BY GARRY CLARKSON

SECOND EDITION

In the time it takes you to read this, four children will lose contact with their father.

By the end of the day another 100 children will have lost contact not only with their fathers, but also grandmothers and grandfathers they dearly love, because of the Family Courts in the United Kingdom.

By the end of the year, the number of children affected will be in the region of 36,500.

Since the Labour government came to power in 1997, around 300,000 children have lost all or partial contact with one parent.

'I'm a father and that's what matters most.
Nothing matters more than that. Nothing!'
GORDON BROWN MP, CHANCELLOR OF THE EXCHEQUER

Introduction

The civil rights group Fathers 4 Justice (F4J) was launched in December 2002. Since then it has become the world's leading equal parenting group, with a franchise extending as far as Australia, Canada and the United States. From Spiderman at Tower Bridge through to Batman at Buckingham Palace, with the flour-bombing of the Prime Minister in the chamber of the House of Commons and the massed ranks of protesting Father Christmases, the campaign for truth, justice and equality in family law has captured public imagination worldwide, catapulting the issues surrounding family law to the top of the media and political agenda, and inspiring thousands of disenfranchised parents and grandparents to take positive action for change.

Applauded and derided in equal measure, our eye-catching and provocative campaign has succeeded in making visible that which had been hidden from public view for over 30 years: the systematic failure of Britain's family courts in their duty of care towards separating families and children. This failure is now widely acknowledged by judges and politicians alike, although the precise causes of that failure, and the remedies they demand, remain the subject of heated debate.

The Government's response to this so far has been lamentable: a cynical and PR-driven succession of sham inquiries, pilot schemes and cosmetic reforms (contained in the Children (Contact) and Adoption Bill) which utterly fail to address the crisis in family law. The gender apartheid in Britain's family courts, which ruptures the parental bonds of thousands of children annually, is having a catastrophic impact on the life of this nation, and its effects are becoming increasingly apparent throughout society.

While the Government's reaction has been akin to rearranging the deckchairs on the Titanic, Fathers 4 Justice has advanced sensible, concrete proposals for substantive legislative and institutional reform which strikes at the very root of the problem: the Blueprint for Family Law in the 21st Century, first published in June 2004 and presented here in a revised and updated edition, sets out our vision for a new, fair and family-friendly private law family justice system in this country.

This pioneering, ideas-led document outlines a radical and visionary framework for a first-class family law system which not only reflects our society as it is today, but looks forward across the coming decades. The Blueprint sets out the principles of a system which is truly just, open and equitable, built on a new foundation of parental rights intertwined with responsibilities – a system which really does put our children first.

Fathers 4 Justice

"The fastest growing pressure group in the country, if not the world."
THE TIMES, 19TH FEBRUARY 2004

Who are Fathers 4 Justice?

- Founded in December 2002 by Matthew O'Connor, Fathers 4 Justice (F4J) believes that Britain is needlessly creating a nation of children without parents and parents without children.

- F4J is now the world's leading equal parenting group campaigning for a child's right to see both parents and grandparents. With several thousand members, an established network of regional groups in the UK, and thriving international chapters in Holland, Canada, Australia, the United States and Italy, F4J continues to grow.

- Who belongs to F4J? F4J's membership represents a complete cross-section of society, including teachers, doctors, company directors, barristers, childminders, policemen, and prison officers. Many are fathers who see their children, but have suffered at the hands of the Family Courts in the past and who don't want their children to inherit the same unjust system. A substantial proportion of our members are women, grandparents and other family members, represented in our Purplehearts section.

- While some commentators have condemned F4J out of hand, casting us variously as 'misogynistic bullies [who] don't deserve justice' (Yasmin Alibhai-Brown),[1] or 'immature, egotistical show-offs'(Deborah Orr),[2] others have chosen to engage in dialogue and inform themselves about the issues: having heard from F4J members, family lawyer Marilyn Stowe, a previously outspoken critic of Fathers 4 Justice, acknowledged that that F4J represents *'men who had practised what successive governments had preached, taking an active, sharing role as a parent only to find themselves suddenly expunged from the daily lives of their children'.*[3] *For Jenni Murray, presenter of Radio 4's Woman's Hour, and Maureen Freely, a journalist who has written extensively on the family courts, we are the new Suffragettes.*[4]

Why direct action?

- F4J is based on the Greenpeace model and inspired by the examples of celebrated civil rights movements across the World. F4J is committed to a twin-track strategy of 'Publicity and Pressure,' combining non-violent direct action and civil disobedience to raise public consciousness, with a coherent political message and forceful behind-the-scenes lobbying of MPs and decision makers.

---

1 Yasmin Alibhai-Brown,'Misogynistic bullies don't deserve justice', The Independent, 22nd November 2004
2 Deborah Orr, 'Immature, egotistical show-offs - why don't these men grow up?', The Independent, 22nd May 2004.
3 Marilyn Stowe, 'Outraged fathers who made me think again', The Times, 6th April 2004.
4 Jenni Murray, 'The men who yearn to change society', Manchester Evening News, 13th April 2004; Maureen Freely, 'Move over, Mrs Pankhurst', The Guardian, 15th September 2004,

- By exposing the family courts to the glare of publicity, or as Ghandi put it: *'making the injustice visible',* F4J has stimulated public debate and placed the problem of a fatherless nation firmly on the political agenda.

- Over the past 30 years, despite the best endeavours of parenting groups, there has been a progressive erosion of a parent's right to exercise his responsibilities towards the bringing up of his children. The situation is now at crisis point: a generation of children are growing up without the love, care, influence and guidance of their fathers.

- High-profile voices are now calling for a change in the law, including Sir Bob Geldof and Prince Charles. In a seminal essay published in 2003, Geldof wrote: Family Law as it currently stands does not work. It is rarely of benefit to the child, and promotes injustice, conflict and unhappiness on a massive scale. [...] It is creating vast wells of misery, massive discontent, an unstable society of feral children and feckless adolescents.'[5]

- Our members experience a living bereavement when courts fail to respect their bond with their child. We feel helpless, frustrated, disenfranchised, and angry. We want to nurture and protect our children, but instead find ourselves marginalised or excluded from their lives altogether by the State.

- Our position: Fatherlessness is *the* child welfare issue of the 21st Century. ALL decent parents and grandparents have inalienable rights to share in the care and upbringing of their children and grandchildren, and the breaking of the bond between child and parent is a grotesque travesty of natural justice. The systematic exclusion of parents from the lives of their children by the family courts in this country is tantamount to abuse.

---

5 Bob Geldof, 'The Real Love that Dare Not Speak its Name: A Sometimes Coherent Rant', in: Children and Their Families: Contact, Rights and Welfare, edited by A. Bainham, B. Lindley, M. Richards and L. Trinder, Oxford 2003, pp. 171-200 (pp. 172, 182).

Why purple?

Purple is the international colour for equality. Purple flags are a common sight at F4J events.

Who are the 'Purplehearts'?

- Purplehearts is the support group for grandparents, wives, partners, friends and relatives of fathers affected by contact disputes. The sub-group was set up in January 2004 in recognition of the love and support provided to fathers by friends and relatives. The group also supports non-resident mothers experiencing contact problems, and those adults who, as children, have suffered the unnecessary loss of a parent.

Uncovered: A Family Justice System in Crisis

Whether or not we've been personally touched by family break-up, we can all empathise with the hurt and upset that besets a family when parents separate. And while the reality is that most of us know somebody – a friend, family member, or perhaps just a colleague – who has experienced difficulties seeing their children following relationship breakdown, the true scale of the problem has been disguised and played down by the Government.

Embedded within the mine of government statistics is one that should rock any modern society, and yet it receives little attention. The statistic that doesn't reach the headlines is that 100 children everyday lose all or partial contact with a natural parent each day and that for 40 of these children, in less than two years, that parent-child relationship will be completely severed. 100 children a day is one child every fifteen minutes. It is 365,000 children over the last decade.

All the underlying social dynamics suggest that this is a worsening problem. Relationship Breakdown is rife. The divorce rate is touching 1 in 2. There is a move away from rearing children within marriage. The UK has seen a twofold increase in the number of lone parent families, half of who rely on income support to get by and the number of contact cases has risen by 1000 times over the past 3 decades.

It is statistics like these that should put the family at the top of any responsible government's agenda.

Some Basic Facts and Background Information about the Social and Empirical Dynamics

DIVORCE & SEPARATION

About 55 per cent of couples in England and Wales divorcing in 2003 had at least one child aged under 16 - a total of 153,527 children affected by divorce alone. Of these, two-thirds of them were aged 10 or under, with more than one in five aged under 5.[6]

---

6 ONS Population Trends 117 (Autumn 2004)

In 2003, 41.4% of all live births (257,200 children) were registered to unmarried parents. Of these, under 64% were registered jointly by parents living at the same address, and almost 18% were sole registrations.

Recent research suggests that relationship breakdown among cohabiting parents of children under 5 is almost three times higher than that of married parents. An estimated 88,000 under-fives alone were affected by the separation of their unmarried parents in 2003.[7]

- Over 40% of marriages now end in separation.

- In 2003 69% of divorces were granted to the wife.[8]

- The average cost of divorce is £13,000, with more expensive divorces exceeding well in excess of £30,000 or £50,000 [9]
- Around one third of couples sell the family home to fund their divorce.[10]

- The Legal Aid bill for child contact and residence disputes was £133million in 2003-04.[11]

2001 Census figures published by the Office for National Statistics revealed that:

- Only 65% of the 11.7 million dependent children in England and Wales live with both their natural parents:

- Nearly one in four (2,672,000 dependent children) live in lone-parent families - 91.2 per cent of which are headed by the mother.

- More than one in ten (1,284,000 dependent children) live in a step-family.

LIFESTYLE PATTERNS – THE CHANGING ROLE OF WOMEN AND MOTHERS
Source: BBC Survey 'Going Solo – Single Life in the 21st century'

- 50% of the workforce are women.

- The proportion of single women has doubled from 18% in 1979 to 35% in 2001

- Among women aged 18 to 49, the proportion of single women cohabiting more than quadrupled from 8% in 1979 to 35% in 2001.

- According to The London Fertility Clinic, around 30% of the clinic's deliveries are from single heterosexual women. It has noted a month-on-month increase in this figure since the clinic was set up.

---

7 Harry Benson, 'What interventions strengthen family relationships? A review of the evidence', Bristol Community Family Trust, February 2005. The research was reported in The Times 5th February 2005.
8 Source: National Statistics Online
9 According to the results of a survey commissioned by Norwich Union, reported in The Guardian, 18th June 2003.
10 Ibid.
11 Legal Services Commission Annual Report 2003/04, p. 81.

CONTACT ORDERS & OUTCOMES FOR CHILDREN

- Some 67,184 contact orders were made in 2003, up from 61,356 in 2002, and 55,030 in 2001. That's around ten per cent of the nation's birth rate. This was a 50% increase over the last 5 years from 42,000 in 1997 and a 100% increase in contact orders over the last 10 years. In 1993 just 27,780 orders were made. A minority of these will be repeat applications.

- Many contact orders actually *weaken* the parent-child relationship. Substantial parenting time, sufficient for the parent-child relationship to flourish, is ordered in only a minority of cases.

- In many cases, wholly inadequate and inappropriate orders are made: providing only for indirect contact (letters, cards, presents etc.), or for supervised contact in circumstances where there are no child safety issues.

- 50% of all contact orders are flouted. (THE TIMES NEWSPAPER 2003).

- 40% of mothers admit stopping contact to punish a former partner. (DEPARTMENT OF SOCIAL SECURITY 1998)

- As a result, 100 children every day lose partial or total contact with their fathers.
- Government does not gather any further data about the specific character of contact orders made by the courts, and no records are kept on the outcomes for children who have been subject to contact orders.

- *"40% of fathers had no contact with their children after 2 years."*[12] (Bradshaw and Millar, 1991) This figure has often been quoted by Dame Elizabeth Butler-Sloss, President of the Family Division. In a speech given in 2003, she asserted that: "60% of fathers have little or no continuing relationship with their children post-separation."[13]

- Over 20,000 children every year use 300 contact centres affiliated to the National Association of Child Contact Centres (NACC). This equates to 100,000 contact sessions. Around 30-40% referrals are from the courts. (DCA)
- From 2003 to 2006 £3.5m will be provided to pay for 15 new supervised child contact centres. (DCA)
- CAFCASS, the Children and Family Court Advisory and Support Service, handled 33,803 private law (i.e. routine contact/residence) cases affecting 53,697 children in 2003-04.[14]

- The funding of Cafcass, The Children and Family Court Advisory and Support Service has risen from £73 million in 2002 to £107 million for the year 2004-2005.[15]

---

12 Bradshaw, J. & Millar, J. (1991): Lone Parent Families in the UK. DSS Report 6.London: HMSO
13 Dame Elizabeth Butler-Sloss, 'Are we failing the family? Human rights, children and the meaning of family in the 21st century', The Paul Sieghart Memorial Lecture, British Institute of Human Rights, King's College London, 3rd April 2003. This speech is published online by the Department for Constitutional Affairs.
14 CAFCASS Annual Report and Accounts 2003-04, p. 23ff.
15 CAFCASS Business Plan 2004-05, p. 15

CHILDCARE

- Up to a third of all childcare is carried out by fathers. (EQUAL OPPORTUNITIES COMMISSION)

- There are 5 million unpaid carers in the UK. (EQUAL OPPORTUNITIES COMMISSION)

- There are 13 million Grandparents in Britain who provide childcare worth more than £1 billion a year – that equates to 82% of all children receiving some form of childcare from a Grandparent. (THE ECONOMIC AND SOCIAL RESEARCH COUNCIL)

- In two generations, the proportion of children cared for by grandparents has jumped from 33% to 82%. (THE ECONOMIC AND SOCIAL RESEARCH COUNCIL)

- Nearly 1 in 4 Grandparents has experienced family breakdown in at least one of their sets of grandchildren. (THE ECONOMIC AND SOCIAL RESEARCH COUNCIL)

FAMILY VIOLENCE & ABUSE

- 1 in 6 men and 1 in 4 women suffer from domestic abuse over a lifetime. (STUDY NO 191 – BRITISH CRIME SURVEY 1999)

- Domestic violence against men has risen 81 per cent since 1999 (Scottish Executive 2004)

- Female violent crime has also risen by 140 per cent in 10 years. Women convicted for serious assault, murder and robbery more than doubled between 1993 and 2002. (Scottish Executive 2004)

- Women are five times more likely to report domestic violence than men. (STUDY NO 191 – BRITISH CRIME SURVEY)

- Every year around 150 people (120 women and 30 men) are killed by a current or former partner. (SAFETY AND JUSTICE PROPOSALS 2003)

- There are over five hundred women's refuges in Britain. Only three exist for men, two of which opened in 2004.

- 65% of total child abuse (neglect, sexual, emotional and physical) is committed by mothers, whereas 8% of child abuse is committed by fathers. (NSPCC)

According to research published by the Home Office, **homicides of children by their natural parent are committed in roughly equal proportions by mothers and fathers.**[16]

The biological father is the least likely person to abuse his children, and all types of abuse increase significantly when biological fathers are absent from the family.[17]

---

16 F. Brookman and M. Maguire, Reducing homicide: a review of the possibilities. Home Office Online Report 01/03 (2003), p. 16.
17 Anthony CLARE , On Men: Masculinity in Crisis (London, 2000), p 186.

- Research published by the NSPCC in 1992 found that in neglect, physical and sexual abuse cases, children were over twice as likely to be living with their natural mother alone.[18]

OTHER RELATED FIGURES

- The Government's National Suicide Strategy identified suicide as the biggest cause of death in men aged under 35, of whom 65% are fathers. In general, men are 3 times more likely to kill themselves than women.

- An estimated one in 50 under 16 youngsters are forced to leave their home every year. This equates to around 15,000 youngsters a year one in four of which blame family breakdown as the cause of either being thrown out or leaving. (CHILDREN'S SOCIETY)

- 50,000 children go missing every year (PARENTS OF ABDUCTED CHILDREN TOGETHER)

The Cost of Family Breakdown

FINANCIAL COSTS

Direct Costs: £15 Billion   Total Cost £30 Billion

Family breakdown hits hard in the pocket both of the individuals concerned and of the Nation. The legal aid bill alone matches the NHS drugs bill each year. The cost to every family experiencing divorce is currently estimated at £13,000, with many divorces exceeding £50,000. In around one third of cases this cost results in the family home having to be sold. The economic hardship caused by family breakdown forces many parents onto benefits, increasing the burden on the taxpayer.

In 2000, the Family Matters Institute, in a report commissioned by the Home Office, concluded that the direct cost of family breakdown to the nation was £15 billion, a figure which doubles to £30 billion when the indirect costs of extra welfare payments, poorer health, lower productivity and higher crime are factored in.[19] Based on these figures, the cost of family breakdown amounts to 10 pence on the basic rate of income tax.

One can only guess at what the real costs are now, four years following this study.

---

18 Susan Creighton, Child Abuse Trends in England and Wales, 1988–90 (London, NSPCC, 1992).
19 The Cost of Family Breakdown, Family Matters Institute, London, 2000.

SOCIAL COSTS

The social harm caused by the breakdown of the parent-child bond was highlighted in the United States in 2001 by President Bush:

"Over the past four decades, fatherlessness has emerged as one of our greatest social problems. We know that children who grow up with absent fathers can suffer lasting damage. They are more likely to end up in poverty or drop out of school, become addicted to drugs, have a child out of wedlock or end up in prison. Fatherlessness is not the only cause of these things, but our nation must recognize it is an important factor."

President George W. Bush, 7th June 2001

The social costs of family breakdown are equally reflected in Britain: there is an abundance of research to suggest that the absence of a father may be associated with mental health problems, truancy and educational underachievement, drug and alcohol dependency, youth offending, and teenage pregnancies.

According to a report by the Audit Commission in 2004:

a) 1 in 4 teenagers – about 1.25 million - had broken the law in the past 12 months.

b) 70% of this crime was carried out by fatherless children and young adults under the age of 18.

c) 84% re-offend within 2 years.

d) Britain now has the second highest rate of young offending in Western Europe.

e) The cost of teenage crime to the taxpayer is estimated to be over £10 billion per annum, with the cost to London's economy alone put at £3.3 billion.

The intentions of Parliament, European Law and the United Nations

INTRODUCTION

The Children Act 1989 was supposed to herald a new dawn in the handling of private law contact and residence cases. The intent of the Law is to encourage both parents to continue to share in their children's upbringing even after separation or divorce. The Lord Chancellor spoke of this intent when, in 1999, he said:

'The underlying philosophy of the Children Act is that parents have a shared responsibility for the upbringing of their children, even after the relationship between the parents has broken down. This reflects the Government's belief that children generally benefit from a continuing relationship with both parents.'

Rt Hon The Lord Irvine of Lairg – 8th May 1999

The Minister's briefing to Parliament in the bringing forward of the Act was:

'In some cases, the order will provide that the child will live with both parents... More commonly, however, the order will provide for the child to live with both parents, but spend more time with one than the other.' 'If such an order is practicable, there is no reason to discourage it'

The overriding principle of the Children Act is that the *'best interest'* of the child is paramount. The Family Law Act 1996 directly tied the 'best interest' principle to the child maintaining a meaningful relationship with her parents:

> *'children have the right to know and be cared for by both parents, regardless of whether their parents are married, separated, have never married or have never lived together'*

> *The general principle, in the absence of evidence to the contrary, is that the welfare of the child will be best served by:*
>
> (i) *his having regular contact with those who have parental responsibility for him and with other members of his family;*
> (ii) *the maintenance of as good a continuing relationship with his parents as is possible'*

Family Law Act 1996

It is hard to conclude Parliament's intention was anything other than that parents, separated or otherwise, should share in the day-to-day care and responsibilities of raising their children. Yet courts make these 'shared parenting' orders in fewer than 1% of cases.

The Achilles heel of the Children Act 1989 is that the principle of the child's 'best interest' remains undefined: it can mean anything a judge wants it to mean.

Many may feel that it is appropriate for judges to be given broad discretion to decide what is best for each child on a case-by-case basis. While this is understandably appealing in theory, in the absence of a judicial framework it begs the obvious question: How effectively do judges use their discretion?

Evidence from judges themselves suggests that when judges have unfettered discretion, even apparently straightforward contact cases often go badly wrong. Senior Family Court Judge Mr Justice Munby highlighted these failings in a widely-publicised judgment in April 2004:

> "There is much wrong with our system and the time has come for us to recognise that fact and to face up to it honestly. If we do not we risk forfeiting public confidence...Responsible voices are raised in condemnation of our system. We need to take note. We need to act. And we need to act now."[20]

F4J routinely sees cases where judges make manifestly perverse judgments about what constitutes a children's best interests. It is common to see orders for perfectly ordinary, decent parents to be **allowed** to see their children for just a few hours a month, or to have 'contact' only through letters and presents. Of course, in the looking-glass world of our family courts almost any kind of contact is deemed to be 'meaningful'. In one of the most perverse judgments of recent times, Lord Justice Thorpe permitted a mother to veto **all contact** on the basis that she got depressed when dad and daughter spent time together.[21]

The Children Act left a loophole by not bringing the intent of Parliament for shared parenting through into clear judicial guidance as to the evaluation of a child's best interests. The Family Law Act 1996 sought to close this loophole by linking the child's best interests with having a relationship with her parents in the normal case, and by providing a legal principle of contact. This section of the Family Law Act is yet to be brought into force. The consequence of this is that 300,000 children have not had the benefit of this legal safeguard and have lost partial or total contact with their fathers over the past eight years alone.

It is vitally important for a child to retain a meaningful, loving relationship with both parents, and it is a failure of the legislature to not provide, in the 21st Century, the legal right for parents to contribute to the day to day care of their children. F4J calls for the urgent enactment of legislation that provides this right through a legal principle and presumption of contact through the current Children Bill.

---

20 Published as: Re D, F v M, Neutral Citation Number: [2004] EWHC 727 (Fam), 1st April 2004. The full transcript of the judgment is available on the UK Court Service website.
21 'Contact ban for 'hated' father', The Guardian, 23rd May 2003.

INTERNATIONAL PERSPECTIVES ON THE ROLE OF FAMILIES, CHILDREN AND PARENTS

International thinking on the importance of the family in society is perhaps best summed up by the United Nations' *Universal Declaration of Human Rights*, which states at Article 16(3):

> *"The family is the natural and fundamental group unit of society and is entitled to protection by society and the state."*

The *European Convention on Human Rights* also contains key articles:

- Article 8 *states that: 'everybody has the right to respect for his private and family life'*

- Article 5 of the 7th Protocol states that: *'spouses shall enjoy equality of rights and responsibilities in their relations with their children, as to marriage, during marriage and in the event of its dissolution'*

UNITED NATIONS CONVENTION ON THE RIGHTS OF THE CHILD

- Article 7(1) - *'The child shall be registered immediately after birth and shall have the right from birth to a name, the right to acquire a nationality and, as far as possible, the right to know and be cared for by his or her parents.'*

- Article 9(3) - *'parties shall respect the right of the child who is separated from one or both parents to maintain personal relations and direct contact with both parents on a regular basis, except if it is contrary to the child's best interests.*

- Article 18 - *"Parents will have the primary responsibility for the upbringing and development of the child."*

UNTED NATIONS UNIVERSAL DECLARATION OF HUMAN RIGHTS

- Article 16(1) - *'men and women of full age...have the right to marry and found a family. They are entitled to equal rights as to marriage, during marriage and dissolution.'*

EUROPEAN CONVENTION OF CONTACT REGARDING CHILDREN

- Article 4(1), p24 - "As it is such an important human right, obtaining and maintaining regular contact between the child and his or her parents should only be restricted or excluded where necessary in the best interests of the child... contact may be restricted or excluded only where necessary in the best interests of the child...it must be beyond any doubt that such restriction or exclusion of what essentially is a human right is necessary in the best interests of the child concerned....the necessity of a possible restriction or even exclusion of the right provided in Article 4 paragraph 1 shall take into account the following elements: 'There shall be no other less restrictive solution available; the possible restriction or exclusion shall be proportional; the necessity of the restriction or the exclusion shall be duly justified. The more the right of contact is to be restricted, the more serious the reasons for justifying such restriction must be.'

COMMENT: Children and their parents have inalienable rights to see each other that have been woven into the fabric of human society for more than 6,000 years and are enshrined in common law. Parliament's intention, and that of the United Nations and the

European Union, unequivocally underlines the fundamental importance of a child retaining a meaningful, loving relationship with both parents, and the State's joint responsibilities to promote this and not interfere with it unnecessarily.

"Most family cases are not intellectually particularly demanding"

Judicial Studies Board

What happens to parents in the Family Courts?

The conventional wisdom - some may call it common sense - that parents are generally the best people to bring up their children, but this gets lost in the UK's family courts when separating parents turn to the State for help in negotiating the future of their children.

In the vast majority of cases, parents turning to the Family Court do so to help resolve private disputes over how they should rearrange their lives following separation. Typically, these are normal people who at the end of their relationship are frequently hurt, angry and anxious about what the future holds.

Were the family courts to look upon these cases from the perspective that the child, in the general case, benefits from both parents continuing to care for her, then judges would see their role as twofold: a) to help parents make the transition into a post-separation caring arrangement; and b) to dissuade parents from seeking to undermine each other.

Instead of the *'best interests = two parents'* model described above, a *'winner-take-all'* paradigm dictates the culture of our family justice system: whereby one parent is awarded the prize of 'residence', while the other – invariably the father – is relegated to a subordinate and more-or-less marginal role in his child's life.. It has also become axiomatic that any parental conflict is resolved by the removal of one of the parents. Since the courts award residence to mothers in around 95% of cases, the invariable outcome is that:

(i) mothers have a de facto veto (also known as the 'gatekeeper' role) over the father-child relationship

(ii) the onus is placed on fathers to prove why they should continue be involved in their children's lives.

In 1986, the Law Commission highlighted the flaws in this judicial thinking:

> "It is hard to maintain a parent-like relationship with a child who is only seen from time to time... there is a tendency to assume that if access is not working, it should be reduced, whereas some of the factors mentioned would point in the opposite direction."
>
> Law Commission Working Paper 172 - 1986

Almost by definition, parents who turn to the family courts are in conflict. In failing to shift their thinking towards the 'best interests = two parents' model, and seek to resolve conflict rather than inflame it further, the courts have failed in their duty to implement the Children Act as it was intended by Parliament.

Family Courts make family conflicts worse

The adversarial nature of the Family Court automatically pitches wife against husband, and father against mother, whilst, at the same time, expecting everyone to act at their most reasonable when the emotions, fears and uncertainties of the moment make them least able to so do.

The tendency of family court proceedings to exacerbate parental disputes was highlighted in a key report to the Lord Chancellor by the Children Act Sub-Committee in 2002:

> "The court process is stressful for both parents and children, it is expensive for those who are not publicly funded; it is slow and adversarial. It tends to entrench parental attitudes rather than encouraging them to change. It is ill adapted to dealing with the difficult human dilemmas involved, notably when it comes to the enforcement of its orders."[22]

Being adversarial, contact and residence hearings all too often focus on the dispute - i.e. what the parents are upset about -, rather than focusing on the needs of the child. In the *winner-take-all* culture this translates into:

- Courts attempting to act as a superordinate parent.

- Courts feeling the need to apportion blame in parental disputes. 'Facts' are decided on the balance of 'probabilities' rather than conclusive evidence.

- Orders for contact being made on the basis of what a mother will tolerate, rather than for what is appropriate for a child to maintain a meaningful relationship with her father.

- The best interests of the child being compromised to achieve maternal cooperation. It could be argued that the mother's best interest has replaced the child's best interest principle.

- Breaches of contact ignored to pacify a recalcitrant mother.

- Contact levels repeatedly reduced in the face of an implacable parent.
- Contact eroded over successive hearings, often over a period of years

- The use of 'cooling-off' periods, where judges stop contact for months or even years to, as one judge put it, "allow mother to calm down".

- Ordinary parents being placed in contact centres when no child safety issue arises

What types of Order are made?

The Government promotes the statistic that, while only a few hundred contact orders are refused each year, over 60,000 are granted. This is true, but these figures mask the troubling

---

22 'Making Contact Work: A Report to The Lord Chancellor on the Facilitation of Arrangements for Contact between Children and their Non-Residential Parents and the Enforcement of Court Orders for Contact', Children Act Sub-Committee of the Advisory Board on Family Law, February 2002.

reality that the vast majority of these orders fail to provide for any meaningful level of contact, and that around half of all orders will be flouted by the resident parent in any case.

No less a source of concern is the admission by the Department for Constitutional Affairs admits that it does not collect any statistics whatsoever on the level and type of contact that is ordered. Furthermore, no longitudinal studies have ever been conducted on the outcomes for children passing through the family courts. **The blunt fact is that the legislature has no means of knowing whether the best interests of children are being protected by the family courts.**

Common Types of Court Order

- **Indirect Contact Orders:** Typically, these 'allow' for the sending of a birthday or Christmas card. May also include the exchange of letters and photographs.

- **Supervised Contact Orders:** 'Allow' for parent-child contact in church halls and community centres, often on alternate weekends for as little as a couple of hours..

- **Unsupervised Orders non-staying contact:** Father and child will be allowed some limited time together, usually on a Saturday. Often, the time available contrains the development of the relationship, particularly if the child partakes in extra-curricular activities.

- **Unsupervised Orders overnight contact:** These mark a step towards the resumption of a normal parental relationship between with the child. Often, though, overnight stays are too infrequent and too short for the relationship to become firmly re-established and for the child to feel truly *'at home'.*

- **Shared Residence Orders:** Where the child spends bountiful amounts time with both parents and quickly grows to regard both parents' houses as his home. Despite Parliament's intention that this would be the *'common form of order,'* these orders are made in less than 1% of cases.

How long does it take, and how much does it cost to get a Court Order?

If a father finds that 'contact' is denied by the resident parent it, it will usually take 2-3 months for the issue to come to court, during which time there may have been no contact with the child whatsoever.

In a substantial number of cases where contact is denied for no good reason, the resident parent gets legal aid to defend her actions. Conversely, the Legal Services Commission frequently looks on such cases as 'unwinnable' from the non-resident parent's perspective and will refuse legal aid to a qualifying father. Most fathers use whatever savings or capital they have left, spending £2-3,000 in legal preparations and around £1,000 a day for a barrister in court to secure an order which has a 50% chance of being broken, little chance of being enforced if broken, and with no guarantee that he won't have to expend similar sums for similar reasons at some future point.

What Judges have said and done to Parents in Britain's Family Courts...

5-year 'Breathing Space' for a two-year-old

In the case of 'G' (A Child) [2003] EWCA Civ 489 in Northampton County Court., HHJ Mitchell recognised that prior to any contact mother *'went to pieces'*, and so ordered a **five-year bar** on further contact proceedings concerning a **two-year-old** child, on the basis that *"everyone needed some peace and a breathing space."*

Prison for giving his children Christmas presents

In 2000, a judge sentenced a father to four months in prison for giving his children Christmas presents during a scheduled contact meeting, in breach of the court order.

Seeking more than two hours contact is "being too possessive"

A judge said in relation to a father who sought more than two hours contact per fortnight that *"it may well be that the father is being too possessive."*

One day's contact per year plenty for two young children

Lady Justice Hale, in a judgment made in the Court of Appeal on the 13th February 2003, stated: *"Father should be satisfied with one day of contact per year...father should appreciate that any happy contact, no matter how brief, no matter how infrequent, is of benefit to the children."*

If you want to see your children don't go to court [but if you don't...]

Ibidem: "The way to increase contact is to reduce pressure on the mother, contact improves when mother is not under pressure, bringing the matter to court puts mother under pressure."

If you see your children, make sure they don't enjoy it

In another recent judgment, the Judge observed that whilst the child enjoyed seeing the father, this also upset the mother. This in turn led to the child feeling guilty for having good times with his father. The outcome was that the father was prevented from seeing his child entirely as it was judged not to be in the child's best interest.

A mother can veto a child's relationship with her father

In the case of A-M (A CHILD) [2003] EWCA Civ 762, LJ Thorpe on appeal from HHJ Ludlow – Chelmsford County Court permitted a mother's veto on all contact, commenting: *"This is a truly tragic case in which the mother suffers from an emotional and psychological disability that prevents her from any normal response to the prospect of a relationship between E and her father. The extremity and intensity of her disability is illustrated by her quite extreme reaction to endeavours by the experienced court welfare officer to read to E quite unobjectionable communications from her father, or even to show her the photograph of her father....Judge Ludlow has wrestled with this problem for over two years.....In the end, although the judge has reached the unhesitating conclusion that the responsibility for this impasse rests entirely with the mother, nonetheless the judge has abandoned any further endeavour to strive for progress in making the barren order refusing direct or indirect contact between father and daughter.....I would only end by expressing the hope that sooner or later light will fall into the dark places, and that there will be a happier outcome than any I can see as we sit here today."*

No sanctions for those making malicious allegations of sexual child abuse

In the case of A v A [2004] EWHC 142 (FAM), Mr Justice Wall found that the father had been falsely accused by his ex-wife of sexually abusing his daughter, allegations which had also been made to close friends and the vicar, but then criticised the father for not putting it behind him. He stated: *"It would be hoped that father might have been able now to put this matter on one side. It seems that he is not yet able to do so... the father would inevitably feel intensely bruised and battered by the allegations of sexual impropriety...despite his understandable sense of outrage at the allegations he had really learnt nothing from the whole process."*

Such judicial imbecility is common currency in our family courts, and many F4J members have similar stories to tell. It simply beggars belief that such people should be allowed to bear responsibility for the future of our children. The Observer journalist Nick Cohen recently wrote:

"We should urge Lord Falconer to cram the bench with lawyers who haven't been contaminated by decades of secrecy. If he runs out of legal cronies, there's always his milkman, postman, lady who does and teenage children. Anything and anyone will be better than the status quo."[23]

Family Law descends into Violence...

In a case in 2003 concerning an 11-year-old child who was refusing to see his mother, a Judge held a father confined in the courtroom while he sent Court bailiffs to snatch the child from his home. Within two minutes of his order being made, bailiffs forced entry into the house and spent 4 hours smashing down the boy's bedroom door before removing the child, later described as extremely traumatised by the experience, from the home.

---

23 [2] Nick Cohen, 'Families denied justice', *The Observer*, 16th January 2005. Cohen is no friend of F4J, but has championed the cause of families whose children have been taken into care or put up for adoption by the family courts.

Two days later the judge admitted that he had acted unlawfully and placed the homeless child under an interim care order. Following a period of assessment, where the boy was kept in a care hostel away from his family over Christmas, Social Services returned the child to the home from which he had been snatched.

Despite a promised investigation by the President of the Family Division, none has taken place - no disciplinary action has been taken against the judge – he continues to preside over family cases.

Now, even the judges admit – we are getting it wrong

'We failed them. The system failed them...we need to act. And we need to act now.'

MR JUSTICE MUNBY, AFTER A FATHER ABANDONED A FIVE-YEAR BATTLE TO
MAINTAIN CONTACT WITH HIS SEVEN-YEAR OLD DAUGHTER, APRIL 2004

Might the cases detailed above be nothing more than rare examples of judicial eccentricity?

Even if they were, it doesn't lessen the irreparable damage done to the parents and children involved. However, in just over 18 months F4J has received tens of thousands of enquires from desperate parents and grandparents, all telling despressingly familiar, heartbreaking stories of family court failure.

Now we find that the voice of F4J has been joined by family court judges who have sought to highlight how the family justice system fails children and families.

On 1st April 2004, Mr Justice Munby took the step of publicising a case that would otherwise have been hidden from public scrutiny in order, and in doing so he exposed the way in which, over a period of five years, the family justice system had overseen the destruction of a father-child relationship.

The Judge, who called for sweeping changes to the way courts deal with applications for contact, said:

> "Those who are critical of our family justice system may well see this case as exemplifying everything that is wrong with the system. I can understand such a view...there is much wrong with our system and the time has come for us to recognise that fact and to face up to it honestly. If we do not we risk forfeiting public confidence...Responsible voices are raised in condemnation of our system. We need to take note. We need to act. And we need to act now....we failed [this family]. The system failed them.'"
>
> HON. MR JUSTICE MUNBY – 1 April 2004

MR JUSTICE SINGER – Family High Court Judge

> "The system isn't working in the best interests of the children."

DAME MARGARET BOOTH – Family High Court Judge (retired)

> "Emphasis is on children needing both parents. This does not come over as clearly as it should in this jurisdiction...our country does not easily learn from what others have done successfully...we are years behind...the time has come to remove our blinkers."

LORD JUSTICE THORPE – Family Appeal Court Judge

> "precisely the sort of case that needs to be considered by policy makers who are surveying the deficiencies in the courts' current powers."

ELIZABETH BUTLER-SLOSS DBE – President of the Family Division

Answering the question she posed in her Paul Sieghart Memorial Lecture in 2003, '*Are we failing the family? Human rights, children and the meaning of family in the 21st century?* the President answered:

> *"Yes. We are failing the family. We are failing its most vulnerable members, children"*

'*The judiciary now admits that the law acts **against** the best interests of children. How can good parents sit back and do nothing?*'
GARY BURCH, PARLIAMENTARY CO-ORDINATOR, FATHERS 4 JUSTICE

When even judges state that the judicial system is failing in its statutory duty to uphold the best interests of the child, it is clear that the time for meaningful reform is not just overdue, but an urgent necessity. In the interim, the spectre of further miscarriages of justice hangs over every order that is currently being made in the family courts..

'If you tolerate this then your children will be next.'
MANIC STREET PREACHERS

What happens to Fatherless Children?

A report by Civitas, published in 2002, blamed 'fatherless families' for increasing crime, drug-taking, and educational failure among abandoned offspring.[24] The report said that children from fatherless families are:

- Are more likely to live in poverty and deprivation
- Are more likely to have problems in school
- Are more likely to have problems of socialisation
- Have higher risk of health problems
- Are at greater risk of suffering physical, emotional or sexual abuse
- Are more likely to run away from home
- Are more likely to experience problems with sexual health
- Are more likely to be on income support
- Are more likely to experience homelessness
- Are more likely to offend
- Are more likely to suffer long term emotional problems
- Are more likely to suffer from psychological problems

There is now a substantial academic consensus that children do better when they have their father actively involved their lives. Children perform better at school, they integrate better into society, and their long term emotional health is improved. Conversely, children who are denied access to a loving, decent father suffer from this privation. With the benefit of this body of longitudinal research, it is the responsibility of the Government to look again at fatherlessness as a Child Welfare issue.

---

24 Rebecca O'Neill, Experiments in Living: The Fatherless Family, Civitas, London, September 2002.

The Government's Catch-22 approach to the crisis in family law

'Any court that does not enforce its own orders is a sham.'
LORD FILKIN, MINISTER FOR THE FAMILY COURTS, JANUARY 2004

Is Government in a double bind? Until recently, Government has taken the view that little can be done when a resident parent is prepared to flout a court order by refusing to facilitate contact:

> *"when one parent refuses to cooperate with all attempts to facilitate contact there is nothing the State can do"*
>
> Children's Minister Margaret Hodge – Feb 2004

and:

> 'The position of the government is that Parliament's intention was that shared residence should NOT be a common form of order, but that was not the same as saying that shared residence should not be a common form of arrangement. By its very nature though, shared parenting requires a high degree of cooperation between parents...cases that reach the court arena have inevitably gone beyond the stage where this level of mutual cooperation can be achieved.'"
>
> Children's Minister Margaret Hodge – Nov 2003

The Minister's comments expose the Catch-22 faced by non-resident parents, whereby an application to court to share in the care of your children is regarded as evidence, in itself, of why you cannot be allowed to share care of your children.

- The only right a non-resident parent has is to make an application for contact under Section 8 of the Children Act.

- The only right a grandparent has is to apply to court for permission to make an application to see her grandchild.

- The Minister confirms that in cases where a mother seeks to remove a father from a child's life, the court will not intervene.
- The Minister has stated that mothers should not face imprisonment for repeatedly flouting contact orders *"Fining or imprisoning the mother is not in the interests of the child."*

- Conversely, the Department for Education and Skills, has actively encouraged local authorities to prosecute 7,500 parents of truanting children last year. At least 10 mothers have been given custodial sentences as a result. **Why is it then that the government will prosecute mothers for not sending their children to school, but not do the same when they don't allow the children to see their fathers?**

One case that powerfully demonstrates how the historical approach to contact and residence disputes works *against* the best interests of the children, is that of a Plymouth family where the father was denied access to his three daughters for 6 years because of maternal hostility to contact. The case involved 133 court appearances in front of 33 different judges. The father was imprisoned for 129 days for breaking 'no contact' orders, and the case cost the taxpayer in excess of £750,000.

The result? When the children were old enough to assert their true wishes, they voted with their feet and went to live their father. Now, the eldest daughter seeks to sue the State for failing to protect her relationship with her father.

This case illustrates just how little the Courts know about the outcomes for children, how protracted litigation can economically cripple the family, and how courts abrogate their responsibilities to protect the best interests of children by postponing contact issues until the child is old enough to assert her wishes.

'...there are some cases, and I don't know how many there are, in which domestic violence is being used as an excuse to restrain contact'
LORD FILKIN, MINISTER FOR THE FAMILY COURTS

Domestic Violence, Abuse, False Allegations, and the Family Courts

Fathers 4 Justice welcomes Government initiatives to eradicate violence in the home. However, there is another side to the 'DV' coin which receives almost no attention.

While there has been a sea-change in opinion making it socially unacceptable for a man to hit a woman, there has been no corresponding effort to make it unacceptable to use a false allegation of Family Violence to subvert a parent-child relationship.

It is apparently perfectly acceptable to make a false allegation within family proceedings, and indeed this practice is extremely widespread. Conduct which in any other circumstances would be considered a serious crime, is routinely dismissed as being understandable at an emotionally-charged time: a response to the 'distress' of the proceedings.

By the same token, a mother who implacably stops contact between child and father is treated as someone who is upset and needs time to 'cool off', rather than someone who is failing to put the needs of the child first.

All decent parents want their children to grow up safely and happily. But the Government's approach to this issue raises a paradox. To date, Government concerns about child safety have been focused on the risk supposedly posed to the child by its father, to the exclusion of almost everything else.

The Government's policy of seeking to promote 'safe' contact betrays the prejudice that 'contact' parents are presumed to be a risk. However, research shows that a child just as likely to be killed by her mother as by her father, and that the majority of violence towards children in the home stems from the mother/resident parent, with the risk increasing dramatically in lone-parent households.

There is currently no policy to tackle (or even investigate) the emotional harm done to children who are denied contact, despite Government research showing that around 40% of resident parents stop contact in order to get back at their former partner. And as the case of A v A (set out on page 18) shows, it is all too easy for a mother to raise a specious 'child safety' concern in a family court in order to stop 'contact'.

The failure to look at Child Protection in a gender-neutral way puts children at risk. Further, the adversarial nature of the Family Court provides a powerful incentives to level false allegations against the other party.

Is there evidence of an institutional Gender Apartheid in Government Departments and the Family Law Industry?

- The DCA's PSA8 Committee was tasked with investigating ways of increasing 'safe' contact between children and their fathers. The committee consisted of nine women - many from women's rights groups - and just one father.

- Government funds women's groups to the tune of millions of pounds each year, The only funding any fathers' or equal parenting group has ever received is a Home Office grant of £150,000 spread over 3 years.

- The funding given to women's groups is often used to lobby those very same politicians and civil servants for further funding and policy development.

- There are over five hundred women's refuges in Britain. Only three exist for men.

- Government funding of £5 million for the Marriage and Relationship Support (MARS) grant programme saw money given to groups whose agenda was at odds with the purpose of the programme. Not one group representing fathers received any funding.

- The Government's Families and Children Study 2002 describes the family as consisting of: a mother, children and, optionally, mother's partner. Even where fathers were acting as primary or sole carers, the report described the father as the *'mother-figure'*.

- Delaney and Delaney (1990, p156) commented: *'The dominance of women in family services, and the corresponding scarcity of men, is among the most powerful of all the forces which exclude fathers from the lives of their children today, for in this we see the outward and visible sign of what begins to be perceived as an essential truth: that in family life, men are an irrelevance at best, and at worst a danger.'*[25]

- A study by Newcastle-based Children North East in 2004 found that institutional sexism is damaging the educational prospects and social development of young people, and that unconscious practices disregard the needs of men and fail to recognise the role of fathers. In other cases, conscious discrimination labels men as 'dangerous oppressors' or 'perpetrators'.[26]

- A report in 2002 by the Fawcett Society, the Equal Opportunities Commission and Fathers Direct called for a 'gender audit' of government departments and public services to address the marginalisation of men as fathers. The NHS was criticised for not publishing a single piece of literature aimed solely at fathers.[27]

Speeches by ministers and other Government communications make little or no mention of fathers rights, little funding of fathers groups and no policies to address the problem of the 40% of fathers who lose contact with their children within 2 years. Why are separated fathers not appearing on the Government's radar? How does the Government reconcile its policy towards fathers in family courts to DfES and DTI initiatives that encourage fathers to spend more time with their children?

---

25 DELANEY, TJ and DELANEY CC, 'Managers as Fathers: Hope on the Home Front', in: LR Meth, Men in Therapy: the Challenge of Change (New York, 1990), p. 156.
26 Barry Knight, A Question of Balance: Including Fathers in Services - Learning from the work of Fathers Plus 1997 – 2004, Children North East, 2004.
27 Men and women: who looks after the children? Report on three joint seminars, Fathers Direct / Fawcett Society / Equal Opportunities Commission, November 2002

CAFCASS – The Weakest Link - failing Children and their Families

CAFCASS, the Children and Family Court Advisory Service, prepares reports for court providing recommendations on how childcare arrangements should be apportioned between separated parents. Prior to 2001, court reporting was performed by the Probation Service, with former probation officers reporting on the welfare requirements of children. In April 2001, this function and the probation staff that performed it, were incorporated in to the CAFCASS.

The establishment of CAFCASS was intended to herald a new dawn for separating families and their children. Since its creation, its Chief Executive was suspended for a year and then dismissed, its Chairman resigned, and the entire board was sacked following a highly critical report by the House of Commons Constitutional Affairs Select Committee.

As a reporting service to the Family Court, CAFCASS suffers from the same deficiencies that stem from the *'winner-take-all'* system. In the absence of the principle that in the general case children should be brought up by both parents, CAFCASS has assumed the role of a super-ordinate parent, pronouncing judgment on the way normal families conduct their lives.

The agency's roots in the Probation Service have imbued it with a culture which is redolent of an organisation more used to dealing with criminals rather than helping ordinary people going through a relationship breakdown. Fathers commonly report having been made to feel 'criminalised' or 'under suspicion' by CAFCASS reporters.

Whatever the reasons, CAFCASS is widely seen as routinely failing children and families. It has no guidelines as to what constitutes a meaningful level of contact. It is deluged with cases. It has a huge backlog. Cases involving genuine child welfare issues readily get lost in the plethora of run-of-the-mill contact disputes. As a result, perfectly normal fathers are routinely denied access to their children, while cases where there are real risks to children slip through the net.

Here are a few other facts about CAFCASS:

- Many Family Court Reporters are former probation officers used to dealing with criminals, not children and their parents.
- An ongoing recruitment crisis has led to what many argue is the appointment of even more inadequately trained and inexperienced FCRs.
- 75% of Family Court Reporters are women.
- CAFCASS has no minimum training requirement. Many reporters have received little more than two days' training (less than a Parking Warden) before working on active cases.
- The 2003 Parliamentary Inquiry commented that *'CAFCASS' failure to establish even a minimum training and professional development strand appears to us to be one of their more serious shortcomings.'*
- There is NO defined training budget.
- There are NO defined guidelines on minimum recommended contact.

- Before 22nd April 2003, there was NO complaints procedure whatsoever. It continues to have no guidelines on how complaints should be handled.

- NO records are kept on the outcomes for children subject to its recommendations. The Parliamentary Inquiry commented: *'In the absence of data, the identification of what might be best for any particular child in any particular case is fraught with difficulty.'*

CAFCASS' internal problems since its creation have been given greater corporate priority than the promotion and protection of the interests of children and families. Its continued involvement in private contact and residence cases raises serious welfare concerns for those children involved.

"I look at this baby – as bald, wrinkled and scrunched up as an old man – and something chemical happens inside me."
TONY PARSONS, MAN AND BOY

A Blueprint for Family Law in the 21st Century

The family courts in the United Kingdom are in urgent need of fundamental reform. While the government and the professionals involved continue to demonstrate their resistance to any kind of radical progression in thought and practice, F4J has advanced coherent, sensible proposals for legislative and institutional reforms which will provide the children and families of this country with a family justice system which really puts their interests at heart.

The Blueprint for Family Law in the 21st Century sets out the key principles of a new family law framework for the 21st century. The Blueprint is based upon a core set of principles which we call the **Critical Triangle**, three integral elements that are the foundations of the Bill of Rights for the Family, and underpin the 'flow of family justice':

THE CRITICAL TRIANGLE

- **LEGAL PRESUMPTION TO PARENTING TIME**
  A LEGAL RIGHT TO SEE YOUR CHILDREN

- **ENFORCEMENT**
  STRONG INCENTIVES TO AGREE

- **MEDIATION**
  PARENTS MOTIVATED TO REACH OUT OF COURT SOLUTIONS

A Bill of Rights for the Family

INTRODUCTION

In the last 30 years we have seen an unprecedented degradation of the importance of parenting. Parents today are routinely vilified for the 'anti-social behaviour' of their children, but state interference in family matters - of which the systematic removal of fathers by the family courts is only one dimension - frequently leaves parents feeling undermined, confused and powerless to address the challenges they face in raising their children.

The erosion of the family, and of the rights and responsibilities of parents, must be reversed. A Bill of Rights for the Family is urgently needed to achieve this end.

PARENTING TIME AS A HUMAN RIGHT

At the heart of the Bill of Rights is the principle that the relationship between parent and child is a fundamental human right for both, and should be subject to State intervention only in very special circumstances, where there are justified concerns for the child's welfare.

The Bill of Rights introduces the principle of proportionality which requires that, when the State intervenes, then any reduction in the parent-child relationship should be cogent and proportionate. Cogency requires that the reasons for curtailing a parent-child relationship are based on sound evidence, proven beyond reasonable doubt. Proportionality requires that any curtailment is proportionate to the concern, is appropriate to the child's welfare, and can be reversed when it is in the child's interests to so do.

BILL OF RIGHTS PREAMBLE

This Bill recognises that children and their parents have inalienable rights to enjoy a loving, meaningful relationship with each other.

These rights extend to separated families, where both children and parents should be supported in maintaining a close ongoing relationship, except in circumstances which raise substantial concerns for the welfare of the child.

The Bill recognises and respects the contribution made by all family members in the raising of children, and underlines the importance of upholding and promoting these relationships for the benefit of the child.

This Bill places a duty upon the State to promote the role of the family in the upbringing of children, whether the family is intact or otherwise, and to protect children from the loss of contact with a parent through the actions of others.

Where the State seeks to intervene in the relationship between a parent and child, the necessity for intervention shall be shown to be cogent and proportional.

BILL OF RIGHTS ARTICLES

ARTICLE 1
Every child has the right to a meaningful loving relationship *(the bond)* with both their parents and grandparents.

ARTICLE 2
Every child has the right to know their parent's identity.

ARTICLE 3
Children of separated parents shall be presumed to be cared for equally by their parents, save for instances where there is a proven risk (to the criminal standard of proof) to the child (presumption of shared care).

ARTICLE 4
Both parents have the right to be treated equally and fairly in the eyes of the law, regardless of gender. (equality of parenting role).

ARTICLE 5
Grandparents have a legal presumption to grandparenting time with their grandchildren.

ARTICLE 6
The natural parents of a child will have automatic Parental Responsibility for the child in law.

ARTICLE 7
The family is the desired, natural and fundamental group unit of society and is entitled to protection by the State.

ARTICLE 8
With rights come responsibilities. All parents and grandparents have a duty of emotional and financial care to their children and grandchildren. Parents have a duty to co-operate over parenting arrangements for the children, save for instances where there is a proven risk of harm to the child or parent.

ARTICLE 9
There will be an open, accountable and transparent system of family law.

ARTICLE 10
All working parents have the right of access to flexible working arrangements and affordable childcare. State benefits will be apportioned equally between parents, or relative to the agreed division of parenting time.

Parenting Time – The New Parentshare Scheme

The language of family law in the UK has been contaminated by the prejudices (particularly with regard to fathers) and assumptions which characterise current practices.[28] A new language is needed for family law – a language which is free from the taint of gender prejudice, and which reflects the new thinking towards family and parental relationships following separation.

'Contact' will be replaced by the term 'parenting time'. Parenting Time arrangements between parents will be set out in a **ParentShare Plan** (PSP). The ParentShare Plan will evolve over time to accommodate the changing circumstances and needs of both parents and children.

ParentShare Plans can either be agreed by parents directly or, where agreement is not reached, though a mandatory **Parenting Session** (mediation) with a **Parenting Advisor**. Solicitors shall have a positive duty to advise clients of their responsibilities under the ParentShare scheme, and to refer clients engaged in disputes over parenting arrangements to a Parenting Session.

ParentShare Plans will replace *'Contact Orders', rendering the terms 'contact' and 'residence' redundant.* ParentShare Plans will take into account the age of the child and the working commitments of both parents. Plans are supported by time-linked guidelines that help the parents and Parenting Advisor to decide how best to adapt the equal parenting presumption (a 50/50 starting point) to an apportionment that best suits the family.

The ParentShare Scheme aims to foster a co-operative and consensual relationship between parents. The key to ParentShare planning is to assist parents in taking advantage of non-adversarial dispute resolution services, whilst ensuring that the core principle that the child needs *both* her parents remains at the centre of the decision-making process. Critically, Parental Advisors will have the appropriate professional skills and training to tackle the anger and animosity between separating couples that often blocks agreement.

David Price, a retired district judge who ran a child mediation scheme at Wandsworth County Court, commented that *'anger resulting from the break-up was the main stumbling block to the parents agreeing over anything...I would suggest that unless parental anger is specifically dealt with at the beginning of the process, not only will they not hear the other's words, they will not heed the advice given by those trying to help them.'*

Parenting Advisors will support parents and guide them towards working together minimise the disruption and emotional impact of relationship breakdown on their children. Disputes will be dealt with in the first instance by the Parenting Advisor, or referred to the new Family Magistrates Service if the parents are unable to reach agreement.

---

28 This is explored by Bob Geldof in 'The Real Love that Dare Not Speak its Name', p. 175 ff.

The whole purpose of the ParentShare Scheme is to motivate and support parents in reaching co-operative parenting arrangements without the intervention of a court, while providing strong disincentives (and, ultimately, sanctions) to those who may seek to enter into 'battles' over the children.

Abusing the ParentShare Process

In certain circumstances a parent may try to subvert the ParentShare process: for example, by demonstrating **implacable hostility** (unreasonably refusing to cooperate with the process of facilitating the alternate parent-child relationship), or by engaging in **parental alienation** (consciously or unconsciously convincing children that they do not want to see the alternate parent).

It has long been accepted that the attitude of a parent towards a child's relationship with the other parent can have a direct and detrimental influence on the child:

> 'If a mother's attitude to the father is negative she may wish the children to reflect the same feelings towards him.'[29]

Attempting to subvert the ParentShare process in order to undermine or take revenge on the other parent will be considered a child welfare concern which a Family Magistrate shall have a duty to address. A range of therapeutic interventions will be at the Magistrate's disposal: ranging from parenting education programmes to more directed behavioural adjustment therapies to help bring about a change in the parent's attitude.

The New Family Support Service

Since its inception, CAFCASS - the Children and Family Court Advisory and Support Service - has been beset by fundamental problems of both management and practice. CAFCASS itself was created to address shortcomings in the former Family Court Welfare Service, but it has made little progress in this respect. It is a backward-facing organisation, rooted in the Probation Service and poorly equipped and motivated to tackle the challenges faced in reforming the family justice system. CAFCASS has lost the confidence of the very people it sets out to serve, and it has become synonymous with the failings of family courts. It is a measure of its failure that the Conservative Party is committed to abolish CAFCASS if it comes into government.

To promote the development of a new culture of conciliation and co-operation in post-separation parenting, we propose to replace CAFCASS with a new **Family Support Service** (FSS), which will have responsibility for operating the ParentShare Scheme and managing the Parenting Advisors.

---

29 W. OPIE, Barriers to Father's Involvement in Child Care Within the Two Parent Family and Policy Suggestions to Remove Them (Unpublished Masters thesis, University of Bristol, 2002).

The Family Support Service will be responsible for all cases where no child welfare issues are present, save for the lack of agreement between parents over Parent Sharing. Public law cases involving legal Guardians will will not fall within its remit. Where concerns about the child's welfare are raised, Parenting Advisors will be responsible for referring these risks to the appropriate agency (usually the local Social Services).

The FSS will offer parents high-quality state provision of mediation services, free at the point of delivery. The skills profiles of Parenting Advisors shall be based on those practicing in the field in jurisdictions where directed mediation/co-operative parenting systems operate successfully. The FSS shall be responsible for maintaining quality of practice and for re-training suitable existing CAFCASS staff prior to their being deployed as practicing Parenting Advisors.

The FSS will not be a cosmetic rebranding of CAFCASS: it will be an entirely new organisation, with a new culture, and operating to open and properly audited standards to ensure that it delivers the service that parents and children expect and deserve.

The New Family Magistrates Service

The goal of the ParentShare Scheme is to help parents avoid resorting to court to resolve disputes over their children. Indeed, it should be understood by parents that resorting to court without good reason will amount to a failure on their part to put their child's interests above their own.

As a result of ParentShare, it is expected that the number of cases requiring judicial input will fall by as much as 90%. (BASED ON THE EMPIRICIAL FINDINGS OF JURISDDICTIONS WHERE SUCH SCHEMES HAVE BEEN IMPLEMENTED)

Where parents do not agree, or where there are allegations raising child welfare concerns, the family will be referred to the new **Family Magistrates Service (FMS).**

Family Magistrates Courts will perform four basic functions, working to a short case timetable of just a few weeks:

- Resolution of ParentShare disputes
- Enforcement of ParentShare agreements
- Implementation of the Fast Track Justice scheme
- Referral of particularly intractable cases to new High Court Family Judges

All decisions of the FMS will be made on the basis of the best interests of the child as set against the same time-linked guidelines that Family Advisors work to.

Family Magistrates will be recruited *from the local community in a 'judgment by peers'* model. Applicants will be required to conform to a set of family-orientated criteria and will receive specialised training in contemporary family law. Three magistrates will sit on each case, so that a balanced judgment is arrived at. Magistrates will be under a duty to set out clearly and fully the reasons for any order they make which deviates substantially from the expected norms of parenting time division.

Uncooperative parents will be referred to the new **Family Magistrates Service (FMS).** Parents attending court can be legally represented at this stage, but legal aid will only be provided in a minority of exceptional cases, at the discretion of the magistrates. Parents choosing not to have legal representation will be able to attend with the assistance of a lay helper or friend, and will be supported by the Court through the proceedings.

Enforcement

In recognition of the crucial role that parents play in their children's lives, and the likely harm caused to a child who is unreasonably denied this relationship, the FMS will operate a straightforward, swift and no-nonsense *'three strikes and you're out'* sliding scale of tariffs for offenders:

1) Failure to agree a Parent Share Plan (PSP)   **Referral to Family Magistrates Court**

2) Failure to adhere to a PSP

**Parenting Probation
Electronic Tagging
Community Service**

3) Repeated failure to adhere to a PSP   Automatic three-day **Custodial Sentence**

It should be noted that it is the responsibility of *both* parents to make ParentShare arrangements work – and that a repeated failure to make yourself available to care for your child will be equivalent to failing to make your child available for care with the other parent in accordance with a ParentShare plan.

Cases coming before the Magistrates will be those where the parents have failed to co-operate over parenting plans. This essentially makes the FMS an enforcement service for ParentShare. As such, the 'no order' principle present in the Children Act 1989 will not apply as an order at this stage would, by implication, be a necessity.

FAST-TRACK FAMILY JUSTICE

A substantial complaint of those enduring the current system is the excessive time that it takes for outcomes to be reached. All too often contact is stopped unilaterally by one parent, and by the time the court has got to grips with the problem, months or years may have passed and substantial harm caused through severance of the parent-child bond.

These shortcomings need to be addressed if harm to the child is to be minimised. Under these proposals, allegations that raise child welfare concerns that would likely curtail contact should come before a Family Magistrate within 14 days. The magistrate will make an assessment of the prima facie case and decide whether there is a requirement for further investigation. Cases where harm or risk of harm is found would be referred to the appropriate child protection service and passed to the Family High Court as a public case, and, where necessary, to criminal justice services.

"Publicity is the very soul of justice"
BENTHAM

An open, transparent and accountable system of family justice

Currently, family proceedings must be heard in closed court. Advocates of this model claim that it is against the best interests of the child for publicity to be given to a case involving her. The President of the Family Division has argued that children would be subject to 'teasing and bullying'.

Those that believe that family proceedings should be more open include lawyers and journalists who have championed the cause of parents in child protection proceedings who have been wrongly accused of harming their children. The recent high-profile exposure of multiple miscarriages of justice in cases involving mothers wrongly convicted of killing their children has pointed up the terrible consequences that can ensue when the justice system is not open to public scrutiny.

OPEN JUSTICE IN SCOTLAND

The objections to 'open justice' in the family court fall away when it is considered that Scotland, while operating under the same 'best interest of the child' principle as in England and Wales, has an open system of public proclamation, and there is no evidence to suggest that Scottish children suffer as a result.

MPs FALL FOUL OF CHILDREN ACT PRIVACY

In 2004 the Solicitor General, Harriet Harman, fell foul of the privacy requirements of the Children Act when she passed on material from a 'Munchausens' case, drawn to her attention by her sister, to the Children's Minister Margaret Hodge.

At the same time, the Guardian Newspaper highlighted the fact that hundreds of MP's had unwittingly broken the law by taking up Children Act cases on behalf of local constituents. Martin Salter, MP for Reading West, said the law needed to be updated, stating: *'If the law prevents me taking up cases on behalf of my constituents then the law must change.'*[30]

OPENNESS IS ESSENTIAL

In New Zealand, Principal Family Court Judge Peter Boshier is a vocal advocate of greater openness in court proceedings. Here too, it is now widely accepted that the objections to Family Cases being reported are not well founded.

The new Family Magistrates Service, and all other family proceedings, will operate an open, transparent and accountable system of justice without reporting restrictions, save for the anonymising of children's names.

Openness will break the *omertá which currently operates in the family courts* [31] – *the conspiracy of silence* that has allowed miscarriages of justice to go unobserved - replacing this with a judicial process which is open to the *'disinfectant of sunlight'.*

---

breaking law in children's cases', The Guardian, 29th March 2004
ohen, 'Families denied justice', The Observer, 16th January 2005

Fathers 4 Justice welcomes the Government initiatives towards the eradication of Violence in the Family. It is, however, anomalous – and wholly unacceptable - that there is no corresponding concern for the harm committed to parents and children when contact is denied or when a false allegation is used to stop contact.

Government research shows that 40% of resident parents use the children as weapons against a former partner. This behaviour is routinely overlooked by judges, but it is time that this is seen as a form of abuse like any other.

In the same way that Society is facing up to the issue of violence within the family, we need to accept the fact that violence and abuse, whether physical or emotional, is not gender-specific:

- 30 of the 150 people murdered annually by a partner are men
- Around half of the children killed every year in the family are killed by their mothers.
- The Family Justice System is widely acknowledged to be grappling with an ever increasing number of cases of emotional abuse caused to children by resident parents who stop contact for no good reason, or who alienate their children against the non-resident parent.

F4J believes that the key to achieving effective protection against family violence and child abuse is for the protection system to be founded on evidence-led, gender-neutral solutions.

Under these proposals, the term Family Violence will be adopted, to move away from the physical man-on-woman connotation that Domestic Violence has assumed.

Fast-track family justice seeks to bring cases of alleged family violence to the fore as early in ParentShare proceedings as possible. A fast-track approach separates normal cases from those where allegations of abuse arise. Allegations can then be considered rapidly, reducing the risk to children from perpetrators of abuse and avoiding interruptions in parenting arrangements where allegations are found to be without foundation.

Under these proposals there will be amendments to the Domestic Violence, Crime and Victims Act providing specific protection for victims who lose their relationship with their children as a result of a false allegation. A new offence of knowingly making a false and malicious allegation in relation to a child would be created that would act as a deterrent to a parent who is motivated behave in this way.

For full details of F4J proposals on the issue of Family Violence, please refer to the F4J paper 'The Domestic Violence Bill and Family Breakdown'.

When should a parent be denied access to their children?

The vast majority of parents - those towards whom this Blueprint is primarily directed - are normal, devoted carers who want the best for their children. The sad truth, though, is that there are bad parents – mothers *and* fathers - who are prepared to abuse a partner and/or child to serve their own ends.

The operation the ParentShare and fast-track processes seeks to identify quickly cases where there is risk of harm and to establish where that harm stems from. Where there is a clear harm, or risk of harm, stemming from one or both parents, this can be flagged up early and passed to the appropriate agency.

The New Family Rehabilitation Service

The function of ParentShare will be backed-up by therapeutic services to assist families in transition or conflict. Family Rehabilitation works on the *'best interests = two parents'* principle, providing services of increasing degrees of support and intervention to assist in the establishing of ParentShare arrangements, and helping the family evolve these arrangements over time as the needs of the children and parents change.

Specific programmes will be provided for parents who have abusive histories, to help them address these issues and to help to move the parent and child safely to a point where their relationship can be put on a more normal footing.

Services will also be provided for children and other family members who, at times, need support in adapting to changing family circumstances.

General Parenting Issues

GRANDPARENTS

The role of grandparents, who are often also the victims of family break-ups, is frequently overlooked. The Bill of Rights for the Family envisages grandparents playing a more pivotal role in family life, and affords them a legal presumption to contact with their grandchildren. Grandparents currently provide childcare worth more than £1 billion a year.

Today, the only right a grandparent has is the right to ask a court for permission to make an application to the court to see her grandchildren. The Bill of Rights for the Family affords grandparents the legal presumption to contact with their grandchildren, in acknowledgement of the importance of grandparents at the heart of the family and the benefits they can provide to parents coping with a growing family.

RE-LOCATION OF PARENTS AND REMOVAL OF CHILDREN FROM THE JURISDICTION

As parents separate the, issue of one parent seeking to move away to another part of the country, or even to another part of the World, is becoming increasingly common.

The prevailing orthodoxy in the family courts (reinforced by case law such as Poel v Poel and Payne v Payne) is that the parent's right to a new life elsewhere outweighs the child's right to be cared for by both parents. In the case of *Payne v Payne,* the daughter, who was being cared for 40% of the time by her father, was removed to live in New Zealand with her mother.

Relocation is one of the most common sources of heartbreak and disruption for both parents and children, and we believe it is routinely exploited by resident parents to rupture the relationship between children and their non-resident parent. Only in very rare circumstances is the non-resident parent able to prevent a move away.

The co-operative parenting principles of the new Bill of Rights for the Family will mean that it will not be possible for parents to move children from the general home vicinity without the consent of the other parent. Where consent is forthcoming, ParentShare would require that a workable ParentShare Plan be established setting out parenting time sufficient to afford the child a meaningful relationship with the parent who has moved away.

Family Centres

Britain's family courts have become dependent upon Child Contact Centres (CCCs) to maintain relationships between non-resident parents and their children in circumstances where there are no welfare concerns which would justify supervision of the contact.

Under our proposals, *Contact Centres will be replaced by 'Family Centres'. These will have a very narrowly circumscribed role, limiting their use to* cases where there is a proven risk to the child.

The removal of normal cases will allow Family Centres to provide appropriate services for cases where there is risk. Focussing on real cases of risk will help avoid circumstances where dangerous parents slip through the net.

One of the main criticisms of the existing network of Contact Centres is that the environment they provide is inappropriate for its purpose, making parenting time awkward and artificial. Family Centres will be suitably furnished and equipped so that parents and children can spend time together in conditions which are much more home-like, and offering a range of leisure opportunities.

Parenting Advisors trained in managing parental conflict will also be able to rely on the Family Centre network to manage handovers where the parents have become implacably hostile to each other.

The Department for Family Affairs and Minister for Family Life

There are currently five separate government departments dealing with children and family related matters including the Department for Education and Skills, the Department for Constitutional Affairs, the Department for Work and Pensions, the Department of Health and the Home Office Family Policy Unit. The spread of responsibility, with layer upon layer of bureaucracy, has acted as a barrier to coherent and effective policy development and co-ordination when it comes to children and families.

In order to place the family at the heart of government policymaking, we propose the creation of a new Department of Family areas Affairs headed by a Secretary of Sate for Family Life.

The DFA will engage in 'joined-up' thinking about children and families, co-ordinating and implementing radical reform and ensuring that all government policy and legislative programmes conform to the Bill of Rights for the Family.

The position of Secretary of Sate for Family Life will subsume that of the current Minister for Children. This new cabinet position will acknowledge the recognition that children's welfare and well-being is best served by the family, and that their successful development depends first and foremost upon the love, care and support of their parents, siblings, grandparents and other relatives. The aim of the department will be to defend and vigorously foster these relationships for the benefit of the child. The family will be promoted as a cross-generational institution at the heart of society, and one that transcends changes in the relationship between a child's parents.

The Family Support Service and Family Magistrates Service will come under the department's control, as will the new position of Family Ombudsman, who will have responsibility for reviewing the operation of these services, and the power to establish appropriate policies and protocols designed to achieve positive outcomes for children. The Department will also be required to collect complete records of cases going through the FMS and to commission on-going research to monitor the outcomes for those children over a period of one, two, five and ten years.

New thinking for a new Ministry

Family policy has been hijacked by government apparatchiks and academics. The people who really matter – the families themselves – have been increasingly sidelined.

We need a new vision for the family and for family policy making. A new generation of advisers will be brought to the DFA, with parents actively and proportionately represented. The Minister for Family Life will be responsible for invigorating and energising the department with a dynamic new creative vision, and for driving the implementation of the Bill of Rights for the Family.

Encompassed within this new department will be the following agencies:

- The Family Magistrates Service   (replaces the Family Division)
- Family Support Service   (replaces Cafcass)
- Family Benefits Service   (replaces the Child Support Agency)
- Case Review Service   (new)

ACCOUNTABILITY

The Department of Family Affairs and the services under its control will be accountable to the Family Ombudsman and to a cross-party parliamentary committee who, together will strictly monitor the performance of each service and the implementation of the Bill of Rights. The Department will make public the following information on a yearly basis:

- Number of ParentShare Plans agreed.
- Analysis of parenting time splits.
- Number of ParentShare Plans broken.
- Analysis of reasons why PSPs broken.
- Number of cases sent to the Family Magistrates Court.
- Number of Community Service Orders given.
- Number of Custodial Sentences.
- Report on the outcomes for children.
- Report on the number of Case Reviews.
- Report on compensation paid.
- Report on the outcome of the Public Inquiry.

Recognising good parents - FAMILY AWARDS

The DFA will recognise the work of nominated parents, grandparents, other family members, children and carers in an awards ceremony every year.

STUDY INTO THE COSTS OF FAMILY BREAKDOWN

The DFA will commission urgent research into the costs of family breakdown.

Addressing the Past

CASE REVIEW SERVICE AND COMPENSATION FOR LOSS OF FAMILY LIFE

Parents considered 'non resident' under the current system of family law will be able to apply to the Case Review Service (CRS) have their cases re-examined if they have lost contact with their children or still have limited parenting time with them.

If a possible miscarriage of justice and/or loss of family life is found to have taken place without good reason, the case will be referred to a Case Review Officer who can ask the Family Magistrates Court to re-open the case under the new Bill of Rights for the Family.

The CRS will also conduct a review of such cases to assess the loss of family life and what compensation or remedies might be appropriate.

PUBLIC 'TRUTH & RECONCILLIATION' INQUIRY

The children and families who have suffered injustice under the current Family Law System require help to move forward with their lives and to come to terms with the injustices that they have suffered.

Under these proposals, a 'Truth and Reconciliation' Inquiry into Divorce and Family Justice since the Second World War will be conducted along the lines of that undertaken in South Africa following the collapse of apartheid. Judges, family law professionals, civil servants, parents, children (many of whom will now be adults) and other relatives may be called to give testimony in public at the inquiry.

The purpose of the inquiry is to investigate and understand how the injustices of the family law system arose, and and what lessons must be learned to prevent these recurring in the future.

Distribution of Benefits – the New Family Benefits Service

Today, under the Child Support Agency a parent who provides no care for his children pays 100% of the child's maintenance requirement. Where care is shared, the amount due is reduced by 1/7th for each night the child stays with the maintenance bearing parent, whilst the other parent at no time is required to make reciprocal payments.

These rules leave a responsible parent sharing the care of his children with a doubled burden of maintenance. For example, where care is shared equally between the parents, the maintenance-bearing parent bears the cost of feeding and clothing the child whilst in his care but also pays 7/14th of the CSA child maintenance assessment to the other parent.

Falling under the umbrella of the Department of Family Affairs, **The Family Benefits Service (FBS)** will replace the Child Support Agency. The FBS will be responsible for implementing an equitable and efficient system of child support. The new service will avoid the problems that have bedevilled its predecessor, since the majority of cases that are currently handled by the CSA will be dealt with by parents themselves through ParentShare.

The FBS will be responsible for ensuring the division between *both* parents of benefits such as the Working Families Child Tax Credit, based on the amount of time a child spends with each parent as set out in the ParentShare Plan.

The link between maintenance and parenting time acknowledges equality between the parents. All benefit calculations will take into account the ability to pay from each household and the number of children each parent is responsible for.

PROVISION OF AFFORDABLE CHILDCARE, FLEXIBLE WORKING and PARENTAL LEAVE

The DFA will undertake a review of the issues of flexible working, childcare and parental leave. The goal will be to provide a set of childcare-friendly measures that will assist parents in successfully establishing a sound work/family balance.

The DFA will work with the DTI to investigate appropriate measures for extending the scope of family-friendly working practices that also meets the competitive needs of the economy.

A flexible workforce needs flexible and affordable childcare The DFA will undertake a review of all existing childcare provisions with a view to providing radically improved, affordable childcare facilities including nursery places for pre-school children and increased crèche facilities in the workplace for all working parents regardless of gender and ability to pay.

Also to be reviewed will be the current arrangements for maternity and paternity provision. Amongst proposals to be considered will be the ability for families to combine their parental leave entitlements and for parental leave to be available at times other than during early-years care.

These proposals underline a determination and commitment to support working parents and their children in the new social order of the 21st Century.

Further Reform

A NEW LANGUAGE FOR FAMILY LAW

The language that has grown up around family law has itself conspired to work against co-operative parenting. For example, the terms 'resident parent' and 'contact parent' immediately put the parents on an unequal footing. A new language is required to reflect the realities of equality-based co-operative parenting and the principles enshrined in the Bill of Rights for the Family.

THE FAMILY AND ADVANCES IN MEDICAL SCIENCE

The DFA and other agencies will be responsible for considering the implications of medical advances in relation to the Bill of Rights. For example, the Human Embryology and Fertilisation Authority would need to consider the function of fertility services and genetic science as they relate to the Bill of Rights. The right of the child to know its natural parents would also require that DNA testing be available without the need for joint parental consent.

FINANCES, PROPERTY AND BELONGINGS

The aim of these proposals is to place both parents in the best position possible to continue to provide care for their children. The conciliatory nature of the ParentShare scheme will help parents come to financial arrangements relating to the dissolution of their partnership.

The emphasis on **two** *parents* will lead to a greater number of consent arrangements over money on an equitable clean-break basis. As with current procedures relating to the assets of the couple, the child's needs will remain paramount, this being placed within the context of both parents' needs to provide home environments for the child in the normal case.

An equitable basis for the division of assets will lead to reduction in the sort of financial disputes which currently are often the catalyst for acrimony between parents. It will also lead to a reduction in the number of non-molestation and ouster applications that arise where the grievance is financially motivated rather than through a genuine risk of harm.

ADOPTION

In the recent case of Re J [2003] EWHC 199 (fam), a young mother sought to have her baby adopted. Whilst mother identified the father to Social Services she refused permission for him to be contacted. Social Services took the view that the father should be consulted prior to adoption proceedings and sought permission of the court to breach their duty of confidentiality to mother and contact the father. The court took the view that the father's consent could be dispensed with, on the puzzling basis that father, who had not been aware that he was a father, had not hitherto played a parenting role in the baby's life and that, on this basis, he should be precluded from so doing in the future.

This case amply illustrates the cavalier disregard that the courts currently demonstrate towards fathers and their influence on a child's life.

Under the new Bill of Rights, such situations would not arise as there would be a duty on adoption services to take reasonable steps to obtain consent from both parents in circumstances where the adoption of a child is being considered. The requirement for dual-consent can only be dispensed with in exceptional circumstances with the permission of the Court.

ABDUCTION

The Bill of Rights will place a duty on all agencies to operate in accordance with its Articles. This will place a duty on the Criminal Justice Services to approach family related crimes, such as abduction, in an equal and fair way.

Currently, what amounts to a two-tier approach to alleged abduction appears to have arisen (mirroring the gender apartheid which operates elsewhere in the family justice system), where cases of mothers who remove their children from the family home and disappear to another part of the country, or even go abroad, are dismissed by the Police as civil issues. The father faces a lengthy, and expensive, quest to locate and re-establish contact with his children. But if a father removes his children from the home, on the other hand, this triggers prompt action on the part of Police and other agencies to ensure the immediate location of the children and their return to the home. Prosecution of the father invariably ensues.

Under our new proposals, the movement of children from their home will be governed by the operation of ParentShare Plans. An attempt by one parent to circumvent these parenting agreements would give rise to the involvement of the Family Magistrates who, in cases of actual abduction, could order the involvement of the police to recover the child.

The myth of the 'deadbeat' dad

Fathers who have limited or no involvement in the upbringing of their children have become demonised as 'Deadbeat Dads', whilst mothers are often held up as paragons of virtue, 'Madonna Mums' no less. There is an increasing body of research which suggests that the reasons for the absence of a father from his children's lives are usually much more complex than simply negligence on his part: he is more likely to have been thwarted by a hostile ex-partner or by his experiences at the hands of the family courts.

A further significant contributing factor is the widespread denigration of masculinity and men – young men in particular – in our society as a whole. The media is saturated with images – fuelled in large part by disinformation propagated by women's groups (many of them substantially government-funded), suggesting that men are either feckless or violent. Separated fathers are regarded with particular suspicion, if not outright hostility, and these prejudices are readily reproduced inside the family courts.

Low self-esteem and negative self-image are widely recognised to be key factors contributing to other types of delinquent behaviour, but there is little acknowledgement among policy-makers that this might play a part in the absence of some fathers.

Until society, and the courts, give a clear message that fathers are as important to children as mothers, and treats them accordingly, it is not surprising that some fathers fail to rise to their responsibilities.

Britain, with one of the highest levels of teenage pregnancy in Europe, also has large numbers of teenage fathers. Without suitable encouragement and support, they can all too easily drift out of their children's lives.

Under these proposed reforms, the DFA will be responsible for investigating ways in which young parents can be encouraged to participate fully in the upbringing of their children. For example, the DFA will seek to foster responsible parenting attitudes among young fathers, drawing on best practices from other parts of the world, such as the pilot scheme operating on the east coast of America where young fathers are subsidised to stay in education and supported in their parenting role. The cost of such schemes will be offset by the savings to society as a whole derived from increased family stability and more positive outcomes for the children involved.

PARENTING CLASSES FOR YOUNG ADULTS

It is important that children, as they grow, see their future role as parents in a constructive and positive light. Parenting and family issues are subjects that should be integrated into the national curriculum to build an understanding of relationships and familial responsibility.

TRANSITIONAL INTERIM PHASE TO THE NEW DEPARTMENT OF FAMILY AFFAIRS

There will be an interim phase before the Bill of Rights is enshrined in legislation.

During this time, it will be possible for certain measures to taken independent of new legislation. For example, new Practice Directions should be issued to all Family Court judges concerning Children Act proceedings with regard to the issue and enforcement of court orders. This will include the introduction of the penalties highlighted within this blueprint.

BUDGETARY SAVINGS

The reforms outlined in the Blueprint will result in dramatic cost savings to the UK taxpayer – in the order of several billion pounds annually. Whilst a detailed cost analysis is required, substantial savings will come from the following areas:

SAVINGS

- The scrapping of legal aid for parents in disputes over parenting time.

- The scrapping of Cafcass (apart from Public Law Cases).

- The scrapping of the Child Support Agency.

- The scrapping of the Family Division Courts and Judges.

- Massive reductions in court time as in number of cases are dramatically reduced.

- Massive reduction in parental spend on child psychologists, psychiatrists and other 'experts'.

- Massive reduction in parental spend on legal advice.

- Reduction in numbers of Child Contact Centres.

- Reduction in direct and indirect costs of family breakdown.

- Reduction in young offending, teenage crime and anti-social behaviour resulting from fatherlessness.

- Reduction in pre-school childcare costs as fathers and the paternal grandparents play a greater role with childcare, helped by flexible working patterns introduced by the Department for Trade and Industry.

COSTS

- Launch of Department of Family Affairs.

- Launch of free ParentShare Scheme.

- Launch of Family Support Service.

- Launch of Family Magistrates Courts

- Launch of Family Benefits Service

- Launch of Case Review Service

- Increase in free Childcare provisions

- Compensation for loss of Family Life

- Investment in Family Centres

CONCLUSION – A LEGACY FOR OUR CHILDREN

There will come a time – and this time is fast approaching - when we will look back with utter disbelief on our current system of family law and the catastrophic impact this has had upon the lives of children and families. And we will ask ourselves: "How could we have allowed this to happen?"

This, and other questions, are being put *here* and *now* by Fathers 4 Justice. If the intention of Parliament in the 1989 Children Act was that children should retain a meaningful, loving relationship with both their parents following separation, how we have managed to produce a reality in which children are routinely removed from decent, loving parents and grandparents, and family law has come to fail the very children whose 'best interests' it purports to serve?

The 'child's best interest' principle has become an empty mantra to justify and disguise the multitude of sins concealed beneath the cloak of family court secrecy. Any system that fails to be open, accountable and transparent is open to abuse, and our current system of family law has been grotesquely abused.

Without question, our society is undergoing dramatic changes in family dynamics and structures, and in the alignment of opportunities for both genders. Where once the roles of each gender were clearly defined, now they are blurred: fifty per-cent of the working population are now women; according to the Equal Opportunities Commission, up to a third of all childcare – an upward trend - is now carried out by fathers.

Is it so unreasonable, then, when women enjoy equality of opportunity in every other sphere of civil life, that fathers now demand equality – with a fifty-fifty division of parenting time as a starting point - in post-separation parenting?

Discrimination on the grounds of race, gender or sexuality is now universally accepted to be completely untenable on any grounds, and our society is much the better for this. How, then, can it be that over the past thirty years the systematic removal of fathers from their children's lives has become the acceptable face of family law, with the full sanction of government? The last vestiges of Victorian patriarchy have long since been expunged, to be supplanted by no less iniquitous orthodoxies which privilege mothers: the pendulum has swung full-tilt to the opposite extreme, and now dictates that 'Mother Love' is the only valid parental presence, while fathers are regarded as being, at best, of marginal importance.

The emerging movement for equal parenting is not just a British phenomenon, nor even is it restricted to the English-speaking nations: it manifests itself in post-industrial countries across the globe where legal thinking in the sphere of the family has fallen far behind the prevailing social realities. The clamour for reform is building worldwide.

The moment for change has come: nobody, having read the body of evidence presented here, can be left in any doubt as to the urgency of the need for wholesale reform of family law in the United Kingdom. This 'cold rubbish...so stupid, so brutish in its implementation' (Sir Bob Geldof) must be consigned to the dustbin of history. It has already blighted the lives of a whole generation of fathers and their children, and the fallout from this will continue to be felt for decades to come.

Evidence of the effects of fatherlessness can be seen every day on the street corners and housing estates of modern Britain. A nation of lost children growing up in 21st century families where relationship breakdown is rife, where transient stepparents pass in and out of children's lives, where 1 in 4 teenagers is now a criminal, where ASBO's are dished out like confetti, where teenage pregnancies are on the rise and where the fallout of this disastrous piece of social engineering is becoming more alarming by the day.

Enough. We must act now. The old laws are redundant. Legal professionals increasingly state that they have no confidence in them. The judiciary state that they have no confidence in them and most importantly the parents, many of whom have given testimony in this document, have no confidence in them. We must recognise that the time for change has arrived. Now is the time for the pioneers of family law in the 21st century to make the emboldened vision set out in this blueprint a tangible reality for our children with a new Bill of Rights for the Family – a legacy our children will enjoy free of the injustices of the old laws.

Matt O'Connor, Founder, Fathers 4 Justice

"I couldn't get my boy out of my mind: how sick he'd been and how wrong it felt to be leaving him and Victoria behind. ALL my instincts were telling me that my place was at home with them, at least until I knew for sure Brooklyn was going to be all right."

DAVID BECKHAM, MY SIDE

ABOUT THE AUTHORS

Matt O'Connor, Founder, Fathers 4 Justice

38 Year old Matt O'Connor created the Fathers 4 Justice campaign after a difficult divorce which found Matt struggling to maintain contact with his two children Daniel (9 years of age) and Alexander (7 years of age). His baptism of fire in Britain's secret family courts ignited the creative spark that would result in one of the most high profile campaigns of recent years. Ironically Matt and his ex wife Sophia had resolved their problems outside of the legal process by the time he had set the group up and the boys now spend weekends with him on his Suffolk farm.

A designer, marketing and public relations man by trade, Matt was able to use the valuable experience gained in campaigning in the Anti-Apartheid movement, CND and Amnesty International when he was younger and weave this knowledge together with that gained working on numerous international multi million pound food and drink brands. It was this potent mix that led to the creation of the now infamous 'superheroes' campaign and the establishment of Fathers 4 Justice as a household name and international campaign brand.

Since then Fathers 4 Justice has been increasingly recognised for its achievements in creating awareness about the problems of fatherlessness. In January 2005 Matt was shortlisted amongst 20 other people for the Royal Society's Great Briton of the Year Award. Elsewhere he was listed in GQ Magazine's Top Ten Communicators in the UK and Britain's 100 Most Powerful Men in the UK and in Esquire Magazine's 50 Most Influential Men in Britain Under 40.

Matt runs his successful design company from Suffolk alongside Fathers 4 Justice and as well as attending public speaking engagements about civil disobedience and civil rights campaigning, he has started work on a book about Fathers 4 Justice and will shortly launch the Fathers 4 Justice Foundation which will help young offenders from fatherless families.

Gary Burch, Political Co-ordinator, Fathers 4 Justice

Since it's inception in December 2002, Gary Burch has been instrumental in developing the group's political and public relations strategy and is a member of the group's management team. A 39 year old software design consultant, Gary lives in Surrey with his wife Jeanette. He has two daughters he hasn't seen for over 4 years.

Michael Cox, Legal Advisor, Fathers 4 Justice

Michael is a 41 year old Barrister from Hythe, Southampton. He has five children and is married to Beth who is a primary school teacher. Michael advises Fathers 4 Justice on all legal matters relating to the campaign and is a member of the group's management team.